INTERVIEWS BY STEVE DUBB
FOR THE DEMOCRACY COLLABORATIVE

Conversations on
Community
Wealth
Building

Conversations on Community Wealth Building
Interviews by Steve Dubb

©2016, The Democracy Collaborative

For more information, or to order copies, please contact
The Democracy Collaborative:

Washington, D.C. Office:
The Ring Building
1200 18th Street NW
Suite 1225
Washington, D.C. 20036

Cleveland Office:
The Hanna Building
1422 Euclid Ave.
Suite 616
Cleveland, OH 44115

Web: www.democracycollaborative.org
Facebook: fb.me/democracycollaborative
Twitter: @democracycollab

Cover Design and Interior Typography by
Kate Khatib, Owl Grammar Press

This book was typeset in Adobe Garamond Pro and Avenir Next.

Table of Contents

STEVE DUBB

Introduction

Community wealth building is a community-based, economic development strategy that aims to democratize the ownership of wealth from the ground up. It is an asset-based approach that addresses economic inequality and poverty by building upon existing local talents, capacities, capital, and expenditure flows to develop community-owned businesses that are anchored in place and can sustain the local economy for the long haul.

At The Democracy Collaborative, we have been drawn to community wealth building institutions because our mission is to develop a vision of a new economic system where shared ownership and control creates more equitable and inclusive outcomes, fosters ecological sustainability, and promotes flourishing democratic and community life. As part of this work, we have sought to study, support, explore, and document growing efforts to build economic institutions at the local level, which we understand to be one important vector of this struggle.

The interviews in this volume stem out of this work. Here you will find stories of people pursuing a range of strategies that are making a positive difference in communities across the United States. The strategies include social enterprises, cooperatives, employee stock ownership plan (ESOP) companies, community land trusts, community development financial institutions (CDFIs), community development corporations (CDCs), and community organizing. Everyone we interviewed in their own way is not only working to improve their own communities, but is also contributing to a broader movement towards social and economic justice, rooted in community-controlled land and enterprises.

We launched what we now call our Community Wealth Building Initiative in 2005, when we wrote our first book of community wealth building. Published by the Aspen Institute, our book was titled *Building Wealth: The New Asset-Based Approach to Solving Social and Economic Problems.* In that book, we highlighted the promise of community wealth building, while being forthright regarding the continuing challenges. Our study concluded that a "new and potentially important wealth-building paradigm is clearly emerging in diverse sectors and communities, but it is not yet fully formed."[1]

Indeed, it was not merely that the sector was not fully formed, as even the term "community wealth building" was new. It was so new that in the book we used the phrase "community asset-based approaches" at least as often as we did "community wealth." Even more telling is the fact that until March 2005, two months before launch, the working title of the Community-Wealth.org website was "assetstrategies.org."

The fact, however, that we chose the title *Community-Wealth.org* for our website and used "community wealth building" to describe our work among colleagues and to the broader public proved fortuitous, as more and more people over the years have come to identify themselves as part of a movement to build community wealth that is in anchored in community economic institutions, the hallmark of an inclusive, systems-based, community wealth building approach.

While we launched the website in May 2005, it took another 18 months before Ted Howard, our President, came up with the idea of interviewing key community wealth building leaders. The first of these interviews, conducted in December 2006 and published in January 2007, was of Ron Phillips, the CEO of Coastal Enterprises, Inc. (CEI), a Maine-based community development corporation (CDC) and community development financial institution (CDFI). Since then, I have conducted "C-W Interviews" of nearly three dozen leaders. Turns out that when we introduced the Ron Philips interview as the "first in a continuing series," we weren't kidding!

There are a number of ways one could introduce these essays, such as tracing the interviews by year or organizational type. In this essay, however, I have instead decided to highlight key themes raised by the interview subjects themselves. In some cases, of course, people do follow form—in other words, social enterprise leaders talk about non-profit ownership of businesses and community development financial institution (CDFI) leaders talk about ways to raise capital. But in many cases, community development leaders, regardless of the particular approach pursued, highlight common challenges. So you will find CDFI leaders talking about the importance of community organizing and community organizers talking about the importance of capital. More importantly, you'll find threads of a common conversation throughout—namely, a conversation of how we rebuild community, rooted in local economies that work for people.

It would be impossible to cover every theme that the people interviewed in this volume discuss. What I have sought to do in the comments below is tease out a dozen themes that highlight some of the critical issues community wealth building leaders raised, which also reflect common issues in the field and broader community wealth building.

Access to Capital: Getting access to capital is a common refrain and so it is not surprising that both the first interview, conducted of Ron Phillips in December 2006, and the most recent interview, conducted of Michael Shuman in September 2015, touched heavily on this theme. For Ron Phillips, key challenges include having access to flexible, subsidized capital to sustain operations; policies that create a regulatory environment conducive to community wealth building; access to private capital; and generating data on impact, or, as Phillips puts it, "making a difference at the community level." Shuman argues for shifting the ways capital can be invested economy-wide. According to Shuman, "Fixing our capital markets is critical to reconnecting residents of a community to ownership of the businesses operating within that community. That, in and of itself, doesn't redistribute wealth. But it matters a great deal, because the Fortune 500 companies under the current system have too much capital and community-based businesses have too little."

Tensions in the work: Community wealth building advocates may often, like Michael Shuman, seek to promote fundamental economic change, yet they must also operate in a world that requires compromise as part of the work. Ron Phillips works for a CDFI, Tony Brown worked for a consortium of anchor institutions (and is now a consultant), and Melissa Hoover directed a national association of worker cooperatives (and now leads its foundation arm), but all three pointed to similar tensions in their work. Phillips, for example, acknowledged that "achieving scale while not losing contact with the community is a tension that will probably persist."

Brown who led the Uptown Consortium, an institution that invested over $100 million in University of Cincinnati loan funds to support community development, highlighted the complicated negotiation that goes into a "university community partnership." As Brown explains, "we were honest up front about our redevelopment priority areas. Out of self-interest they are contiguous to the hospitals and university. We then work with the established neighborhood groups to do an effective plan. We use the plan to work with the community to do visioning and design charrettes that at least gets us to a shared vision."

Hoover, founding executive director of the U.S. Federation of Worker Cooperatives, noted that tensions are inherent in worker co-op development too: "When you are talking about running a business, you are dealing with a myriad of compromises that you have to make to be in the marketplace… It's a compromised form. I don't think of that as a bad thing—but it's not pure. You are operating on principles that contravene the principles of business as usual and there's a struggle there. Organizations pursuing social justice goals would do well to take that in mind."

Organizing the community: A number of the people interviewed highlighted the importance of community organizing. Eric Weaver, CEO of the Opportunity Fund, a large CDFI, has an MBA and might seem an unlikely advocate of community organizing. Yet Weaver found his early stints in community organizing invaluable. Weaver points out that he "had worked with low-income tenants and as a relief worker in El Salvador. This background was beneficial to help me figure out what partnerships made sense for us to bridge that gap between mainstream financial institutions and people who had not been comfortable with using those institutions."

Stephen McCullough, then CEO of Bethel New Life (and now COO of Communities in Schools), considers community organizing as central to the work of Bethel. "Community organizing is really about community block organizing and outreach to institutions, like the police... We work block-by-block, beat-by-beat, connecting police to residents in the community identifying trouble issues and working to resolve them. And we do the same thing with schools.... Without that grounding framework, we would have a much more difficult time getting our programs out in the community and making sure they are successful and people take advantage of them."

A related theme coming out of these interviews is that while, for sure, community organizing can and does involve advocacy work, the confrontations are really the tip of the iceberg of much deeper community-based, relationship building work. Paul Hazen, who directed the National Cooperative Business Association, which mainly works on co-op development outside the United States (and who now heads the Overseas Cooperative Development Council) noted that, "The approach that we take is a very bottom-up approach. Starting at the local level, we help people address their own problems. In the United States, we have had too much of a top-down mindset where folks come in and say, there is a need over here." Rev. Barry Randolph of the Church of the Messiah in Detroit talked about this work as ministry. "Ministry is community building. The Gospels mean the Good News. We are to go out and spread Good News. But we are also to *be* good news. The way we are good news is supporting, rebuilding the community, and changing the mindset of the community by making the world a better place. That is what ministry is to us. Ministry is not a religious concept as much as it is about changing mindsets."

Rethinking the CDC: The Community Development Corporation (CDC), which exists in nearly every major city in the United States, is perhaps the community wealth building institution *par excellence*. And yet, CDCs face an increasingly challenging environment. No longer foundation favorites and having often become overcommitted (largely due to funding availability) to housing development, the CDC movement is in the midst of a reformulation of its goals, with an increasing emphasis on a comprehensive approach to community building, harkening back to the origins of the community development corporation coming out of civil rights organizing in the 1960s.

Seema Agnani of Chhaya CDC in New York City (who in 2014 left Chhaya to become policy director of the National Coalition of Asian Pacific Americans for Community Development) remarks that Chhaya called itself "a CDC because we are about institution building—not just providing services, but putting things in place that provide long-term stability." Agnani notes that in New York City, "We can't look like a traditional CDC. There is no more land left to develop." The environment in the Eastside of Detroit, where Maggie De Santis has worked for the past three decades, couldn't be more different. Yet, like Chhaya, the Eastside organization she founded (from which she retired in 2016), has likewise sought a balanced approach: "we have spawned organizations that are bringing block grants in and building homes, we built the shopping center, and we've created programs that are 20 years old and still serving kids. It's the sum total that causes people to recognize that the Eastside is a strong part of the city."

Bernie Mazyck, executive of the statewide South Carolina Association for Community Economic Development (SCACED), highlights the importance of leadership development. "We have a number of folks in our field who have been elected to local offices and the General Assembly in our state. Along with the broad definition of leadership development, the ability to grow leaders with the minority communities has been very positive."

Building social enterprise: Social enterprise can come in many varieties. One is a nonprofit that owns a subsidiary business, typically as a tool for helping those with barriers of employment gain job experience on-the-job. The case of Sweet Beginnings in Chicago's North Lawndale neighborhood is a typical example. Brenda Palms-Barber explains that her effort began with data collection. From a survey conducted between 2001 and 2003, "we learned that 57 percent of adults in North Lawndale had some kind of criminal background.... Out of the situation, a social enterprise, Sweet Beginnings, was born. We've been operating for three years—we are generating a little over $200,000 in sales." In the first four years, approximately 200 people came through the business, with recidivism rates of 4 percent (compared to a statewide average of 55 percent). The business continues to operate to this day.

Equal Exchange provides a different model. Equal Exchange is one of the nation's leading worker cooperatives, but, it also sees itself, according to Rodney North, as a for-profit social enterprise. "By choosing a for-profit social enterprise model, we have to explicitly balance the interests of farmers, workers, investors, customers, and the environment," North remarks. North also sees part of Equal Exchange's role as changing the culture of business, which is why the group regularly accepts invitations to speak at business schools and business conferences.

Incubation and Acceleration: Particularly when working with low-income communities with limited resources, outside technical assistance can play an important role. Two C-W Interviews highlighted two ways to provide this support. Hilary Abell, then CEO of a nonprofit called WAGES (now Prospera) notes that, in their approach, the nonprofit subsidizes the manager's salary and works closely with the manager. "The co-op is covering all of its operations," Abell mentions, "but we do cover the key role of the manager until the incubation period ends... After the incubation period, the co-op board takes over." Abell herself remains active in co-op incubation, wrote a Democracy Collaborative study in 2014 on the challenges of incubation (*Worker Cooperatives: Pathways to Scale*), was named an Echoing Green Fellow and has cofounded Project Equity to build out the incubation ecosystem in the San Francisco Bay Area.

Carla Javits of San Francisco-based REDF operates a social enterprise accelerator, which works with existing businesses to increase their scale. "We select a pretty small number of organizations," Javits notes. "During that period of time we agree on objectives in such areas as employment, revenue growth, and other business objectives. We provide financial support in the form of grants and also very hands-on business assistance. This business assistance ranges from marketing to business planning to infrastructure. Every year, both REDF and its partner organizations have a mutual conversation about how things are going and we renew and refine the partnership on an annual basis." In 2015, REDF was awarded a two-year, $7-million federal Social Innovation Fund award to expand operations to a national scale.

Land: Community control of land is also a critical element of community wealth building. Two strategies are the land bank and the community land trust. A land bank is a public authority designed to avoid private speculation and facilitate public reuse of property. A community land trust is different than a land bank in that it is usually a community-based nonprofit that intends to hold land in perpetuity for some public purpose, most often permanently affordable housing.

Land banks have seen considerable expansion due to the Great Recession, with land banks now operating in roughly 120 U.S. cities. As Dan Kildee, who as Genesee County treasurer in Flint, Michigan helped launch a national land banking movement (and, who since 2013 has represented Michigan's Fifth District in Congress) notes that the Great Recession has also forced land banks to take on new roles. "The most significant," Kildee noted, "is managing rental properties. We have a goal of stabilizing those properties and not just selling those to the first buyer. In order to do that, we have had to develop in-house capacity to be a benevolent, 'good-guy' landlord. We put the proceeds from the rentals right back into improving the housing.... Another thing we didn't expect initially is that we would become a developer. We thought the market would soak the properties right up directly. But we've had to become a catalytic developer. We've done several buildings that have spurred other private development."

Land trusts, like CDCs, come out of the civil rights movement. "The leaders of the first community land trust all came out of the civil rights movement," recalls Burlington, Vermont-based John Emmeus Davis. Slater King, a first cousin of Martin Luther King, was president of the first community land trust in Albany, Georgia. Today, there are 240 land trusts in the United States. Land trusts share the equity accumulation to balance giving a fair return to the homeowner with preserving future affordability. A common formula is that in return for purchasing at a substantially reduced price, the homeowner agrees that he/she will receive 25 percent of the equity gain, with the other 75 percent of the equity gain going to the trust. As Davis also points out, in a down market, community land trust housing is significantly more stable than traditional housing, to say nothing about housing that relied on subprime financing. "CLTs across the country reported a foreclosure rate of only 0.56% at the end of 2009," Davis explains. "This compared to foreclosure rates reported by the MBA [Mortgage Bankers Association] of 3.31% among homeowners holding prime mortgages and 15.58% among homeowners holding subprime mortgages."

New Models of Community Wealth Building: We have also seen the emergence of many new forms of development. One is the emergence of the *union-co-op*, a form of organization that combines worker cooperatives with union organization and which was co-developed by the Steelworkers, Mondragón (the Spanish-based worker co-op network) and the Ohio Employee Ownership Center. Rob Witherell of the Steelworkers explains the logic of the approach, "Why do unions exist? Why do people try to create cooperatives? At the most basic level, in both cases, it is about workers helping each other out to create a better life for themselves."

Another new model is the development of what Kate Sofis of San Francisco-based SFMade calls a local *manufacturing omsbudsman.* "By digging deep, we can take a broad wrap-around model: land use and real estate, hiring (working with the city's workforce development programs), education and business advising for the companies and an emerging youth program. It is a combination of being able to work in all of these areas as well as have partnerships with the city, which makes our model particularly viable," Sofis explains. Across the Bay in Oakland, José Corona of Inner City Advisors (who recently left ICA to become Director of Equity and Strategic Partnerships for the City of Oakland), has operated a business incubator with an equity focus. "Of the companies we serve, 58% are minority-owned businesses and nearly 50% are women-owned," Corona says. "The people they employ are 58% from minority populations. The median revenue of our companies is about $460,000. The average wage is $14.50 an hour, and 64% of the employees have health benefits."

Public markets may not be new, but they are gaining new attention. As Ramón León of the Latino Economic Development Corporation of Minnesota, which has led the revitalization of Minneapolis' Lake Street and now operates statewide, observes, "One thing that has been forgotten in much of the United States is that public markets are community development tools. They are a very important part of the community. There are many aspects to this work: real estate, loans, community organizing, training, business incubation, facility development, business development, and market management."

On the capital side, one of the primary innovations has been the rise of impact investment and mission investing. The term was originally coined in 2007 by the Rockefeller Foundation, but quickly spread through the foundation world. As Lisa Hagerman observes, even by 2009, The More for Mission network had grown to include ninety foundations representing $34 billion in total assets." As of year-end 2008, $1.3 billion of that $34 billion was committed to mission investing.

Transnational Influences: As Ai-jen Poo, director of the National Domestic Workers' Alliance, reveals, U.S. organizing of "care workers" owes a considerable debt to immigrants from the Philippines and Hong Kong.

As Ai-Jen emphasizes, "Many of the Filipina workers were accustomed to such standards and a set contract and established paid days off and such. When they came here, they were taken aback by the lack of protections and standards. And the lack of respect and recognition that this work was real work. They immediately asked the question: the rest of the workforce isn't organized either. We need to organize together. So they began to organize Latina and Caribbean workers. That was the origins of Domestic Workers United."

Rey España of the Portland, Oregon-based Native American Youth and Family Center (NAYA) has helped expand the group's educational and community wealth building activity to the extent that NAYA is now one of the nation's leading urban Indian organizations. España highlights the centrality of culture to NAYA's work: "At NAYA we have a clear mission to work in partnership with the community and promote cultural identity and education. The organization prides itself in incorporating traditional Native values of respect, community, generosity, and kindness." España also speaks to his personal connection this work. "I grew up in East Los Angeles, California in a Latino or Mexican household. My indigenous side comes from my dad's side. He comes from Yaqui people in northern Mexico... My folks were bilingual (English-Spanish) and some of our cultural practices were a mixture of Latino and Indigenous/Native cultures. How I relate to this is that I identify as a Chicano, which is a Mexican-American *and* indigenous worldview.

Education and Advocacy: Blake Jones of Boulder, Colorado-based Namasté Solar and Raquel Pinderhughes, author of the *Roots of Success* green jobs curriculum, both speak to the centrality of education in community development work.

Jones, CEO of Namasté Solar—who directs a worker cooperative that employs ninety people as of 2014—notes that, "Each hired employee goes through a twelve-month candidacy period. They then become eligible to purchase one share of voting common stock. During that candidacy period, they have a candidate curriculum to follow. They have to talk to different people in different teams to learn background information, our history, and how we do things and why. There is a curriculum checklist. They have to check all of those line items. They also have a mentor who helps guide them and helps answer questions. The mentor helps connect them to different resources or people who can answer their questions."

Pinderhughes works with much more disadvantaged populations but has succeeded in creating curriculum for populations with barriers to employment (such as past incarceration records). Pinderhughes points out that, "There are very few, if any, other environmental curriculums out there designed for adults with lower levels of education.... Our pedagogical approach doesn't just provide information on the environment, we connect that information to people's concerns and hopes and we try to inspire people to become activists—the justice aspect is very important to our organization. The fact that it focuses on issues of justice is important. People working with our student population deeply care about justice. They don't want a curriculum that is just about global warming. They want a curriculum that focuses on equity and justice. They know that will be more relevant for their participants. The fact that we do this is important."

John Tyler, CEO of the National Community Reinvestment Coalition, emphasizes the role of education for advocacy. "The Community Reinvestment Act is very simple," Tyler points out." It is only one-and-a-half pages long. But it doesn't mince words. A bank doesn't just have an obligation—it has an affirmative obligation to meet the credit needs of communities. That means the bank must actively pursue opportunities to investment in those neighborhoods. And, just in case there was any doubt, Congress added the words 'including low and moderate-income neighborhoods.' It was a great law on paper, but it wasn't being enforced. Our idea was to get more information into the hands of community groups so they could really use the law, and to ratchet up its enforcement."

Planning for the Future: Rosalind Greenstein, who used to direct the land trust program at the Lincoln Institute for Land Policy and now teaches urban planning at Tufts University, highlights the challenge of implementing community land trusts, which requires acquiring land before gentrification occurs. "The conundrum, of course, is that you don't know in advance that prices are going to go up and it's hard to raise money to get ahead of the curve. How do communities escape this dilemma? They do it with civic leadership and vision."

John Logue, the late director of the Ohio Employee Ownership Center, made a similar observation about employee ownership. "The failure to plan for business succession is the number-one cause of *preventable* job loss in this country." Logue added that, "What you're asking for is a city to say is that, 'We want to build an economy that is inclusive of working people in our community.' You're asking a Chamber of Commerce to say, 'We are more interested in developing businesses at home than in chasing smokestacks from major publicly traded corporations.' You're asking for the press to say 'We celebrate the success of locally owned businesses not just when they sell themselves but in their rootedness to the community and their contributions to the local United Way.' Again, planning for the long haul is key if you want to have an impact."

Changing the system: One last key theme is the need for systemic change. Emily Kawano, Co-Director of Wellspring Cooperative Corporation, is helping build a network of worker cooperatives linked to anchor institution spending in Worcester, Massachusetts, but this work is informed by her vision of building what Kawano calls a solidarity economy. The goal, Kawano says, is the "transformation of the system, based on principles of democratic ownership, equity in all dimensions (race, class, etc.), sustainability and democratic decision-making and control." Kawano also links this broad perspective back to her specific co-op work, adding that "Transforming the entire economy system... requires building practical, on-the-ground alternatives."

Hitomi Igarashi, Board Member of the Seikatsu Club Insurance Cooperative Union in Japan, makes a similar observation, "One single person cannot change the world, but if we can work in larger numbers in solidarity, in cooperation, we can change the world, such as for example when we started a milk company. We can't do that as individuals."

Ed Whitfield, Co-Managing Director of the Fund for Democratic Communities in North Carolina, notes that the question of how to truly transform our present economic system looms large in his foundation's work with the Southern Grassroots Economies Project. "In 2010 and 2011, we asked ourselves how is it that we can focus our work more sharply?... We ended up pretty quickly deciding that cooperative solutions would be among the best solutions to those economic questions. They are rooted in that spirit of self-reliance. It wasn't honest for us to say that if you have a giant jobs march that the federal government will do something good. We wanted to be as up front and honest as possible. We talked about the fact that, yes, there is resistance work that is needed. There are powerful people, places and forces where you can be crushed if you don't. Advocacy is needed because you need to steer resources. But in the final analysis, you need to build community power so communities can be self-reliant and do things for themselves… I often talk about this approach as RAD—resistance, advocacy and doing-for-ourselves."

Closing Thoughts

There is, in short, a wide range of deep thinking and conversation in the world of community wealth building and a growing realization that systemic solutions are needed to meet the scale of the challenge. To understand that scale of our challenge, consider that according to pre-Great Recession data by Ed Wolff, an economist at New York University, as of 2007 the top one percent of households owned 9.4 percent of housing assets, but 38.3 percent of stock and nearly half (49.7 percent) of investment (that is, business) assets. If you can envision a community where the top one percent of households owned half of all housing value, you would get a picture of our actual business world today.[2]

Moreover, the concentration of wealth is getting worse over time—rapidly so. A Pew Study in 2013 found that the bottom 93 percent of households lost $600 billion in assets between 2009 and 2011, even as the top seven percent gained $5.6 trillion. Wealthier families lost housing wealth too, but made up for that with growing business assets.[3] Adding to these challenges are a growing racial wealth gap, with the median white family having 16 times the wealth of the median black family.[4]

The importance of this work cannot be overstated. Our nation's growing concentration of wealth has corrupted our political system, enabling those who hold the ownership to literally call the shots. Thus, for example, in the fall of 2013 the state of Washington approved a subsidy of $8.7 billion over 16 years for the Boeing Corporation, a state guarantee of $500 million-plus a year until 2030 to keep production in the Seattle area.[5]

The challenges that we face are immense, even as positive examples are proliferating. Hopefully, reading these interviews will help inspire us to reflect on our work, deepen our resolve, expand our efforts to generate the infrastructure and ecosystem to support community-based economic development, adopt innovative strategies, and help make community wealth building a central organizing principle of economic development strategy in communities across the nation.

June 2016

Notes

1 The Democracy Collaborative at the University of Maryland, *Building Wealth: The New Asset-Based Approach to Solving Social and Economic Problems*, Washington, DC: The Aspen Institute, Nonprofit Sector Research Fund, 2005, page 120.
2 Ed Wolff, *Recent Trends in Household Wealth in the United States: Rising Debt and the Middle-Class Squeeze—an Update to 2007*, Working Paper no. 589, Annandale-on-Hudson, NY: Levy Economics Institute of Bard College, March 2010, http://www.levyinstitute.org/publications/recent-trends-in-household-wealth-in-the-united-states-rising-debt-and-the-middle-class-squeezean-update-to-2007, accessed Nov. 22, 2015.
3 Richard Frey and Paul Taylor, *A Rise in Wealth for the Wealthy; Declines for the Lower 93%*, Washington, DC: Pew Research Center, April 23, 2013.
4 Laura Shin, "The Racial Wealth Gap: Why A Typical White Household Has 16 Times The Wealth Of A Black One," *Forbes*, March 26, 2015, http://www.forbes.com/sites/laurashin/2015/03/26/the-racial-wealth-gap-why-a-typical-white-household-has-16-times-the-wealth-of-a-black-one, accessed Nov. 22, 2015.
5 Danny Westmeat, "Tax Breaks for Boeing: We're Number 1," *The Seattle Times*, November 13, 2013, http://www.seattletimes.com/seattle-news/tax-breaks-for-boeing-wersquore-no-1/, accessed Nov. 22, 2015.

Community Development Corporations

Four interviews of community development corporation (CDC) leaders form the first section of this book. The community development corporation emerged out of the 1960s civil rights movement as a potential vehicle for community-based business development as part of a comprehensive community building strategy. Some CDCs have had success in this area. But many others have ended up focusing on affordable housing development and management, social services, and community building (parks, streetscape improvement, etc.). The federal program that helped create the CDC, the Office of Economic Opportunity (OEO), was eliminated in 1974, yet the number of CDCs has grown from a few hundred then to 4,600 by the mid-2000s and CDCs have expanded to cover nearly every city and many rural regions. The interviews here—from leaders of Chhaya CDC in New York City (Agnani), to Warren/Connor Development Corporation in Detroit (DeSantis) to Bethel New Life in Chicago (McCullough) to the executive director of the statewide trade association of CDCs in South Carolina and current president of the national association (Maczyk) highlight some of the many challenges inherent in the CDC mission of rebuilding communities "block by block, brick by brick."

Seema Agnani

*For fourteen years, Seema Agnani served
as the Executive Director of Chhaya
Community Development Corporation
(Queens, NY). Founded in 2000 to
serve New York City's rapidly growing
South Asian community, high land prices
have forced Chhaya to innovate in its
affordable housing strategy. Rather than
developing new housing, the CDC has
worked with City officials, architects, and
homeowners to improve and legalize New
York City's growing market (which now
numbers over 100,000 units citywide) of
"in-law" or "informal" housing.*

*As of January 2015, Agnani became
the Director of Policy and Civic
Engagement for the National Coalition
for Asian Pacific American Community
Development (National CAPACD).*

Interviewed in 2007

Steve Dubb: Your CDC aims to serve the South Asian community throughout New York City. Could you begin by explaining how you define South Asian?

Sema Agnani: Basically, we consider South Asians to be people who emigrate from India, Bangladesh and Pakistan or countries that border that region. This includes Sri Lanka, Nepal, Afghanistan, and Tibet, as well as the diaspora who immigrate to the United States via the Caribbean or Africa. In New York City, the main population groups are from India, Pakistan, Bangladesh, and those who come to the United States after having migrated to the Caribbean.

SD: *Between 1990 and 2000, the South Asian population in New York City nearly doubled from 113,000 to 216,000. What factors are behind this rapid growth?*

SA: Although there has been a South Asian community in the United States since the 1920s, the first wave of immigrants—the first large wave—came in the 1960s. Initially migrants were primarily from India. Since the 1980s, the number of immigrants from Bangladesh has grown more.

There are a lot of factors behind the recent growth in the South Asian community. Many people are coming in through family visas. Also, companies—particularly tech companies—bring in experts. The Bangladeshi migration is different. Many of them came in through a diversity visa program that awards slots by lottery to countries that are under-represented in the immigrant pool. Indians and Pakistanis used to come in through diversity visas, but their numbers are now too great a percentage of the immigrant population to qualify. There are also a lot of people who come into the United States using visitor visas and overstay their visas—leading to a large percentage of undocumented immigrants.

SD: *Are there other cities that have experienced similar growth? Which ones?*

SA: The South Asian population in New Jersey is huge. People are now going straight to New Jersey. There are pockets growing in all areas, such as Atlanta, Georgia; Houston; and Dallas. All of these cities have pretty significant populations. Seattle also has a good-sized population. The coasts, especially California, also have large populations. Chicago has one of the largest South Asian communities in the country. It is very spread out and growing. New York, Chicago, and Los Angeles probably get the biggest numbers.

SD: ***What would you see as the main issues facing South Asian immigrants today—both in New York City and nationally?***

SA: The number one issue is immigration reform. It is going to really impact our community. We have such a mixed bag of documentation statuses—often within the same household you will find both documented and undocumented immigrants—that's a huge challenge.

There are also big class differences within the South Asian community. The high-end group is fairly well off. The other is not—it's pretty extreme. Language is an issue. Education is an issue. A rising high school dropout rate is emerging as an issue.

In New York City, two other big issues are housing overcrowding and job opportunities. In the city, for example, you will meet cab drivers that are engineers by trade, but they have to get recertified in the United States and that's not easy. Overcrowding is a big issue—despite the myths, immigrants don't want to live in these close quarters, but they have limited options. You have multi-generational households living in very cramped conditions—it's complicated and stressful for the family.

SD: ***What were the origins of Chhaya CDC? How has the organization's relationship to Asian Americans for Equality (AAFE), from which it emerged, evolved over time?***

SA: Before I was at Chhaya, I worked for AAFE. The idea of Chhaya initially was to broaden AAFE's work to involve more South Asians—in other words, we saw a need and were trying to meet it.

We had a health care program—that was the first program that we tried to broaden. We sought to enroll people in Medicaid and Child Health Plus. There was a Bangladeshi population in Chinatown where AAFE was based and so we started to work there—in Manhattan's Lower East Side. Concurrently, AAFE opened an office in Queens—we started to work on fair housing in Queens.

The problem we encountered was that these programs were dependent on staff that spoke Bengali, Urdu, and Hindi. When the staff with these language skills left, the programs left. So then we started to organize the leadership of the South Asian community to build something that would be more lasting. This involved leaders of community-based organizations, business owners, and others who we knew were visible in the South Asian community. This group eventually coalesced into an advisory committee that later evolved into being the first Board of Directors of Chhaya CDC.

We had a pretty strong initial group. One woman was working for the Queens Borough President's office. One guy was working for Deutsche Bank. One was from Fannie Mae. It worked well. We had the expertise of AAFE, community leadership, and an institutionalized body to make sure it continued. Eventually Chhaya set up its office in Queens.

Chhaya was initially set up as an affiliate of AAFE. We formally separated in 2005, but that was the idea all along. The relationship with AAFE is still strong, but we no longer have a formal legal relationship. We still refer clients to them—they have such a broad array of services. They also still have a South Asian clientele of their own as well, although it is not very big.

SD: *Why did you decide to spin Chhaya CDC off as a separate organization?*

SA: We decided to spin it off after 9/11. You're in a crisis situation and you have two communities with very different issues. In Chinatown, there was severe economic loss and a lot of people who lost families in the attacks. The South Asian community, by contrast, was under suspicion and attacked by federal government immigration policy trying to root out terrorists. AAFE had to respond to what was happening in Chinatown—that's their base.

It should also be noted that there are many other differences between the two communities. There are many issues in common, but many differences culturally—most obviously language-wise.

SD: *How did Chhaya CDC come up with its current priority programs? And how do these priorities evolve over time?*

SA: We're working in the context of Queens with a mixed combination of owners, renters, co-op rentals, and so-called "single-family" homes, which are often jointly occupied by two to three families. We are trying to respond to all of the predatory lending. That requires education, outreach, trying to prevent people from losing their homes through foreclosure prevention work.

We can't look like a traditional CDC. There is no more land left to develop. We call ourselves a CDC because we are about institution-building—not just providing services, but putting things in place that provide long-term stability.

One key issue is the issue of illegal conversions. A lot of owners are renting out basements, attics, garages, first floors, wherever there is space. It is happening all over the city, but especially in Queens. It's related to predatory lending. People get mortgages that they cannot afford so they rent out part of their homes to supplement their income.

In a sense, what this means is that an informal form of affordable housing has been created. We are working with the City to produce a report on this issue. The lowest number I have heard is that there are 100,000 units of "informal"—we prefer the word "informal" to "illegal"—housing in the city. The high estimate is 300,000 units.

The impact it has on the family is frustrating. When we first started doing tenant rights work, 60 to 70 percent lived in these informal units. We spent our time going to hearings and just buying time for tenants before the inevitable displacement occurred. Owners themselves were also in the dark about what their responsibilities were. We found it was too expensive to use the system and too time consuming.

So we are working with New York City's Housing Preservation and Development Office (HPD) to look at potential administrative solutions to ease the burden on the owners and make it easier to legalize the rentals, provided it is safe. We're also working with the Architectural Institute of America. So we have adopted a two-pronged approach of policy advocacy within the city and actual assistance to owners.

The idea with the owners is to get them the resources to do the renovation work to bring their rentals up to code. So we are placed in the role of mediating between the owner and the tenant and trying to get them to come to an agreement.

Of course, if it's both illegal and unsafe, the tenants need to find different housing. But we don't want to be in the business of evicting tenants. In an ideal world, we'd have access to transitional housing—but it's hard for the tenants anyway.

"We call ourselves a CDC because we are about institution-building—not just providing services, but **putting things in place that provide long-term stability**."

SD: *You mentioned earlier in this interview that South Asians often faced federal government hostility after 9/11. How specifically has 9/11 affected the South Asian community?*

SA: The discrimination was there. The increased level of policing has had a large impact. Not as much any more in Jackson Heights in Queens—more so in Midwood in Brooklyn among the Pakistani community, where regular sweeps still go on. It creates an atmosphere of distrust and fear. Everybody knows someone who was disappeared. A lot of the businesses went under after 9/11—staff weren't around; people weren't going out and buying. Kids were being beaten up. Women and girls were being harassed if they were wearing a hijab.

As for the CDC, we tried to help people who could access federal assistance for business interruption suffered in the aftermath of 9/11, such as taxi drivers and restaurant workers. With cab drivers in Manhattan, we were able to document the revenue loss. In Queens, it was hard to show. We also did education—"know your rights" kind of stuff.

SD: *Many of New York City's CDCs, such as Mid-Bronx Desperados and Abyssinian CDC, are based in the city's African-American community. Do you work with these groups? What obstacles, if any, has Chhaya, and more broadly Asian CDCs as a whole, encountered in breaking into the CDC community both in New York City and nationally?*

SA: AAFE has a great relationship with the New York CDC community. AAFE was set up around the same time as Abyssinian. The relationship is very good. There is a lot of distrust among the different New York City communities, but not among the leadership.

Nationally our relationships are also strong. Because of the work of the National Coalition of Asian Pacific Americans for Community Development (National CAPACD), Asian American CDCs are becoming more and more visible. Some of our members like AAFE have been around for thirty years.

The problem is subtler: it's that the Asian American community is like the third or fourth thought—it happens in this movement as well. But it's changing slowly.

In our own work, our workshops are very diverse. Because it's Queens, people of all ethnicities attend our events: we get African American, Latino, and white participants. We even had a Canadian immigrant at one of our recent events.

SD: What languages do you work in?

SA: We have staff members who speak Bengali, Urdu, Hindu, and Nepali. We also have volunteers who speak Tibetan and Tamil.

SD: Chhaya CDC has decided to serve New York City's entire South Asian community rather than a specific neighborhood. What was the strategic rationale for doing this?

SA: Because the community is so spread out, there is no single neighborhood base. It was a very conscious decision that we made to call ourselves a citywide group. We went into every commercial corridor we knew of. That made it obvious we couldn't stay sealed in one part of the city.

Now it feels like it's becoming more neighborhood-based (in Jackson Heights in Queens). There are benefits—there is a lot more you can do and you can be more strategic. So some of our programs may become more neighborhood-focused. Our homeownership program will remain citywide, however.

SD: How does your citywide scale affect your ability to be accountable to the neighborhoods you serve?

SA: Through partnerships we work throughout the city. That's how we work in Brooklyn, for instance. We thought about making Chhaya a membership organization, but it seemed like an overwhelming task. We remain accountable by staying engaged with the community. We continually do studies and research surveys. With individual services around the community, we're trying to do it a little differently, based on the responses we receive. We are still figuring things out as we go along. With community development, there are lots of models. It's good to mix it up a little bit.

SD: *What do you see as the main benefits that CDCs provide immigrant communities? How does working with an immigrant community change the kind of work a CDC must do?*

SA: I think we do the same things as CDCs that serve established communities. The needs are the same. They get a little bit more complex in immigrant communities because of immigration status issues, cultural and language issues. But fundamentally it's not different. These are working people who are peacefully living in the city and need access to resources and stability.

The amount of displacement people experience can dramatically affect their lives. As a CDC, what we can do is provide some kind of stability here.

SD: *How has the CDC community responded to growing immigration in the United States?*

SA: It's a mixed bag. There are those who've done well to adjusting to the shift in population and those who haven't. For those who don't respond, because they don't respond, they're kind of stuck. So either you pressure them to do it or do it yourself. New York City is about sixty percent immigrants and their children. If you don't respond to it, you're making a bad business decision.

SD: *Historically many immigrant communities have established a variety of "self-help" mechanisms to pool capital and develop businesses or establish services to support community members. Do you find such mechanisms in the South Asian community and, if so, how does the CDC work to leverage these resources?*

SA: The faith-based community is very large and diverse. We work with faith-based institutions to do outreach, but we would never place our organization within one group. We very consciously keep a balance between Hindus, Muslims, and Christians.

As for the business community, the South Asian business community is strong. There is the Jackson Heights South Asian Business Association, for instance. They're pretty strong and politically connected. There are gender politics that play into this as well. A lot of our staff consists of women, while a lot of the business community is male and conservative. It's not easy, but we are building trust and some business leaders are more progressive than others.

For instance, some of our English classes happened in a print shop. In terms of capital resources, they do exist. They have facilities—lending pools. We advise the people we work with that if they are seeking, for instance, help with a down payment, that might be an available source. Within the Islamic community, there is a whole separate Islamic financial system based on principles of Sharia law.

SD: *What do you see as your CDC's role in building wealth? What other groups do you work with to achieve your wealth-building goals?*

SA: We see our role as informing people of the different ways you can conserve and save. In terms of employment, hopefully moving forward we will offer basic job training. The South Asian community is not accessing many public resources. The percentage of south Asians benefiting from Section 8 or Low Income Housing Tax Credit housing is very, very low. There's a lack of information.

SD: *Do you work with limited equity co-ops, mutual housing associations, community land trusts and other forms of "shared equity"?*

SA: We're trying to find out more about how to convert rental units into co-ops. A lot of units in Queens were built with the plan to convert into co-ops at some point. So we would like to encourage people to look into establishing co-op housing, particularly buildings that provide two-to-five family homes. It would be great to shift that.

SD: *Does Chhaya CDC generate significant earned income?*

SA: Right now, we're highly dependent on foundation support. In large measure, this is because we have had only a short period after the separation from AAFE. One possible source of earned income is development work, but because of the lack of land to develop I don't think it's going to happen. We could charge fees to clients, but we don't want to do that. We are trying to get U.S. Department of Housing and Urban Development (HUD)-certified, which would help. If we are able to assist owners with housing renovation work that gets them up to code, we might be able to earn some income for that.

SD: *What government policies have been most helpful in sustaining your work? What are the biggest government obstacles that you face?*

SA: To date, we also have not accessed much public contract money. We might be able to access Department of Youth & Community Development money. That would be the appropriate source, but it's very political and it's hard to access. The other possible city agency is Housing Preservation and Development. To date we haven't gotten much money, but that's what we're looking to do: contract work with owners, neighborhood improvement work.

For our members, FEMA assistance to date was the most helpful. There is also a city "Jiggetts" housing assistance program [named after an earlier state supreme court case] that has been helpful for members seeking to catch up on back rent.

In terms of obstacles, proving eligibility is not easy. If you're paid in cash, for instance, documenting everything is challenging. Another problem that immigrants face is that public housing is located in parts of the city that people don't feel comfortable living in.

SD: *New York City in recent years has become very much a "hot market" city. The city used to own thousands of parcels of vacant land or boarded-up properties, but no more. How has the rise in land values affected your CDC's work?*

SA: Organizations are getting creative. There is a lot more renovation work of existing property. The definition of CDC work is also broadening. It's not necessarily building development any more. For us, the CDC movement is much broader than bricks and mortar. It comes through these different types of wealth building strategies: employment capacity, stable housing. I see that as community development work. The illegal conversions work we do best fits this—we are legalizing affordable units that are there.

SD: *You've mentioned that in many respects immigrant CDCs are similar to any other CDC, but surely there are also important differences.*

SA: Language and immigration—the way that you do the work changes dramatically when you have to work with people with varying immigration statuses. You need to figure out which people qualify. Communities also want to stay together. Our seniors need environments that are supportive. And there are also cultural issues you face. People respond differently. You can't have a traditional counselor ask a

"With community development, there are lots of models. **It's good to mix it up a little bit.**"

South Asian woman for family financial information. That would be seen as betraying her family. Nuances like that. Having an immigrant organization doing this type of work is needed if this work is going to be done properly.

SD: *You serve on the national board of National CAPACD. What are some of the movement's national priorities?*

SA: One priority is simply to build up the capacity of Asian-American community-based organizations. A second key objective is to inform the broader CDC movement of how to be a little more aware and understanding of our organizations, and communities. We are advocating with intermediaries within the movement to be more responsive to the needs of Asian and Pacific Islander communities.

SD: *Are there specific objectives that National CAPACD has?*

SA: Well, one is building up the capacity of our organizations—this involves training and technical assistance. Second, there is the political aspect of our work. We would like the federal government to be more responsive. Right now, there are set-asides for Native and African-American communities. We don't expect a set-aside, but we want to make sure resources are invested in the communities in accord with population size. Right now, it's just not holding up.

SD: *A lot of Chhaya CDC's work centers on housing, but many CDCs, including Asian Americans for Equality, have branched out to do more business development work. Is this a direction you anticipate following in the future? How will you decide to take on new directions, such as individual development accounts or commercial development?*

SA: We haven't talked about commercial development, but we have talked about developing a community center—a one-stop-shop type of thing. There is a need for transitional housing, so we have

ideas about that as well. IDAs [individual development accounts]—
we definitely need to do that because of our homeownership work.

SD: *In the current "immigration debate," most of the focus has
been on undocumented Latino workers. But as you have
mentioned, the South Asian immigrant community is likewise
affected. How is the South Asian community affected by and
responding to this debate?*

SA: We have a community of very mixed status. In New York City in particular there is a good percentage of people with expired visas. So it's going
to have a great impact. The family visas issue will also have a great impact.

Housing will also be greatly affected. Right now, you effectively
have undocumented housing—illegal immigrants in illegal housing. Even if someone in the household has legal status, often there
is a family member that is not. Giving people legal status will enable
them to speak up and secure basic human rights. So you have a lot
of the same issues as with the Latino community.

SD: *What do you see as the most important challenges or opportunities facing immigrant-based CDCs today? Where do you think
the National CAPACD and Chhaya should focus its energies over
the next 5-10 years?*

SA: There are unbelievable opportunities for National CAPACD and
Chhaya. For Chhaya, there is no other organization in the city or
even nationally doing this type of work and the need is immense.
The infrastructure is there. The federal government and foundation
world has done some good work in putting this in place. For us, it's
about building capacity and accessing that—I see a lot of opportunity as long as we stay on track.

As for National CAPACD, I feel it's really coming of age. We've
been steadily building it since 1999. In addition, the founding organizations are in a much better place. The networks are even stronger
now. We have a lot of executive directors who are very seasoned. I
think our biggest asset is that it has a lot of member organizations
that are strong in their community base. And I think the country
is trying to find ways to adjust to the new immigrant population.
We're in a good position to play a leadership role in that arena,
because we have the expertise and know-how.

Maggie DeSantis

Maggie DeSantis is a Founder and President of Warren/ Conner Development Corporation, a Detroit-based community development corporation noted for its "comprehensive" approach to community development that combines commercial development, service delivery, and community organizing. Since it began operating in 1984, Warren/Conner has played an important role in redeveloping Detroit's Eastside. Signs of revitalization include the development of the 60,000 square-foot Mack Alter Square Shopping Center, a revitalized Warren/ Conner Shopping Center, and hundreds of new homes.

Warren/Conner owns its 30,000 square-foot, renovated headquarters building and also serves as landlord to a number of service agencies. Warren/Conner is the parent corporation to a number of subsidiary groups, including a youth development program, a workforce development group, a community organizing and capacity-building group, and three real estate subsidiaries.

In 2015, DeSantis announced her intention to step down from leading Warren/Conner in early 2016, but said she intends to remain active in Detroit community development.

Interviewed in 2008

Steve Dubb: What were the origins of the Warren/Conner Develop-
ment Corporation? How has the organization's relationship to
the community from which it emerged evolved over time?

Maggie DeSantis: The organization started after a two-year process. In the early
1980s, I was working with the Southeastern Community Association
(SECA) to develop a community plan. This organization is the result of
that work. I lived in the neighborhood and I was working with another
agency. That agency assigned me to work with SECA and help them
develop a plan. The plan we created called for the development of a
coalition of businesses, residents, and institutions in the area. We asked
a hospital that was being built at the corner of Warren and Conner to
support our effort and to our surprise, they said yes. That led to a two
year planning process. And then they loaned us the initial $56,000 that
was used to hire me. So the initial board was a coalition of businesses,
residents, and institutions. It has always been a coalition of organizations and a coalition of those three segments of the community.

SD: *Your board, with its designated business, institutional, and*
residential representatives has a somewhat unusual structure.
What benefits has this multi-stakeholder model brought to your
organization?

MD: Well, it is hard to say what a normal CDC board structure is. A traditional CDC that does affordable housing might have a lawyer, an
architect, a real estate broker, and a few community representatives.

We have always had more of a community leadership type of structure. You get a much broader agenda and a much broader way of
thinking about things that way. It really came out of that initial planning process. If we were going to have far-reaching impact, we knew
that you couldn't do that with a board that is insulated and is focused
only on bricks and mortar, or that is only residents or only business
or institutions. It is not necessarily easier, but people kind of know
that the board is diverse and it has a lot of leaders on it. There is a fair
amount of credibility that is attached to that.

SD: *Your organization has a number of affiliate groups or pro-*
grams, including a youth development group, a workforce
development group, a community organizing or capacity-build-
ing group, and three real estate subsidiaries. Could you explain

*briefly how each of these developed and how you coordinate
their activities so that they support each other?*

MD: Warren/Conner is now set up as the parent corporation. The affiliates
originally started as programs of ours. The programs developed out
of that initial planning process in the early 1980s. The youth program was developed with local institutions and the local police and
is now a separate subsidiary. The workforce development was created
out of an economic development plan in the late 1980s and early
1990s. The community organizing and capacity building program
was formed out of a community planning process through the Casey
Foundation's "rebuilding communities initiative" in the mid 1990s.
The real estate pieces—the original decision was that our bricks and
mortar were going to be commercial rather than housing.

   We came to a point where we were a nonprofit that sponsored
different programs—it became very cumbersome: to some we were
economic development, to some we were organizing, to some we
were youth. As we got to the point of thinking about leadership
succession and survival beyond the current executive director, we
decided that each of those programs should have its own board,
its own identity, its own tax status, and its own executive director.
Warren/Conner is the sole owner of the subsidiaries but each one
has its own separate tax status and can raise its own money and the
board is in charge of the mission. We've negotiated operating agreements between the parent and the subsidiaries over how decisions
get made and who has authority over what.

   The restructuring process—we made that the basis of our 2002-
2007 strategic plan. We just finished our new strategic plan going
forward for the next five years. It was developed by all of the boards,
and is going to be presented to the WCDC board in the next couple
of weeks. It is really five separate plans with some integration on
some issues we are working on in common.

SD: *What are your priorities going forward?*

MD: Our youth program and workforce development are going to go citywide. There is a big emphasis on collaboration to work with other
organizations to be more effective. We've changed our philosophy
about community organizing a little bit. Traditionally we've worked
with helping block clubs—now there is a focus of uniting block clubs

into associations so they can have more influence. There is not a lot of change in the basic way that we do the work in the community—just a lot more emphasis on collaboration and a larger geographic scope for two of them and then a big emphasis on entrepreneurship, on developing more earned income, and tapping more into individual contributions so we can reduce our dependence on foundation grants.

SD: *The resident ownership model you use for one of your real estate subsidiaries is rather unusual. Could you discuss the resident share-ownership structure of Detroit East CDC? Specifically, how does this work and what financial return, if any, do resident owners receive?*

MD: Basically, it's a for-profit shareholder cooperative, which means that regardless of the number of shares you own you still only have one vote. We've got institutional owners with a lot of stock, and resident owners with a little stock, and they all have one vote. The real gist of it is that it's like a closed corporation in many ways—if we want to sell more stock, it has to be tied to a specific project. Some have donated the stock to Warren/Conner. Mostly they hold on to it.

At one point, it owned eight acres of property, but it also had a huge debt load. So it formed a partnership with Eastside LAND, Inc., another of our subsidiaries, to make that package of land attractive for brownfield redevelopment and investment by a developer-partner. Now there's a shopping center there that wouldn't be possible without that initial investment by our shareholders in the late 1980s.

Detroit East CDC still owns one building. We are doing a rehab of that building. The corporation has spawned a great deal of development. The shopping center is a 60,000 square-foot very attractive shopping center. The equity raised through Detroit East CDC allowed us to buy the land and hold out for it to be developed in a way that would benefit the community. The members haven't gotten much of an economic return, but what they've spawned is pretty incredible. And they probably will end up making an economic return on the one building that the corporation still holds.

We are not looking to sell the entire building, but rather we are looking for a partner who buys an ownership share. We have to continue to reduce the debt. In the weak Michigan market, the hardest part is finding a tenant.

SD: *What is the membership and size of Detroit East CDC?*

MD: It has about 200 resident members and five institutional members, and it has roughly $200,000 in initial investment equity.

SD: *If you had to choose three accomplishments of Warren/Conner's work that you are most proud of, what would be?*

MD: There is no one specific thing. Anyone who knows the Eastside is always amazed at the level of development, even though we haven't done everything ourselves. Between our organizing, advocacy, and bricks-and-mortar work, we have spawned organizations that are bringing block grants in and building homes, we built the shopping center, and we've created programs that are twenty years old and still serving kids. It's the sum total that causes people to recognize that the Eastside is a strong part of the city and everyone recognizes that. It relates to our influence and existing as an advocate, more than anything else.

SD: *Shifting gears and thinking nationally, obviously there has been tremendous growth in CDCs and CDFIs and the community wealth building movement more generally since Warren/ Conner was founded in 1984. What do you see as most important changes brought about by the growth of CDCs and CDFIs?*

MD: There's been growth, but there is also stagnation. If you start where the industry or movement started in the 1960s—clearly there is now a community development industry or movement. If you compare with the mid-1990s to where we are now, there is definitely stagnation. A lot of traditional funders are starting to question whether the movement is at an impasse. There has always been a debate within the movement between brick-and-mortar and comprehensive work. There is a huge crop of people like me—of founding visionary executive directors—that in many ways defines community development. You have to be a little bit obsessive to want to do this. You fight really big odds. So you have the personalities that don't always think about succession. So there is a question of what will happen when this generation starts to die or burn out. The 1990s—there aren't as many people who have the same kind of emotional make-up as the sixties generation did—too few to really sustain the community development industry without a lot of intervention. And then you have cities that are older and older and older, and funders who are less and less

"It is not necessarily easier, but people kind of know that the board is diverse and it has a lot of leaders on it. **There is a fair amount of credibility that is attached to that.**"

---

willing to make that investment. You have a federal government that is backing away—that started in the early 1980s but they are backing away more. The national organizations that used to exist—like the National Congress for Community Economic Development and the National Community Builders Network—they disappeared. So the Center for Community Builders (and the National Alliance of Community Economic Development Associations) is trying to resurrect that national voice. But it's really a much more localized voice and it varies from state to state.

SD: *For Warren/Conner, what impact has declining federal support had for your work?*

MD: Our strategic plan talks about more entrepreneurship. We were never that reliant on federal funding. The 1980s spawned a generation of CDCs that were more entrepreneurial. The real issue is whether your revenue portfolio is balanced so you're not relying on any one source. Our response is to make a strategic plan to balance earned revenue with government contracts and foundation funding.

Right now, we've got a ventures committee that is working to create ventures. There are several options we are looking at. We decided to take the two buildings we own and convert them into profit centers—we're working to attract tenants that pay market-rate rent. We are looking to buy a convenience center in the community that we helped build. We are looking to start a wholesale product distribution business. We have a campaign slogan "I'm an Eastsider" and market products with that slogan to various retailers. So there are a number of ways that we are trying to get serious about entrepreneurialism. We are furthest along on the building piece since we already own the buildings and know how to do real estate.

SD: *Another area, which involves not declining federal support, but rather federal financial deregulation, has led to the rise of a predatory lending industry that strips away the assets and wealth that community development groups try to build. How has the Detroit Eastside and the community Warren/Conner serves been affected by the foreclosure crisis? At the level of policy, what do you think can be accomplished in this area?*

MD: Because we really don't do housing, we really have not gotten directly involved in the foreclosure side. We are trying to partner with organizations that are involved in it. The impact in our neighborhood has been horrible, terrible. Every day we see the impact of it. In the neighborhoods we try to work in, it's bad.

We know there are a lot of people working on it. The only thing I think that is going to make a difference—this is me speaking, independently of my role at Warren/Conner—is that we have to have a moratorium on foreclosures. The houses are emptying out and they are being bought en masse by absentee investors. They are not going to have a mechanism to pay attention to the neighborhoods. It's just bad, what's happening.

SD: *Are there specific areas where Detroit CDCs and community organizations need to focus their efforts to better develop capacity?*

MD: The only strategy that has kept the city from dying completely in these last fifteen years are the CDCs, but folks don't understand that. We don't market ourselves. Detroit has never had a progressive community development atmosphere.

The industry is dying in the city. Michigan is probably the state with the worst economy in the country. When Michigan gets sick, Detroit is on its deathbed. The local Detroit funders are reacting and many are not supporting community development. There is a lot of withdrawal of funding. Instead, there is a strategy of targeting. The city picked six neighborhoods—almost none of them have viable CDCs. They were picked for other reasons. The older CDCs like us will make it, but there are CDCs that are dying off.

Some funders get it. Others do not. They've gone to other cities—they are trying to import what they see as other city's solutions, but the problems of Detroit are more severe and different. Detroit used to be inhabited by two million people spaciously. Now

"The only strategy that has kept the city from dying completely in these last fifteen years are the CDCs, but folks don't understand that. We don't market ourselves. **Detroit has never had a progressive community development atmosphere.**"

---

it has 900,000. So the level of vacancy is stunning, much worse than other cities—that's going to require more radical strategies, and there are too few leaders in Detroit willing to go there.

SD: *Your organization does a considerable amount of commercial development, but also does a considerable amount of community organizing. As you know, there has been a long-standing debate regarding how to balance development and organizing and these goals are often seen as contradictory. How does Warren/Conner achieve this balance?*

MD: We've never seen them as contradictory, although obviously it does create a dynamic tension. We are straight up about it—we say to funders, "This is our members' and constituents' priority, and this is what we are funding." With our Rebuilding Communities subsidiary, our community organizing program, Casey gave us eight years. When that dried up, we were faced with the harsh reality of how hard it is to raise money for organizing. It is a challenge.

It's what we're supposed to be doing, so the real question is how we find the resources for it. The balance is more of a funding challenge than anything else. I frankly think that the CDCs that say they feel they don't need to organize are copping out—they just don't want to do it.

SD: *Presumably, the argument that CDCs make who don't organize is that it is hard to organize against a target who is also a development partner.*

MD: Well, that's true. The bottom line is you can't organize around everything. You have to be more strategic and creative about where you get resources. You can't ask for money for people you organize against.

It also boils down to your philosophy of organizing. Some follow a consensus model. Others follow the more confrontational Alinsky model. We define our organizing as relationship-based. Some would say that is not real organizing. But it is certainly better than no organizing. Also, the model of organizing that is appropriate depends on the community.

SD: *One area of considerable discussion in the CDC community has been the issue of scale. Scale is seen as necessary for accessing greater amounts of capital, but can also mean larger organizations that may (or may not) become disconnected from the communities they serve. You mentioned that in its strategic plan, two of Warren/Conner's affiliate organizations plan to expand their scale to extend citywide. How has Warren/Conner sought to build scale while retaining community responsiveness?*

MD: Some of it has to do with the decisions you make. The one affiliate that really retains a strong relationship with the community is not one of the ones that are going citywide. I think part of the reason this is so is that we recognize that.

Another part of it is whether you are going to remain philosophically committed to the people you serve. That's not just a geographical question. For workforce development, we are now citywide but we've never lost the commitment to serving the hardest to employ. In the youth program, we have the ability to go citywide but we generally choose to go into schools that have the most at-risk kids. Sometimes the most philosophical of problems are invented by academics, who would rather study than *do*.

Steven McCullough

Steven McCullough served as President and CEO of Bethel New Life from 2005 until 2010. Bethel New Life is a faith-based Lutheran community development corporation in Chicago that has played a leadership role in its community work. Since 1979, Bethel New Life has played an important role in redeveloping Chicago's Westside, with a focus on Chicago's Garfield and Austin neighborhoods. To date, Bethel has helped bring $110 million of investment into Chicago's Westside, placed over 7,000 people in living-wage jobs, and developed over 1,000 units of affordable housing. But Bethel is perhaps best known for its transit-oriented development work, which combines energy efficient homes, brownfield redevelopment, schools, shopping, and jobs in a combined and mutually reinforcing effort.

Since leaving Bethel, McCullough has remained active in community development; in September 2015, he became Chief Operating Officer of Communities in Schools' national office.

Interviewed in 2009

Steve Dubb: What were the origins of Bethel New Life? How has the organization's relationship to the community from which it emerged evolved over time?

Steven McCullough: The organization started out of the Lutheran Church thirty years ago. It started with members of the congregation seeing the deterioration of the housing market and housing stock in West Garfield Park and deciding to make an investment in rehabbing a three-unit building. That is how the organization began as a church ministry. It grew from there, and then it got into employment services. They weren't able to rent or own a home without having residents who were gainfully employed. So the organization grew by filling gaps where the public sector and private sector were not present. That includes a lot of services and coordinated efforts that require real focus and attention the church can provide. The original capitalization was $9,000. Today we have a $13.5 million budget, with 250 staff in the organization.

SD: *Does Bethel own the facilities it develops? What are its asset holdings?*

SM: We have about $40 million in assets. That includes three independent living facilities, assisted living facilities, and different program sites. We own those facilities as well.

SD: *Does Bethel generate income from rent revenue on the buildings it owns?*

SM: We do. Not on all of our property, but we do generate rent income from the people we lease to—churches, nonprofits, for-profit businesses—things like that.

SD: *You started your career in the private sector but then moved into community development. What prompted you to make this shift?*

SM: Throughout my career, I have always been doing work in the community, whether on a volunteer basis or as a paid staff person. The motivation was always there. At the point that I decided to shift, I just wanted to apply my knowledge and skills to a productive use that would impact people's lives. I worked for Quaker Oats for eight years and then did consulting for Accenture, but I just felt that helping

"The original capitalization was $9,000. Today we have a $13.5 million budget, with 250 staff in the organization."

people produce products wasn't where my spirit was at. I wanted to have a direct impact on people and community. The opportunity to switch career tracks came at a perfect point in time. I hadn't bought a big car or a big house. I didn't have the trappings that would keep you in a corporate lifestyle. So it came at a point where I said to myself, it was either now, or I would forever hold my peace.

SD: *In a summer 2006 letter that you placed on Bethel's website, you note that in your first year as Bethel's president, the organization developed "a new mission statement, board members, bylaws, and staff." That sounds like a lot of change. Could you give some of the background as to why a new direction was needed at that time?*

SM: A couple of things: first of all, I succeeded the founder. Mary [Nelson] is very much a part of Bethel and remains very active doing consulting work and things like that. Mary is extremely entrepreneurial. I'm much more process-oriented and operational by nature. So I felt I needed to make sure we have a really good engine that wasn't centered on an entrepreneurial framework. I am more of a person that wants to have a structure and process and know we are producing the outcomes we are committed to. A lot of that push to change was to really narrow the focus of the organization and provide a framework of: Here's where we need to operate effectively from a governance perspective and staff perspective. That involved a big culture shift in the organization. While all of this change was happening we were going through personnel changes—the board was changing at the same time. We decided to take that year and do our best to transform the organization to a model that could be effective without Mary as the lead.

SD: *In particular, you mention that cuts were made in cultural arts programming and multi-family rental property management.*

Nonprofits are not always known for their ability to cut programs that are not working, so can you discuss what problems Bethel faced at the time and the impact of the changes you made?

SM: I have a couple more to add to that list. There are other areas we have transitioned out of over the last two years—we got out of doing Head Start programming. This past summer we got out of supportive housing. In both, we found a partner organization to take on responsibility for the programs and kept services in the community. But the change has created a lot of internal angst in the organization.

Here's the thing with Bethel—we are the largest CDC in the area. We are the only true CDC in the area that also does service programming. It is difficult to do service programming when you're constantly under-funded. Government doesn't pay the full cost. Over the last three to four years, a lot of our unrestricted dollars came from housing. That money largely went away. We have declining donations and earned income. The programs that we chose to exit were always subsidized programs. We always had to put additional resources over and above the main sources, because we wanted to make sure we were producing a quality product. When the economic crisis hit, our ability to generate unrestricted dollars also took a hit. These are programs that are well regarded and a lot of Board members are tied to them emotionally. A lot of our staff members are also tied to them emotionally. But it was necessary to keep the organization as a whole on solid ground.

From July 2005 to today, we've dropped about $4 million in programming. As a result of that, we are much more stable. We don't have to subsidize so many programs. But it wasn't easy or popular.

SD: *Being more forward looking, could you discuss Bethel's current strategic plan and the community of choice framework that you use? As I understand Bethel's strategic plan, Bethel has chosen to focus on three key issues—housing, education, and wealth building—and work in four central areas—workforce development, investment, asset building, and asset retention—to advance on those issues. How does this work in practice and what progress do you see Bethel as having made?*

SM: We just had our strategic planning retreat. We wanted to respond and be responsive to the economic crisis. We just had our retreat this

September, from which we will develop our next strategic plan. When reviewing our current strategic plan, I think we were successful—out of that came some good stuff. We really beefed up our foreclosure prevention work. We are really providing good resources to residents who are challenged in terms of their ability to be homeowners.

We also have developed our Community Savings Center, in partnership with Park National Bank and Thrivent Financial for Lutherans, to offer banking products that are cheaper and more accessible than mainstream banking. We have the largest matched savings account in the state. So, on the wealth building aspect, we did really well.

In terms of education, we also did really well. We have staff embedded in one elementary school and one high school. We are doing after-school programming and mentorship. We have an alumni program working with families and students in financial aid packages and retention in college.

The only area that has been really challenging is housing. With the economy and the housing market, we really weren't able to produce what we wanted to with that particular strategy. But it allowed us to reframe and take a run on it in a different way. Our work now centers on making sure that properties don't get abandoned and become blight on the neighborhoods that we work in. It's a mixed blessing. It's unfortunate that a housing market took that turn for the worse. But it has also allowed us to be even more engaged as an organization in the community.

SD: *What are the demographics of the neighborhoods you work in?*

SM: We work mainly in two communities: Austin and Garfield Park. Garfield Park has 40,000 to 50,000 residents and Austin has 120,000. Both are predominately African American (about 90 percent), but with a growing Latino population, which right now is at about eight percent. The last two percent is everyone else. The age breakdown is interesting. We have a huge elder population and a huge youth population and a small adult population in the middle. Unemployment was 12 percent in 2007, back when the city average was about eight percent. Both have since gone up.

In terms of education, we're below city average in graduation rate and above the city average in terms of truancy. Overall, as a community we have the highest rate of recidivism in the state. There is a high level of crime and high gang activity. But the other interesting thing is that over the past ten years we've seen a growing middle class. Looking at income there has been a shrinking of the low-income population and a rise in the middle-income population. It's about a 10 percentage-point swing, which is significant.

SD: *Could you discuss Bethel's work with ex-offenders?*

SM: About six years ago, we started to do specific work with folks coming out of prison. We called it, "Welcome Home"—we give them a paid internship to work within Bethel in various capacities (facilities, administration, food service)—every area that is not sensitive to having a record. We give them a two-month paid internship and at the same time they are getting work experience and full time job search, and hopefully at the end they get gainful employment. Every six to eight weeks we bring in a new class and put them through the same process. We've been able to hire quite a few ourselves—I can't even count how many—and we've been able to place others into other workplaces. The most difficult thing to do is to get a job when you don't have one. So that's the goal: put people in a position of strength. Give them a track record. We're looking to expand that. We want to do more and bring on more employers—and just be able to do more.

SD: *Bethel, of course, is known for its work in transit-oriented development and green building and, in particular, the Bethel Center and Beth Anne Center projects. Can you discuss these projects? Also, more broadly, how and why did transit-oriented development and green building become a priority for Bethel?*

SM: Transit oriented development came first. It came out of an effort to save the green line, which is the elevated line that runs through the West and South sides of the city and goes through downtown Chicago. In the mid-90s, there were a huge amount of issues with the transportation line—declining infrastructure: the rail was crumbling, there was no money to subsidize it. And the second thing was declining ridership—not as many riders as the Chicago Transit Authority (CTA) expected, although it was still very much in use. The administration of CTA wanted to shut it down. Bethel and the local government—namely, the closest suburbs (Oak Park and

River Forest) came together in a coalition to save the green line from being dismantled. Out of that, there was a need to demonstrate that this line could not only sustain itself, but that it could thrive. As a community, this came out of a community effort, there was a decision to design a project that showed that residents in the city and the suburbs do use this line, that the green line not only provided access to transportation but could serve as a building block for the local economy.

The Bethel Center came out of that—it took over 10 years from initial concept to actual opening. The reason for that was mainly because we had to justify the market—that is, we had to demonstrate that there was a market that wanted and needed various types of services. That was one factor. The other was that government and private sector were not going to make that investment. It was sited on a huge brownfield. Bethel never had enough money. It took 10 years, but we were able to do it. We used state money, federal money, and New Markets tax credits—over time we just put it together. So we finished construction 2005 and opened the doors in 2006, and it really is an example of the community's effort to revitalize its main source of public transportation and use that as a tool to attract families to use transit and keeps cars off the street. The other way it anchors the community is that within the center there are a lot of services—we have the Community Savings Center, a branch of the attorney general's office, a child care center, a dry cleaner, a coffee shop, an employment center, and a community technology center—these were things that were missing in the community that people wanted to bring back.

The green technology was laid on top of that. When we did the Bethel Center and subsequently all of other construction, it came out of a mindset that we need to find ways to lower the cost of living so we could have housing and businesses be more accessible. One of the ways to do that is to incorporate green technology in your construction. When we built the Bethel Center, it was a LEED (Leadership in Energy and Environmental Design) Gold-certified building. We were one of the first and we paid a premium for that. None of the contractors knew exactly what they were doing—they had these concepts, but they hadn't been market-tested. Looking back, I'm not sure if it was worth pursing a Gold certification—at the time, being a first mover, you pay a price for that.

"When we did the Bethel Center and subsequently all of other construction, it came out of a mindset that **we need to find ways to lower the cost of living so we could have housing and businesses be more accessible**."

SD: *How have achievements in "green" development assisted Bethel to meet its community development objectives?*

SM: A couple of ways: one is that we want to demonstrate that this kind of development can be done in very low-income communities. I think we've been able to demonstrate that. I also think we can demonstrate to residents that using green technology can really save you money on your monthly utilities. When we do housing development, one of our points is you're not only looking at your price point, but at how much of your monthly budget is going to go to utilities. I think we have made a difference in that regard.

Although we haven't gotten to scale, we also demonstrate that jobs have been created around the maintenance and construction of green buildings. It's a viable opportunity that is now at our feet, where we can take advantage of putting people to work on green projects.

SD: *Bethel has worked with both DePaul University's Chaddick Institute for Metropolitan Development and the Center for Urban Research and Learning at Loyola University. Can you describe the partnerships you've developed? How effective have they been?*

SM: Universities play a big role. Not only do they help with the evaluation of programs, but they also help us design and implement new programming. The work with DePaul involves trying to work with youth, leading community change. We are engaging youth in visioning what their community would look like and really instilling a sense of ownership and leadership in the community from that perspective—and that's been effective.

The Center for Urban Research and Learning (CURL) has been in and out of various programs. Most recently they worked with us designing curriculum for what was then our Head Start staff. They helped us identify training needs and link resources to us. They also do a lot of research that we use relative to housing and they are always a source of interns and post-graduate employment as well. That connection is strong. Not only with DePaul and Loyola, but Northwestern University as well.

SD: *One feature of Bethel that is particularly impressive is Bethel's high use of volunteers. How has Bethel been able to achieve and maintain this high level of volunteer involvement?*

SM: We do have a lot of volunteers. We have about 11,000 to 12,000 volunteer hours. What that means is it could be a project over a weekend or an extended project. We come out of a church—we're a church-based organization. Out of the Lutheran Church, we are connected with Lutheran churches across the country and particularly in the Chicago region there is always one big project going on. The other source of volunteers is the corporate-based—either directly or through the United Way.

SD: *You mentioned that Bethel had the largest individual development account (IDA) program in the state. How large is it and how do you integrate matched savings programs into your broader wealth building objectives?*

SM: We have 425 matched savings accounts and we're constantly doing financial literacy training as well. We try to develop a pipeline of people to buy a home, start a business, or begin a college education. It is also tied into our housing development and rehabilitation work and matching families to those opportunities. The one area that we haven't gone deep into is small business development, and that has been a high area of interest, so we partner with small business development centers to support these entrepreneurs.

SD: *Could you talk a little about the work that Bethel has done in community organizing, such as policy work and voter registration? More broadly, how do you balance community organizing and community development?*

SM: Community organizing is really about community block organiz-
        ing and outreach to institutions, like the police. So that's about
        what works. We work block-by-block, beat-by-beat, connecting
        police to residents in the community, identifying trouble issues and
        working to resolve them. And we do the same thing with schools.
        So community organizing is more of a relationship-building piece
        and bridge piece than organizing toward a political end. That fits
        into everything else we do. Without that grounding framework, we
        would have a much more difficult time getting our programs out in
        the community and making sure they are successful and people take
        advantage of them.

        We also do voter registration. That's another way to connect to
        institutions. There is a big gap to cover to connect community
        members to politicians, whether it is at the city, state, or federal
        level. And gaining access for our community—providing a voice
        to politicians is important. We are also working on the census and
        designing it to make sure that we get everyone counted.

SD: *Could you talk about the sustainability of Bethel itself? How*
        does it successfully raise funds to maintain its operations? To
        what degree does earned income help Bethel?

SM: About 60 percent of our budget is government based, about 20
        percent is from corporations and foundations, about 10 percent
        is individual and church contributions, and about 10 percent is
        earned income. We definitely want to see less dependency on gov-
        ernment revenue and a bigger part from individual and church
        income and earned income. That's the work. We have to make sure
        that we are not biting off expenses when we do programming and
        make sure we get the most revenue from what the funder requires
        and what we require.

SD: *Shifting gears and thinking nationally, obviously there has*
        been tremendous growth in CDCs and the community wealth
        building movement more generally since Bethel New Life was
        founded in 1979. What do you see as most important changes
        brought about by the growth of CDCs?

SM: At a national level, CDCs have become kind of like their own
        industry. The value they have brought to the national conversation

"We work block-by-block, beat-by-beat, connecting police to residents in the community, identifying trouble issues and working to resolve them. And we do the same thing with schools."

is a voice for low-income neighborhoods that thirty years ago were abandoned and under-resourced, underdeveloped, and neglected. What CDCs have done as a whole is bring some local stability in terms of investments in housing, jobs, and retail to communities that would never have gotten them. Especially in the inner city, but also in rural communities, CDCs have made a difference in bringing in dollars that wouldn't have come otherwise. They have been catalytic in their impact.

The future—now everyone has woken up and seen the value in a revitalized inner city and are starting to make those investments. The role of a CDC is evolving, it is always evolving.

The other thing CDCs have brought is their innovation—both in the types of projects they take on as well as financing. CDCs structure government and private source revenue and make those projects work. CDCs have brought a wave of innovation that never would have otherwise existed. Those are a couple of things. This has happened for the past thirty years, but especially the past ten. Financial institutions and banks look to CDCs to be their advance team in terms of market development. Once CDCs can demonstrate the market is a viable one, you tend to see additional investment from banks. It could lead to gentrification in some areas, but if done well it could lead to stabilization of a local economy. That's the good that comes out of a CDC. It's what a CDC that is really focused on building up residents and assets in a community can do.

SD: *For Bethel, what impact has the federal government had for your work? The past decade has seen federal cuts, but now there are potential new funding streams.*

SM: For the most part, the new funding has yet to be seen. On the upside, there is a huge potential for investment that CDCs could potentially take advantage of. The whole green technology policy thrust and green investments are welcome and need to be part of the future for CDCs to be in that kind of work. The challenge with that, from my perspective, is that I have yet to see the market for green development actually take off yet. You have the training programs, but the jobs aren't really there yet. Are there jobs at the end of the rainbow? Are there actual projects that create the number and scale of jobs that are needed? Or that put the economy in the direction that the Obama administration wants in terms of green infrastructure?

In the past, we've seen efforts to promote CDCs in the government. Bush's faith-based initiatives weren't really new money, but a re-framing. I have that the same type of skepticism about where we are at today. It is way too early to judge. For CDCs, right now, it's great in terms of visibility and exposure. But, at the end of the day, there is very little in terms of resources being dedicated to the work that is being done. At Bethel, we've been able to work with federal officials to get money, but a lot of that is an exception to the rule. We're in a big "let's wait and see" time. Let's see from a federal perspective how the administration is moving forward and how Obama's ideas of investment in the inner city are going to play out in terms of investment in transit-oriented development and greening of the nation. I'm very encouraged that some of the departments are talking to each other and doing joint planning to move forward. I am looking forward to seeing proposals that actually put money out on the street and make it accessible for CDCs to invest in neighborhoods. I also hope the Administration will encourage private sector investment. CDCs do not work in isolation, but with government and the private sector. When there is an absence of one, CDCs don't invest as effectively.

SD: *Another area, federal financial deregulation, has led to the rise of a predatory lending industry that strips away the assets and wealth that community development groups try to build. How has the Chicago Westside and the community Bethel serves been affected by the foreclosure crisis?*

SM: It's been very devastating. We've seen a huge spike. We're a HUD-certified counseling agency and we see quite a bit of situations where

"At a national level, CDCs have become kind of like their own industry."

families are in foreclosure or at the brink. The challenge is identifying who actually owns the property—the loans have been packaged and repackaged so often that is hard to find who is the loan servicer and who you can actually talk to. If you can get that cleaned up, that would help.

Another related challenge is that we're in a market with declining home values. It adds even more difficulty in terms of putting foreclosed homes back on the market. Part of the challenge is pushing banks to work with CDCs and government to identify properties and come up with creative solutions so those properties don't go abandoned. When abandonment occurs, that opens up the block to drug activity and more gang activity. It becomes a higher crime neighborhood and that's really destabilizing. We need the private sector to give us the tools and information and work with CDCs and government to turn that into an opportunity for stable housing.

SD: *Is Bethel participating in the federal government's Neighborhood Stabilization Program (designed to assist cities to put foreclosed property back into productive re-use)?*

SM: Yes, we are an approved developer for Neighborhood Stabilization Program (NSP) dollars in the first round of funding (NSP 1) and we are part of a consortium with the Chicago Rehab Network (CRN) that has submitted a proposal in the "NSP-2" round.

SD: *Are there specific areas where Chicago CDCs and community organizations need to focus their efforts to better develop capacity?*

SM: This is a tough sector in terms of keeping people and building capacity. One big thing is the human capacity need for CDCs to hire and retain talent. We are always getting picked off—either by government or the private sector. The life cycle of a new person in the CDC world is very short. That's one, a human capacity need. Two, there is a financial capacity need. We need flexible financial products that we can use to do things like complement Neighborhood Stabilization Plan funding to invest in small business where banks have basically pulled out and are retrenching. Somebody needs to fill the gap. CDCs can do that, but we need the financial and investment support to make that happen.

SD: *One area of considerable discussion in the CDC community has been the issue of scale. Scale can boost organizational capacity, but can also mean larger organizations that may become disconnected from the communities they serve. Given Bethel's large size, how has Bethel sought to build scale while retaining community responsiveness?*

SM: That's what we talk about all of the time. I think the way we are handling it is two-fold. One, we've got to be smaller. That's what we've been doing over the past three years. We need to get to core operations in terms of programming that allows us to be less about service and more about community development. I think the environment has evolved so that we have enough partners that we can hand off a lot of the programming. In the past we were the only ones who could do it. The big thing that has changed is that we have more partners in the community now that we can work with. So you can be more nimble and creative—other organizations and institutions and churches can pick up the weight and be just as effective and that allows the CDC to be really creative. We are at a size where I feel we can do work that no one is doing like financial services, the elder care programming we are doing—and at the same time be responsive to community needs like the foreclosure crisis and drug and violence activity in the neighborhoods. It requires a strong administrative staff that can really manage well, and then you need a great program staff that knows and is engaged with the community. That takes times to build up. I believe there should be a stage in the CDC life cycle where it needs to get smaller in order to be more effective and focus on those things CDCs bring that no one else does. And that is the innovation piece—bringing solutions to communities that haven't been thought of or created for residents to have access to resources that improve their lives. CDCs can get too big to be relevant. That's the tension that every CDC should have and it is a healthy tension to have.

SD: *What are your priorities going forward?*

SM: Coming out of our strategic planning retreat in September, we identified five areas. The first is around continuing to support our elder community. In this community, you are either really young or really old. Our elder community is growing—it needs more support so residents can stay in the community. The second is around youth—making sure youth have access and opportunity to resources that make them competitive in the workplace, as well as education. The third area is building resident leadership—identifying leaders—youth, elders, and everyone in between—really developing the next wave of leaders. The fourth is around policy and that involves work to develop policies that benefit residents and community; for example, there is a lot of work done with formerly incarcerated individuals around expunging of records—that needs to be policy that is engaged with the community. And the final area is around stewardship of the community's assets as well as the organization's assets. We need to make sure we are highlighting the effectiveness of our programming and the community's efforts to improve the community research, analysis, and promotion of what works well and what needs to happen to improve the community. Those are the five directives we are going to be working under beginning in 2010.

SD: *If you had to choose three accomplishments of Bethel New Life's work that you are most proud of, what would be?*

SM: We're most proud of the jobs we have been able to create both internally as an organization and externally. Number two is our work around elders in the community in providing really excellent support. The third area would be around our work in bringing financial resources to the community in a way that is affordable and accessible and turning those into tangible assets, whether it be housing or business, and thereby moving people forward. Those are the top three. That's Bethel's legacy to date. There is a lot more we are working on and can do, but I point to those as we've really increased the community's quality of life in those areas.

Bernie Mazyck

Bernie Mazyck has served as President and CEO of the South Carolina Association of Community Development Corporations (SCACDC) since 1998. Founded in 1994 when the state had only four community development corporations (CDCs), the statewide association has helped grow the CDC movement to the more than seventy CDCs that operate in South Carolina today, twenty-eight of which are active association members. To date, SCACDC and its member CDCs have developed projects valued at $96.8 million, with a statewide economic impact of $156.6 million. Mazyck has also been active in the CDC movement at the national level. Since 2011, he has served as Chair of the Board of the National Alliance of Community Economic Development Associations (NACEDA).

Interviewed in 2011

Steve Dubb: What were the origins of the South Carolina CDC association?

Bernie Mazyck: The initiation of CDCs in South Carolina started with grassroots leadership development or neighborhood leadership training. In the early 1990s, I was working for a community foundation that had a neighborhood small grants program and part of that was to provide training and technical assistance to neighborhood leaders that they felt was important for their own issues. Ironically, similar types of activities were under way in different parts of the state, which were being supported with different players.

With the groups I worked with, part of the leadership development program was exposing them to how community development organizations that are community-based could help transition a low-wealth community into one that is more prosperous, either through job creation, housing development, or entrepreneurship development. After we exposed the leaders to several models, they became very interested in CDCs and encouraged us to help them to put such an organization in place. Similarly, that was happening in a couple of other places in the state. As we in the Low Country were made aware of these other groups, and as part of our training, we invited folk out of North Carolina and folks in Pittsburgh who had experience creating a state association as a way to support what we believed to be a new movement of CDCs. Although there were only four CDCs at the time, they felt it was important to create an association; and that was organized as the South Carolina Association of CDCs in June of 1994.

SD: Can you discuss the growth of the CDC movement in South Carolina over time and what programs have been most important in supporting this growth?

BM: As a result of the fact that we were so small when we began, we reached out to the North Carolina Association CDCs, which had a four-to-five year head start on us. What were the key programs they put in place? Who were their key funders? One key funder for SCACDC was the Mary Reynolds Babcock Foundation out of Winston Salem, North Carolina. One of the banks was Branch Bank and Trust (BB&T). As we went about the work of putting the corporate structure in place, we also began to focus on public policy.

In North Carolina, the CDCs were being supported very well by the state legislature. They were able to convince the North Carolina General Assembly to dedicate a pretty significant allocation not only to CDCs but other types of community-based economic development organizations. We wanted to follow suit and educate legislators in South Carolina regarding the benefits of investing in community economic development.

Community organizing and advocacy were early priorities. We began to have these new CDCs meet with key members of the legislature. One of the activities that we launched was to take some key leaders of our legislature to North Carolina and have them see what a mature CDC was able to produce with the kind of support they had received from the North Carolina legislature.

Our goal was to broaden the net of the South Carolina legislature to understand this new type of organization, the CDC. In 2000, the legislation that we were promoting since 1996 finally passed the legislature. It authorized the state to provide $10 million in grants, loans, and tax credits to certified CDCs. From 1994 until 1998, we were largely a volunteer-driven organization. We met and convened and strategized and planned and organized throughout that period. By 1998, BB&T, the Babcock Foundation (who had been following our progress), and the Southern Rural Development Initiative decided they all wanted to invest some startup money in the association. In 1998, the association received its first significant funding. In the interim, we got some support from NCCED (National Congress for Community Economic Development, then the nation's leading CDC association) with the endorsement by the CEO of NCCED. It was in 1998 that an operating budget was developed and a job description was prepared for an executive director or CEO, and the Board decided they were ready to bring on the first staff and reached out to me, and asked that I do that. So I left the community foundation and decided to take this on.

From 1998 going forward is when we started to put programs in place. Grassroots leadership development has continued to be a staple. That involved retreats where we would bring grassroots leaders together to train them on community organizing but also community development and what it takes to put a CDC in place. With the support of the Mary Reynolds Babcock Foundation and the

Federal Home Loan Bank, we put in the Community Economic Development studies program—that is where we got into the nuts and bolts of what a CDC does.

This was our capacity-building program, which enabled the establishment of a number of new CDCs and played a significant role in going from four CDCs in the state to seventy. The way the state legislation was structured, it provided $5 million in state tax credits, while $5 million would be in an appropriation from the state budget. From 2000 to 2004, while the money was authorized, there was no appropriation. In 2005, we got the first actual $1 million appropriation that provided grants to the CDC industry. Appropriations were made in 2005 and 2006. But in 2007, the legislature started seeing changes in the economy and the appropriation at that time ceased. Of the $5 million that was authorized, to date only $2.4 million has been appropriated. We have had the legislation extended three times, so that the legislature is still authorized to appropriate money.

The managing agency was the South Carolina Department of Commerce. They contracted with us to manage the grant program and they still contract with us to provide capacity building training.

We also get much of our funding from non-governmental sources. Some of our funding comes from banks, such as Branch Bank and Trust (BB&T), Bank of America, Wachovia (now Wells Fargo), Carolina First (now TD Bank) and the Federal Home Loan Bank of Atlanta. We've also played a role in attracting other foundation funding. That's the origins, genesis, and process of CDC expansion in the state.

SD: *Obviously, in some places CDCs formed in the 1960s and 1970s, while the development of CDCs in South Carolina is of more recent origin. Does the fact that most CDCs in South Carolina are less than a decade old make them look different than CDCs in other states? If so, how?*

BM: The similarity with other states is that most of the CDCs start or cut their teeth on some kind of housing development. That's largely because of the history of housing in the field, but it is also due to the availability of housing resources.

The difference I would see is that CDCs in South Carolina are more quickly willing and interested to consider entrepreneurial approaches, work on job development, asset development like

"In 2000, the legislation we were promoting since 1996 finally passed the legislature. **It authorized the state to provide $10 million in grants, loans, and tax credits to certified CDCs.**"

IDAs, and might be considered more creative in how they do their work. In other words, they often perceive their mission more broadly than traditional CDCs that have been around longer in other states. That's the main difference I would see.

SD: *Can you talk about your personal history and how you became involved with community development and CDCs?*

BM: Largely, my involvement was limited to my experience with the Coastal Community Foundation, in Charleston, South Carolina. Before that, my focus on community development started with the work that I did with the Chamber of Commerce's job development and workforce development programs. I then moved from that agenda to the community foundation, which gave me the opportunity to explore a variety of models for community development, including the CDC model, the IDA approach, and the community development finance approach. I got exposure through a program at Tufts University as well as at the Kennedy School at Harvard University. I was able to drill down and get more intellectual exposure to community development while I was at the community foundation. I was there for eight years. I would give that experience the lion's share of credit and have since sought to bring that information to neighborhood and community folk that I am working with.

SD: *Do you see any unique challenges CDCs face in the South?*

BM: The biggest challenge with community development work in the South is still that the work is not seen as having the level of importance of traditional economic development. It is also not seen as being as important of a strategy as in other parts of the country, in part because of CDCs' more recent presence. There are those institutions that have supported our work and continued to support our work, including the banking sector. That is largely driven by CRA (Community Reinvestment Act) and how banks are all measured on their performance. They are the easiest sector to tap into for CDC work. The foundations in South Carolina—and there are many more than a lot of people realize—still do not have a lot of information about the impact of community development and CDCs. They continue to fund traditional programs in the arts and culture, but they don't fund as much community development and CDC work as foundations do in places like Maryland, Massachusetts, Ohio, and so on. So the biggest challenge is to get the financing community, funding community, and even government to fully support it. We are making inroads. But it takes a lot of time and a lot of education to bring those players along.

SD: *Can you describe the communities where your CDC members work?*

BM: All of the major metropolitan areas have some presence of CDCs, but South Carolina is primarily a rural state. The majority of CDCs are in rural areas, and then you have concentration in urban areas. For example, Charleston has four CDCs, Columbia has 10 CDCs. Greenville and Spartanburg, which are upstate, have five or six CDCs. And in smaller statistical metropolitan areas (SMAs) like Savannah River, there are two or three CDCs there. The majority are scattered in rural areas of the state. That's where a lot less capacity exists and a lot less community development infrastructure, which makes it attractive in those areas to create such an entity as a CDC.

SD: *At last year's annual conference, a central theme of your conference was on CDCs' role in the green economy. What do you see as the role of CDCs in the green economy?*

BM: I see CDCs playing a leadership role in the green economy, starting with the area where they have the greatest competency—affordable housing, housing retrofit, housing rehab. South Carolina is an old state and has an old building stock. You'll find homeownership in the state is very high—72 to 75 percent—you might find that surprising in a relatively poor state. It is not the amount of homeownership

"The biggest challenge with community development work in the South is still that **the work is not seen as having the level of importance of traditional economic development.**"

that is the problem; it is the condition of the housing stock. What you have is fairly old, dilapidated, and definitely energy-inefficient homes. When you talk with CDCs, especially in rural areas, they secure Community Development Block Grants (CDBG) or Federal Home Loan Bank funds most of the time to rehabilitate existing homes. So the low-hanging fruit that we see is to be the go-to folk for housing retrofits—helping housing stock to be better weatherized, insulated, more efficient HVAC units, to make sure that we have housing stock that could use renewable energy sources. That part is building on CDC strengths and capacity.

We are working to ensure that there is a network of entities that can finance the up-front cost of these energy improvements. At present, most of that work is being financed through utility companies. They have put in place programs for their customers that will pay the up-front costs for energy improvements through a loan. The customer will repay the loan in their energy bill. Theoretically, the amount they are saving because of these improvements will be equal to or greater than the cost of the monthly payments to repay the loan that has been used to pay for the improvements. That's the way we see CDCs getting out front in this and being a leader in the green economy. And of course this will also create job opportunities. Part of the process involves training programs that provide certification for individuals in energy-efficient improvements. We have endorsed and are helping our constituents to secure Builders Professional Institute (BPI) certification. It is those certifications that utility companies are requiring to do the rehab work. So that's where we see CDCs playing a leadership role and try to get out front with the branding, recognition, and contracting of our CDCs and their residents to do this work.

From there, we see some other opportunities for entrepreneurship, where individuals can establish their own construction companies, their own renewable energy companies. Some of that we already see taking place.

SD: *Are there any examples that you would like to highlight?*

BM: The association, with an earmark from Senator Lindsay Graham (R-SC), was able to establish a weatherization and energy efficiency program in partnership with our local technical college. The initial goal was to help them find employment, but we also encouraged them to pursue entrepreneurship opportunities. One of the individuals out of the class is a woman who has taken the initiative to start her own company, called Low Country Renewable Energy Solutions. Its mission and goal is to provide renewable energy products for residential and commercial customers.

SD: *Has SCACDC partnered with any other universities? If so, what have been the results of these partnerships?*

BM: We previously partnered with an HBCU (historically black college/university), Benedict College. And we have also partnered with Clemson University to launch a CDC Certificate Program. The goal there was to take our regular capacity building program and ratchet it up to another level so it could ultimately provide continuing education credits and maybe even college credits in the area of community development. That program ran two years. It is on hiatus, because we want to analyze it further. There are some cultural differences between the community economic development field and the academic field. In academia, you have theory. In community economic development, you have practice. Sometimes the two don't come together. We do see the opportunity to make this work. We are taking time to figure out what are the best opportunities to make these two cultures work together. There is a chance to re-launch.

We also have an on-going partnership with Clemson University to provide technical assistance through Clemson professors participating in our regular training programs. There is also a partnership with the entrepreneurship program at Charleston College. Students from the entrepreneurship program prepared the business plan for

Low Country Renewable Energy Solutions. We are always looking for new opportunities to partner with universities.

SD: *CDCs are best known for their housing work, but a 2008 report from your association noted that six of your member CDCs run IDA programs, seven support volunteer income tax assistance sites (which help residents claim their earned income tax credit refund), 23 provide personal financial education, five provide business loans, and 16 provide a range of other services (including one that supports a grocery store). Do you see this trend of diversification continuing? If so, what areas do you expect to see the most activity?*

BM: We definitely see the diversification continuing. We see the community economic development field evolving. One of the big differences of our program in South Carolina and those of more traditional markets is that we don't have the depth of resources of other markets, so we have had to be more creative in how to leverage resources. In rural communities, where you don't have an abundance of nonprofits, when a CDC is created they may have to address a variety of issues—some social and some economic. Community development finance and entrepreneurship development are key areas for growth. I do see CDCs engaging with non-traditional partners like conservation folks and the agricultural sector. I see CDCs reaching out beyond housing to address entrenched economic challenges in our communities.

SD: *In addition to the establishment of South Carolina's Community Economic Development Fund, could you highlight some of the other policy successes that SCACDC has achieved? What are your policy priorities right now?*

BM: Financial support for IDAs came through a state agency—it's not ongoing support, but it did provide start-up funding. We were involved with the passage of the housing trust fund act that supports local and regional housing trust funds. We were involved in an effort to recapitalize the conservation bank that provides money for rural areas of South Carolina. Those are some of the additional policy successes we have had.

        As for future priorities, we are looking to pursue a state-earned income tax credit (EITC) and funding for micro-business development. Both of those issues are on our radar screen. Shifting gears and thinking nationally, obviously the last few years have been tumultuous ones.

SD: *Funding, of course, was cut under the Bush administration, then there was a boost with stimulus dollars, and now a new round of cuts is threatened. What do you see as most important challenges CDCs are facing? How are CDCs nationally seeking to meet these challenges?*

BM: Clearly, federal funding is going to be a challenge going forward. With the deficit the way it is, the pressure to cut deep, the elimination of housing counseling dollars, significant strain on HOME and Community Development Block Grants (CDBG) and the questions being raised of the efficacy of HOME, [1] with those challenges it is going to be more important than ever for CDCs to make their case to a broader array of partners. We have a successful record. I think we are going to have to make our case to the private sector more. The banking sector does value us, but we'll have to make our case to venture capitalists and other types of investors. We're going to have to be entrepreneurial in how we do our work. We're going to have to have earned revenue as part of our funding structure. That will demand new skills, such as: how do we raise venture capital and generate earned revenue?

That conversation has begun with National Alliance of Community Economic Development Associations (NACEDA) and other CDCs in the country. Clearly in South Carolina we are already beginning those conversations with the construction sector, the development sector, social entrepreneurs, and private sector businesses, so they can see the value of CDCs in community economic development work. In a number of states, CDCs are working to create state tax credits to serve as incentives to attract investment from the business sector and others. Based on the challenges that we see at the federal level, we have to look to other ways to capitalize our work.

---

1. In the spring of 2011, *The Washington Post* ran a series critiquing the HOME program. See: Debbie Cenziper and and Jonathan Mummolo, "A Pattern of HUD Projects Stalled or Abandoned," *Washington Post*, May 14, 2011, https://www.washingtonpost.com/investigations/a-pattern-of-hud-projects-stalled-or-abandoned/2011/03/14/AFWelh3G_story.html.

"One of the big differences of our program in South Carolina and those of more traditional markets is that we don't have the depth of resources of other markets, so **we have had to be more creative in how to leverage resources**."

SD: *As you noted above, HOME has been attacked recently in the press. In your opinion, how well has HOME worked?*

BM: HOME has worked very well. What came out in the *Washington Post* article is all about context and what is happening on the ground. At a 50,000-foot altitude, certain things will jump out at you. But when you look on the ground level you can see the circumstances that exist, and they can be explained. That's the case with many programs. Community economic development projects require an array of funding partners. If any of those partners are slow or fail to play their role, it puts the whole program on the slow track. We are quick to indict the program, but it requires a deeper understanding of the issues and complexities of community development.

SD: *The last decade, of course, has seen the rise of a predatory lending industry that strips away the assets and wealth that community development groups try to build. How have South Carolina and your member CDCs been affected by the foreclosure crisis?*

BM: Much like many other states, we have been affected. The downturn in the housing sector has affected us as well. But in South Carolina, the community development field got ready. We studied the foreclosure data and convened meetings to educate our constituents about the issue. We got our heads focused on the causes of foreclosures in South Carolina and made sure we had folks ready to use NSP dollars when the program rolled out of Washington. We were prepared to execute NSP. We also have a good network of folks working on loan modification. We have a system under way in the state that is working very hard to address the issue of foreclosure. It is operating. We still have foreclosures. But we are working very hard to resolve them. We may be a little better off than some states because we had a good group of folks working on the front end to prevent folks from going to foreclosure. We still have many challenges associated with the foreclosure issue. It is affecting our homeownership pipeline, but we are fortunate that we have an infrastructure that is working to address that.

SD: *The Neighborhood Stabilization Program (NSP) is designed to assist cities to put foreclosed property back into productive re-use. Can you discuss SCACDC's work in NSP?*

BM: We're on the other side of first round of that program, in that we are converting foreclosed housing stock back into housing opportunities for others. In some cases, this has meant rental housing. We are now on the other side and we are starting to see the ultimate impact or benefit of the reinvestment. It is going to be a long haul. It is my hope that we will be able to stay the course and be very active. We are realizing it's going to take a little longer than we initially thought.

SD: *What are your priorities going forward, both at the state level and at the national level?*

BM: For both levels, it's going to be capital, funding, and finance. That's got to be a top priority. It is all about sustainability, especially during this economically questionable period. I think, going forward, the priority is going to be to continue to make the case for our relevance. We need to be able to articulate very clearly the impact that we are having, so that we can become and continue to be a main institutionalized player to bring about prosperous communities across the state and across the country.

SD: *If you had to choose three accomplishments of SCACDC's work that you are most proud of, what would they be?*

BM: We always put at the top of the list our CED Act, the community economic development legislation that we got passed. That puts policy in place that makes our work in the eyes of many in South Carolina legitimate. I would also say the association has been able to market and present CDCs as a key player in building prosperous communities. We are seeing more institutions coming to us requesting our expertise. The third one would probably be growing leadership in many parts of the state and also across demographic areas. For South Carolina, leadership is often viewed as the property of a certain select group of folk. We have been able to expand the definition and provide a broader range of leaders in state policy development and state economic development strategy.

SD: *Anything else you would like to add?*

BM: In South Carolina, when it comes to issues of race and class, the CDC work in South Carolina has brought to bear leaders in the African American community that shows there is talent within that community and success in that community. Although CDC work is not an exclusive benefit to the African American community, it has elevated minority leaders in the state. We have a number of folks in our field who have been elected to local offices and the General Assembly in our state. Along with the broad definition of leadership development, the ability to grow leaders with the minority communities has been very positive.

Community Development Financial Institutions

In this section, we feature three interviews from leaders in the community development financial institution (CDFI) industry, which includes a mix of for-profit and nonprofit community development banks, credit unions, venture funds, and loan funs—all of whom focus on lending to underinvested areas. The CDFI movement grew out of the moving against redlining, a practice in which the Federal Housing Administration, from the 1930s until the 1960s, literally drew a "red line" around communities of color, creating "do not lend" areas. Even after the law changed to ban housing discrimination, informal practices of "redlining" continued, leading community activities to create their own banks. In 1994, the federal government created the CDFI Fund in the Treasury department, which provides some federal funding (as of 2015, roughly $250 million a year) to support CDFIs. Since the CDFI Fund has been created, assets under management by CDFIs have grown from less than $4 billion to over $64 billion. In 2000, Congress also approved the New Markets Tax Credit program, to support commercial development in low-income neighborhoods. Some CDFIs actually grew out of CDCs; such is the case with Coastal Enterprise, which Ron Philips founded and still directs. Eric Weaver, based in Silicon Valley, operates a CDFI that has been a leader in microenterprise development and the promotion of matched-savings accounts (also known as individual development accounts or IDAs). Mark Pinsky served as CEO of Opportunity Finance Network, a trade association of community development loan funds, from its founding until June 2016. Pinsky is now in the midst of writing a book on the history of the CDFI industry.

Ron Phillips

For nearly thirty years, until his retirement in 2016, Ron Phillips served as CEO of Coastal Enterprises, Inc. (CEI), a Maine-based community development corporation (CDC) and community development financial institution (CDFI). Founded in 1977, CEI provides financing and technical assistance to job-creating small businesses, natural resources industries, community facilities, and affordable housing. CEI's primary market is Maine, but, in recent years, it has expanded several programs to northern New England, upstate New York, and beyond. We interviewed Phillips to get his perspective on CDCs, CDFIs, and overall trends affecting community wealth building nationwide.

Interviewed in 2006

Steve Dubb: *Obviously, there has been tremendous growth in CDCs and CDFIs since CEI was founded in 1977. If you had to choose only three main accomplishments, what would you pick as the three most important changes brought about by the growth of CDCs and CDFIs?*

Ron Phillips: CDCs have come a long way since their origin in the '60s as an outgrowth of the civil rights movement and the War on Poverty. Combined with community development banks, credit unions and loan fund entities—many of whom became CDFIs—community-based development and finance entities number over 4,000 today, managing billions in housing, real estate and small business assets and investments. If the goal of the CDC/CDFI industry has been to achieve some measure of *scale, permanence*, and *impact*, today we could certainly say these have been its three main accomplishments.

First, by *scale* we mean the ability to take on increasingly significant development finance projects. For example, hundreds of thousands of units of affordable housing have been created by these institutions helping to change the economic prospects for millions of individuals, families and children. CDCs/CDFIs are also developing charter schools throughout the United States. Many are involved in rural development, revitalizing and creating new enterprise natural resource ventures. To back up these organizations national intermediaries have sprung up like LISC (Local Initiatives Support Corporation), Enterprise, or HAC (Housing Assistance Council), aggregating capital and providing the technical and capital vital to urban and rural CDCs/CDFIs to pursue their mission.

Second, by *permanence* we mean entities that are financially sound, well managed and capable of functioning in a market-like economy. Certainly, CDCs/CDFIs are at different levels of capacity and self-sufficiency—a Self Sufficiency Index (SSI) or percentage of revenue from earning assets. The greatest challenges to the CDC/CDFI field has been the need for a steady flow of subsidized funding. Achieving a high SSI level is not without its challenges. Within that framework, however, CDCs/CDFIs have become increasingly self-sufficient, as development finance institutions generating needed capital for core operations and ongoing community development.

And finally is the question of *impact*. In the end, do CDCs/CDFIs make a difference? Studies are beginning to show that these grassroots institutions are essential in the community development process. They identify needs, manage and leverage capital to help fill the gap between those with resources and opportunities, and people and places left out of the economic mainstream. The record now speaks for itself. The CDFI Data Project, among other national surveys and assessments, is showing the impact these institutions are having in underserved neighborhoods and rural regions. Truly the CDC/CDFI field is an industry today, a permanent fixture of the community economic development landscape.

SD: *CDCs and CDFIs have grown in strength in a period of generally declining federal support for community development. What impact has declining federal support had for your work?*

RP: While it is true that federal funding has declined over the years, in another way this retrenchment has caused CDCs/CDFIs to branch out to alternative sources. Indeed, CDCs/CDFIs have gone through several cycles of federal government reductions from the '70s on, so recent experiences in budget cuts (for example, the Strengthening American Communities Initiative, which in our view has been a White House bid to gouge many of the most vital resources for community development) are not new. Alternative funding needs have thus resulted in more discipline in managing assets, as well as striking out to identify other sources. These include state funding programs and mechanisms to capitalize the industry, foundations, individuals, religious institutions, banks and, in recent years, private socially minded investors. With respect to the social investment market, the Social Investment Forum, a membership organization of money managers, is now reporting increased levels of community investment. The Calvert Foundation in Washington has been among the leading intermediaries to serve as a bridge between private, socially oriented capital and CDCs/CDFIs.

SD: *Another area, which involves not declining federal support, but rather federal financial deregulation, has led to the rise of a predatory lending industry that strips away the assets and wealth that community development groups try to build. Coastal, along with Self-Help and others, has been a leader in the anti-predatory lending movement. At the level of federal policy, what do you think can be accomplished in this area?*

RP: Congress and the federal regulatory agencies have been slow to effec-
        tively eliminate predatory mortgage lending. The Office of Thrift
        Supervision and others have promulgated some regulations and
        restrictions on mortgage lending practices. Fannie Mae and Fred-
        die Mac have raised the bar to a great extent in terms of acceptable
        secondary market purchases. Citigroup has also made considerable
        progress from its earlier history and abuses by, for example, capping
        fees at three percent. But much work lies ahead, and the burden of
        progressive legislation has fallen to the states. The Center for Respon-
        sible Lending in North Carolina has been among the leading advo-
        cates of state-based legislative strategy to eliminate predatory mort-
        gage lending. In CEI's case, the study we completed in February 2006
        identified upward trends in Maine. Our goal is to pass legislation in
        Maine's upcoming legislative session that would effectively deal with
        primarily out-of-state, non-bank mortgage companies like Amer-
        iquest—which was already the subject of a national class action set-
        tlement involving some 2000 Maine homeowners. By passing strong
        state laws, we can send a signal to Congress that nationwide action is
        needed, action that builds on but does not reduce effective state law.

SD: *Are there specific areas where CDCs and CDFIs need to focus
        their efforts to better develop capacity?*
RP: There are four fundamental challenges to the future growth of the
        CDC/CDFI industry. Firstly, access to *flexible, subsidized capital* to
        sustain operations and provide the needed capital to initiate and
        develop high impact projects. These sources, as indicated above, have
        traditionally come from the public sector, and from the private sector
        such as foundations. The second challenge is *policies* that create a reg-
        ulatory environment conducive to community development. CRA is
        the most dramatic example of regulation that provides incentives for
        banks to target some of their capital to underserved and under-banked
        people and places. Other potential regulatory issues and opportuni-
        ties involve the environment. Communities are facing a wider threat
        of global warming. CDCs/CDFIs must engage in policy initiatives
        to ensure the resources necessary for "green" affordable housing, for
        example. The third challenge is *private sector leverage*. The govern-
        ment and charitable giving comprise essential legs to the stool of com-
        munity development. But they are not the only legs. Private capital

markets must increasingly flow to support the rising development capacity and impact these organizations are already demonstrating. Many CDCs/CDFIs are working at creating an "asset class" that can be more acceptable to Wall Street-like investors. There has been some success in this regard, and Opportunity Finance Network's CARS rating (CDFI Rating and Assessment System) is beginning to make inroads among money-center banks and investment institutions. The fourth challenge is *impact*. CDCs/CDFIs must continue to show that there is indeed show both the social and financial return on investment, that they're making a difference at the community level, and that they're a necessity in the community development landscape.

SD: *Your organization describes itself as both a community development corporation (CDC) and a community development financial institution (CDFI). This presumably simplifies coordination of development and finance in your case, but how well do these sectors coordinate more broadly? What could be done to improve coordination?*

RP: These two approaches are not easy to balance. In a nutshell, CDCs, by definition, are rooted in the community. While endowed with local knowledge, they bear the costs of identifying and raising money for community development projects. CDFIs, while making much needed capital available, often are there only at the transactional stage of development. Both are required and many CDCs and CDFIs share qualities of each. However, the CDC tends to be in the riskier, subordinated position when it comes to investing; the CDFI is often in a more senior position, or at least better secured along with the bank. Furthermore, CDCs are running programs involving much deep subsidy and grant funds, such as technical assistance, counseling and training programs. Coordination between the two becomes an internal management challenge to maintain solid asset liability policies and guard against draining much needed capital for reserves, while at the same time benefiting from the reinforcement programs that protect asset managers. For example, a loan to a business owner is enhanced if she or he can benefit from technical assistance in planning, marketing, or pricing of a product. So too the stability of revenue from a family if housing or job counseling is available.

"It's not clear to me that you can have scale in a 'small pond' (though you can have impact). **What stikes me is the confusion between scale and impact.**"

SD: *This year, after thirty-five years, the National Congress for Community Economic Development shut its doors. What impact does the demise of this trade association have for the CDC movement? Is there a need to create a new trade association or will existing groups fill in the gap?*

RP: The demise of NCCED was truly a sorry moment. The official act of dissolution came in the summer of 2006, without much notice except for the few who felt its symbolic significance. Was it the end of the civil rights dream embodied in NCCED that for so many years carried the banner of social justice? Or was it time for the organization to step aside as others had evolved and matured to go the next step? The reasons for its unraveling as the place where the many could come together to form a greater whole are still not evident; little has been written about it. While certain organizations are assuming responsibility for the legacy of NCCED, it certainly has not found a steward of its rich history and special purpose in advocating for community-based economic development.

A case could be made that since NCCED closed its doors, a vacuum has been created in the CDC/CDFI field. Perhaps, if this vacuum becomes more pronounced and felt across the board by past and future leaders, a meeting will be called to indeed evaluate and perhaps to rebuild from its ashes a new NCCED-like organization that can stand on the shoulders of other national groups and represent the challenges that lie ahead for the field. And perhaps these challenges, in addition to dealing with continued racism and widening gaps between the rich and poor, can also turn to the international stage and serve as a place to bring our brothers and sisters together in a global environment to reach across borders, race, ethnicity, and religion, and work on the world stage for peace and justice.

I do believe there is a gap, a hole, left by them. Other intermediaries can only fill a piece of it. There is a place for an organization that gathers in all of the best of the trade associations and is one big tent.

SD: *One area of considerable discussion, particularly for CDFIs, has been the issue of scale. Scale is seen as necessary for accessing greater amounts of capital, but can also mean larger organizations that may (or may not) become disconnected from the communities they serve. As the CEO of a statewide community development organization, how has CEI managed to build scale while retaining community responsiveness?*

RP: This is an excellent question, somewhat addressed above as one of the three goals CDCs/CDFIs have been pursuing as their industry has grown. With respect to the potential disconnect between scale and community, it's not clear to me that you can have scale in a "small pond" (though you can have impact). What strikes me is the confusion between scale and impact. National intermediaries project significant "scale" numbers, but a closer look leaves much to be desired. For example, LISC describes the important role it plays in fostering childcare. But many other organizations are involved in childcare facility development, and they're not national. CEI is one; Self Help is another. And we each have done a considerable job in our respective regions. You don't necessarily have to be national to achieve scale because it's a question relative to your market.

Nevertheless, even if a community group achieves some kind of impact in their area, it's difficult to achieve any kind of scale, and the natural tendency is to broaden the range of targeting communities. Often local groups must stay in their communities and do not have the capability nor desire to go further. So the answer to this question of achieving scale while not losing contact with the community is a tension that will probably persist. At CEI we've tried to have it both ways, broadening our market reach while, in fact, concentrating more in some of the communities in Maine. Groups like LISC, which support local CDCs, and CEI, which is now affiliating with other CDFIs in rural New England, are perhaps the best models of maintaining connections with the grassroots, while trying to achieve some measure of scale in their product lines.

CEI also works closely with trade associations, such as in the fisheries, or welfare groups, or women's groups, to align our financing products better to these communities of common interest. Another question is also raised regarding the nature of community. Certainly, place is of paramount importance, as are the people in it. Geographic "impact area" as the original CDC concept described it, is still relevant to focus resources, and most federal and many private funding sources are looking to have deeper "impact" on place. But another way to look at community is a group with a *shared interest*. Thus, a farmer, fishermen, people who work in the woods, elderly, people with disabilities, all represent a community. Geography is another way to help define how that community will further its interests. In community development, another form of community has been economic sectors and how to improve their aspirations.

SD: ***Your organization, like many CDFIs, was founded in part through capital from religious/social justice organizations. Today, again like many of your counterparts, your main sources of capital are foundation and government-based. Beyond bringing in more resources, how has the shift in your sources of funding affected both CEI and the CDFI industry?***

RP: First of all, many foundations have limits to their funding. CEI has experienced this with the Ford Foundation, for example, which was a prime supporter of CEI for many years (and is still invested with us, and to some extent, supports our latest venture into triple bottom line investing). The major sources of capital for CEI now are bank investors and, through the New Market Tax Credit (NMTC), non-traditional investors like GE Capital, or Plum Creek Timber. We're now reaching out to individual social investors, and hope to open up significant resources for both grants and investment dollars. That said, we've not let go of the government, and will continue to advocate for community development programs from U.S. Department of Housing and Urban Development (HUD), U.S. Department of Health and Human Services (HHS), U.S. Department of Agriculture (USDA), Small Business Administration (SBA), and others.

Further, we do continue to approach foundations—especially those who have not given in rural America, where foundation funding is notably slack—and among those who are contemplating

Program-Related Investments (PRIs). PRIs have not expanded as a source of "giving" among foundations, and we believe that there's promise if new wealth, family foundations, and intergenerational wealth transfers occur.

SD: *CEI has raised over $25 million for community development equity investments. Thinking less in terms of job creation numbers and more in terms of qualitative impacts, in what cases is community development venture capital most helpful as a wealth-building tool? Where are its limitations?*

RP: CEI is among a very few CDCs/CDFIs that operate venture capital subsidiaries. We're managing some $35 million now, less than 10 percent of our total capital under management (about $370 million when counting the $249 million NMTC). There are several important reasons why we believe engagement in the venture capital area is worthwhile.

First, there's a market for smaller scale venture capital, particularly in rural areas. While there may not be substantial deal flow initially, over time, and with changing economics of rural regions (for example, the baby boomer retirement and second careers), there are new opportunities. Next, venture capital creates jobs. It's difficult to start or expand promising companies without that kind of capital. Banks turn to us for the resource, and its availability nurtures new relationships in the market we otherwise might not have. Third, venture capital opens up new investor connections and ones that cross-fertilize with other CEI financing programs. For example, TDBank North America is an equity investor, but also, a major NMTC investor. This familiarity with CEI across product lines (we don't just do microloans, for example, but can engage in much larger and more sophisticated financing deals) expands our investor base. Fourth, in addition to social benefits of job creation, equity investments can generate much-needed earnings to support core operations.

SD: *Part of CEI's philosophy is to pursue triple bottom line returns (economic, equity, environmental). How stringent (or how flexible) are you regarding these criteria? Can you provide a couple of examples of how you've negotiated trade-offs that arise between, say, equity and environmental returns?*

RP: We're not purists by any means, so we will invest in companies that might not be stellar environmental performers. But we try to offer information on ways to, for example, cut energy costs. The real question is whether trade-offs in the short run may mean more dire consequences in the long run. We've seen fisheries investments sometimes suffer due to a focus on short-term gain.

Eric Weaver

*Eric Weaver has served as the CEO of
Lenders for Community Development
(now known as Opportunity Fund),
a community development financial
institution based in San Jose, California,
for the past twenty-three years. Since
its formation in 1993, Lenders for
Community Development has disbursed
over $5.6 million to more than 2,300
savers through its individual development
account (IDA) program, the nation's
largest. The group has also made over 600
loans worth over $8 million to support
local microenterprise and has directed over
$115 million in community investment
into affordable housing and community
facilities.*

Interviewed in 2008

Steve Dubb: Could you explain briefly the origins of Lenders for Community Development?

Eric Weaver: It came out of the Community Reinvestment Act (CRA), when Bill Clinton was first elected to office and CRA was starting to be enforced more strongly than it had been. Local banks were looking for ways to invest in low-income communities. The local community foundation, which is now the Silicon Valley Community Foundation, convened the local banks to discuss whether they could do something collaboratively. They put together a loose group. I was hired just out of business school to put together a lending consortium.

We initially created a for-profit multi-bank CDC with a focus on loans to small business and affordable housing. The goal was for banks to be able to make some (CRA-qualifying) loans that they might not be able to make on their own.

SD: So I guess that answers where you got your initial capital from.

EW: Our loan capital came from banks. And most of the operating dollars initially came from banks. Then we started to get funding from other funders, mainly for the micro-lending. We really launched the programs in 1995 and five years later we converted the organization into to a nonprofit. We did this for a couple of reasons. We realized that micro-lending would require continuing subsidy and the IDA program we launched in 1999 was entirely grant dependent. So we decided to convert it to a nonprofit.

SD: What are some of the unique challenges of working in the Bay Area?

EW: In many ways, we are very fortunate to be working in a place where there is a strong funding community and interest in the issues we work in. But there are challenges being in an area with such a really high cost of living, especially housing, and pretty poor public transit. It is a difficult place to be poor. So it is a "good news, bad news" situation. We have a stronger employment base, but if you're in low-wage employment or not employed, it's an extremely hard place to get by.

Another challenge is that it is a very multiethnic place with a lot of different cultures. You have to be pretty creative about who you partner with and be able to offer services in multiple languages. It

> "My experience as a community organizer was **as helpful if not more helpful** than my MBA background."

can also be a challenge in terms of our cost structure. It's a more expensive place to do business. You pay more for rent and salaries, so it's hard to run as efficient an operation as you might in other parts of the country.

SD: *Your background as a community organizer with a Stanford MBA is a little unusual. Can you explain how this has background contributed to your work?*

EW: The background in community organizing turned out to be surprisingly helpful at the beginning of this process. We started out with fifteen different banks that were all part of this effort who we were asking to cooperate with each other, even though they were all competing with each other in the market. My experience as a community organizer was as helpful if not more helpful than my MBA background. I had worked with low-income tenants and as a relief worker in El Salvador. This background was beneficial to help me figure out what partnerships made sense for us to bridge that gap between mainstream financial institutions and people who had not been comfortable with using those institutions.

SD: *You mentioned that you converted to a nonprofit to be able to accept grant money, but did this shift from for-profit to non-profit status bring any challenges?*

EW: Surprisingly few. There were a couple of reasons we started out as a for-profit. The main one was that the banks providing the capital understandably wanted to have a lot of control. They were really new at doing community investing. They weren't sure what they were getting into. As a shareholder, you own it. You have a lot of control. At that time, there was less familiarity with the concept of social enterprise and hybrid organizations. If we started out as a nonprofit, it was feared that we might be seen as not caring if these loans didn't need to be repaid or that what we were doing wasn't a real business.

When we got a handle on what this was and when we got an individual development account (IDA) program, it made sense to convert. By then the bank investors had more comfort that if you were a nonprofit you could still run a business-like operation. The banks gave up a little control. We did set ourselves up so that the banks are the members of the nonprofit. Major decisions need their approval and they also elect the board. But they were very comfortable with the transition. There was obviously an approval process with the Internal Revenue Service, but nothing that we weren't able to work out.

SD: *One of your organization's largest programs is your Individual Development Account (IDA) program. Am I correct that it is the nation's largest?*

EW: We have more enrollees and more graduates cumulatively than any other IDA program in the country. EARN in San Francisco has a similar number of active accounts and they are growing fast. We helped them get off the ground, and they are sort of a sister organization. We have the most historical information on savings patterns.

SD: *How has IDA program been funded?*

EW: It started out as a collaboration with the Center for Venture Philanthropy, which is part of the Silicon Valley Community Foundation. They did most of the fundraising for the first 1,000 accounts. They raised private money and county money. Catholic Charities helped us get funding from the Office of Refugee Resettlement. And there was money from the federal program, Assets for Independence Act (AFIA). Once the Center for Venture Philanthropy finished its engagement, which we had anticipated from the beginning, we took over the lead role in fundraising. We have had a large grant from the Knight Foundation. We get an AFIA award every couple of years. We are working with United Way Silicon Valley to fund IDAs for single moms. We've also been able to use our earned income through the New Markets Tax Credit to generate matching funds for the IDA program, which is pretty unusual for an IDA program. Once people understand this, they really get invested in it. For instance, we are working with a person who on her own organized a donor circle to help raise money for the IDA program in San Mateo County.

"At the end of the day, there is also an issue around trusting people to use the money wisely.... There are other things people need savings for—**after receiving financial education and having saved dutifully for two to three years, we ought to trust them**."

SD: *What do you see as the role of advocacy for IDAs? What is needed in terms of funding to meet the demand?*

EW: To meet the demand, a lot would be needed. We're not an advocacy organization ourselves but we work very closely with groups working for that like CFED, New America, and the Asset Policy Initiative of California. We view our role as generating the outcomes and data to show why this is good public policy. We're involved in advocacy, but I wouldn't say we're leading the charge. I would say what is going to be needed is expansion of AFIA, and changes to the rules (for example, experiment to enable broader uses of matching funds, not just the three traditional uses—children's education, retirement accounts). Allow people to save for a family emergency fund. There is going to be an ongoing role for some kind of on-line vehicle for smaller donors to match the savings of IDA savers. I think that has a lot of promise.

SD: *Are there broader challenges, beyond needing more money, that the IDA field faces?*

EW: There is definitely an infrastructure challenge. It's a relatively complex program to operate. With no disrespect, the average social service agency might find it pretty daunting. If you have 1,000 active accounts and hundreds more open every year, and many withdrawals for asset purchases, and having controls to verify the money is going to where it is supposed to, it's pretty complicated. CDFIs might have a bigger role to play as the field grows. Citibank is the only large bank playing a major role. There are others, but more need to jump in. As people in low-income communities have more access to technology, there can also be more use of technology in terms of getting statements, etc. I don't want to push the education to an on-line platform. That may be needed in some places, but I think face-to-face is more powerful.

At the end of the day, there is also an issue around trusting people to use the money wisely. This gets back to AFIA, where the money can only be used for three purposes (education, homeownership, or starting a small business). There are other things people need savings for—after receiving financial education and having saved dutifully for two to three years, we ought to trust them.

In Great Britain, their Child Savings Accounts have no restrictions on how you spend the money. We ought to look in that direction.

SD: *When Child Savings Accounts were proposed earlier this year in the presidential campaign, the concept developed a high level of opposition.*

EW: Part of this is due to a mistake in a speech by Senator Clinton where she overstated the cost of the program. But it's fascinating to see the kinds of things that emerge in opposition to this idea. Obviously, the cost is something we are concerned about. But the federal government is subsidizing asset accumulation for 401(k), preferential capital gains, mortgage deductions to the tune of hundreds of billions of dollars. AFIA is just a few million dollars. I find that argument hard to understand.

There was a bipartisan effort in California to introduce child savings accounts. What shot it down right out of the box was anti-immigration concern, that this would encourage people to come to California and have children. The Republican cosponsor backed off immediately. I thought this was crazy.

SD: *Your organization also operates a large micro-lending program. What do you see as the impact of these loans on community development?*

EW: We really look at that in a quite systematic way. We're using the Aspen Institute's "Microtest" methodology.

On an annual basis we do surveys of our customers. We look at what's happening at the business level and the individual level. We look at changes in revenue and net income, employment, whether or not health care is being provided, business retention, household income and wealth.

SD: *Do you target your lending for specific neighborhoods?*

EW: We have to feel that it's a business that is not going to be eligible for conventional financing. We either lend to a family that is low or moderate income or to a business in a neighborhood that is low or moderate income that would provide services needed by that neighborhood. Sometimes, in partnership with a city or community-based effort we might target a certain neighborhood in our marketing, for instance. This might happen, for example, if someone is putting up a loan loss reserve for loans made in a particularly low-income neighborhood.

SD: *You've been known to say that micro-lending in the United States requires subsidy. What is a reasonable level of subsidy that should be expected?*

EW: We're not aware of a mission-based micro-lender in the United States that is able to cover all of their costs through income in the program. There are many reasons why it's more difficult here than in the developing world. First, it is either impossible because of legal barriers or frowned upon to charge the kind of interest rates that international microfinance charges. Right out of the box you have less income. Also, if you're willing to pay those kinds of interest rates, there is credit available in this country. So if I'm charging 40 to 50 percent interest, there are other ways people can get the money without having to spend time getting technical assistance from us and answering all of the questions that we have.

Also, it typically has not worked in this country to do peer lending. I think that is cultural. I think that peer lending works in villages where there is deep knowledge of your neighbors. Here people move around and keep to themselves more. When you can't use peer lending, you have to do old-fashioned underwriting. That drives up your costs.

Another issue is concentration of borrowers. In a lot of developing countries, you have a higher percentage of people who are self-employed. You can quickly sign up borrowers. Here you have got to market. There is a lot of noise—a lot of other kinds of credit available. It's costly to get to the customers.

Doing business in this country is also more complicated and more regulated than in the developing world. So there is a higher need for technical assistance, which can also drive up costs.

So, it is more challenging economically to scale it and make it pay for itself. We see the same kinds of positive impacts on household well-being, wealth, and income. The argument I make is that maybe it is not appropriate to measure U.S. micro-lenders by comparing them with international micro-lenders, but instead we should compare micro-lending to other things we do to help people improve their economic circumstances, such as job training, affordable housing, and community colleges. I'm not denigrating any of these things. I'm just saying maybe it's a better comparison point. What we run into all of the time is someone who knows international micro-lending and thinks it's so cool that it can make a profit and then declares that since micro-lending doesn't make a profit in the United States, U.S. micro-lending doesn't work. If profitability is the only criterion, then job training doesn't work, affordable housing doesn't work. All of these things require philanthropic or governmental subsidy to do what they do.

SD: *What amount of subsidy is required to make micro-lending in the United States work?*

EW: If you're lending in a high-cost area, you're going to need more subsidy than in a low-cost area. There are two measures that get used a lot. One is called the "cost" rate—the dollars you spend per dollar under management. So if you have a portfolio of $1 million, how many dollars do you spend in a year to manage that? Rates in this country range—ours is between 30 and 40 cents. You might have a small number that have a more efficient cost rate than us, such as Acción Texas and Acción New York. They focus less on technical assistance. But you need to look at a lot of variables such as where are you lending, how much add-on service (or technical assistance) you are providing and, how much risk you're taking on.

The other measure is the self-sufficiency ratio—that is, what percentage do you generate through earned income? We're not aware of a program that is at 100 percent. Some would claim to be up in the '70s and '80s. You need to be careful and look under the hood and see what costs are being included. There isn't a magic number there.

Someday there may be an organization with franchisees that provide the exact same services throughout the country. Then you could compare apples to apples.

SD: *Your organization also operates an affordable housing and community facilities lending program and has used New Markets Tax Credit to support some of your larger projects. Could you explain briefly how you were able to access New Markets monies and how they have assisted with financing specific projects?*

EW: The New Market Tax Credit gives a tax credit to investors that provide funds for loans or equity investments in businesses that are working in low-income communities—it could be for-profit or nonprofit businesses. We've focused on nonprofit community facility projects. It's new. It's got a lot of regulations. It's pretty complex. The cost in terms of legal and accounting fees that you need to pay to do a deal tend to drive practitioners to do larger projects. Because of the baseline fixed costs for lawyers and accountants, if you tried to do a $500,000 project, you would eat up the subsidy in fees. It has also tended to be used more for real estate than working capital type loans. It's a place-based program. If you make a loan to a business, there is a concern that it could move. A building can't move, so that gives people more comfort. It's tended to be used mostly for commercial real estate, either for-profit or nonprofit.

It has certainly allowed us to do some larger projects that have had a transformative effect on neighborhoods.

SD: *Could you discuss an example, such as the National Hispanic University project?*

EW: The NHU was the first New Markets tax credit project in the Bay Area. We provided a loan to finance a new campus building for a nonprofit, community-based university whose mission is to educate low-income Latino students. It was operating out of an old elementary school and bursting at the seams. It was not able to provide a quality experience from a facilities point of view. They were able to fundraise quite a bit of grant money but not enough. But we were able to provide a low-interest loan over seven years. It gives them seven years to raise the rest of the money. Once they do refinance, there will be money left over at the end. We will share some of that

"The big tension for us is achieving greater scale without sacrificing impact. And to what extent we want to place priority on one or the other. **We're leaning on the side of impact**."

---

with the university in the form of a grant. So this will help them build the endowment and strengthen their financial bottom line.

SD: *More broadly, could you comment on how Lenders for Community Development seeks to coordinate its IDA, micro-lending, and community development finance activities so that they support each other?*

EW: We feel it all coheres from a mission standpoint—to improve the economic well-being of working people by giving them the means and the know-how to invest in their own future. So that really starts with affordable housing and other services that people might need to stabilize themselves economically. That's why we do the real estate lending and community facilities such as child care. We provide access to financial education and a place to save. We work so that it doesn't cost you money to save and through the IDA program give low-income people an incentive to save. Low-income people, since they pay little income tax, they don't have much of an incentive to save. They don't have the same incentive that upper income people have. We also provide access to appropriate credit—appropriate versus predatory credit—so they can use it productively.

How much do the programs work in tandem? We have had a good bit of overlap with IDA savers using IDA savings plus a loan to start a business. There are certainly been some neighborhoods such as in East San Jose, where we provided all three types of service and feel we've had some impacts.

SD: *What are your priorities going forward?*

EW: We're in the middle of that discussion. The big tension for us is achieving greater scale without sacrificing impact. And to what extent we want to place priority on one or the other. We're leaning on the side of impact. So if you have to choose between doubling the number of people we serve versus really having a transformational impact, we would go towards the latter. It's hard to talk about an overall organizational goal, but by programs: with IDAs, we want to expand the uses so it is something that brings the opportunity to save to a broader universe of people, as well as broadening the universe of people who support it by donating through an online platform.

　　With micro-loans, there we are focused on scale. There are real efficiencies that can be gained by going to 500 loans a year versus the 200 we are at.

SD: *If you had to choose three accomplishments of your work that you are most proud of, what would they be?*

EW: I would say being part of proving that low wage workers can save and use money responsibly, whether it is saved or borrowed, use money in a productive way. I would say pioneering a model that relies on private sector dollars to do microfinance in the U.S. The last one is having created a healthy high performing organization where people with high ideals can put them into action and have a satisfying career.

SD: *Shifting gears and thinking nationally, obviously there has been tremendous growth in Community Development Financial Institutions (CDFIs) since Lenders for Community Development was founded in 1993. What do you see as most important changes brought about by the growth of CDFIs?*

EW: It's a whole new way to invest in working communities. Prior to the dawn of the CDFI, you were going to have a purely private sector approach and start businesses and hopefully that would trickle down to everybody or government income supports. The CDFI is kind of a hybrid where you are providing financing, but it is very much targeted at benefiting the low-income sector of the community. It's not waiting for the trickle-down. It is using business principles. It opens up a lot more avenues—try to bring more economic opportunity and economic justice. It doesn't replace the traditional means. It's just another vehicle.

SD: *CDFIs have grown in strength even during this decade, in a period of generally declining federal support for community development. How? What impact has declining federal support had for your work?*

EW: Federal support is not the only driver. As the industry develops more capacity, you may have faster growth. In our case, federal CDFI funds had a really transformational effect in terms of our confidence to invest in growth and our capacity to take on more growth. I think CDFIs can keep growing with or without federal backing, but they will grow a lot faster with it. I think it's a good investment in resources.

I think it should also be noted that CDFI funding hasn't declined as much as some areas. That reflects a bipartisan agreement that this is a good way to use federal dollars.

SD: *Another area, which involves not declining federal support, but rather federal financial deregulation, has led to the rise of a predatory lending industry that strips away the assets and wealth that community development groups try to build. How has Lenders for Community Development and the communities you serve been affected by the foreclosure crisis? At the level of policy, what do you think can be accomplished in this area?*

EW: Payday lending, the big thing is that they found a way to get around usury laws. They got all of their interest charges considered to be fees, which is unfortunate. The credit card industry is a great example. There is more and more creative financial wizardry. Now credit card companies can make money off of customers who don't pay all of their bills because they have assessed them so many fees that by the time the customer declares bankruptcy, the company has already made money off of them.

In terms of policy, I am not one who feels that credit is inherently a good thing. A lot of these predatory lenders hide behind the fact that you're giving people access to credit, but if it's a bad loan that they foreclose on, that's not a good deal. Re-introducing usury laws and capping the fees payday lenders charge is definitely in order. We definitely need to extend safety and soundness regulations to non-bank mortgage lenders. The idea that they could make loans without documenting whether people have the ability to repay is crazy.

I see no downside to dramatically regulating the credit industry. Not that it will happen. Banks are also getting into this with overdraft charges.

SD: *Are there specific areas where CDFIs need to focus their efforts to better develop capacity?*

EW: Mortgage lending. CDFIs are going to be less likely to go down the same road again, which the private sector, after a few years of caution, will. I'd love to see especially community development credit unions grow—they are the best suited to provide alternative credit loans and combat predatory consumer lending.

SD: *What do you see as the most important challenges or opportunities facing CDFIs today? Where should the CDFI movement be focusing its energies over the next five-to-ten years?*

EW: We're in the midst of what is going to be one of the biggest periods of stripping away of wealth from low- and moderate-income households in a long time. CDFIs need to rededicate themselves to programs and products that can begin to turn that around. That includes financial education so that people learn not to do that again. It's alternative products. It's advocacy. One of the soapboxes I'm on these days is that we really need to rethink and revisit our national obsession with home ownership. Certainly a lot of what has happened recently has to do with a lot of bad actors. I think what made it easy for these bad actors to take things as far as they did is this notion that homeownership is the Holy Grail and something everybody should have.

I'd love for everyone to own a home if it was beneficial to them, but the reality is homeownership is quite risky even in the best of times. The real estate market is far more volatile than other markets. Given the fact that low-income people don't really enjoy the home mortgage interest deduction, it's not clear that this is best for them. CDFIs have been supportive of permanently affordable rental housing. It is a much more efficient use of public dollars to provide safe and decent housing. Some of us have lost sight of this. This whole asset-building movement is too fixated on home ownership. That's the single most important asset-building opportunity you can give somebody—housing is your biggest expense, then they can save enough to do homeownership responsibly. We need to be doing that debate.

SD: *What about shared equity such as land trusts or limited-equity cooperatives?*

EW: Land trusts are certainly worthwhile, but I am less supportive of limited equity cooperatives. I used to develop limited equity cooperatives. I never saw what the big deal was. I see it as all of the responsibilities of homeownership with none of the potential upside. Rental housing run by a mission-driven nonprofit that is well organized and capitalized is actually a better opportunity for most people. With limited equity cooperatives, do people do better than having their money in a security deposit? I hear a lot of talk about it these days, but I want to see models that show that they really provide significant economic benefit for people to justify the complexity.

Mark Pinsky

Mark Pinsky served as CEO of Opportunity Finance Network (OFN) from 1995 until 2016. OFN is the nation's leading trade association of community development financial institutions. Through 2007, OFN members had originated more than $19.8 billion in financing in underserved urban, rural, and Native communities. In this interview, Pinsky discusses the state of community development finance, the movement's vision and policy initiatives, and current challenges faced by CDFIs in this period of economic crisis.

Interviewed in 2009

Steve Dubb: What is the status of the Opportunity Finance industry today? In what ways have community development financial institutions (CDFIs) been impacted by the global financial crisis?

Mark Pinsky: The Opportunity Finance industry is healthy and sound, though we are certainly experiencing some level of stress from what's going around us in the marketplace. Balance sheets remain strong. We expect some CDFIs to be in trouble as the year goes on, although we haven't seen any yet. Right now, every ecosystem we exist in—whether it is the economy, the policy arena, or our own ecology of development finance—are all in the midst of a once-in-a-lifetime transformational change. It's a volatile and turbulent time. It's a challenge to keep our feet on the ground.

Jim Collins, the author of *Good to Great*, spoke at our conference last December. Before the conference, he spent some time studying our industry and looking at the data. He's a mountain climber, so he used a mountain climbing analogy. He said, "If you're climbing Mount Everest and you're not fully prepared, but you're at base camp and a storm hits, you can probably survive, but if you're at 27,000 feet you're dead if you're not prepared." In some ways, he said to us, "You work at 27,000 feet—you have to be always prepared." We have these attributes by necessity.

If you look at airlines, Southwest has done well in a very difficult industry. The point Jim made was that the companies that are really successful are as disciplined in good times as in bad times. It means they are able to manage in bad times without missing a beat. That's why Southwest was able to make gains in market share after 9/11. And that's part of the reason why community development finance has held up so well during the crisis. There is something true about this—our role is increasingly important—from a financial point of view, but also from a media or policy point of view. I get asked these days by the press, "How come you're able to be successful?" The answer is that we never stopped being responsible—it's not really more complicated than that.

Of course, we're not invulnerable to the economic turmoil. To the extent there are drags, it's the economy, which makes lending more difficult. There will be some loan funds that may not survive. But I think we will be all right. By and large, the industry will be just fine.

SD: *You just had your annual conference this past December and a follow-up event on Rethinking Risk and Reward in February [2009]. Can you discuss some action items or main themes that came out of those conferences?*

MP: A few themes came out of the conference. These are difficult times ahead. Policy is going to be really important. No surprise there. The really big one is the sense of dedication to being part of the solution in a way that we haven't been before—in a bigger picture way. In part, it is about seeking to bend the moral arc of the universe towards justice. We need to impact the way the financial system operates—Lord knows we do. At our conference this past December, I talked in my speech that we need to disprove Gresham's Law—that instead of having bad money chase out good money, we need to have a system that allows good money to drive out bad.

This is what our forum in February on Rethinking Risk & Reward was about. We need to engage our industry, the consumer advocacy industry, labor, community development folks, regulators, and others. What does that mean? It means that we need to decide what we think about financial markets and how do we think about bending the moral universe. That was just the start of the conversation. We think we will be reinventing the financial industry for years and possibly decades. There are some fundamental things that we think have to be true. Reward has to be directly tied to risk. Protecting consumers needs to be a fundamental notion of prudence in financial markets and not a convenience or add-on. It is possible to pursue profit too hard. Profit in the absence of regulation can take you to places that are catastrophic. The decision of a few people at rating agencies can have an incredibly leveraged effect. The forum on the 25th [of February] was very rewarding and I think it was a successful day. We have a lot to learn and we have a lot to teach. There is the mystification of what went on in the markets that only the smart people could figure out, but really the problems were pretty simple.

SD: *If the problems are, despite superficial complexity, at their heart pretty simple, without being simplistic, what do you think of as the solution or solutions?*

MP: I don't think there is *a solution*, but I think we can be part of the solution. We've created a financial system that is so clever that it has

"We need to disprove Gresham's Law—
that instead of having bad money chase
out good money, **we need to have a
system that allows good money to
drive out bad**."

divorced risk from reward. People were taking risk without opportunity for reward and getting rewarded without taking risk. That's capitalism: broken. If you take a lot of risk, you should get a lot of reward, but when those two things are dissociated, it tends to misalign every reasonable incentive that you would expect to find. It makes it hard to manage things as basic as price risk or even price an asset. We have lost confidence in our ability to know what an asset is worth. We've spent so much time deceiving ourselves to make one-plus-one equal four. We thought there were alchemists who could make this equation true. We deluded ourselves —we as a financial system—into thinking you can get gold from hay. We know that isn't so. We should've known better.

What can opportunity finance do right now? First of all, just continue to demonstrate that is possible to be prudent, sound, and safe and lend to low-income people, as we have been doing successfully for thirty years. It works. We were right then and we are right now. The answer is not to run from those markets, which is what has happened. If we don't have a financial distribution system that gives everybody the opportunity to access credit on fair terms, even if we are not going to replicate the problems of the past, we are certainly not going to have growth that is inclusive. The credit system is not doing the things the credit system is supposed to do.

SD: *In December [2008] at the Opportunity Finance Network conference, you asked some critical questions, such as "What must our global financial system do and be if we are working toward a sustainable and inclusive prosperity?" and "How does the nation align capital with social, economic, and political justice?"*

What do you see as key components of answers that begin to address those questions?

MP: We need to take a seat for ourselves at the table of financial system reform. We are in the process of redefining financial markets. It happened in the 1930s and it happened in a way in the 1960s and it is happening now. This is comprehensive. If we come out of this with a system that is like the old one, we're in a lot of trouble. But we have an opportunity to think differently about the role of the credit system and the financial system.

The other piece is to take the importance that is now attached to the work that we do and figure out how to leverage that on Capitol Hill and across executive agencies and figure out how to leverage the credibility we have earned to strengthen our movement and our capacity. We need to become a core part of how the credit system works—whether at U.S. Department of Housing and Urban Development (HUD), U.S. Department of Agriculture (USDA), or Small Business Administration (SDA). We need to leverage the policy success we have had with the CDFI Fund and apply that success in other venues.

One of the ideas in the policy book that we issued is to create an investment bank to finance community development research and development. We need to do things like that.

That's what we need to do in the policy arena. In local communities, we simply need to go about being disciplined in good times as in bad times. We need to provide those anchor financing services—we need to build our capacity without losing a sense of mission and purpose. Not just policy. Maintain the discipline. Continue doing what you're doing. As you get bigger and more noticed, you can lose your sense of purpose. Part of my job is to keep people focused on the right things.

SD: *You've proposed a federal bond guarantee for CDFIs? How would it work and what would be its impact?*

MP: The notion of the bond fund is that it would free up $1 billion a year for five years to provide a pool of money, with repayment amortized over forty years, to support further CDFI lending. What it would do is enable CDFIs to be part of the lending solution. It would give CDFIs the liquidity that has pretty much dried up and enable them to lend. It would give the federal government the authority to guarantee bonds for five years up to a total of $1 billion a year, which it could do through as many as five issuers. That number could go up. But let's assume the number is $1 billion and that Opportunity Finance Network would be one of those five bond issuers. Suppose we got a federal guarantee of $200 million for a bond issue. We would take the bond issue revenues and place it in CDFIs. They would lend into communities, get paid back, and re-lend it (since the bond debt is for a forty-year term).

In our industry, there is a grim joke going around that in today's economy the market of low-income communities is growing rapidly. We think we could use more than $1 billion, but we would be happy if the legislation passed and provided a billion.

SD: *You've talked about establishing an affirmative fiduciary responsibility of all financial institutions to invest at least one tenth of one percent of their assets in CDFIs. Again, how would it work and what would be its impact?*

MP: That's my big hairy audacious idea. The next stage of opportunity finance will be making it a credentialed asset class in capital markets. There was a time when we thought we're not like capital markets and should be separate. Well, now we're doing better than a lot of asset classes. We need to get rid of the idea that CDFIs are an alternative when nothing else works. Something like this is going to have to be in place. It debunks the idea that this is an oddball kind of thing to do. It is simply not.

SD: *Are there any ideas from outside the United States in community finance that you would like to see implemented here?*

MP: We always watch microfinance internationally and the ability to scale that in the United States. Acción Texas is trying to bring that to scale. It's a good question. Honestly, we have not spent a lot of time looking into that.

SD: *One of the sources of CDFI funding has been from the banking sector. Presumably that has taken a nosedive. How has this impacted CDFIs?*

MP: There is no question that the economic crisis has had an impact on our lending. That's coming from a number of sources. Banks are

"In our industry, there is a grim joke going around that **in today's economy the market of low-income communities is growing rapidly**."

not picking on CDFIs [by reducing their lending to CDFIs]; they are not lending to a lot of former borrowers.

We're also affected by the fact that most of the foundations that make program-related investments have seen their endowments shrink. And almost all investors have less money to lend. It is a tough time for liquidity. That's why gaining access to the bond market is so important. That's also why we want CDFIs to have access to funds from TARP [Troubled Assets Relief Program] as well.

SD: *Has there been any tracking of the impact of the economic crisis on your membership to date?*

MP: This week we are going out with a survey. Within the next three or four weeks we'll have pretty substantial data of what's going on. That's within our industry. Some of the Fed banks are trying to get someone to write a paper to look at the effects of the change in liquidity on community development finance broadly defined—in other words, it would cover CDFIs, but not just CDFIs.

SD: *To step away from the current economic crisis, over the long haul, there has obviously been tremendous growth in CDFIs since OFN was founded in 1985. If you had to choose only three main accomplishments, what would you pick as the three most important changes brought about by the growth of CDFIs?*

MP: The first is just the proof of concept that this has worked. The second thing is demonstrating the potential or viability of what we call opportunity markets—markets outside the mainstream— markets of people of color or markets of communities of mixed income. There was this presumption that they don't behave or grow as economies the way more conventional markets do. We've been able to prove that was not the case. One of the consequences was that predators came in, but in the long run it is a positive change. The third thing was the growth in this industry coupled with the performance of the industry has the potential to change thinking about how the financial industry as a whole should function. We haven't fully realized this potential yet, but I think we are beginning to do so.

SD: *Cdfis grew in strength during the eight years of the Bush administration, a period of generally declining—or, at best, anemic—federal support for community development. How did this occur?*

MP: There are a series of stories one could tell about why this happened. One is that CDFIs were never a product of the federal government. The fund was designed to support what we do without taking the industry over. There is no other program that works the way it does. It invests in the balance sheets and invests in the ability of organizations to pursue their strategy. This is really different from most federal programs—so much financing is project based.

We understood, even though we weren't always so good from a political perspective, that CDFIs had a diverse base of support. There was a time when the Democrats didn't like us when the first [President] Bush liked us. And then when Clinton liked us, the Republicans didn't like us. But the bottom line in Congress is that we provided the early-stage financing for that multi-family development or child-care center in your district. We were able to make the connection. Everyone knew these were special deals. Everybody was a little surprised. We had a very rich and broad and deep bipartisan base in Congress. That's critical. That's why we survived.

If you can find more than five people who say that in 2001 they would have told you that CDFI Fund would still be around in 2009, somebody is lying. People didn't think it was possible, but it was possible. We underestimated the depth of the support we enjoyed. That's the story.

One of the most important moments in our industry was in 2005 when the Bush White House led this effort that was going to be called the Strengthening America's Communities Initiative, which would have consolidated CDBG [Community Development Block

Grants] and other community development programs and cut funding by one third. I am told it was known inside the White House as the Strangling America's Communities Initiative.

It was a lot of hot air. What I call "Popcorn policy." There was a kernel of truth in it, but it was surrounded by a lot of hot air. We found out that the emperor had no clothes. They couldn't win a fight on this. When we challenged them and they backed off, it was a huge signal to people on the Hill that we had the political clout and know-how. It was then when we went from keeping CDFI funding at a minimal level to expanding it. We didn't have much of a lobbying presence, so it was definitely not K Street. It was grass-roots. Our success is in the fact that we have so many people around the country willing to mobilize to support us and we have great compelling stories. We weren't going to roll over and die. We had real data and real results that showed that we're really important.

SD: *How do community development financial institutions coordinate with community development corporations (CDCs) and other community groups? What could be done to further improve coordination?*

MP: There was a time, maybe fifteen to twenty years ago, when ties between CDFIs and community organizations were somewhat strained. CDFIs were at least in appearance—if not in fact—interjecting themselves between community organizations and their sources of capital. It took a while for them to understand that we could add value and leverage resources that they could not, because of our ability to manage capital and take on risk. Over time that's become a healthy relationship and it is different in every community. What's going on in Washington and a lot of banking places and funding places is that CDFIs, because of their solid balance sheets, are viewed as the wisest place in which to invest. That's great that we have resources, but if we don't have strong community partners, we can't place the money.

Community development finance has to also be about charter school developers, multi-family housing developers—many of who are really struggling right now—or supporting small business. We can't succeed without all of those things going on. If we don't have a foundation of strong community-based organizations out there, there is very little we can do. Money alone doesn't solve

"If we don't have a foundation of strong community-based organizations out there, there is very little we can do.

Money alone doesn't solve a thing."

a thing. The hard work gets done on the ground where you have a CDC developing rental housing or a community-based organization developing a charter school. We can't do the development; we just do the financing.

SD: *A few years ago, OFN developed CARS—the CDFI Assessment Rating System [since renamed Aeris]. How would you assess the rating system's effectiveness?*

MP: CDFI Assessment Rating System is a rating system for investors, but it is rooted in twenty or so years of work in financing and articulating and putting into play best practices in community development finance. Since we're largely unregulated, we felt it was important to set up a system that would provide strong industry standards.

We use a Capital, Assets, Management, Equity, and Leverage (CAMEL) structure. We also look at impact performance and risk—no other rating system does this. We will soon be at fifty rated CDFIs and thirty subscribers or investors who are using the systems. Subscribers include mutual funds, banks, socially motivated investors, and foundations.

CARS is really at the epicenter of our strategy, as performance has always been key. Having an effective rating system has been at the center of that effort. It is never more important than now. For investors to make a decision in this environment, they absolutely need a third-party investor tool that is beyond reproach. It is playing an increasingly important role. Banks, foundations, and others are losing staff. Part of losing staff means a greater reliance on third-party ratings. CDFIs are more important than ever for folks trying to do development finance of any kind. So there are fewer people to do it and greater need. CARS is fundamental to our industry and development more broadly. We've been approached to make CARS available for use for other kinds of investing opportunities beyond CDFIs. It hasn't happened yet, but we think that will eventually happen.

SD: *What more do you see that needs to be done to expand the CARS effort?*

MP: Our focus is increasing the efficiency. It has been an experiment. It is small scale. We've been working on restructuring how we staff it. That's well on its way. It will be a year or two until we master that. It's also important to appreciate that it is a market system—you need buyers and sellers. It's been a little bit of a seesaw—as there are more subscribers, more CDFIs want to get rated. As more CDFIs get rated, more investors want to subscribe. Managing growth requires us to make this market. We're getting there. It will put us in a position to increase the efficiency of capital flows to CDFIs and from CDFIs to communities, particularly as the economy starts to get better and more financing becomes available.

SD: *One area of considerable discussion for CDFIs over the past few years has been the issue of scale. Scale is seen as necessary for accessing greater amounts of capital, but can also mean larger organizations that may (or may not) become disconnected from the communities they serve. How have OFN members sought to build scale while retaining community responsiveness? Has the crisis at all put this discussion on hold?*

MP: The fundamental issue is that we weren't providing a solution that was commensurate with the problems of wealth and inequality that we are trying to address. A few years ago, we sought to investigate if there was any way to create a financing system that would get us closer. Little did we know how right that conversation was. But we wanted to start that conversation and we did.

One key question that we would come back to our members with is: What was core? What did they absolutely have to do themselves and what could they do through a partnership with others or through other sorts of systems? This was an important step to develop systems that were more productive or efficient in their use of resources.

I think we can safely say that this discussion has enabled us to increase the volume of our financing. When we started six years

"The greatest wealth building effect that we have has come through **our ability to create healthy economies in places that didn't have healthy economies.**"

ago, we did $1.3 billion in new financing. Last year we went to $5 billion. So something is going right. The demand for our financing is growing, so there is the need to pursue scale. The challenge is resources. This is why we have pushed for an innovation fund. To help people that have great ideas, but need some investment capital. The industry is ready and able to pursue it—we just the need the resources to do it. I think the resources will be there. We just need a little bit of time.

SD: *How would this Innovation Fund work?*

MP: We've been kicking around an idea to create a fund that would allow for some grant money and some investment money for promising ideas. Money to support things that would allow a lot of CDFIs to take advantage of them if they worked: a bond fund is one of them. A lot of ideas wither on the vine. The Innovation Fund would be working capital. Some ideas would require grant funds while others could be financed through loans. We haven't developed a formal proposal yet, but we are working on this.

SD: *What has been the impact of CDFIs on wealth building? How far back have those efforts been set by the crisis?*

MP: Obviously, pretty much everyone has been set back by the current crisis. I have certainly lost wealth in my own 401(k).

But I think we create wealth in a number of ways. For instance, more CDFIs are participating in programs that support individual development accounts (IDAs). Folks like the Opportunity Fund of San Jose, California, are trying to link IDAs to financing. We also create wealth through support of small businesses, by supporting community-based entrepreneurship that creates real wealth, as opposed to the phantom wealth on Wall Street. The greatest wealth building effect we that have has come through our ability to create healthy economies in places that didn't have healthy economies.

SD: *Some Opportunity Finance Network members pursue a triple bottom line return (economic, equity, environmental). How successful have these members been? Do you see the practice spreading?*

MP: I do see the practice spreading. I think the leaders are probably Shorebank and Enterprise Cascadia, but there are a number of others: MACED (Mountain Association for Community Economic Development, Sustainable Jobs Fund (SJF), The Reinvestment Fund (TRF) in Philadelphia. It's gone past the experimental stage. How do we build a system that is going to build over time? I think it is a successful strategy. I think it is going to grow—not at a rapid pace, but a steady pace.

SD: *What are Opportunity Finance Network's priorities in green investing? What is Opportunity Finance's role in this area?*

MP: Green finance is how we would define it. It brings us back a little bit to that innovation fund. We're used to using pass-through grants where we provide flexible capital to our members: we've done this with lending for child-care facilities and small business finance back in the 1990s. We could provide some innovation capital, some working capital, with a fair amount of flexibility. That's the approach we are trying to take right now. We don't know what the best thing is. Part of the reason we do it this way is to get a number of people to work on this and identify two or three areas that really work well, which we can then take to scale.

SD: *Opportunity Finance Network's strategic plan expires in 2010. While obviously the end result will depend on the members, do you have any thoughts about what might come out of the next round?*

MP: The next strategic planning round will be launched in Charlotte, North Carolina, at our conference this year and we expect to have a new strategic plan by the middle of 2010. I do a lot of thinking about that.

We are certainly in a period now of making sure that we are stable and secure and sound. We want to continue to pursue high-value financing, which we call scale, and credential what we do. Things like pursuing that idea of having an affirmative obligation of financial institutions to dedicate one tenth of one percent of their assets to opportunity finance will become more central. And of course making sure that we are focused and we earn and keep the respect for what we do.

SD: *Is there anything else that you would like to add?*

MP: We are very invested in taking advantage of this policy moment both for good reasons and bad reasons. The current economic crisis brings us many opportunities, such as the ability to get more federal funding for the CDFI Fund, but there are real threats to us in terms of financial system reform. Policy is critically important. It is what we have worked towards for a long time.

Community Investment and Institutional Strategies

This section highlights three different approaches to investment. Tony Brown is a business consultant who for a number of years directed the Uptown Consortium, an early anchor institution-based strategy of community development. The Uptown Consortium, which brought together the University of Cincinnati, the zoo, and three hospitals, invested hundreds of millions of dollars at low interest rates in seven nearby underinvested neighborhoods. Lisa Hagerman examined similar "mission investing" (or what is increasingly called "impact investing") in the foundation community. Michael Shuman has been a leader in the "crowdfunding" movement and was one of the architects of the federal Jobs Act (and various state-based offshoots). The JOBS Act, passed by Congress in 2012, has helped create new ways for "non-accredited" investors (that is, the overwhelming majority of Americans who are not millionaires) to invest small amounts of capital in local businesses.

Tony Brown

*From 2004 to 2009, Tony Brown served as CEO
and President of the Uptown Consortium, based
in Cincinnati, Ohio. The Uptown Consortium
was founded in 2003 as an alliance of the city's
public university (the University of Cincinnati) and
four leading nonprofit groups (Children's Hospital
Medical Center, the Cincinnati Zoo & Botanical
Garden, the Health Alliance of Greater Cincinnati,
and TriHealth, Inc.). The group aims to develop
a mixed-used (commercial, retail and residential)
approach to community development in the Uptown
neighborhoods where the university and nonprofits
are located.*

*With an annual operating budget of $3 million
and a capital budget of $100 million, the Uptown
Consortium is a precedent-setting effort that
illustrates the potential for nonprofit hospitals and
universities to employ an anchor-based approach to
community wealth building. To date, the trustees of
the University of Cincinnati alone have allocated
$100 million from the university's $1 billion
endowment to support the effort, helping leverage
over $400 million for community renovation work.*

Interviewed in 2007

Steve Dubb: Could you explain briefly the origins of the Uptown Consortium?

Tony Brown: Officially they formed when they hired me as President in 2004. But a year before, they got together on an informal basis and hired an urban planner, John Alschuler, who specializes in community development finance, to help them to determine what their common needs and interests were. I was hired more or less to implement the Uptown Strategic Plan that Alschuler developed.

SD: Why was the Uptown Consortium led by nonprofits? Why wasn't the corporate community involved?

TB: There is a broader private sector effort that is focused in the central business district called 3CDC. Proctor & Gamble, Federated, and other businesses are leading a similar renaissance in the central business district. There was some initial thinking among the universities and hospitals that they would combine with 3CDC. But Dr. Nancy Zimpher (President of the University of Cincinnati) and Jim Anderson (CEO of Children's Hospital) felt their interests were somewhat different than those downtown and didn't want their interests to be overshadowed. They felt there was enough institutional wealth among the public university and area nonprofits that they could sustain their own direct effort. So that was the tactical decision.

It helps to understand Cincinnati's geography. If you stood at the corner of Vine & MLK, you'll see the hospital, the University of Cincinnati, and the zoo. Within a half-mile radius, all five of the (Uptown Consortium) institutions converge, so that's a pretty powerful physical presence when you look at the Uptown area and our dominance in healthcare and higher education.

SD: What level of commitment is required to be one of the five members of the Uptown Consortium? Could you detail the level of financial commitment of each of the partners?

TB: Collectively they all have pledged to invest $75 million. This was separate from a University of Cincinnati endowment investment allocation of $100 million. Our big three—Children's Hospital, the University of Cincinnati, and the Health Alliance—have all committed capital funds. Tri-Health and the Zoo haven't committed capital funds but have provided operating support. We have been successful in using the members' commitment to raise $52 million in New Markets Tax Credits and another $18 million from some local banks.

SD: *Uptown Consortium's website notes specifically that the University of Cincinnati has invested to date more than $50 million of the $100 million it has allocated from its endowment. Is investment a metaphor or is it a real investment? In other words, how does this investment process work? Is it a donation from its endowment or does it get a return? If it does get a return, what level of return are the trustees expecting?*

TB: We get very flexible, low-interest loans. I can access it directly from a member. It is at four percent, with interest-only payments due. The source of repayment is the goal of what we are doing with the money. In other instances, we might borrow directly from the New Markets Tax Credit fund.

SD: *Presumably 4% interest is not a market-maximizing rate of return. How do trustees view this?*

TB: There is a double-impact type of return. One, they want to see an improved environment around their edges. Then there is the reality that to set a high rate of return makes it very difficult to invest into low-income communities. If they can do good and use an amount of capital that won't impact their plans but will still provide enough to finance investment in the community plan, then it works. The endowment financing has been a good way to access capital in a way that a for-profit developer couldn't do.

There is accountability to the endowment trustees—they know what the targeted rate of return is and how it is going to impact the portfolio performance.

And there are tangible benefits as well. This year at the University of Cincinnati they had their largest enrollment rate ever for their freshman class. They attribute that to the fact that they spent $1 billion in creating a beautiful campus and they have invested in the rough edges. So they are benefiting by getting a higher rate of students who are admitted to enroll.

SD: *Increasingly, universities, hospitals, and other nonprofits are defined as "anchor institutions" because they are largely place-*

based and cannot easily move. This creates a potential for action, but also creates obstacles. As you know, often universities, hospitals, and similar "anchor institutions" are seen as not being very responsive to the community. What steps have been taken in Cincinnati to try to involve smaller community groups and break down this divide? To what extent have these efforts been successful?

TB: It's an excellent question. One of the things that I always have to work at is to extend our efforts to let the community know that our approach is one of collaboration and not of a big brother that knows it all. One of the ways we have done this is that we were honest up front about our redevelopment priority areas. Out of self-interest they are contiguous to the hospitals and university. We then work with the established neighborhood groups to do an effective plan. We use the plan to work with the community to do visioning and design charrettes that at least gets us to a shared vision. We come up with redevelopment principles. And the work we have done has occurred without controversy, which shows strong community consensus. If a project is consistent with the redevelopment plan, we get community support. So you do a parking garage, for instance, but you wrap it with other uses, such as an office building or housing. As a result, the community is not looking at the back end of a parking garage but instead the parking structure is wrapped with other uses that make it appealing.

For instance, we put up parking garages in the neighborhood business district in a way that serves as a catalyst for neighborhood revitalization. The additional space provides capacity for commercial retail.

SD: Could you provide any examples of how this works?

TB: One is when the University of Cincinnati decided they would do a part of their campus called Varsity Village. The campus sits in a bowl. They wanted to place the parking garage adjacent to the campus. So they dug the parking garage into the hillside and put ground-level retail and student housing above. If you're facing south, you will see the neighborhood business district and the new student housing. If you look north, you see the University of Cincinnati campus. So this allowed the University to build a parking garage and give the community partner air rights. The University got two benefits: retail and housing for the students, with the commercial and housing development owned by their community partner.

"Within a half-mile radius, all five of the (Uptown Consortium) institutions converge, so **that's a pretty powerful physical presence when you look at the Uptown area**."

A second example is what we did with Children's Hospital. It's headquartered two blocks away from the Avondale neighborhood business district. The plan in Avondale aimed to get more employees to support the neighborhood business district and make it more pedestrian friendly. So Children's Hospital agreed to build a 100,000 square-foot office building and a 1,400-space parking garage. The parking garage also provides parking for a 45,000 square-foot retail office building and is helping generate more foot traffic between the main campus and Avondale—this only two blocks away from the heart of a largely African-American community that had previously had problems with disinvestment, boarded-up properties, and crime.

SD: *Clearly, the riots that took place in Cincinnati in 2001 were at least one of the factors that led to the formation of the Uptown Consortium. How has the Uptown Consortium sought to address race- and class-based divisions in Cincinnati?*

TB: I think the issue of the racial disturbance probably had a bigger impact in the central district. It was a less of an issue in Uptown because it is more diverse. Their rationale was less a response to the disturbances than to disinvestment. With that being said, we recognize that the neighborhoods that make up Uptown are our city's most diverse. If we can get it right in Uptown, we can create diverse mixed-income communities and create an environment where that diversity can thrive. We consider ourselves successful if the doctors and PhDs can enjoy the same environment as the mother that lives on welfare and has Section 8 housing and create a quality of life that is the envy of the region.

We just recently did a soft launch of our new website. The whole purpose is to show the diversity of Uptown—black and white, as well as a considerable international presence. You will not find an area of our region that is more diverse than Uptown.

SD: *Are you facing any displacement or gentrification?*

TB: With any redevelopment effort, it is at least a concern. The home-ownership rate in Uptown is very low—24 percent—compared to a national average of well over 60 percent and the city's average of 39 percent. But we have a significant percentage of vacant housing stock. So gentrification has not been an issue so much in Uptown because there is an ample supply of affordable rental housing. Our community has supported the development of market-rate housing.

Can we improve the quality of affordable rental housing? That has been a secondary goal of ours. The primary strategy is to increase the rate of homeownership in the Uptown area and do it in a large-scale way that would convince the employees of the Uptown Consortium to live close to where they work.

SD: *How do you determine the extent to which you are successful?*

TB: One of the internal metrics is to increase the rate of homeowner-ship. We hope to show some increase by 2010. Right now we talk about the number of units we are attempting to build. Another measure is a survey measure of perception and attitude. Every other year, we survey residents, employees, and nonresidents. We ask questions such as, "How is the uptown area perceived?" We also ask about the perception of crime: for example, whether people see Uptown as a safe or dangerous area. We use that metric to test if our public perceives our area more positively. We know that residents give a higher rating than nonresidents. Most nonresidents see Uptown as unsafe and the quality of schools as being unattractive. You still see those negatives among residents, but they have a higher appreciation of the positive amenities.

SD: *One notable feature of the Uptown Consortium were three community planning "Uptown Summits" that were held in 2003, 2004, and 2005. Could you describe the community input process that the Consortium has used? What has worked best about the community input process? What problems have arisen? How has community planning continued since the last summit in 2005?*

TB: It was a way to get some feedback. Initially the CEOs of the consortium brought in an outside planner who interviewed the community. At the first summit, the CEOs reported on the plan and the community for the most part endorsed it, but the community felt it didn't go deep enough in workforce development and education. The plan did address public safety. So the latter summits focused on workforce development and education. What we have since done is we do have a quarterly meeting where we get back together. We also took the community stakeholders that emerged from those summits and sort of embedded them in three committees—public safety, neighborhood services, and community development. So we get ongoing feedback through those committees.

SD: *Prior to working at the Uptown Consortium, you were director of the CDFI Fund in Washington. What made you want to come back to your hometown of Cincinnati from Washington? What were the opportunities that you saw?*

TB: I was impressed by the opportunity to head up the Uptown Consortium. I had been away nearly twenty years and saw the substantial commitment the university and hospitals had made. I talked with Jim Anderson of Children's Hospital and was very impressed. They were offering a commitment to work in a targeted area and were willing to bring resources to that area. I felt it would be a well-funded commitment and it has been. It was also an opportunity to apply a lot of things that I had seen as director of the CDFI Fund in a specific community.

SD: *Are there any lessons that have required "mid-course" corrections at the Uptown Consortium? Describe what some of these challenges have been and how the Consortium has met them?*

TB: The biggest one is that the community asked us to focus on workforce development and education and, in some cases, healthcare disparity. We've become so involved in community development, there's no way we could effectively put the resources or programs in place to have a demonstrable effect on social service delivery in Uptown. The community partners want the money, but often they don't want the accountability and oversight. The mid-course correction was to realize that social service delivery is one area where we needed to

"We consider ourselves successful if the doctors and PhDs can enjoy the same environment as the mother that lives on welfare and has Section 8 housing and **create a quality of life that is the envy of the region.**"

play more of an indirect role. We can create an environment of job opportunities, such as universities working with schools. We can be a bridge for introduction. But we shouldn't have the responsibility of coming up with program initiatives or providing resources in an area that requires millions and where our thousands can only go so far. That's been our biggest change—the others have been refinements.

SD: *How does the Uptown Consortium interact with the business community and local government?*

TB: The business community in general gave the Consortium instant credibility as a top-tier organization on day one and that's by virtue of its members. It so happens that four out of five are ranked within the city's top seven employers. The University of Cincinnati employs more than Procter & Gamble and General Electric. And the Zoo is our leading tourist attraction with over 1 million visitors a year. So we got instant credibility.

   After we raised our investment capital and local government saw us make sizable investments, we gained the respect and credibility of the City as a valuable community development partner, so much so that we work closely with the City to coordinate our plans. The magnitude of our investment can sometimes outpace the local government. But you can't do community development without working with the City.

SD: *What lessons does the Uptown Consortium hold for anchor institutions that might want to lead similar efforts in other cities? What do you see as the most important ones?*

TB: Lesson number one is to know the business opportunities. And the second lesson is to gain the financial commitments to execute. I think the early market assessment of bringing in Altschuler to get a determination of what the opportunities are, and how they can make a difference (that his report outlined) was key.

It allowed me to say: "If you want to hire me, here is the magnitude of the operating capital and here is the investment capital that is needed." It required demonstrating the market opportunities and what that meant. For instance, I could make some estimates that $100 million would leverage $400 million of development—and this is the type of impact you'll have.

The CEOs know money and budgets. So I could say: "If you think $10 million is a lot of money, this is what we can do. But if you want to see ten blocks improve and you would like to see that tomorrow, here's the budget of buying and demolishing 10 blocks and rebuilding." So they understood the magnitude of the investment required.

SD: *What do you see as the most important challenges or opportunities facing the Uptown Consortium today? Where do you think the Uptown Consortium will focus its energies over the next five to ten years?*

TB: The most important one is our credibility. To get projects out of the ground. As we complete what is on the drawing board, that strengthens our credibility, so folks know that it is not a smokescreen.

Our challenge really is the growing pains. As we are successful in one neighborhood, the expectation that we can make it happen elsewhere adds growing pains. We are taking on speculative real estate, but there is a lot of risk involved and sometimes we're out there before we get commitment from local government. So the biggest challenge is to maintain real time data as we budget for each project. The longer the time from product to market—the higher the carrying costs in terms of title, interest, and so forth. So capacity and delivery is our biggest challenge.

Lisa Hagerman

*Lisa Hagerman was the Director of
More for Mission, based at the Initiative
for Responsible Investment at Harvard
University. More for Mission is a research
and advocacy initiative dedicated to
promoting the concept of mission investing
and influencing foundations to take up
mission investing practices. More for
Mission's network of foundations includes
ninety mission-driven foundations
representing $34 billion in total assets.*

*Currently, Hagerman is the Director of
Programs at DBL Investors, which she
joined in 2011. She leads the strategy and
implementation of double bottom line
practices working with DBL Investors'
portfolio companies across workforce
development, environmental stewardship,
community engagement, and siting
initiatives.*

Interviewed in 2010

Steve Dubb: Tell us about your background. How did you become interested and involved in the movement for mission investing?

Lisa Hagerman: My background includes ten years of banking experience, three of which were at Wells Fargo, where I was provided an opportunity to work with their community development department and promote the Bank's minority lending initiatives. I have always had a strong interest in community development and regional economic development issues. My work with Belden Daniels of Economic Innovation International, a Boston-based consulting firm that builds privately capitalized community equity funds, provided an opportunity to work on directing private capital towards funds having social, environmental, and economic impact. My doctoral work with Tessa Hebb and Gordon Clark at Oxford University on the Pension Funds & Urban Revitalization Initiative, a four-year project sponsored by the Rockefeller and Ford Foundations, was an opportunity to examine this practice from the public pension fund perspective—under the name of economically targeted investing. It is exciting to be working with foundations and see the potential for significant institutional dollars to flow into the underserved markets.

SD: Tell us about More for Mission—how it began, its goals, your work, who is involved.

LH: More for Mission has now been in existence for just over two years. We started in September 2008 and were initially housed at the Institute for Responsible Investment of the Boston College Center for Corporate Citizenship and are now at the Initiative for Responsible Investment of the Harvard Kennedy School, run by David Wood. We were founded with the financial support of three foundations—pioneers in the field of mission investing: the Annie E. Casey Foundation, F.B. Heron Foundation, and the Meyer Memorial Trust. This initiative was originally called the "2% Campaign"—that is, advocating that foundations allocate two percent of their endowment assets to mission-related investments. When I was brought on to manage this effort, we changed the name to "More for Mission." We found that two percent was too high of a hurdle for the larger foundations and too small for the smaller foundations, some of which may be at 100 percent of their investments aligned with the mission of the organization.

In the spring of 2010, our Funders Circle expanded to seven foundations, which, in addition to the three co-founders (Annie E. Casey Foundation, F.B. Heron Foundation, and Meyer Memorial Trust), now includes the Cleveland Foundation, the Mary Reynolds Babcock Foundation, the Jessie Smith Noyes Foundation, and the W.K. Kellogg Foundation. We are glad to have our supporters across different types of foundations (private and community) and across regions of the country—showing this is a national movement. At the same time, our home moved from Boston College to the Harvard Kennedy School.

SD: *Is Veris Wealth Partners, for example, one of those groups?*

LH: Yes. Michael Lent, a Partner with Veris Wealth Partners and Trustee of the Edward W. Hazen Foundation, moderated a panel at More for Mission's national conference in September on the dynamics of the foundation/consultant relationship and balancing organizational goals. In particular, we are reaching out to the large institutional consultants to better understand the landscape and breadth and depth of offerings in mission investing or more broadly responsible investing. The More for Mission website includes a section listing of consultants—both dedicated mission related investment consultants and the large institutional consultants with a dedicated mission related or responsible investment team. Sandra Urie, CEO of Cambridge Associates, was the keynote speaker at More for Mission's national conference. In collaboration with Cambridge Associates, we offer our foundation members access to Cambridge's proprietary listings of approximately 270 fund managers offering public and private mission-related funds across asset classes and strategies, including community investing, ESG investing, and double bottom line real estate.

We want to show that mission investing is a viable field with foundation investors, investment intermediaries, and a growing base of consultants in the industry.

SD: *Are other types of institutions getting into the mission investing space? Universities? Hospitals? Pension Funds? Others?*

LH: Yes. Other institutional investors have taken up mission investing but under a different name—for example, targeted investing for public pension funds and faith-consistent investing for faith-based investors. More for Mission created an Affiliates Circle in Spring 2010 to show that this is a concept across institutional investors addressing the opportunities targeted investing can bring to their investment practice and unique institutional goals. More for Mission seeks to collaborate with other institutional investors including public sector pension funds, faith-based organizations, and university endowments. More for Mission affiliates include: The International Interfaith Investment Group (3iG), the Interfaith Center on Corporate Responsibility (ICCR), the Responsible Endowments Coalition (REC), and Teachers Insurance and Annuity Association—College Retirement Equities Fund (TIAA-CREF).

I think that whatever the language used—whether it is faith-consistent investment for religious investors or targeted investing for pension funds—it's a way to show that mission investing is a concept that extends beyond the foundation sector and that there could be opportunities in the future to leverage co-investment.

SD: *Is there anything analogous to More for Mission among universities, where, for example, universities get together like foundations have—or are they all doing their own thing?*

LH: I would say the Responsible Endowments Coalition (REC), part of More for Mission's Affiliates Circle, is similar in trying to bring university endowments together. However, REC is unique in their important work with student organizers on responsible investment training, and having students participate on university endowment investment committees helping to establish responsible investing programs at the university.

There seem to be a lot of terms associated with socially conscious forms of investing—impact investing, double and triple bottom-line investing, socially responsible investing, PRIs, MRIs, etc.

SD: *What do you see as the important distinctions among these categories? At its most basic, what is mission investing?*

LH: More for Mission's constituents are foundations that are "mission investors." We define a mission investor as a foundation seeking investment opportunities that align with the mission of the organization, whether that be through market-rate, mission-related investments (MRIs) that broadly support the mission of the organization while seeking market-rate returns, or below-market, program-related investments (PRIs) structured to create specific programmatic benefits, and for a private foundation can count towards the five-percent payout requirement. MRIs use the other 95 percent of foundation endowment assets towards investments seeking financial returns while having social and environmental benefits to society.

At its core, mission investing is driven by investor intent and aligns with an investor institution's goals and objectives. A mission investor's goals are different than, say, a public pension fund, which has a fiduciary duty to reach targeted returns meeting benefit obligations while also seeking alternative investments having economic development impacts in their state. Every investment has impact; it depends on the investor's intent as to the nature of the investment—targeted financial returns while also having social and environmental benefits. A mission-driven foundation investor's reason for being is rooted in their mission furthering their unique institutional goals. That said, each foundation may have its own self-definition and has an overall concept of mission investing particular to its own unique mission and investment goals.

SD: *Can you give us some specific examples of the types of investments that are being made in this space?*

LH: Some mission investment examples come from our recent national conference at the Harvard Kennedy School as highlighted on a panel on mission investing across asset classes. DBL Investors, a venture capital firm that spun out of JP Morgan in 2008, has invested in innovative companies like Tesla Motors, SolarCity and Revolution Foods that are creating quality jobs for lower income people while addressing climate change and serving healthy lunches to our nation's school children—especially in disadvantaged areas. The first fund (Bay Area Equity Fund I) will create over 5,000 new jobs, many of which are entry-level, high-quality jobs with livable wages, stock option programs and quality benefit packages. DBL Investors portfolio companies are also leaders in employee programs, community engagement and environmental stewardship. For example, SolarCity (the largest U.S. installer of residential and small commercial solar power systems) has partnered with the City College of

"We define a mission investor as a foundation seeking investment opportunities that align with the mission of the organization."

San Francisco and Young Community Developers to offer a solar training program for economically disadvantaged residents of the Bayview/Hunter's Point neighborhood of San Francisco. The program is the first-of-its-kind scholarship program funded by a privately held solar company. One of More for Mission's co-founders, the Annie E. Casey Foundation, enjoyed top quartile returns in the Bay Area Equity Fund I that it has now reinvested in DBL Investors Fund II from the alternative asset allocation of their endowment.

Another example, that also presented at the More for Mission national conference, is State Street Global Advisors, which has developed a Community Investing Index Strategy, which is a mission investment product in publicly listed stock. The Community Investing Index Strategy seeks to match the return and characteristics of the U.S. Community Investing Index. Created in 2005 by the F.B. Heron Foundation in collaboration with Innovest Strategic Value Advisors [now MSCI ESG Research] the Index is comprised of approximately 330 large and mid-cap companies across sectors that show proactive engagement with economically underserved populations in rural and urban communities. The methodology evaluates a universe of companies across three pillars of community performance: strategic alignment, workforce development and wealth creation, and community engagement & corporate philanthropy. The Index is a trademark of the F.B. Heron Foundation and has been licensed for use by State Street Global Advisors.

An example of a fixed-income mission investment is Community Capital Management, a fixed-income portfolio manager. Meyer Memorial Trust is an investor in Community Capital Management, as it allowed them to meet a geographic focus in the state of Oregon and address the foundation's programmatic areas of affordable housing, community and economic development. In this case,

Community Capital Management replicates the Barclays Aggregate Bond Index to construct a portfolio targeting the State of Oregon and economic development activities in Oregon. For Meyer Memorial Trust, Community Capital Management custom created a portfolio of single-family agency pools that target low- and moderate-income borrowers in Oregon, financing small business loans in low- and moderate-income communities. Many of the businesses within Meyer Memorial Trust's portfolio are located in historically underutilized business (HUB) zones or are women-owned businesses.

SD: *The mission-investing field seems to be gathering a lot of momentum. Is it growing? How many institutions are involved? How much money are we talking about?*

LH: The More for Mission network now includes ninety foundations representing $34 billion in total assets. In some cases, foundations are at less than two percent of endowment assets in mission investing and in others they are at nearly 100 percent. In terms of dollars committed to mission investing we conducted a survey in the fall of 2009 showing that, of respondents, $1.3 billion dollars was committed to mission investing at year-end 2008 or 4.7 percent of respondents' aggregate assets. We are now in the process of tabulating results from a 2010 survey to be able to show the growth in mission investing. There are also a growing number of organizations helping different types of investors at various stages of this practice. More for Mission continues to collaborate with other learning networks, investor circles, and affinity groups (e.g. PRI Makers Network, Global Impact Investing Network (GIIN), Confluence Philanthropy) to build the field.

SD: *Do mission-related investments generally provide returns at below-market rate, or at market rate? Is this really a sound investment strategy for a foundation or an institution?*

LH: We are trying to help foundations think about moving beyond traditional grant making and use their endowment assets in ways they further their mission. These investments span both below-market PRIs and, in particular, using endowment assets in market-rate MRIs. For some foundations, with the downturn in the economy, their PRIs ended up being the best performing part of their portfolio. Getting comprehensive data on returns can be a challenge—we aim to improve on this. On MRIs, Luther Ragin, Chief Investment Officer, at the F.B. Heron Foundation, presented data received from Cambridge Associates at More for Mission's national conference. The data compared public equity ESG Managers to Cambridge Associates Manager Universe over a four-year time period showing ESG managers were at par and in some cases outperformed traditional managers in the Cambridge Associates database. A similar comparison was done for private equity clean-tech deals and private equity real estate managers.

SD: *According to the Social Investment Forum, over $2 trillion total is invested in socially responsible investment, but sometimes the portfolios of screened funds are difficult to distinguish from a standard S&P Index Fund. How would I know a mission-related investment when I saw it?*

LH: What makes an investment a mission investment is that in some way, shape, or form it is driven by a financial return, at least on the market-rate side, but also has ancillary social, environmental, and economic impacts. Investments across the mission investing spectrum have a common distinction—they either tightly or loosely align with the foundation's broader mission or programmatic objectives and geographic focus. In public equities, they can know that their investments are not running contrary to their mission, unlike a famous case, profiled in the *Los Angeles Times* in 2007, where one side of the foundation was investing in petroleum companies while their grant-making side was funding grant programs to improve health disparities caused, at least in part, by the effects of these companies. So it is really about how much these investments are loosely or tightly meeting a foundation's mission, programmatic, or geographic interests.

SD: *As you know, a major issue and challenge for economic development and community building in low-income neighborhoods is the lack of access to capital. Does mission investing offer a new source of such capital? What kinds of projects does mission investing provide financing for and what are other kinds of projects for which deeper levels of subsidy are required?*

"What makes an investment a mission investment is that in some way, shape, or form **it is driven by a financial return, at least on the market-rate side, but also has ancillary social, environmental, and economic impacts**."

LH: PRIs meet specific programmatic objectives. A guarantee is another way that a foundation can use their endowment to get capital to entities that would not otherwise receive a loan from a conventional lender. These instruments are examples of getting capital out to areas that have historically lacked access to capital. Thinking of the spectrum, and depending on programmatic interests, a foundation can move from a grant to a PRI—this ultimately gets more capital into distressed low-income communities in a more sustainable way.

SD: *Are there policy implications? Are there things that the government can do to help expand mission investing—either carrots or sticks?*

LH: For the foundation community, it is not per se about prescribing any particular mission investment standard but about disclosure and modifying the 990-PF [nonprofit Internal Revenue Service form for private foundations]. Bill McCalpin, Interim President at the F.B. Heron Foundation, published an article on the topic three years ago for the NYU Charity Law Center [can be found in the selected readings in the resources section of the More for Mission website]. The article, "A Standard for Disclosure: Endowed Foundations, Investments and Institutional Mission" proposes the use of the IRS 990-PF to publicly disclose how investments relate to mission. The article's objective is to advance a proposition (and invite critical discussion of it) the proposition being: "As a matter of expected, good practice, an endowed grant-making foundation should disclose—regularly and publicly—how its investment strives to advance the institution's mission." What it proposes mirrors advice on the investment of charitable funds that the Charity Commission for England and Wales has provided to the charities it regulates.

SD: *Where do you see this field going in the next ten years?*

LH: I think we are on a solid path to the foundation community integrating a higher percentage of their endowment assets with institutional goals, values, and missions. Foundations are increasingly seeing the practice of mission investing as an investment discipline helping achieve mission objectives across thematic interests, populations served, and geographies—and with a guiding mission investing policy statement and the right resources will soon say, of course, why shouldn't we consider this?

Over the next ten years the field will expand for the better—with more interest and a convergence from the various players: mission-driven foundation investors committing capital, quality mission-driven investment vehicles realizing financial returns and deploying capital in challenging underserved markets (may be catalyzed by investor demand), and large institutional consultants expanding the breadth and depth of services in this area (may largely need to be driven by client demand). There will be a need for continuing education at the foundation trustee level, breaking down silos between investments officers and program officers, and structuring in some cases smaller mission investment committees with external consultants. There will also be the potential for co-investments across institutional investors—for example mission-driven foundation investors, Taft-Hartley pension funds, faith-based investors, and university endowments.

SD: *Anything else you would like to add?*

LH: We are all part of a larger movement to expand the field and get more capital into investments having both financial returns along with social and environmental benefits. Success is when there is no longer a need to persuade foundations that this is a goal.

Michael Shuman

*Michael Shuman is an economist, attorney,
and globally recognized expert on community
economics. He is one of the architects of
the crowdfunding reforms that became the
Jumpstart Our Business Startups Act (JOBS
Act), signed into law in April 2012. He is
the author of nine books, including* Local
Dollars: Local Sense, The Small-Mart
Revolution, *and* Going Local. *In 2015,
Shuman's newest book,* The Local Economy
Solution, *was published by Chelsea Green. It
presents the stories of twenty-eight "pollinator"
enterprises that are nurturing local businesses
in self-financing ways. Additionally, Shuman
is a fellow at Cutting Edge Capital and the
Post-Carbon Institute and is a founding
board member of the Business Alliance for
Local Living Economies (BALLE). Shuman
has also advised countless communities
on strategies to increase local economic
multipliers, and just completed (with Gwen
Hallsmith) a handbook on local investment
opportunities in Vermont.*

Interviewed in 2015

Steve Dubb: *Could you talk about your background and how you became involved in the "buy local" movement?*

Michael Shuman: Since 1982, after completing Stanford Law School, I've been trying to connect communities to the world. I spent my first ten years mobilizing cities to get involved in foreign policy through a nonprofit I started called the Center for Innovative Diplomacy. We published a *Bulletin of Municipal Foreign Policy*, which went to thousands of local elected officials across the United States, and showed how cities were promoting peace through nuclear-free zones, fighting apartheid in South Africa through divestment campaigns, and opposing the Contras' war through Nicaraguan sister cities. With support of the Kellogg National Leadership Program, I began to see how these municipal tools could promote North-South development cooperation. I then studied the work of a group based in The Hague called Towns and Development, and wrote an evaluation of their work in a book called *Towards a Global Village*, (Pluto, 1994). I was generally very enthusiastic about the European city-to-city movement, except that I felt that their theory and practice around sustainable economics fell far short of their (and my) aspirations. That led me to start thinking about community economics.

This was also around the time that I moved from San Francisco to Washington, and began working at the Institute for Policy Studies—first as a visiting fellow, then as a paid fellow, and then as director for six years. During this time, I wrote *Going Local* (Free Press, 1998), the first of four books on localization. *Going Local* laid out a theory of local economics. The next book, *The Small-Mart Revolution* (Berrett-Koehler, 2006) showed how local businesses were competing successfully against global corporations. I then concluded that the most difficult challenge local businesses faced was getting needed capital, so my next book, *Local Dollars, Local Sense* (Chelsea Green, 2006) focused on local investment.

The most recent book, *The Local Economy Solution*, suggests that communities can carry out economic development more effectively by focusing on local business, and that self-financing pollinators offer the cheapest way for them to do so. The book encourages the local economy movement to ensure that more and more of its work depends not on foundation grants, but rather on sound business structures.

SD: *You've done a lot of consulting studies on local procurement. Just how much of an economic difference does local procurement make?*

MS: What these studies do—and I've authored about twenty of them—is look at what would happen to a community, city, or region if the presence of local industry grows. What would happen if you increased local purchasing by consumers, businesses, and government procurement and local industry expanded accordingly? Some of these studies look at a 10 percent, 20 percent, or 25 percent shift of the entire economy. Some look specifically at localization of food sectors.

It turns out that even a very modest shift generates a huge number of jobs. For example, Leslie Schaller, Brad Masi, and I did a study of metro Cleveland five years ago looking at the impact of a 25 percent shift toward local food. We found that this shift would generate 27,000 new jobs, $250 million more of tax revenues, and nearly $1 billion more in wages. The job impact is so profound that it would reemploy one in eight unemployed residents of the region. Food, of course, is just one sector. If you localize other sectors modestly, the job impact can be even more profound.

SD: *Are there cities where you can point to a shift in the right direction that comes out of this work?*

MS: We still need better proof that the results our studies predict actually occur. That said, there are some interesting success stories. One comes from Hardwick, Vermont. *The New York Times* did a front-page story in 2008 about a concerted effort to build local food businesses in a town of 3,000 people. At a time when nearly all rural communities were losing jobs because of the recession, Hardwick had created 100 new jobs.

It's also useful to look at regression analyses that have evaluated the differences between communities with a high density of local business and those with a low density. One study published in the *Harvard Business Review* in the summer of 2010 found that local-business communities have a higher per capita job growth rate. Two other studies, one from the *Economic Development Quarterly* and another from the Federal Reserve of Atlanta, found that local business communities have higher per capita income-growth rates. In other words, if you want to reduce inequality, growing local businesses is one important tool.

"Communities can carry out economic development more effectively by focusing on local business, and self-financing pollinators offer the cheapest way for them to do so."

SD: *In your most recent book, you describe a group of enterprises that you call "pollinators." What is a pollinator business? How do you define the approach?*

MS: A "pollinator" is a social enterprise with an explicit mission to support other local businesses—and it does so in a way that is self-financing. What I argue in the book is that pollinators are increasingly carrying out the functions of local economic development, which I organize around "P" words: planning, people, partners, purchasing, purse, and policy-making.

Planning involves several different activities. It includes helping local business plan to become more efficient. It includes "place making." It also refers to economic development planning, which means identifying dollar leaks in your economy—all of the instances where residents are unnecessarily purchasing outside goods and services—and then preparing plans to plug those leaks through new, import-substitution local businesses.

People is about entrepreneurship. How do we mobilize people to lead or staff new leak-plugging local businesses?

Partners is about building teams of local businesses that are more effective and more competitive working together than working separately.

Purchasing is about buy-local initiatives by individuals, businesses, or government agencies.

Purse is about local investments. How do you tap short-term savings in banks and credit unions or long-term savings in pensions for investing in local business?

Public policy is where the government gets involved. And here, my top goal is frankly very modest: Government agencies should stop subsidizing nonlocal competitors over local business in the name of economic development.

SD: *Could you give me some examples of pollinators?*

MS: Sure. An example of an interesting planning pollinator is a company based in Washington, D.C. called Main Street Genome. It helps local businesses become more profitable by studying different parts of their business, identifying inefficiencies, fixing them, and then splitting the savings with the companies. Right now, they are working with a couple of hundred restaurants in Washington by studying their supplier invoices. When Main Street Genome finds price differentials with a given supplier, it renegotiates the supply contracts, and typically shaves about 10 to 15 percent off the total bill.

If we look at people pollinators, a really good example is Fledge, a business accelerator in Seattle. There are more than 1,000 incubators in North America today, and nearly all of them depend on government grants or foundation money. But Fledge uses a different model. At the end of its incubation work, Fledge takes a couple of percentage points of equity in the beneficiary company. The company can then buy back that equity by paying a royalty payment on gross revenues over several years.

An example of a partnership pollinator is Tucson Originals, which represents about fifty restaurants. Tucson Originals buys foodstuffs and kitchen equipment in bulk for the members, which brings down input prices and strengthens the entire the local restaurant community.

A good example of a purchasing pollinator is the loyalty card sponsored by a company called Supportland. Every time you use the card at a local business, you get a discount and points that apply to future discounts at other local businesses. There are 80,000 Portland residents that are actively using this card, and Supportland is now spreading to other cities on the west coast.

A good example of purse pollinator is the work of a colleague of mine, Jenny Kassan, who used to work for Cutting Edge Capital and is now working independently. She's an attorney who is helping local businesses create local stock issues—through direct public offerings—and charges significantly less than mainstream law firms.

"It turns out that **even a very modest shift generates a huge number of jobs.**"

SD: *The Democracy Collaborative, of course, has as part of our mission the goal of reducing wealth and income inequality. To what extent do localist efforts address the nation's rapidly growing wealth and income gaps?*

MS: I too am deeply committed to this goal, and one of the best ways localists can improve social equality is by ending what I call "investment apartheid." U.S. investment laws incentivize all of us to put all of our money into Fortune 500 companies. If you're in the top one percent of wealth holders or income earners, you're allowed to invest in anything anytime. If you're in the other 99 percent, you can't put a penny into a local business unless the business spends between $25,000 and $100,000 for legal disclosure documents. Very few local businesses can afford their lawyer bills. The result is that even though local small businesses constitute more than half the economy, and many are highly profitable and competitive, they receive far less than half of our banking capital and almost none of our long-term capital from pension funds.

Fixing our capital markets is critical to reconnecting residents of a community to ownership of the businesses operating within that community. That, in and of itself, doesn't redistribute wealth. But it matters a great deal, because the Fortune 500 companies under the current system have too much capital and community-based businesses have too little. The more capital that moves from Wall Street to Main Street, the more we will finance those businesses that can reduce inequality. Remember, studies show that growing local businesses reduces poverty and inequality.

SD: *You were actively involved in the effort to pass the Jumpstart Our Business Startups Act (JOBS Act). But as you know, the JOBS Act, as passed, is a bit of a mixed bag. What would you say are its strengths and in what ways would you have liked it to have turned out differently?*

MS: What I initially argued for in 2009, in an article I wrote for the Federal Reserve, was a $100 exemption in securities law. The idea was that any American should be able invest $100 at any time with no legal paperwork. A $100 investment won't affect anyone's life savings. You probably only would make a $100 investment in a company you knew and care about—like your local co-op. So this proposal was all about making it easier for local, small-scale investing.

What happened next was that a congressional committee started looking at crowdfunding options, and it decided that any American should be able to invest, not $100, but up to $10,000. And they did not want to limit this to investment in local businesses. They wanted to open up the law so that anyone could invest up to $10,000 in any business across the country.

I had two qualms about these changes. First, $10,000 was starting to get into territory where grassroots investors could lose significant chunks of their life savings. Second, allowing people to invest over long distances defeated the whole point of local investment. And the two issues are intertwined. If you get to know a company in your own backyard, you're much less likely to get snookered in some kind of Enron-like fraud. The farther away a company, the less transparent it is, the more we should want the law to require the company to provide a boatload of facts and figures. The closer the company is, the easier it is for a local investor to get to know the manager and the workforce, and the less one needs all that legal mumbo jumbo.

The JOBS Act then moved to the Senate, where the maximum investment was pared back to $2,000 and a bunch of new legal requirements were added (for example, that stock can only be sold on an internet portal licensed by the Securities and Exchanges Commission). As a result, it's not at all clear that raising capital through the JOBS Act will be cheaper and easier than existing pathways to raise capital. It all depends on the final rules promulgated by the SEC. Under the terms of the JOBS Act, the SEC was supposed to have issued regulations in December 2012, seven or eight months after the bill was signed. It still has not done so [for the crowdfunding section, also known as Title III] three years later, and in my judgment, this inaction has effectively sabotaged the JOBS Act. The companies that set themselves up to run portals to implement the act have run out of money and are going out of business. [*NOTE: federal regulations for Title III were finally promulgated after this interview in October 2015*].

But what has happened next is more than a dozen states have passed their own versions of the JOBS Act. Each of these state laws only governs transactions within the state—which means, by definition, they are only facilitating local investment. So I would argue that we are kind of creating a system for local investment that is cheaper and has less potential for fraud than whatever the JOBS Act ultimately manifests. So I am happy right now.

SD: **Could you talk about the role of anchor institutions in buy-local strategies?**

MS: Well, in *The Local Economy Solution*, I write about examples of companies and institutions, such as Zingerman's Community of Businesses in Ann Arbor, that incorporate economic development into their business behavior. Whenever large anchor institutions begin to do this, they can have a very profound effect on the local economy. I write about the Oberlin Project, where David Orr has been recruiting in the greater Cleveland area foundations, universities, sports teams, and government institutions to redirect their purchasing and investment locally. It's a great model. By definition anchors are large, and when they lead, others follow.

SD: **Could you talk about your role in helping form one leading organization in the localist movement, the Business Alliance for Local Living Economies (BALLE)? What is the current state of play for localism today?**

MS: I was actively involved in the founding of BALLE and was on the board for about seven years. Every one of the founders brought different skills to the table, and I suppose mine was a theory about how and why local businesses matter for economic prosperity. In the early years, we were a tiny organization with a tiny staff. At one point in 2009, we received a couple of grants that allowed us to expand and I was hired (after resigning from the board) to develop an economic development program for BALLE. But the board and the executive director did not see eye to eye, so my job changed direction and scale. I continued to work on a few economic development projects for

BALLE, but it was pretty clear that BALLE was moving in a different direction, so I left at the end of 2010.

This economic development work is still important, but now it has to be done outside BALLE. And this is one reason I wrote the new book. When you look at the eighty or so networks affiliated by BALLE, the typical network is 50 percent dependent on foundation funding. BALLE networks that figure out how to self-finance their activities are going to have more impact, hire more people, and accomplish more. The pollinators book presents BALLE network leaders with twenty-eight business models that they might consider bringing into their organizations. In fact, two of the models are from existing BALLE networks.

It is not just BALLE affiliates that need a solid business model. The same argument applies to communities affiliated with AMIBA (American Independent Business Alliance), with the Main Street program, or with microenterprise associations. No matter what your focal point of local economy building is, you should look at the pollinator models for ideas about how to wean yourself off of unreliable foundation or government grants.

SD: *The idea of buying local is a lot more visible today than when you wrote Going Local. What has caused this? What would you say some of the leading achievements of the localist movement have been?*

MS: There is no question that the localization movement has made huge strides. There used to be a saying that you know you've made it when you're on the cover of *Time Magazine*. Well, it was March 2007 when *Time* had on its cover "Forget organic, eat local."

You know, I visit forty or fifty communities each year to speak, many in deeply conservative areas, and every place I go, I see signs that say buy local, eat local, bank local. I have never seen the sign, "We are not local—buy from us." We have won the war of ideas.

We have also won the war of research findings. There is now overwhelming data and analysis that local businesses are the best contributors to economic development. In fact, there are so many studies all pointing in the same direction that they are getting boring.

So, real accomplishments? The changes in securities law we just discussed stands out. It's hard to appreciate the impact right now because these laws have changed recently. But we have laid the table for a huge shift in capital out of Wall Street.

We also have documentation that in many cities, particularly those with good local business alliances, that "local first" campaigns have made a big difference in the bottom line of local businesses.

One of the reasons for these successes are that the economies of small scale inherent in local business are a lot better than anyone thought. If local business goods and services were significantly more expensive than their global competition, the buy-local movement would have backfired. But in fact buy-local campaigns almost always move consumers in the right direction. That's because local businesses have one consistent flaw—they are poor marketers of themselves. Buy local programs turn out to improve consumer awareness about great local goods and services that they otherwise were overlooking.

Another cause of our success is that there is just a lot more distrust of Fortune 500 companies. The economic collapse of 2008 sowed doubt. Occupy Wall Street deepened it. Lots of people with diverse political perspectives are thinking about more ways to support businesses in their community.

SD: *Is the movement making any inroads in the field of economic development?*

MS: Not fast enough. Again, I think the intellectual argument has been won. All of the evidence right now weighs in favor of *local* economic development. But other factors are leading economic developers to continue doing what they have always been doing. Some simply aren't aware of the new research that shows that the old "attract and retain" strategies are counter-productive. But even if they were aware, at the end of the day many economic developers are driven more by politics than economics.

Politically, you get better press if you can announce one global company that moves in and creates 1,000 jobs. That's page A-1 news. If you have one hundred successful local projects each producing ten jobs, that's page D-7 news. Because of this, the uninformed public believes that big outside attractions are the only kind of economic development that's real and worth having. That's what also drives economic developers and the politicians that support them.

"Even though local small businesses constitute more than half the economy, and many are highly profitable and competitive, **they receive far less than half of our banking capital**."

Economic developers deepen this public misunderstanding by always being able to point to a few minor programs they have—say, a small microenterprise fund—that support local small business. But it's a little bit like what used to be called in fairy tales an "elephant-mouse" casserole. When you add one elephant and one mouse in "equal" proportions, it still tastes an awful lot like an elephant. That's why economic development, despite a few minor initiatives aimed at local business, is largely about supporting global corporations—and not taking good care of the local economy.

I think it is time for those of us in the local economy movement to fight back. We can't say it is okay for a city to pay millions for outside business *and* support local business. The pie is too limited. Every dollar wasted on outside attraction is a dollar that cannot be invested in local economic development. Every hour spent wasting time on international trips is an hour not spent down the block.

SD: *What do you see as the potential of the localist movement going forward?*

MS: I do believe that the pollinator models are the future of our movement. The more, city by city, we reorganize economic development around pollinator models, the more we will be able to carry out the right kind of economic development, focused on local businesses, without depending on unreliable streams of government or foundation money. Once our movement is financially more independent and has more resources, we can then fight politically with greater effect.

SD: *Could you talk about the role of public policy in providing a supportive environment?*

MS: Public policy can and should support pollinators. But the most important agenda item for public policymakers is to stop destroying local business. Defund attract-and-retain policies and use the savings for local economic development—that would be an incredible first step.

SD: *Anything else in terms of policy?*

MS: In *The Small-Mart Revolution*, I presented a list of about fifty local policies that would be useful for local economic development. Let me mention just two that cost little or nothing: move your city's banking to a local bank or credit union; and overhaul procurement, so it results in the fair reward of municipal contracts to local businesses.

At the state level, I would continue to prioritize overhauling securities law. States also should look at creating public banks like North Dakota's. And they too should reform their procurement practices.

SD: *If you were to highlight some key accomplishments of your work to date that you are proudest of, what would they be?*

MS: I think getting the JOBS Act passed, even though it was flawed, provided a foundation for getting some excellent state securities reforms passed. I played a very active role in promoting the reforms in Maryland, Colorado, and Oregon, and an indirect role in the other states. Having spent most of my life aligning myself with losing causes, this recent experience is a bit disorienting.

SD: *Is there anything else you would like to add?*

MS: I do think a surprising difference between smart local businesses and smart Fortune 500 businesses is that while Fortune 500 businesses are trying to build global empires, local businesses are happy to share their best ideas with entrepreneurs worldwide. We therefore need to connect similar businesses all over the world—so that local restaurants learn from one another and local smelting companies learn how to undertake more efficient small-scale steel production. That level of specificity, information building, and network building will enable us to make the localist revolution truly global.

Social
Enterprises
and Innovation

There are few terms in the community wealth building world with more varied definitions than the phrase "social enterprise." The most classic version is a nonprofit-owned business that employs the people it is training in actual business operations. Others look at social enterprise businesses to also include for-profit businesses that generate a "double bottom line" of economic and social returns (or, if environmental goals are part of the business model, a "triple bottom line"). The interviews here highlight both models. Brenda Palms-Barber in Chicago, Carla Javits in San Francisco, and Rey España in Portland work for nonprofits that operate or support nonprofit-owned social enterprises. By contrast, Kate Sofis of San Francisco and José Corona across the bay in Oakland have both supported networks of for-profit businesses, which, in addition to earning profits, focus on developing living wage jobs in low- and moderate-income communities and in communities of color.

Brenda Palms-Barber

*Brenda Palms-Barber is Founding
Executive Director (since 1999) and
CEO of the North Lawndale Employment
Network (NLEN), a workforce
development nonprofit agency that focuses
on helping former offenders reintegrate
to the workplace. In 2004, NLEN
launched a social enterprise called Sweet
Beginnings, an urban honey farming and
natural skin care manufacturing business
that trains and employs former offenders
and others with significant barriers to
employment. The recidivism rate for
former Sweet Beginnings employees is four
percent, compared to the national average
of 65 percent. In this interview, Palms-
Barber discusses the community impact of
North Lawndale's large former offender
population, the development of the social
enterprise, the promise of green jobs, and
the challenge of spreading the model to
other cities.*

Interviewed in 2010

**Steve Dubb: What were the origins of the North Lawndale Employ-
ment Network? Could you discuss how you became involved?**

Brenda Palms-Barber: The North Lawndale Employment Network (NLEN)
was really started by a community movement. The conversation
was facilitated by the Steans Family Foundation, which decided to
invest its assets into one neighborhood and one community. Rather
than save the world, they decided to go deep into focusing on one
community for ten years and see what kind of positive impact they
could have on the conditions of North Lawndale. When they met
with community leaders and residents, they asked them what were
the most pressing issues. Two bubbled up quickly: housing and
employment. Since there were a number of housing efforts already
under way, the Steans Foundation decided to focus on employment.

Because a number of local agencies were already providing some
degree of employment services in addition to their core business,
participants in the conversation determined that it would be best
to create a network of organizations that already provide employment services, rather than form a new organization. Further, they
decided to create NLEN to help build capacity of these agencies in
North Lawndale that were providing employment services. They
also gained significant interest from City Hall, which was willing
to support a training program through a welfare-to-work contract.
This planning process occurred more than a year prior to my arrival
at NLEN.

Eventually, the leadership group managing the development of
the network decided the time had come to hire an executive director. They had over sixty applicants and conducted eleven interviews,
but they didn't select any of those candidates. They decided to take
the search national. At that time I was working in Denver, Colorado, as a program officer and associate of the Denver Workforce
Initiative at the Piton Foundation, in partnership with the Annie
E. Casey Foundation, located in Baltimore. My work addressed
employment barriers for people in low-income communities, and,
in particular, looked at how they access informal networks to gain
employment leads. Ultimately, I was working to eliminate—or at
least reduce—poverty.

Prior to the invitation to interview, the Steans Foundation had
asked me to conduct a workshop for the North Lawndale group, and

I did one on informal networks in low-income communities and how to link to jobs. I was really taken by this group of people trying to wrestle with the issues of unemployment in a long-suffering economically disadvantaged community.

So when they called and asked me to put my hat in the ring and apply for the job as executive director of the new organization, I said I was not sure, but that I would give it a try. I initially didn't think I was a strong competitor for the job. I was a Northwest suburban girl. I was born in Tacoma, Washington. I had lived in Tucson and Denver, but I had a small-town-girl feel and didn't think they would see me as a good fit culturally. I doubted whether they would think I was able to be effective in urban Chicago. But I went in for the interview. I toured the community of North Lawndale and was interviewed by a six-member panel. I shared my experiences and hopes, and listened to their dreams and visions of a thriving, economically strong community where residents work and can care for their families. I left the interview impressed with the group and inspired by the thought of working with and impacting this very special community. And so, three weeks later when they offered me the job, I accepted.

SD: *Could you discuss the organization's early development? Could you explain how the organization has changed since you became executive director eleven years ago?*

BPB: When I accepted the position, I didn't know that the 501(c)(3) tax classification letter from the Internal Revenue Service was not even in place yet. NLEN was clearly still a movement. Today, we are a well-established, 501(c)(3) nonprofit in good standing.

I recall my former boss in Denver asking me, "Are you sure you want to move to Chicago in February?" It was a huge leap of faith. I'm really glad that I took that leap. I saw the North Lawndale community group as stakeholders and trustees, and my role was to help them realize the vision they had established for North Lawndale.

There were some challenges, although their strategy seemed right—creating a network to build capacity. It was clear that no local organization's real focus was employment. It was an add-on for all of those that offered those services. The neighborhood had an unemployment rate that was three times higher than the City of Chicago. In the civil unrest of 1968 after Rev. Martin Luther

King Jr. died, North Lawndale was devastated. There were fires and destruction that led to many businesses leaving the community. North Lawndale was once a thriving commercial, industrial, and residential community—Sears Roebuck was based there, with several other corporate headquarters. But after the civil unrest in 1968, they left. The community has never fully recovered.

There are lots of issues. Unemployment is one of them. It was clear that the nonprofits there had a heart for service. But they weren't doing employment in a direct way. So I spent my first couple of years working with existing groups to build their capacity. I was able to secure grants through NLEN and give sub-grants to other agencies. But ultimately, if the subcontracted agencies didn't perform, it would impact my ability to raise additional revenue. So eventually we ended up transitioning toward a direct service model.

After talking with community folk, we started to hear a theme. "My husband is coming out of prison—I really want to find a job for him." Or, "My son is coming out of prison. He needs a job." The impact of incarceration has been huge in this community. It isn't just that it is one of the ten most challenged neighborhoods in the state. It became clear that there was something else driving this unemployment. I commissioned a study—with the help of a local foundation—to figure out what was the impact of incarceration locally. It was a landmark study called *Drugs, Crime and Consequences*. To do this, we worked with two police districts (10 and 11) and the Illinois Dept. of Corrections to collect data. In 2001, asking them to pull data on former offenders from the North Lawndale zip code was like asking them to go to the moon. But in two years we were able to collect that data. That was when we learned that 57 percent of adults in North Lawndale had some kind of criminal background. It was shocking. So we realized that you can't help people get jobs in North Lawndale without adjusting programs to meet the specific needs of people with criminal backgrounds. That led us to create our first training program, which is our flagship program that we now call "U-Turn Permitted," in recognition of our belief that people can turn their lives around.

So we set out to create a community-level, community-driven response to the training needs of former offenders. There were other organizations offering trainings. But we were accessible. We met with

"The impact of incarceration has been huge in this community. It isn't just that it is one of the ten most challenged neighborhoods in the state. **It became clear that there was something else driving this unemployment.**"

former offenders—sort of a one-stop approach. We found a community church to help, United Baptist Church, and the Annie E. Casey Foundation gave me a $200,000 grant to launch the program. We were off and running. That program continues to this day.

That changed NLEN to a direct service provider. We knew that we were ultimately accountable for our participant outcomes. In the other model, we had to assume all responsibility and accountability but with little control. We also received WIA (Workforce Investment Act) funding for a youth prevention program.

But then when 9/11 happened, there was another big jolt for my agency. Prior to 9/11, we were doing a pretty "OK" job equipping our clients to be competitive in the labor market, getting and keeping their jobs. After 9/11, things changed significantly because of what was called the Patriot Act. It forced a variety of employers to start doing background checks. People with backgrounds who had held jobs for years were suddenly dumped back into the labor market because their employers found out that they had a record. Before, employers may have suspected an employee might have a record, but they were willing to look the other way, if the employee was performing well. There were so many former offenders losing their jobs we began to see a huge influx of people looking for jobs. We were overwhelmed by the demand for their jobs and the lack of jobs. That led to the demand for Sweet Beginnings.

SD: *Could you tell us a bit about the demographics of North Lawndale and the surrounding area that you serve?*

BPB: Roughly, we have about 40,000 people that live in the community. Of that, 60 percent are female head of households. Their average income is about $20,000 a year. That's because you have a lot of single-headed households, but you also have a high elderly population. The high school dropout rate is 70 percent. There are some really good efforts that are starting to affect that, but it is right now still between 70 and 75 percent. Unemployment continues to be around 26 percent. It is predominately African-American—about 92 to 93 percent. And second to that you have a growing Latino presence and probably about one percent white.

SD: *Could you discuss the formation of your social enterprise Sweet Beginnings? How did the business get its start?*

BPB: As a first time executive director I had the privilege of participating in a program designed to build capacity of new executive directors. It was nearly a year-long program. One key issue was that nonprofits should be sustainable. They asked us: "What is your sustainability plan?" NLEN didn't have one, and it was clear that we needed one. North Lawndale clearly had challenges related to employment. Nearly everyone expected me to fail, since there had been several efforts that failed before. Because I was an outsider, people thought maybe I was coming in for just a couple of years and then head out. That, too, had happened before in the neighborhood. I wasn't trying to leave. I knew that having a sustainable nonprofit organization would be hugely important. How do you do that? You need to diversify your funding streams.

One way is an earned-income strategy. I spoke with my board about how to support the nonprofit through a business strategy. We spent time thinking about what kind of businesses we could launch that would allow our clients a viable work experience regardless of formal academic training or achievement. At the same time, however, this issue came up around the time of 9/11 and this great loss of jobs in our neighborhood. And another issue—one of the bigger reasons that men and women with criminal backgrounds have difficulty getting jobs besides low skills and education—is the stigma of having been incarcerated. So we decided that we needed to prove to the hiring community that people who come through NLEN are not high-risk employees. These individuals have demonstrated that they have a good worth and good work ethic. They want to work. They just want a job.

As an employer, we decided we would absorb the perceived risk and do it through an enterprise. We thought about a landscaping business. But we knew that there were already a number of large and small landscaping businesses in our neighborhood. What would be our competitive advantage? We rejected that idea. We thought about a home delivery service, where we would go to the local store or pharmacy and bring your groceries or prescription to your front door. But on second thought, who is going to feel comfortable having a former offender deliver groceries to their home? I thought about a temp agency, too, but the profit margins were too low to have a sustainable business.

One day, we were discussing potential business ideas and a friend of mine mentioned, "I have a friend who is a beekeeper." She told me that although she didn't know much, she knew that it was a profession that is passed on by word of mouth. As I learned more, I found out that with beekeeping there is the ability to teach people with a wide range of learning styles. The more I met with beekeepers, the more I thought about connecting former offenders with urban agriculture and working with nature. But many people were skeptical.

I had breakfast with a good friend of mine, Paula Wolff at Metropolis 2020, a Chicago-based policy think tank. I wanted to talk to her about the idea. Like so many others, I expected her to say something like, "What are you thinking?" But she listened, and paused, and said, "Well, what a sweet beginning for those people." Right away, I knew, "That's the name." We talked with the Illinois Department of Corrections about the idea and in time they awarded NLEN with a $140,000 seed grant, with the caveat that the business would agree to hire former offenders. After two years of piloting the social enterprise, it was time to revisit the business plan. The Boeing Company Employee Volunteer Council spent a year working with the NLEN Board and staff to develop a comprehensive business plan for the next two years.

SD: *Could you discuss the performance of Sweet Beginnings? How has it done in terms of income generation?*

BPB: The idea was launched in 2003. We spent 2004 and 2005 in farmers' markets—we were kind of testing the idea of "If you build it, they will come." In other words, "Will people buy honey produced by former offenders?" So we ran a pilot and tested the feasibility. We learned that people loved honey, loved local honey, and especially loved local urban honey. You have this wonderful mix of floral nectar types in urban honey. We knew that the quality of our honey was excellent. We had chefs from local high-end restaurants buy the honey. We knew we were on to something.

That's when in 2006 we went into a serious business. That's when I learned that the profit margins on honey were thirteen percent, which makes it hard to be sustainable. So that's why we began to focus on cosmetic products where the profit margins are 60 to 80 percent. There the profit margin is sufficient to have a stable business.

So it is a lot more than beekeeping. You have manufacturing. We are doing shipping and receiving. There is production, sales, marketing, website management, customer relations, and everything else that is involved in any business. So Sweet Beginnings was born. We've been operating for three years—we are generating a little over $200,000 in sales. We are at a point where we are hiring a professional sales team to provide sales training. We are talking to UPS (United Parcel Service) to create a training program around shipping and handling.

We have also purchased manufacturing machinery. We used to hand-make everything. Now we are looking at increasing our volume. The demand is growing, so we have to build our capacity. It is exciting to see this idea taking a foothold in the marketplace. We are distributing our products in about eleven local Whole Foods stores— the first market to pick up our product. Whole Foods is no joke in terms of the scrutiny of our products. When they learned about us, they said, "You're one of the cleanest cosmetic lines we carry." They also love the social purpose. But we had to focus on a quality product. You have to have that. People like the idea of contributing to a social purpose, but helping former offenders is not on many people's top ten causes list: we are not saving puppies or children. If helping former offenders doesn't move you, we don't want that to matter. We want you to love our beeline products and love our honey.

The other things people will ask is how do the former offenders like bees? Their job prospects are so dim that they are willing to work with bees, even if they are afraid of them. Twenty-five percent of their time is spent working in the apiary and the other 75 percent is spent on the production side.

SD: *Is there flexibility for those who are afraid of working with bees to spend 100 percent of their time on the production side?*

BPB: Yes, we do have that flexibility for those who cannot work with bees for whatever reason, including allergies. We want to assign work projects where our employees will experience the greatest success during their ninety-day employment experience with Sweet Beginnings. Working with bees is not for all!

SD: *Could you explain the process of creating a new social enterprise, from capital formation to finding qualified management to the recruitment and training of employees?*

BPB: We've been really fortunate. Our first grant of $140,000 was from the Department of Corrections. The second was a grant for $96,000 through the City of Chicago—the Mayor's Office is very interested in our work. After that, we inspired the City to think about funding social enterprises more broadly. We were able to get a $200,000 transitional jobs grant to support our worker wages—and then, after that, I have also had some success raising dollars from local and national foundations including the W.K. Kellogg Foundation, Oprah's Angel Network, The Garfield Foundation, and the Field Foundation, to name a few. There were those with doubts initially, but our social enterprise is seen as a viable solution to a huge social issue. Our results in reducing the recidivism rate are impressive—we're at 170 people having gone through Sweet Beginnings and we have a recidivism rate of less than four percent.

In terms of staffing, we are way understaffed. We have a board of managers who are wonderful thought leaders and volunteers. The chair of my board of managers was formerly on the Board of Ben & Jerry's Ice Cream. Jennifer Henderson is her name—she gets the triple bottom line and ensures that we do not lose focus. I also have a phenomenal person who does marketing, Phil Adams. And our beekeeper, John Hanson, has been beekeeping for over thirty years. He used to head the Illinois Beekeepers Association. Such a thing exists and we are now members! And we have another gentleman, Michael Johnson, a Kellogg (Northwestern business school) grad and a business owner himself; he provides great insight and helps us with our numbers. And we have our CFO. And I have a business general manager, Holly Blackwell. I recruited her from Whole

"It is a lot more than beekeeping. You have manufacturing. We are doing shipping and receiving. **There is production, sales, marketing, website management, customer relations, and everything else that is involved in any business**."

Foods, where she was a buyer. We hire former offenders in supervisory positions, to be team leaders. One team leader for the past eighteen months has been Kelvin Greenwood.

SD: *As I understand it, Sweet Beginnings has a few core employees, but the majority of its employees are there for only a transitional period that typically is ninety days or less. How is this challenge of constant retraining met?*

BPB: It definitely creates an inherent tension for us. We want to give former offenders opportunities to work. How do you take this to scale? One way to do that is to turn over employees every ninety days. Of course, because we stagger entry dates, really it is every thirty days that we get new workers.

Once we are bringing in more sales and grossing more than a half million, we want to be able to extend that workforce stay from the ninety days, which is subsidized, to at least six months. A big driving issue is the subsidy. The limitation on the subsidy payments is the ninety-day period. Many of our workers need more time on the job before they are ready to transition out successfully into the workforce.

So the ninety-day period can be a limitation, but here's what we can do. We know that ninety days is the traditional probationary period to allow a person to prove him- or herself on any job. So, although our ninety-day cycle is challenging, it works on a lot of levels, in terms of our social purpose especially. But in terms of the business it's tough. You're hiring and bringing in new people every thirty days. Once we become more financially sustainable we want to extend it to six months, but it is fulfilling its purposes right now.

SD: *How does placement of employees after the transitional period work? Where do those who "graduate" from Sweet Beginnings go afterward?*

BPB: Most of the folks go into either manufacturing or the service sector. Most of our placements are entry-level jobs and these sectors are most often receptive to people who have had brushes with the law. In general, about 75 percent of the people that we hire go on to unsubsidized employment. Of the other 25 percent, roughly 10 to15 percent go on for additional skills training. They may go on to a technical or vocational school, sometimes they go on to secure an associate's degree, and others go on to try to get work on their own independently. We have a few folks like Clarence Little, who launched his own landscaping and snow removal business. We are very pleased to contract with him to do our landscaping. So that is a smaller percentage. And a little less than four percent return back to prison.

When we talk about education, some of our folks have gone on to work in other social enterprises as well. There is one guy I think of who was not hired as a team leader with us, but he did very well. Because his housing was still questionable and the other nonprofit could offer him stable housing and a job in green construction, he took that opportunity. And he was later hired with them as a team leader. And that's happened with a few of our other guys as well.

SD: *Have you given any thought to "franchising" the Sweet Beginnings model? If so, what would be required to duplicate the model in other cities?*

BPB: That is a great question. It is the next big phase of growth to us, when you talk about taking it to scale. According to the Pew Center and the Urban Institute studies on incarceration in the U.S. and locally, we know there are roughly 700,000 men and women coming out of prison every year. That, coupled with state deficits, sadly says that we have to come up with a better system for how these people re-enter and reintegrate, because incarceration is expensive. That is why we really do want to pollinate this model across the country. We see it happening in a couple of ways. Through the Garfield Foundation, they have given me a grant to codify the model. What are the tools to make this a successful replication model?

The demand is huge. When can we bring Sweet Beginnings to Detroit? To New Orleans? Someone from the Bureau of Indian Affairs asked, "How can we get Sweet Beginnings for the Navajos on the Reservation?" What we are trying to do is make sure we have a solid business model and we also understand the relationship between the nonprofit organization and the for-profit subsidiary. You can't do this work without both.

When workers exit Sweet Beginnings, they still are part of NLEN. Every individual is assigned a code. They go through U-Turn Permitted, they are assigned a coach, and those interested apply for Sweet Beginnings. It is a competitive process, and the coach informs them if they got a job or not. If not, they can explain why and they work on those things. Those hired, once they exit Sweet Beginnings, they still retain their relationship with their coach. We also have three business development specialists whose job is to cultivate job opportunities. We are there for them. There has to be a symbiotic relationship between the nonprofit and for-profit. We see this as a two- or three-year process. We are still improving our internal capacity. We are looking for training partners that we want to bring on board.

Another part of this model and what it would take is a relationship with a community college, so we have established a relationship with Wright College (one of the City Colleges of Chicago). The beekeeping courses that we offer are taught by John Hanson, so he became certified to teach on behalf of Wright College here onsite at our agency. These individuals who were, most of them, very unsuccessful academically, will get a continuing education credit. We think that is a key component for a successful replication. We are doing the work. I want to come up with a nice toolkit. We also have attorneys on board who are helping us think what this franchise model would look like—McDonald's is one of their clients. We are fortunate to have some of the best thinkers.

The short answer of where the Sweet Beginnings model applies, of course, is much simpler. Wherever there are vacant lots and high numbers of former offenders, and a community that cares about these people, we can make Sweet Beginnings happen.

SD: *Could you discuss your Building Beyond: Green Pathways to Success program? What is the program? How has it developed?*

BPB: This program is designed to introduce green collar jobs and what that means to a very Afrocentric community that has been disconnected from these new jobs. It is a skills training program that certifies them in weatherization, so they can secure good jobs after a year of our program.

It's a new program for out-of-school, at-risk young adults between ages 17 and 22. It's very exciting. We have a good track record with local unions, and both union and nonunion construction owners who are looking for workers. We are also working with Community and Economic Development Association of Cook County (CEDA) to do weatherization for the elderly. About 22 participants have gone through the program so far. We are just going into our second year.

SD: *Shifting gears and thinking nationally, social enterprise and green jobs are enjoying increased visibility in the United States. What do you see as steps that groups like yours need to take nationally to build on this new visibility?*

BPB: We do have to continue working at it—it is always really at the bottom. As long as I have impactful numbers and data, and show how we are saving the state money in incarceration costs, and then you continue to keep the stories out there and look at different angles to tell your story. For us, it has been helpful to talk about the impact of the bee on our ecosystem. But it is connected to reentry and incarceration and green is being used in nontraditional ways. It is also important about talking to policy makers about how they fund social enterprises.

There is this new L3C [low-profit limited liability company] model, making it easier for nonprofits to try to fulfill a social good through a social enterprise and how to fund that without it being a tax problem. That would make it easier for funders to support us. It would be interesting at some point to have a convening. We're members of the Social Venture Network and there is the Social Enterprise Alliance. We've done a lot regionally—it would be great to bring these best practices together to have conversations about funding, about scaling up, about measuring impact. We feel that we are very pioneering. That triple bottom line—how do you manage that and grow, it's difficult. To have a forum on which to talk to a national level would be really cool. And out of that you could develop more recommendations for policy that would support this kind of work.

SD: *What are NLEN's main priorities going forward?*

BPB: We are in the middle of starting our strategic planning process for the next three to five years. We serve people from all over the city, but we are still focused on addressing the needs of our community. What we anticipate is becoming a little bit more of an incubator. There is another social enterprise that we are beginning to help launch called UrbanPonics which will grow food to address food deserts like North Lawndale and also create jobs and improve nutrition. How cool to have these greenhouses grow crops in the neighborhood that are not contaminated. To avoid contamination, we are using hydroponics. We are working in partnership with a couple of different universities to develop that. We are becoming this green economic engine in the community where they were lacking jobs. We tried to work with employers and deal with the issue of stigma, but we recognized that the jobs still are not there. So I am focused on using a job creation strategy.

The other focus is going to be launching an entrepreneurial center for former offenders, because I think we learned a lot about how to launch a business and we know the population—so have a micro-lending center for people who want to launch their own businesses. Another leg would be technical assistance and consulting support to other communities.

SD: *If you had to highlight a few key accomplishments of NLEN's work to date that you are most proud of, what would they be?*

BPB: I am really proud that we have unpacked the impact of incarceration in our community. And we forced systems that didn't traditionally talk to each other to do it, such as the police and the Department of Corrections. And we hopefully became a model for other communities. Although there are other communities like ours, very few can say that 57 percent of the adults have had some involvement in criminal justice and then back that up with data.

"According to the Pew Center and the Urban Institute studies on incarceration in the U.S. and locally, **we know there are roughly 700,000 men and women coming out of prison every year**."

We also lifted the importance that three-quarters of the offenses were nonviolent or drug related. This isn't the same in every neighborhood. In another neighborhood, Englewood, a much higher percentage of the crimes were for violent offenses, such as murders. The recidivism rate in North Lawndale is very high because people serve two to three years, get out, commit another crime, and go back. In our little North Lawndale neighborhood, we had heads of police departments, corrections, parole, state, city, and university folks all here once we released this report to talk about what we could do to change the relationship between corrections and the community. I am honored by that body of work.

Secondly, a key accomplishment would have to be launching Sweet Beginnings. Choosing to use my frustration in a way that fostered creativity and a response to the need to create jobs for this population in North Lawndale.

SD: *Anything else you would like to add?*
BPB: I honestly think that the success of the work we have achieved so far rests on the shoulders of hundreds of people. I love the fact that foundations seeded this work—their dollars allowed that our innovative spirit. They have helped us move toward a sustainable model through this earned income strategy. I have really found a tremendous amount of support—the city, the state, who would have thought that the Illinois Department of Corrections would be a significant contributor? But they are. So we stand on many shoulders. It also helps to have to a really committed and smart staff.

Carla Javits

Carla Javits is President of the San Francisco-based social enterprise accelerator REDF [originally called the Roberts Enterprise Development Fund], a position she has held since 2007. REDF was founded in 1997 and is a social enterprise accelerator. REDF conducts this work by providing "equity-like" funding and hands-on business assistance to create and grow "double bottom line" enterprises that earn income while employing people who face high barriers. Under her leadership, REDF became the first California-based organization to receive an award from the Corporation for National and Community Service's Social Innovation Fund competition. With the support of the Social Innovation Fund grant and other donors and foundations, REDF has expanded its operations beyond the San Francisco Bay Area to southern California. In 2015, it won an additional federal Social Innovation Fund ward that will enable it to expand operations beyond California in 2016. To date, the organizations with which REDF has partnered have created job opportunities for more than 9,500 people.

Interviewed in 2011

Steve Dubb: What were the origins of REDF?

Carla Javits: REDF was founded fifteen or so years ago. George Roberts—co-founder and co-chairman of Kohlberg, Kravis, and Roberts (KKR)—and his wife wanted to do something about the growing homelessness in the Bay Area and see that people could get into the workforce and get jobs. They connected with Jed Emerson, a widely known leader in the social enterprise sector, and he took the reins here. At first, they tried a few things that didn't work that well, and then they hit on this idea of supporting nonprofits that employed people who were homeless. Later, the effort expanded to support people with other barriers to employment, such as mental health, addiction issues, or histories of incarceration. Since then we've honed that effort in the Bay Area and now we are expanding our work California-wide. Initially, REDF was part of Mr. Robert's foundation. About six years ago, it became a nonprofit. Mr. Roberts is the Chair of the Board. There is a growing board of directors. We made this switch because there was the sense that we had achieved some important outcomes and we wanted to encourage others to get involved and others to invest in something that we thought was working.

*SD: **What are some of the leading achievements of REDF to date?***

CJ: We have helped a lot of enterprises—more than three-dozen—to either start or expand. We have helped them employ more than 5,700 people. Of those interviewed two years after getting a social enterprise job, three quarters were still working. We see this as an impressive result. Also there are other indicators: income has risen and wages have risen. Those are the outcomes we have seen. Additionally, the nonprofits themselves have earned more than $100 million in revenue. That is revenue that covers costs that would otherwise be covered by government and philanthropy. And, indeed, in a very real sense that is revenue that likely otherwise would have never been dedicated to the sector at all.

Our nonprofit partners have demonstrated their ability to run these enterprises, employ people and help them stay in the workforce. Because we have focused on this one thing, we have learned a lot about how to help nonprofits succeed in this area—both in helping people get jobs that would otherwise not be able to get jobs and also how to support the sustainability of the nonprofit enterprises themselves. There have been a lot of similar attempts around the country. Some have worked out and some have not. This is not easy to do! Over time, we have built the knowledge base of what works. This is another really positive result of REDF's work.

SD: *Could you tell us how REDF structures its support of the social enterprises that it partners with? How do the partnerships with nonprofits work?*

CJ: The way it works is that REDF seeks out nonprofits that either have a business or enterprise of some sort or have a strong focus on work-force development and some ideas of a social enterprise they want to start. We very carefully assess the organizations based on criteria we have developed over the years by working in the field. We select a pretty small number of organizations to get involved with. We like to stay involved for three to five years, although the length of time can vary according to the needs of a specific partner. During that period of time we agree on objectives in such areas as employment, revenue growth, and other business objectives. We provide financial support in the form of grants and also very hands-on business assistance. This business assistance ranges from marketing to business planning to infrastructure. Every year, both REDF and its partner organizations have a mutual conversation about how things are going and we renew and refine the partnership on an annual basis.

We've added some elements to our business assistance that are just getting under way now—one is much more of a focus on employee support to help employees thrive, succeed, and remain in the workforce. Second, we are focused on expanding our business development support. For example, we're now engaging with larger corporations to broker relationships with our partner social enterprises. The idea is to connect them to the supply chain as a way to expand their businesses. We have high hopes for increased success and job growth as a result.

SD: *Could you provide an example of a nonprofit that you worked with and have now exited and talk about how this process worked?*

CJ: One example is New Door Ventures—a San Francisco group that we got involved with fairly early on in REDF's history. It was a shelter for homeless people. The leadership there got the idea of screen-printing t-shirts to employ people coming into the shelter as a way to generate revenue. They started the operation on a shoestring budget with very basic equipment. We started working with them. Over a period of years, we provided millions of dollars. We delivered a whole suite of business services, both to build the infrastructure of the organization and the enterprise (marketing, strategic planning), helping get the right people in place to coach the enterprise leadership, and helping to develop markets for the screen-printed items. That was a tiny start-up at the beginning. It now has a state-of-the-art headquarters building and state-of-the-art screen-printing equipment.

They also set up a second business, a bicycle repair and sales shop in San Francisco. Over those years, they changed their focus from helping homeless people to helping young adults with barriers to employment. Both of their businesses have employed young people who face a lot of different challenges including dropping out of school, histories of incarceration, involvement with gangs, and being in the foster care system.

Around 2006 we ended the portfolio relationship. Our support tapered off over a couple of years. New Door continues to develop these ventures. With REDF's new business development work, seeking contracts from corporations, we have helped New Door secure a screen-printing contract from Safeway. So even though New Door is no longer in our portfolio, our relationship continues. Our work continues to be informed by theirs. They are also participating in a new working group that we formed called the Social Enterprise for Jobs Working Group ("SE4Jobs"). It is a forum for practitioners to learn best practices from one another.

SD: *Could you explain how the organization has changed since you became executive director four years ago? What are some of REDF's priorities going forward?*

CJ: We worked for a couple of years to develop a new strategy that our board adopted for 2011 to 2015—a five-year strategy. We are really excited about it. We have two major goals. One is to expand statewide and help 2,500 more people move into the workforce. The second is to develop a replicable model of social enterprise that can be carried out by many more groups and communities. We are just halfway

"It appears that if people can work in a wage-paying job for six months to a year, **almost all of the things you would hope to improve–job retention, income, etc.–do improve**."

through the first year. We were extremely fortunate to receive a Social Innovation Fund grant from the Corporation for National and Community Service, a program of the federal government that is trying to scale up and establish an evidentiary basis for promising practices. We received a two-year, $3 million grant, which was just renewed for another two years. That has allowed us to issue two requests-for-qualifications to select our nonprofit partners. In the first round, we selected six groups. We are assessing the second round applicants now. Of the first six, there are two enterprises in Los Angeles—that represents our first foray outside the San Francisco Bay Area.

SD: *I noticed on your website that one of your projects involved getting more local produce in high schools. Could you talk about the local produce project?*

CJ: One of the business start-ups is with a nonprofit group called Buckelew Programs, which is based in Marin County. Buckelew serves people with mental health challenges. This is a new business for them. They run a couple of businesses now including a cafe, but they are expanding into this new business line—a commissary that brings fresh produce to institutional buyers like schools and hospitals. They are just settling on a new facility. It should be up and running shortly. Obviously, with the emphasis and focus on fresh local food, institutional buyers like hospitals and schools are more and more interested in accessing that supply. There is a real business opportunity there.

SD: *Is REDF is trying to launch a similar business in Los Angeles?*

CJ: We are looking into this. Having a wider reach helps with replication. We want to see what can be replicated. Different markets have different drivers and cost structures. We want to figure out what can be replicated and what cannot; what can be done nationally or, if not done everywhere, might still be replicated in many more places across the country.

SD: *Could you discuss the other new enterprises that you are presently partnering with?*

CJ: We have six organizations in our portfolio right now. Two are in the San Francisco Bay Area—Buckelew and Community Housing Partnership. The latter has been in REDF's portfolio for several years—they develop, own and manage supportive housing. From their inception they have made employment of tenants a high priority: they run a desk clerk business, an apartment unit turnover enterprise and a pest control business. Basically, they are in property management services. In Los Angeles, we are working with Chrysalis and Weingart Center Association. Chrysalis is one of the better-known nonprofits operating social enterprises in the country. Chrysalis Enterprises currently run three businesses: Chrysalis Staffing, a full-service staffing agency for temporary and temp-to-hire work assignments; Chrysalis Works, a professional street maintenance and cleaning service; and Chrysalis Recycling, which collects recyclables from office buildings, multi-family dwellings and schools. Chrysalis is large and is one of the flagships of the social enterprise arena. We are trying to help them expand existing businesses and start a new business. Weingart is on Skid Row in Los Angeles. They have a focus on workforce development, but have not until now operated social enterprises. We are looking at replicating with them the pest control business developed by the Community Housing Partnership.

Two others are in the portfolio. The Center for Economic Opportunities (CEO) employs thousands of formerly incarcerated people in New York in transitional jobs on work crews doing maintenance projects. They are seeking to replicate that effort both in Oklahoma and in California. We are helping with their California replication. The assistance to CEO also complements an investment in their expansion by the Edna McConnell Clark Foundation.

Cooperative investment for organizations trying to scale can be critical. CEO has started its work in Oakland through an "affiliate" model where it provides support to replicate the CEO model to

Volunteers of America, which is also working with Rubicon Programs. CEO is looking to start up its own enterprise in San Diego. Lastly, the portfolio includes an enterprise called Green Streets—a program of the nonprofit Urban Strategies. Green Streets is a social enterprise that provides recycling and composting services in public housing San Francisco. They are affiliated with Urban Strategies which is the nonprofit subsidiary of McCormack, Baron, and Ragan (MBR), a national for-profit affordable housing development firm. The aspiration is to replicate the enterprise in Richmond, California; Los Angeles, and hopefully in other parts of the country where MBR has properties. That business employs young adults who live in and around public housing.

SD: *How does placement of employees after the social enterprise work? Where do those who "graduate" from social enterprises go afterward?*

CJ: We're not rigid about it—we are trying to figure out what works best in terms of length of employment. That's different for different people who face different kinds of challenges. We are trying to learn what works and what doesn't.

One finding from the data is very powerful. It appears that if people can work in a wage-paying job for six months to a year, almost all of the things you would hope to improve—job retention, income, etc.—do improve. Trying to make sure that people stay in the workforce for six months to a year seems to make a big difference long term. We're focusing more now on employee supports—identifying what helps people make that step into the mainstream workforce and retain the jobs. We want to know what really works in that regard. We are looking at technology, which can pinpoint potential job opportunities by profiling people who employers, even small businesses, want to or prefer to hire. We are not doing a lot with traditional training, such as community colleges, but we are very interested in making that connection. Our perspective on this is that there are a lot of people in this country who can't even get onto that first rung of the ladder. We are really trying to get people well positioned on that first rung so that they can take advantage of opportunities to climb up from there themselves.

"Social enterprise can be a part of the supply chain that generates revenue that offsets what would otherwise be public subsidies and helps employees succeed in the workforce."

There is a tension, of course, in social enterprise. In terms of the individuals, you might want people to move "up and out" after a year, but high turnover can be difficult in many businesses. From a business perspective, you might want to keep people for five to ten years. We are trying to figure that out for different lines of business. We are cognizant of that issue when we are assessing which business niches best fit the social enterprise model. In most cases, most of these businesses have some longer-term positions. So it is a matter of calibrating what percentage needs to be long term and what percentage short term. That is really important. Some of the people in transitional jobs, of course, can move into the permanent jobs at the same social enterprise. So it is really a mix. It is not the case that 100 percent of the employees will be turning over. For some, it makes sense to get in and move on. We are really conscious of that when we are setting up the business— that we are setting these businesses up for at least part of their workforce to be transitory.

SD: *Shifting gears and thinking nationally about public priorities for social enterprise, what do you see as the role of social enterprise? Also, to what extent can lessons learned through social enterprise inform how we should structure national workforce development policy?*

CJ: The big lesson to me is about how to bring people with challenges—mental health, incarceration, and homelessness, etc.—into the workforce. And the short answer is by providing real jobs with a real paycheck and, of course, the appropriate support structures. That appears to have some very promising results and it is worth figuring out how to build on that. A lot of what has been done to date is through wage subsidy programs that are funded by the government. Those are hard to sustain in a time of reduced government resources. Or, you might have public works projects with directives to hire locally. Unfortunately, too often, those result in limited term employment that doesn't go anywhere. Social enterprise, however, if done right, can be a part of the supply chain that generates revenue that offsets what would otherwise be public subsidies and helps employees succeed in the workforce.

On the practical side, the Social Innovation Fund is an important meaningful experiment. In our case, the question is whether public money can be used to spur the development of a whole tier of social results that the public expects. Traditionally, our funds have come from private sources. I think that it is important to assess what public funding can do. One thing it has done is to cause us to systematize what we do. That's been very positive. There are also some challenges. When you get involved with public funding, the money is less flexible, the expected payoff has to be more immediate, and there is less tolerance for risk. Despite these challenges, public policy can play an important role in supporting social enterprise by aggregating and investing the needed capital.

A second thing to look at is how the government interacts with social enterprise in existing business support programs. For example, most social enterprises work in minority communities and employ the people who live there, yet they don't really qualify under the technical definition of "minority-owned business" because they are non-profits. The definition matters as we try to get these entities into the supply chain. Right now, there is a bit of an uneven playing field that doesn't make sense given they are meeting an equivalent social goal. Either the social enterprises need to be incorporated differently or the Small Business Administration definitions need to change.

A third thing is that while social enterprises can generate significant revenue, there are still some costs. There is a need for some ongoing subsidy for the support services. It is a vastly reduced subsidy because of the earned revenue, but there is still a need for some subsidy to cover the training piece and the job readiness piece. I think, over time, these enterprises can become part of the workforce development arena by creating jobs, generating revenue, and partnering with others that provide support funded through subsidy that help people move on and retain jobs long-term.

The obvious incentive on the public side is that social enterprises vastly reduce public costs in others areas, by reducing recidivism, reducing homelessness, and, on the revenue side, by increasing incomes and generating the payment of taxes. For years, REDF has talked about what we call SROI—social return on investment. REDF has tried to develop a meaningful approach to assessing what the social return on investment is for social enterprise, and we continue to push that work forward. For the public sector to invest, it needs to be understood that every dollar provided delivers a return to the public.

SD: *To what degree do you interact with the U.S. Department of Labor and the Workforce Investment Board system?*

CJ: We are a little bit to the side of that. I've served for a number of years on the Youth Council of San Francisco's Workforce Investment Board. We are cognizant of that policy arena. Many of the groups we are involved with have at different times been able to access the funding. The Workforce Investment Act (WIA) system in the United States has tended to shy away from people with the greatest barriers and focus on people who just lost a job this year. So it has to some extent had less relevance for people with greater barriers. I think we are showing we can create a system that delivers benefits for people with greater barriers to employment cost-effectively.

There are other federal programs that we have used more frequently. For example, the U.S. Department of Health and Human Services (HHS) operates a Job Opportunities for Low-Income Individuals (JOLI) program and a Community Economic Development program (CED), both of which, over time, have provided capitalization for some of these businesses. The U.S. Department of Labor (DOL) has a transitional jobs program and some other related programs, but generally this has been more of a private sector play. The place where this comes together with the government is with purchasing. The Center for Employment Opportunities in New York—they use state procurement of building maintenance services. That's a real win-win that can be replicated more widely. Basically, what they are doing in New York is using public resources for public procurement that employ people who would otherwise cost the government a lot of money.

"While social enterprises can generate significant revenue, there are still some costs.... **There is still a need for some subsidy to cover the training piece and the job readiness piece**."

A great example at the federal level is the whole system that exists around the country—through the AbilityOne program of NISH (formerly National Industries for the Severely Handicapped)— which works with hundreds of nonprofits that employ people with disabilities to do work for the federal government—landscape military bases, manufacture military uniforms, destroy documents, and maintain buildings—among other activities.

SD: *How does REDF measure social return of investment and what are some of your recommendations for the field?*

CJ: We are looking at how many people are employed, how long they are employed, wages, and so on. We are also looking at the business itself, including its revenues and the overall strength of the business, and the nonprofit's ability to run the business. Where it gets more challenging to measure impact is on the larger societal scale: the impact on rates of recidivism, for example—things like that. We are looking to do a random-assignment study to provide more of that data in the future. The Center for Employment Opportunities (CEO), for instance, has been analyzed by MDRC [originally named Manpower Demonstration Research Corporation], which is one of the leading evaluators in the field. The results look very promising, demonstrating that crime and recidivism are reduced for people who have gotten into CEO's program. That's one element of it.

The second area where we are looking to improve the analysis of social return on investment is that we are trying to pilot a way for nonprofits to tie financial information to their social outcomes data. What I mean by that is that most nonprofits are using systems and software for accounting and financial management. And they are also using systems to document results for the people they are helping. But we have no systematic way to tie those two data sets together.

For example, take the seemingly simple question of "What's the cost per job?" These days, when asked this question, usually people do their best to put numbers together on a one-shot basis. We are trying to develop a usable, cost-effective way to tie together financial and client data, so that we can deliver better information that ties costs to results. We are just piloting that now, but we believe it shows some real promise.

SD: *How does the Social Innovation Fund program work? Have you found being part of the first round of grantees has provided a useful forum for information sharing with other grantees?*

CJ: We have to match dollar-for-dollar the federal allocation ourselves and our portfolio companies also have to match the money we give out in sub-grants. Fortunately, some of the match can be earned income from the businesses. As for the program itself, the basic focus is to identify promising practices in the community and deliver the evidence and capacity-building support to take these practices to a larger scale.

It is a really interesting effort for the government to work through intermediaries and venture philanthropy groups like ourselves and others like Local Initiatives Support Corporation (LISC), the Center for Economic Opportunities in New York, New Profit, Venture Philanthropy Partners, the National Fund for Workforce Solutions, and the Edna McConnell Clark Foundation, among others. There is a widespread feeling that we need a new model to deliver results with the public dollar. I think this notion that government can work with and through intermediary organizations that also leverage private dollars and are able to work at a direct level with organizations in the community and other actors is a powerful one. It is pretty exciting.

Another benefit of the program is that there is a knowledge network that we have put together. With the latest round of awards from the Social Innovation Fund (SIF), five more intermediaries have been brought into the fold—including the Corporation for Supportive Housing, where I worked for fifteen years. I am really pleased about that. A question and challenge for us is to integrate what we learn through the SIF into the mainstream of what the government does. That is a real effort that we are going to have to make in the coming years.

SD: *What are REDF's main priorities going forward?*

CJ: We want to be in multiple jurisdictions in California, working with a variety of businesses employing thousands of people. We want to learn what works to craft what we learn to be used around the country; and we are going to put everything into that over the next five years. We really do believe this is a powerful way to create some avenues to bring people into the workforce who have been excluded. There are millions of people in this country who want to work, who are capable of working and who aren't given that opportunity. We need a way to do that and this is one promising way to do it.

SD: *Anything else you would like to add?*

CJ: I do think the work that we are doing fits into a larger context to really create more job opportunities, especially for people who may be at the lower end of the income scale. That ranges from the worker-owned cooperative enterprises that the Cleveland Foundation and the Democracy Collaborative are involved with to some of the corporations that have been involved in Business for Social Responsibility, to the Hitachi Foundation's program to identify businesses that provide decent pay, benefits, and opportunities to move up their low-wage employees, to some of the work being done in small business development. We have to harness these investments in companies of all stripes that share these goals of creating jobs and real opportunity for people who have been left out of the workforce. There is much more innovation going on. There needs to be greater investment and attention given to all of these efforts.

Kate Sofis

*Kate Sofis is founding Executive Director
of SFMade, a nonprofit organization
launched in 2010 to support the building
of a local manufacturing base in San
Francisco. SFMade engages directly
with entrepreneurs and growing small
companies, all of whom are headquartered
in and manufacture in San Francisco,
offering industry-specific education,
networking opportunities, branding and
marketing assistance, and "infrastructure"
support, including help with workforce/
hiring, accessing capital, and finding
industrial real estate. By building
strong local manufacturing companies,
SFMade aims to sustain and create job
opportunities for the city's low-income
communities and individuals with less
typical education, experience, or skills.*

Interviewed in 2013

Steve Dubb: Could you talk about your background and how it informed the start of SFMade?

Kate Sofis: SFMade is very much the fruition of several threads of passion that I have had throughout my life: manufacturing, economic development around entrepreneurship, and urban issues. I started my career in high-tech manufacturing in Boston and spent over a decade in that field. When that off-shored, I was determined to continue to work in domestic manufacturing and shifted my focus to more "craft-based" industries—working in ceramic tile and then furniture manufacturing. Along that path I also developed a growing interest in how ecologies of companies work together. The last manufacturer I worked for, a furniture manufacturer, succumbed to the "dot-com recession" in 2001. I remember being somewhat incredulous at the time that, although we still had orders on the books and a viable company, in the end we had to close because we lost access to critical "infrastructure," including capital.

I think, at the same time, American cities had also really given up on local manufacturing, and San Francisco was no exception. I decided if I was going to continue to work in the sector, I would have to reposition my efforts at the broader community or city level, and so I re-tooled, earning a Masters in City Planning and Social Policy at the London School of Economics in 2003, and shifted my career into economic development. Really in hindsight—it wasn't such a large deviation from my path—it was just a shift of orientation—from working inside companies to working with groups of companies.

SFMade is a marriage of manufacturing and economic development and the value of life in the city. We are about the challenges and the possibilities of *urban* manufacturing specifically.

SD: You have described SFMade as a "fresh approach to revitalize and fuel local manufacturers." What are the key elements of this approach?

KS: It is multi-layered, as all things are. The thing we were originally known for, and perhaps what we continue to be most well known for, is our work to harness the power of place—the notion of creating a "local brand" for a city and connecting that to local manufacturers through the use of the SFMade logo and brand. To use an example, it is "San Francisco inside" when you carry a bag that is Timbuk2-made. In the beginning, we were working with just twelve manufacturers who agreed to use the SFMade brand on their products or websites or in their marketing. But SFMade has now grown into a brand that consumers recognize on the West Coast, in New York City, and even at a retail store in Tokyo. That local brand is a very powerful part of what we do. It is the element of what we do which is most asked and talked about by other cities.

A second differentiator of our work, and that of other partner cities, has been a fresh collaborative, instead of competitive, approach to manufacturing economic development. Rather than look outside, trying to throw economic incentives and attract businesses from cities or keep people from leaving, we instead take a look really at who has already chosen to start and grow businesses in San Francisco. Generally, our companies all have a value proposition that allows them to charge a premium that sustains higher wages and land costs. Our goal is to remove any and all barriers to growth and success of these companies. At the same time, if a company starts in San Francisco, but has a business model that requires a scale or cost model that is not appropriate to San Francisco or the Bay Area, we will be the first to help them find a better location. We also work to help San Francisco companies make supply chain connections to suppliers in other U.S. cities when that makes sense.

Overall, we consider ourselves pragmatists when it comes to keeping all or some production local. Many larger SFMade companies in fact have hybrid models. They produce a sizeable amount locally but will partner or co-manufacture as part of their business model. What is fresh about our view, it is not this binary perspective of making it in the United States—let's do it here if we can do it here, but let's not drink this philosophical sauce that we are somehow going to contain 100 percent of supply chains locally nor are most of our companies interested in containing their customer base to the locality. They want to grow locally and to sustain local jobs, and in order to achieve the scale needed to do that, many need to sell to a much broader footprint.

Third, we deliberately have scoped and continue to focus our work within a single city. That has allowed us to go deep and partner with a myriad of city departments. We work most closely with the Mayor, the Board of Supervisors, and the Office of Economic and Workforce Development. But we also work with San Francisco Unified School District, collaborating on our new high school youth programming. We partner with the Planning Department to think through industrial land use policy as well as to collaborate with any of our manufacturers working on a complicated construction project. We even work with San Francisco's MTA (Metropolitan Transit Authority, known locally as "Muni") on parking strategies and thinking differently of how to get workers and customers to far-flung manufacturing areas.

By digging deep, we can take a broad wrap-around model: land use and real estate, hiring (working with the city's workforce development programs), education and business advising for the companies and an emerging youth program. It is a combination of being able to work in all of these areas as well as have partnerships with the city, which makes our model particularly viable. In many other cities— Chicago, for example—there are so many organizations and agencies with deep histories working in manufacturing. This was not the case in San Francisco when we started SFMade. I have yet to meet the organization in a city of our size that has our luxury of having it all under one roof. We can really act as an ombudsman for the manufacturers. While we are independent of the city government, the City is our best partner. We still could have done much of what we done without the City, but that partnership makes us much stronger. So most often we speak of ourselves as a real public-private partnership rather than just a nonprofit.

SD: *How long did it take to form SFMade? Could you describe the different steps that it took to begin to bring your work to scale?*

KS: We had our soft launch—finding twelve seed manufacturers who were already operating in the city who would act as an advisory board—in November 2009. We had great positive feedback. They were all chosen to participate, as they are really emblematic of the scale and diversity San Francisco manufacturing: Anchor Brewing Company—the city's largest brewery and probably best known brand; Ritual Roasters—our largest coffee roaster; an up and coming bag manufacturer, Rickshaw Bagworks; and the city's oldest manufacturer, 113-year-old McRoskey Mattress Company. We had our formal launch in 2010 and really started with a focus on

"The thing we were originally known for, and perhaps what we continue to be most well known for, is **our work to harness the power of place**."

two programs—our local branding concept, embodied in the now trademarked SFMade logo, and industry-specific education and business advising.

Interestingly, we didn't explicitly focus on what many now talk about the most: how this work fosters a strong sense of community. I grew up in hardscrabble Buffalo, where we mostly just sought to create jobs, period. I've been a latecomer of the notion of building community through the economy. I was a bit of a skeptic. But from our launch with twelve companies, we grew rapidly. We had plans to serve thirty manufacturers in our first year; in fact, our network grew to 105 companies by December 2010. Most were existing companies and most referred each other. It was really truly amazing—in that first year, save for an article or two in the press, we spent no resources on advertising or marketing. The manufacturers referred each other to SFMade. They were drawn to us by the notion of community—banding together. I no longer underestimate how powerful that notion is and continues to be. Bizarrely, although it was a recession, we just hit on a theme—the timing was right, the opportunity of the recession got funders focused on job creation. We did not have a hard time getting seed funding. A number of our local banks: Wells Fargo, New Resource Bank, Citibank jumped in quickly. We also had strong initial support from the City—right up to the Mayor. This enabled us to secure funding through City of San Francisco's Community Development Block Grant (CDBG) program. I think the timing and the focus of the work helped a lot—the American psyche was tired of having everything made overseas. The consumer base was really interested in the notion. And the recession was helpful in creating the fire to do something differently to create jobs.

In San Francisco, we have this history and reputation that the economy is about tech jobs and finance jobs for super-educated people. We kind of forget about everybody else. Manufacturing is a counterbalance in the mayor's mind and the public's mind. Tech is harder for young people, less educated people, people whose first language is not English. We have had an exponential growth trajectory. In our first year, we had a $100,000 budget, one staff person (who was me), and 105 companies. By the end of the second year, we were at 250 companies with a staff of three and a budget of $300-400,000. Now we are serving 462 companies and have a staff of five and our budget is just shy of $1 million. Where we are expanding the scope of our work now, we are leveraging partnerships with other organizations and funding those initiatives jointly.

Another new component of our work is connecting manufacturing to the next generation, something I never thought I'd be doing, frankly. Growing up in Buffalo, if you could "get out" and get away from manufacturing in the 1970s and '80s, you did. But modern urban manufacturing is at a much more human scale and we are excited to reintroduce the potential for young people to work for small urban manufacturers or even to start their own business someday. With YouthMade—we are partnering with Juma Ventures to place forty very low-income high school kids over the next year into paid internships at local manufacturers. The model itself of partnering with another nonprofit organization rather than scaling up our own staff is also a hallmark of our approach. In this era of nonprofit organization proliferation, it is important for organizations to think about their growth imprint. It is not only better for us—with Juma, we can secure higher funding than we could independent of each other and we can attract new funders together. In the case of Youth-Made, our primary funding partner is JPMorgan Chase—this will be the first time they are financially supporting SFMade and we are told our partnership with Juma was particularly compelling to them.

Another growth area for us has been partnering with other cities that are engaged in similar efforts. We launched the Urban Manufacturing Alliance (the UMA) in 2011, in partnership with the Pratt Center for Community Development in New York, which now hosts Made in NYC, and is the nonprofit community development arm of Pratt. Together, we secured over $400,000 to support the UMA in its first year. That money is being deployed to create tool kits and deployed to other regions to implement other initiatives.

We have one initiative launching in Chicago, one under way in the Bay Area focused on garment manufacturing, and a third in the New York City region. We are really excited. The UMA is not its own entity; it's not incorporated and it doesn't yet have its own staff, although it has capacity through our joint funding. Part of our work in the next year will be to determine whether it becomes an advocacy organization or a separate nonprofit and, over time, what policy issues or programs are most needed to support the work of organizations like ours working in cities. Again in this area, we are expanding the footprint of our work not by expanding ourselves, but by creating new collaborative structures. The UMA is like a co-op of economic development organizations all focused on the same thing, growing their own urban manufacturing sectors. We currently have engagement from organizations across more than twenty major U.S. cities [as of 2016, thirty-five cities] in the UMA.

SD: *What are the main manufacturing sectors in San Francisco?*
KS: Our major sectors are all consumer product manufacturers. Three large sectors: the largest is "cut and sew" apparel, bags, and leather goods. The secret to that sector and the growth of that sector is that we still have a relatively deep contract garment manufacturing capacity in the city.

We have upwards of fifty companies that have skilled sewers. Some of these are sewing houses that used to make clothes for Levis or the Gap. Their highly skilled sewers hail largely from Hong Kong, mainland China, Vietnam, and the Philippines. The companies that have made it, they have made it because they do short production runs, work with smaller designers. What we see in that sector are young designers who come to San Francisco for school or they come because they are over Los Angeles or New York. We also see larger brands that are on-shoring portions of their product line. That's a growth sector for us.

One of our challenges is that because the workforce is aging and most of the (largely immigrant) women aren't looking at their kids to go into sewing, we have to look at who will be the next generation. Is it some other generation of immigrants? That is what we see in New York. It is no longer just Chinese. You also have garment workers who are more recent immigrants from countries like Ghana or

"In San Francisco, we have this history and reputation that the economy is about tech jobs and finance jobs for super-educated people. **We kind of forget about everybody else**."

Ecuador. We are also looking for an approach that could be attractive to native-born Americans. That is an idea of our youth program—to expose young people to these opportunities. That probably does involve adding more technology to get rid of the most backbreaking work. Garment manufacturing is surprisingly low-tech in high-tech San Francisco. Manufacturers could use computer numerically controlled (CNC) equipment. The technology does exist.

Our second largest sector is food-and-beverage. That has to do with slow-food and farm-to-table and the same thing that has spawned the wonderful restaurants, the Alice Waters of the world. Often, our food entrepreneurs are former chefs who have a passion for chocolate, or coffee, or granola and go off on their own. Sometimes a new product evolves out of restaurants—such as sauces. We always had a lot of beer and wine. San Francisco's history as the Barbary Coast has meant that the city has a long, proud history making beer, and to a lesser degree, distilled spirits. Anchor Brewers and Distillers may be our largest brewery, but we also have Speakeasy and Magnolia, newer growing craft beer brands, both expanding into more space to accommodate their growth. We also have a number of wineries now back in the city. One of the challenges is that once you get beyond really tiny, you need more space than you do in many of the sectors. If you can't find affordable space, we won't keep those guys as they grow. That's an area we are really focused on right now. We have done a lot of work collaboratively with the City on land use.

The third sector is harder to define but could be said to be design-infused consumer products—iPad cases, furniture, jewelry, ceramics—things made out of metal and wood and glass and acrylic and even clay. Bikes are another one. They almost all have a lot of design thought in the product and they are marrying that design with local craft capacity.

SD: *In sectors other than garments, what are the demographics of the workforce? Who works for San Francisco manufacturers?*

KS: In our other industries, it's more mixed. Overall, across all of these sectors, we have 462 companies. At this point, we have an estimated 95 percent of the sector that produces locally in San Francisco participating in SFMade. As a result of this access, when we do our annual data collection and survey, we are able to obtain more detailed data about the nature of these urban manufacturers than is publicly available. We know that people from low- and moderate-income households still occupy 76 percent of the jobs. In food, it's a real mix ethnically. You will find all kinds of people in food and beverage. We find young American-born kids of all backgrounds who have a passion for making chocolate, working next to a father of three from Mexico.

In other companies, the manufacturing capacity is made up of people who came out of the building trades—for example, former cabinetmakers making wood framing for an iPad case. Metalworkers are now milling some component that is going into someone's bag. We are finding a reapplication of trades that we thought might be lost. We are seeing a reemergence of crafts.

One company that exemplifies this "marriage" of craft with technology is Dodo Case: they are use bookbinding technology to make iPad cases. Because of e-books, the originally bookbinding sector had become a dying industry. Now DodoCase has a full bookbindery as a key part of their operations and is actively hiring and training people in the art of bookbinding.

SD: *Could you discuss some of the challenges?*

KS: In food and beverage, it is related to space and size. For some companies, they are expanding. Anchor Brewers and Distillers (the venerable San Francisco craft beer manufacturer) is building a second location—it is on San Francisco-owned Port property, in partnership with the San Francisco Giants, whose stadium is adjacent to the site. If they hadn't secured that very special site and partnership, they might not have been able to expand further within the city. Another SFMade chocolate manufacturer is currently manufacturing on the waterfront as well, but their lease is up soon; we have been in a feverish search to try to find them new space for the past six months and it is not a sure thing that we will succeed.

For the small companies, they need co-packers—help with bottling, commercial-scale baking. The city hollowed out its co-packing and bottling capacity. We don't have a baker or a sauce maker in the city. With the little guys, if they land a contract with Whole Foods or some other large customer, they have to move production out of the city. We at least try to keep them in the Bay Area. It would be good to have modest scale co-packing back in San Francisco. We are working with the City and private sector actors to catalyze that in the next year or two.

We also have real holes in what kinds of materials can be sourced locally—if you are making something about of wood, we have a lot of woodworkers. With metal, we have some but fewer contract manufacturers, and they are all small. But sometimes we can't find contract manufacturers at all—powder coating, plastics, acrylics—none of that is stuff we make in San Francisco. With plastics and acrylics, we make little in the United States as a whole. In this area, we need more contract manufacturers. We need to make it easier for folks to invest in powder coating or laser cutting. Or get someone into the city that can do small-scale manufacturing in these key areas.

I think another complex issue results from decades of separating product design from manufacturing, and that continues to color the sector even as we start to produce more in the United States. Everyone it seems wants to be a "maker," but few want to actually be the manufacturer. We often meet designers and budding entrepreneurs who have designed a prototype product—using fifteen pieces of equipment and 800 hours of their own time at a local hackerspace or in their garage or kitchen. Invariably, with many, their first question is: "Who can make them for me?" We don't have a silver-bullet answer. It used to be that when you wanted to make something, you made it. Or you purchased equipment and hired folks to help you make it, under your direction. You didn't assume someone would make it for you. The current ethos is still often— you can design it and someone else will make it. That is an obstacle:

we have a dearth of people who want to take the hard path of making it in-house. We need to think about education and training and access to capital to help people take that path and be successful. It is harder to get loans for making things than shooting it over the internet to someone else who is going to make it for you.

SD: *Do you see your work intersecting with the environment and sustainability? If so, how?*

KS: We do, although not as significantly as some of our colleagues. For Pratt in New York City, that is a hallmark of their work and they have launched a number of successful initiatives. Their Spec It Green program is particularly interesting, where they have connected the architecture/building industry's appetite for green building products with local manufacturers of those products. At SFMade, we don't screen for companies on environmental goodness. But we know the vast majority of our companies think about sustainability themselves and more than 50 percent have gone beyond "we recycle" or "we manage our energy utilization" to actively thinking about sustainability. For example, one company we work with is Rickshaw Bags. They have a product called the "zero"—it's a bag that produces zero waste. They have literally designed it to use all of the fabric cuttings that go into it. Compared to many other cities, we have a lot of companies who have deeply thought about this.

We are starting to think more now about weaving sustainability more deeply into our practice: we started with educational offerings to the companies. For example, we have a partnership with PG&E (Pacific Gas & Electric). They have been going out and doing energy audits and have been innovative to help their companies to conserve their energy use—that reduces a cost, so it is attractive to many companies. We also have a grant from Google focused on using local manufacturing to reduce the overall carbon footprint in cities.

The other area, although we don't have a lot of traction yet, is supply chain localization. The challenge for us is that we are a small city, an expensive city. It is hard to think about localizing a lot of our raw materials. If garments are a sector, cotton is a big input—not a lot you can do about that in terms of localization. You could have companies think about different materials, really focusing on developing products that intentionally make the best use of locally available materials. But this is a relatively new area for us.

SD: *Has SFMade worked with any businesses with cooperative or employee ownership?*

KS: The short answer is that we had one actual co-op, but it has disbanded (in furniture manufacturing). What we have more of in San Francisco are companies that are setting up stock ownership or phantom stock where if there is a sale of the company, at that point the employees immediately vest and benefit and get a percentage of proceeds. That's what happened when our largest bag manufacturer—Timbuk2—changed ownership a number of years ago. When the company was sold, each employee got an average payout of several years of salary and most of them continue to work at the company today.

Timbuk2 is now majority owned by a private equity firm. But it is important to note that fewer than five of our 462 companies are owned by institutional equity of any sort. The vast majority are family-owned or closely held by two or three people. None of our manufacturers are public. In some ways, family and private ownership—combined with good business models—is the reason why these companies have had the staying power. This is the "stickiness" that keeps the companies here, through multiple recessions and with the higher costs and complexity of doing business.

Another emerging area that we are trying to help catalyze is capital. Last year alone we had 12.5 percent net new job growth. The appetite for capital is increasing. You can't do it all with debt. So we are looking at options like crowdfunding and creating explicit angel networks.

Of our 462 companies, 30 percent are younger than we are and we were founded only three years ago. Of this 30 percent, a quarter of those have launched themselves on Kickstarter or Indiegogo. People are using crowdfunding. It lends yourself to do that if you are making consumer products. I don't think it would work so well with firms like tool-and-die manufacturers.

SD: *Do you worry about family businesses folding as the baby boom generation retires? Do you look at succession?*

"The UMA is like a co-op of economic development organizations all focused on the same thing, **growing their own urban manufacturing sectors**."

KS: We are keeping our eye on family transition. One of our longest running manufacturers is McCroskey Mattress Company. It is third-generation owned and has been operating continuously in San Francisco for more than one hundred years. For companies like this, it is not always clear if there will be a next-generation owner or if other paths make more sense that perhaps engage senior employees in ownership over time. We are actively looking at a variety of tools, including employee stock ownership plan (ESOP) structures, employee buyouts, and occasionally mergers of smaller companies in the same sector to achieve long-term sustainability.

We have a handful of companies that are in this situation, where they will have some real decisions to make over the next decade. Certainly some of the garment manufacturers themselves will find themselves in this position with an aging ownership and workforce. That said, San Francisco, relative to other cities, such as Pittsburgh or Buffalo, has a relatively young manufacturing sector as a whole, so the challenge in this area seems manageable so far.

SD: *What is the role for community development finance in supporting local manufacturing?*

KS: It is a hugely important part of the infrastructure. Anything goes, whether it is a traditional community development financial institution (CDFI) or hybrid CDFIs like Pacific Community Ventures (which makes double bottom line equity investments and has a new loan fund). We are also seeing banks go downstream in terms of the loans they are able to offer. To a company, the general feeling is "I don't care where I get the money." It is all about interest rates and can I get the loan. I am seeing a lot more movement in loan products. We are finally seeing some results in the federal initiative to get Small Business Administration (SBA) loan dollars released.

Sometimes it feels frankly like we are swimming in new loan funds right now. The City just launched two new loans funds and there is a new SBA loan product. There is also a California loan fund. It's all good news generally, although I will also say the landscape of whom to go to for which product is now more complex.

On the equity side, even with the existence of double and triple bottom line funds, if their funds come from institutional investors, there are real limits to the risk they can undertake—especially in deploying capital to companies with less than $5 million in revenue, which is where many growing manufacturers are. And while we certainly have a robust angel community in the Bay Area, a majority of that investment has historically been directed towards technology companies. But we believe that there is a market for patient investment in solid local manufacturing companies. We have already seen indications of this in several of our manufacturers who have prominent angel investors from the tech sector itself; our new Craft Capital initiative will be exploring ways we can target more angel investment specifically into this sector.

SD: *Could you talk about the role of public policy and how SF-Made liaises with City officials?*

KS: What I always tell people is that you can do a lot without your city government if need be. I say that because we hear from some similar organizations that their cities are not yet deeply engaged in manufacturing. But if you can engage your city government in your work, your power to create change rises exponentially. This has certainly been our experience. I have mentioned some of the "transactional" areas we work with the City—on finding low-moderate income workers for jobs, helping companies get through planning and permitting, etc. But our City partnership has also been very important in evolving policy in a number of areas. One notably was business tax reform: until last year, San Francisco had a payroll-based business tax system that intensively taxed labor-intensive businesses like manufacturers and left partnerships, such as law firms, or sole proprietorships—such as real estate brokers—off the hook entirely.

Many administrations had tried to get something changed, but none had the political support to achieve this. Last year, we finally did that in San Francisco, abolishing our payroll tax system and putting this to the voters—electing to change business taxes to be based on gross receipts (consistent now with most other U.S. cities). Manufacturing was a big part of the effort; it provided a lot of horsepower to the public campaign. The measure passed overwhelmingly. That's one example where we got really involved and that made a huge difference. Manufacturing had a real seat at the table.

Another area of policy work is industrial land use and zoning so that we at least have a measure of protection for some industrial space in the city. That has been a huge part of our work. The Eastern Neighborhoods Plan created industrial zones. Hitherto it had been the Wild West, with some real estate developers working to convert former industrial space into live-in lofts. Later this summer, we will launch a second partnership, a nonprofit industrial corporation. It will act like an affordable housing organization but for the provision of industrial space. We intend to start the group under our fiscal sponsorship, but spin it off as a separate organization.

Transportation management has been another area. Parking management must deal with more and more folks in a very small city. We have been very proactive in thinking about this in our work with San Francisco's transit authority—public transit out to the industrial parks in the city. We don't have policy folks. Instead, we scan where the pain points are and deploy staff, often me, into that area and/ or get some grant money from a foundation to get extra capacity in that area. We also view the Urban Manufacturing Alliance as another place that policy can sit. As we move forward to launch the nonprofit real estate organization, we are drawing on policy work from Pratt around nonprofit industrial development from Brooklyn Navy Yard and Greenpoint and using their work to inform our efforts.

SD: *If you had to highlight a few key accomplishments of SFMade's work to date that you are most proud of, what would they be?*

KS: One of the things that we often talk about was our very first collaboration with a major national retailer—Banana Republic (a division of San Francisco-headquartered Gap Corporation). We convinced them two years ago to have a dedicated SFMade station in their flagship store in downtown San Francisco. It symbolized the coming out of the sector. We aren't just a sector of people making funky hats—it was important for proof of concept and a number of small manufactures got lift-off by being pulled into that opportunity.

That payroll tax reform for me was another highlight. There was no doubt in my mind that having manufacturing featured so prominently both behind closed doors and in the public eye was really instrumental in making that change. Seeing the power of our sector in being an organized front was powerful to see.

Also, 30 percent of our 462 companies are younger than we are. We've made it cool again to be a manufacturer. In cities across the United States and Canada, we are seeing others doing similar work now. There is "Made in Copenhagen" and "Fait a Montréal" (Made in Montreal). We helped Pratt re-launch Made in New York and we are also connecting with a sister initiative, Made in Portland. We are inspired that so many folks are trying to do the same thing and we know some have been inspired by us and that's very gratifying.

SD: *How do you see this model working when adopted in rust belt cities?*

KS: I believe our work—with rust belt cities and also in places like Oakland and New Orleans—we collectively have to figure out how this renaissance is going to benefit the Buffalos and Detroits of the world. The advantage that we have in San Francisco includes having a relatively affluent consumer base—which allows a company to launch a new product and guarantee its first market will be local—combined with a city brand that has power, whether that product is on a shelf in San Francisco, in New York, or in Tokyo. That is not going to apply as easily in a place like my hometown of Buffalo. That said, I do think there are some commonalities.

One principle is to dig deeply and have one organization or one initiative of organizations where there is one-stop shopping. That is powerful and needs to be looked at in cities where there are too many organizations for a manufacturer to know where to go.

A second is the wrap-around concept. We provide help with capital, help you find space, help you hire—that has been a really effective model for us. Many weak market cities, such as Buffalo, are smaller than we are. The advantage is that, practically speaking, it is possible to have a one-stop shop. By contrast, there is a different challenge with Los Angeles or New York or Chicago to have a single organization; it just isn't reasonable in cities that large, but I think it would work in many places.

Then there are cross-region supply chains. My hypothesis—and I've always thought about it in Buffalo—is that there is a role to connect first-tier cities with rust belt and other cities with different competencies and cost structures. Part of the solution means that we are not just bringing everything to each city—recreating the competitive urban models of the '70s—but instead we partner with other regions in the United States on manufacturing we can't do. We are starting to pilot that in Chicago. For example, we have a bicycle manufacturer in San Francisco that found a frame builder in Chicago. Part of my hope with the Urban Manufacturing Alliance—which does include some "rust belt" cities like Cleveland—is that we can link supply chains across cities.

As I have thought about Buffalo as a whole, I ask myself, "What do you do about Buffalo?" Growing up here, we just kept to ourselves. The City had this marketing campaign back in the late '70s and early '80s when the city was really struggling economically—that in spite of it all, we were "Talking Proud!" There was something perhaps "patriotic" about that saying as a Buffalonian, but it also sort of implied a "we can do it ourselves" kind of attitude. I always wondered, even in my youth, why aren't we doing more—proactively reaching out—to Toronto, Pittsburgh, and to New York? I suspect Buffalo is not unique. There is a focus on pride of place and lifting ourselves up. That is valuable. But cities like Buffalo would do better to also link with strong market cities and vice versa.

Another key to our success has been diversity. Those rust belt cities that have created some diversity in their manufacturing base, Chicago is a good example, have historically done better cities that have developed largely around one sector and one or two large companies. Somewhere along the way, manufacturing diversity is a key, whether you're New York, Newark, Buffalo, or San Francisco.

José Corona

José Corona was Chief Executive Officer of Oakland-California based Inner City Advisors (ICA) from 2004 to 2015. ICA is a nonprofit technical assistance group that helps build sustainable and responsible businesses that create quality jobs, reinvest in the community, and contribute to building a strong and vibrant local economy. Since its founding, ICA has helped to create and retain over 7,000 jobs in the Bay Area, creating or retaining 2,717 jobs in 2013 alone that pay an average hourly wage of $14.50 and generate over $68 million in total wealth for the local community.

In 2015, Corona left ICA to accept the position of Director of Equity and Strategic Partnerships for the City of Oakland.

Interviewed in 2014

Steve Dubb: Could you talk about your background and how that has impacted your work?

José Corona: I came to the United States in the early 1980s as an immigrant from Michoacán, Mexico. My father worked in agriculture. One of the things that really shaped my passion and where I am now was that I always saw and admired my dad as an entrepreneur. He wanted to make a better life for himself and his family. He was lucky to find a great employer who gave him the opportunity to start the business that he has now. It was sometimes difficult not having my dad around because he worked a lot. But that experience really allowed me to empathize with the entrepreneurial journey that I now see in the entrepreneurs whom we serve. They have similar journeys and make tough choices. They give up and sacrifice a lot for the sake of growing their businesses and creating opportunities for others. That kind of framing not only allowed me to be empathetic to the entrepreneurs but also to really understand the hard work, the hustle, and the discipline around that.

My path here was not straight. It was a winding road. My dad was very much into education. He prioritized that. He wanted to make sure my brothers and I got a good education. He put all of us through college. Back then, I didn't know I wanted to come into this world of economic development.

I graduated from University of California, Davis with a biomedical degree. I went to dental school at UC San Francisco, but then dropped out. It just wasn't what I wanted to do. Then I needed a job and ended up going through the Macy's management development program. I found out about them at a job fair. Long story short, it really gave me the business savvy and the tools around management, around operations, and around how to work at a business. I was running a department and then running a region of stores, focused on operations and shortage analysis. They really gave me the tools I needed to use in my career going forward.

Then I came to the nonprofit world. I reached a point at Macy's where I wasn't patient enough to stay at Macy's. So I put in my notice.

I was a friend of someone running the San Francisco Hispanic Chamber of Commerce. They mentioned the Mission Economic Development Association, or MEDA. That's where I got my first pay stub in the nonprofit world doing development and fundraising.

MEDA does homeownership education, land use planning and much more for the Mission District in San Francisco. That was a great experience to learn about economic development, community development, and how and why communities change. You had to address: How do you deal with gentrification? It was a great time to be there. It was the time of the first dot-com boom and then there was a huge bust that followed. I saw what all of that meant for the community.

That was a great learning ground for me and, from there, I moved here to ICA to pursue more leadership opportunities. I always look at how I can align my values to the work that I do. I am here. I am doing it and enjoying it and having fun.

SD: *Could you discuss the origins of Inner City Advisors? With what vision was it founded? How has it evolved over time?*

JC: ICA was founded on the vision that bringing business and the market to inner cities is a good strategy to address a lot of social problems that exist in inner cities. If you bring businesses to locate here, the hope is that they will be active in the community and address the issues that exist. By bringing in, in some sense, the capital market. Market forces, as Michael Porter believes, will transform the community. That was the basis of Michael Porter's Initiative for a Competitive Inner City. For him, it was a competitive advantage to be located in the inner city: cheaper real estate, transportation hubs, and an accessible workforce.

To some extent, that was true, but the organization has evolved. We have learned over time that just because a company is located in the inner city doesn't mean they contribute back to that community. They might be located there, but for the most part they didn't hire from that community. It really was a real estate play. It was cheaper. We've seen this in many of the communities we work in now, including East Oakland, West Oakland, and Fruitvale. The location of the company by itself doesn't necessarily mean that it has a direct impact on the community.

Learning that, we took that and asked ourselves: "How do we find the businesses and entrepreneurs who are not only looking to locate in the inner city, but who are also committed to impact the inner city in a positive way through job creation?" We are going to find those entrepreneurs and hold them to that by hiring locally and contributing to the community in other ways. First and foremost, this involves hiring locally.

So we help companies in the inner city who are focused on local job creation. It is not enough any more to live in the inner city because inner cities are gentrifying. Just because someone lives in the inner city doesn't mean that person meets the profile of the people we are seeking to help get employed.

SD: *Describe the portfolio approach that Inner City Advisors uses. What businesses are in your portfolio?*

JC: We do have a selection process for companies that we serve, based not only on their business and industries, but on their potential for growth. We try to look at companies that are job creators and employers. We don't work with start-ups. We want to find those that might create 50 jobs in a three-year period—that is the baseline we use. However, we do serve companies at early stages through different programs, such as our Entrepreneurship Institute.

With the Entrepreneurship Institute, we partner with the Mills College Graduate School of Business. We admit sixty to seventy entrepreneurs and try to help them understand their business—go from plan to strategy, and how to focus on growth. The ten-week period of the class allows us to get to know and understand which companies have the most potential for growth.

We have fifteen to twenty companies that we dive deep into their business. We leverage skilled business leaders to work as volunteers and which serve as a de facto advisory board. We look to find people with a lot of operational experiences who provide timely, practical and valuable advice to the entrepreneur.

These entrepreneurs include companies like Revolution Foods, which we have worked with for over eight years. They have grown from five people to 1,200 people. Other major success stories include Blue Bottle Coffee, Give Something Back, Premier Organics, and Numi Organic Tea.

We have a lot of food manufacturing companies. That is intentional. It is an industry that provides a lot of good entry-level jobs with career mobility potential. For us, a good job is one that pays above living wage, offers health benefits, and career ladder opportunities. We believe that a good job has a trickle-down effect on families. We believe that having a good job allows an individual to better support their families.

But in the end, we have to start with helping the entrepreneur and small business to grow first. If they are not sustainable and profitable first, then the good jobs that we seek to create will not be created.

SD: *Could you give an overview of the services Inner City Advisors provides?*

JC: We look at it as three tracks. The first is a capital preparedness track: financial management, operational support, human resources support, among other areas, which help companies to improve their business—all with a focus of having them access capital.

The second track is Talent Management. As we help companies grow and scale, we help them recruit their people and talent from workforce agencies that work with different populations, such as formerly incarcerated, immigrants, and people with lower educational attainment levels—we work with workforce development partners out there to get these companies the staff they need. The Talent Management program helps companies build sound, strategic human resources infrastructure so that they can prepare, recruit, and promote good talent, which we help recruit from partner workforce development agencies.

Our third track is Capital. Through our partner fund—Fund Good Jobs[2]—which ICA created and launched in 2013, we use a hybrid capital approach (debt and equity) to invest in Inner City Advisor companies. We build in job creation and job quality metrics within the covenants of our investments to ensure that good jobs are being created.

SD: *Did you have covenants before the Fund was created?*

JC: We didn't have any covenants. The way we have traditionally worked is that we have demonstrated that we add value. We have helped the businesses we work with connect to a lot of the investment they raised. We added a lot of value to build their business. We built trust.

So before we had Fund Good Jobs, we couldn't enforce covenants. We didn't say, "You are going to get ICA services and you have to do X"—we didn't really do that. But that has been the evolution.

---

2. http://www.fundgoodjobs.com/how-we-work/#our-approach.

Over time, year over year, we have become a lot more intentional and picky about the companies with whom we partner. We want to make sure they share our values—there is no legal way to enforce where they hire from or who they hire. All of the consulting we provide is on a pro bono basis. They don't have to take our advice. They can do something else. And we have seen some companies go in a different direction and we have parted ways and are comfortable with that.

We have come to be a lot better about screening up front for commitment to job creation and for hiring people with barriers to employment. Even now, we have a very trusting relationship with the companies. They see that we are looking out for the best interests of their business. They tell us, "If you are telling us you are working with the target population, we will do it." But it is because we have built trust and demonstrated value to their business. That is the kind of relationship we build over time. And we try to do that better and faster with the new companies we are serving.

SD: *How are you funded?*

JC: About 40 percent of our funding comes from foundations, both local and national. Forty percent of our funding comes from corporations, banks and other financial institutions. Fifteen percent comes from an Alameda County social service agency, and the remainder, about 5 percent, is from individuals.

SD: *You've been at ICA for about a decade. Could you discuss the growth of ICA over that period?*

JC: When I joined in 2004, we used to be called Oakland Advisors. I was the first employee after the organization had gone through a tumultuous period. They were able to secure funding to hire a new director, and that is when I came in. It was only focused on servicing anywhere between eight and ten companies a year in Oakland.

The mission has not changed, but the approach has. We have grown from one to 10 staff and from a budget of $95,000 to $2.1 million. We were 100 percent funded by a few corporations. Now we have a more diverse funding mix. Our reach is broader too. It is not just Oakland, but includes Alameda County [whose county seat is Oakland], Contra Costa County and San Francisco.

We are looking to expand into the Peninsula and the San Jose area and up into the North Bay. We are planning that for 2015 and 2016, but we are doing it carefully and thoughtfully, and in no rush. We have plenty to do where we operate currently. The majority of companies we work with come to us through word of mouth. That is how we get most of our clients, which is great. But we are also trying to be more intentional and strategic in our work.

SD: *Beyond food production manufacturing, what are the main sectors you work with?*

JC: Food production manufacturing is the highest. We also have health care, such as in-home senior care, and supporting kids with autism disorders. Fortunately, both of those are growing sectors—a lot of the nursing in-home care provider jobs are good jobs that can be accessible to people who don't have a high education but have good talent for caring for people. The other that is building is solar, particularly installation, because of the jobs they create and for whom. The rest is a mixture of retail, services, advanced manufacturing, distribution and repair.

SD: *What are the demographics of the workforce of the companies that you support? What are some key indicators of the impact of your businesses?*

JC: Of the companies we serve, 58 percent are minority-owned businesses and nearly 50 percent are women-owned. The people they employ are 58 percent from minority populations. The median revenue of our companies is about $460,000. The average wage is $14.50 an hour, and 64 percent of the employees have health benefits. We are also beginning to track job mobility as part of an indicator of a good job. More to come on this and other indicators in 2015!

SD: *You have mentioned that you like to work with practical, action-oriented tools. What are some of the practical, action-oriented tools that you use? How does it work?*

JC: We use the Eight Factors framework, which was developed by Michael Bush, a former ICA Board member.[3] He is also a savvy,

---

3. http://action.innercityadvisors.org/meet-michael-c-bush-founder-of-the-8-factors-business-framework.

"Of the companies we serve, **58 percent are minority-owned businesses and nearly 50 percent are women-owned**. The people they employ are 58 percent from minority populations.... The average wage is $14.50 an hour, and 64 percent of the employees have health benefits."

committed and serial entrepreneur. It looks at areas such as Mission, Cash, Strategy, People, Culture, Processes, Structure, and Leadership. We look at these areas of a business and dive into them. Whether it is staff or volunteer advisors, we want to provide concrete steps and to give real world examples that businesses can use. We have amazing volunteers, business professionals who have extensive operational experience of running a business. It is simple—can someone provide useful information to an entrepreneur so that she or he can put into practice right away? For that reason, we screen our advisors as carefully as we do the businesses.

SD: *Have you worked with any businesses with cooperative or employee ownership or nonprofit ownership?*

JC: We are exploring nonprofit social enterprise, but we have not worked with social enterprises yet.

Part of our definition of a quality job is to treat employees well. So we have worked with some of our companies to implement ESOP (employee stock ownership plans) ownership structures. Revolution Foods provides stock ownership for their employees. We help them structure that internally and provide the legal support. But, we do that on a case-by-case basis.

With co-ops, we really haven't done much. We have tried to work with a couple but really do not have much practical experience.

SD: *Does your work intersect with the environment and sustainability? If so, how?*

JC: We do, but it is not a focus of ours. It happens to be that most of the companies with whom we work have an angle of environmental sustainability. For us, the impact metric is job creation. We don't seek companies that are environmentally sustainable, but many, such as the solar companies, and others implement sustainability practices into their business because it makes business sense for them and because it is just a value that the entrepreneurs possess.

SD: *How are Inner City Advisor businesses actually linked to capital?*

JC: We work with all banks, including community banks such as Beneficial State Bank, New Resource Bank and other community development loan funds like Pacific Community Ventures and Oakland Business Development Council (OBDC) Small Business Finance. We have great relationships for traditional debt capital. We have links with impact investors and also play in that world.

What we try to do is understand the need of our businesses first and then connect them to the appropriate sources. In a sense, we act almost like an investment bank to our clients, where we convene capital providers to build the capital package and capital stack that makes the most sense for the entrepreneurs. Fund Good Jobs is at the core of this strategy. We are preparing companies so they are well prepared for capital when we get to them.

SD: *How does work with business translate into building community wealth?*

JC: We are becoming better at connecting companies through communities primarily through hiring practices. We believe that having a good job is a first step to increasing an individual's financial position and that of their family. We also support our entrepreneurs in building businesses that build other wealth creation and financial incentive mechanisms for their employees, so that if the business does well, the employees do well too.

This moves the dialogue beyond just wages as a measure of the quality of a job. The more families that are supported by employees that work at the companies we support, the more economically sound families and people are created. That local wealth is then reinvested in the community. We propose these practices and make them aware that they can do it and afford it, and we help them get there. But job creation is where it starts for us.

SD: *Do you track by neighborhood?*

JC: We track results as a whole. We do know that about 80 percent of those 2,700 jobs are in the inner city communities. We are making a huge impact on hiring locally and we are beginning to dig deeper. We want to understand the families that these individuals are supporting: who are they?

What are their profiles? For instance, $54,000 a year (which is the average salary across ICA companies) supporting one person is okay. It is still not good, but it's okay. However, $54,000 supporting a family of four, and in the Bay Area? That is not sufficient. So we are looking at how to improve that. Over time, we expect that the impact reporting will become a lot more robust by looking at a lot more indicators.

SD: *Revolution Foods operates nationally. Is that the norm or the exception?*

JC: They are in the 25 cities. But it is definitely the exception in our portfolio. The vast majority of the businesses we work with are operating and employing only locally, but they distribute more broadly. Blue Bottle Coffee is another example like Revolution Foods, however. All of the other companies have employees located here. They may have sales reps in other states, but 98 percent of their workforce is here.

When it comes to that, when someone has the capacity to expand, obviously we encourage that. If Revolution Foods can have an impact in the Bay Area, they can also have an impact in Chicago, New Orleans, and Washington, DC.

Given the scale of where they are, we can't help them on the scale strategy in those cities, we can only support them in what they do in the Bay Area—at least, not yet.

SD: *Could you discuss some of the leading challenges you face in your economic development work?*

JC: The entrepreneurship and small business development work that we are in—it is not a level playing field. The entrepreneurs that we serve do not have profiles where they can easily access traditional capital. They don't have the profile that a bank or a venture capitalist would look for. And, banks are getting tighter in their lending—particularly for the profile of companies that we serve. We are helping in the capital piece. But there is a lot more to do.

Another challenge is that the economic development that is happening is not benefitting all communities. You see Oakland in the *New York Times* as the number five place in the world to visit; and that is great. But the economic development activity that is happening in Oakland is concentrated in downtown and uptown. That is not benefiting Fruitvale, West Oakland, or East Oakland. So, how do you bring equitable economic development activity in our cities and communities? That is a big challenge.

Finally, technology-based economic development is a big driving force, but it doesn't benefit everyone or employ everyone and does not solve every problem. We need to look beyond technology as well when we are talking about economic development.

SD: *Could you talk about the role of public policy in providing a supportive environment?*

JC: If anything, it is really just prioritizing and investing in the businesses that are already locating here. The same incentives that cities use to attract a business could also support local business in expanding. Why can't you take similar approaches for local businesses if they hire locally? Government and policy has a huge role in creating the environment for someone to grow in their own city. It is often overlooked. It is not sexy. It is not bringing the next Twitter into the world. But how do we grow our next Revolution Foods or Blue Bottle Coffee?

SD: *Do you see the ICA model being adaptable to other cities? What would need to happen?*

JC: It is definitely applicable. Other communities: Detroit, New Orleans, Philadelphia, even Portland have reached out to us. It is applicable and it is needed.

The challenge is to really come in with a sense of humility. ICA is not the sole answer. Detroit has great organizations. It is about understanding who is doing what and how, or if, can the ICA model leverage or supplement what is already happening. We are not so cocky to say that ICA is the answer to all communities. Communities are very different, with different assets and challenges. Oakland is not the same as Detroit or Portland. The best thing that we can do is to share our learning and experiences. We are not attached to the model. It is a simple model and we hope others can adopt it and build upon it. We want to start the conversation about our approach to scaling businesses and talent management as a strategy for the creation of good jobs. This can be a national model, but ICA does not have to be in every city. We actually know that that approach from other organizations has been tried before and has not worked.

SD: *Is there a point of exit in the program or is it open ended?*

JC: There is no exit strategy, yet. We want to keep supporting entrepreneurs as long as they keep being receptive to the advice, keep growing, keep adding jobs and employing from their communities. Whether a business has five or one hundred or 500 employees, here is value ICA can offer, whether it is capital support or talent management.

SD: *If you were to highlight a few key accomplishments of Inner City Advisors' work to date that you are most proud of, what would they be?*

JC: The obvious one for me is that we have a really committed and talented team of staff, board, and advisors that are really in line with the values of not only the entrepreneurs but also the mission of creating good jobs. Everyone is aligned and cares deeply about the mission. I'm proud that we created that team.

I'm also really proud that we really built a network of support for entrepreneurs in the Bay Area. They can tap into Inner City Advisors. Entrepreneurs see us as a valuable piece of that ecosystem. We all have a role in improving our communities and we have empowered entrepreneurs to play a vital role in making our communities better places to live, work and play. So it is not only ICA who is talking about good jobs, but the companies are carrying that message too. And that is what creates a movement.

Rey España

*Rey España has over thirty-eight
years of experience in community
development, including affordable
housing, neighborhood initiatives, small
business development, acquisitions and
turnarounds, workforce employment
and training, community development
financial institution planning, financial
education and individual development
accounts program management, direct
emergency housing and energy assistance
service development, home repair and
weatherization of low income housing,
and education. For the last 10 years,
España has been Director of Community
Development at Portland, Oregon-
based NAYA (Native American Youth
and Family Center), a nonprofit that
has grown over the past decade from
a relatively small nonprofit to an
organization with a nearly $10 million
budget and over one hundred employees
that serves over 6,000 families.*

Interviewed in 2014

Steve Dubb: Could you talk about your background? How did you become involved in community economic development and community wealth building?

Rey España: Well, first of all, I'm just another guy out of East Los Angeles; I spent my early years on a farm and moved with my family into East Los Angeles in 1952. My community development experience probably begins in 1975 in Long Beach, where I directed a nonprofit that primarily focused on social services and workforce development and child development services. Under my direction we moved from youth employment and training to housing rehabilitation. That was my introduction to comprehensive community development— employment and job training. The agency was Latino focused, so we had English as Second Language training, social support for children and their families. That was in the late seventies.

Then I went into the private sector. I had a gym acquaintance that eventually became my employer. He was a typical entrepreneurial businessman. I did a variety of special projects for him for about a five year stretch. He was somewhat of a venture capitalist. He had a number of holdings in steel and ornamental iron manufacturing and I did business acquisition, management, and turnover companies. I set up an import company for him and purchased a gazebo and custom hot tub and deck manufacturing company. It was during this period that I had my first taste of profit-and-loss responsibility and gained valuable insights into private sector and for-profit business practices.

After my private sector experience, I went to work for the City of Santa Monica from 1984 to 1990 in their Community Economic Development department. I served there as the Community Development Block Grant (CDBG) coordinator. I had responsibility for all federal and local dollars for community and neighborhood services and projects, including public service contracts ranging from homeless services, community-based organization supports, and senior services. There was a separate housing unit within the department. I was the overall coordinator of sorts and responsible for federal and local compliance. I did that for almost seven years. Additionally, during that time, I also performed project management on several capital construction public works projects, including a senior service center, a homeless center and shelter for women, and a multi-tenant building that included a community organization support center, two for-profit commercial art galleries. and a food bank operation.

In 1990, I left Southern California and took a job in Multnomah County (Portland, Oregon). I was hired into the Aging Services department. I was hired to be the manager of the County's anti-poverty resources—everything from homeless and emergency housing services, low-income energy assistance to community action programs and CDBG dollars. I was the coordinator of these federal community development dollars and responsible for the implementation of projects. I represented the county and worked with the city of Portland to restructure the homeless singles system of shelter and services.

In 1996, I shifted to special assignments in the County Human Services department and became more involved in planning for aging and disability services and mental health services. I prepared all the Older Americans Act requirement plans and state-mandated plans and contracts. I had an extensive tour of duty from federal projects administrator to the role of coordinating planning for social service delivery in the county.

I resigned my position and left the county in 2003. I had spent nearly thirteen years with the county. I felt I wanted to do something a little bit more hands-on. At first, I worked as an independent contractor for the Latino network, a newly-formed community based organization.

It was prior to leaving the county that I became aware of what was then the Native American Youth Association, or NAYA. I worked with former director Geoff Roth and then Nichole Maher. That's when I became aware of NAYA, the organization. After a year of doing independent contracting with the Latino organization, NAYA had an education position available, so I called Nichole and expressed my interest and she encouraged me to apply. I was hired and have been with NAYA ever since. I'm now ten-and-a-half years in. With my background and experience in general community development—both from a community nonprofit perspective and a city and county perspective—I brought those skills, knowledge and interest to the organization.

At the time of my hire into NAYA, it was primarily a cultural and academic support organization for Native children. They had a very active volunteer recreation and sports program and a pretty active academic support initiative. They had also been involved in some domestic violence intervention work. When I came to the organization, it had less than a $1 million budget. Now we're an organization with 120 (FTE) staff and our budget exceeds $9 million. The needs of the organization when I was first hired indicated interest in certain areas of workforce and housing. I brought in grants and contracts to deliver employment and training services to youth and adults, emergency housing, rent assistance and homeless prevention activities. Moreover, I brought a community economic development and community building perspective of doing community work. Through our education work, we developed a private education facility, the NAYA College Academy, which we operate as an accredited high school with a current enrollment of 86 students. I developed NAYA's capacity in affordable housing. They have acquired a housing portfolio—we became a low-income housing provider and now own 53 units and a new 40-unit project, NAYA Generations, is in the planning cycle. We have established a microenterprise and small business support program. We have established a financial services program and we have launched two social enterprises. We have grown very rapidly.

SD: *What are NAYA's main program areas?*
RE: NAYA has three primary service departments: We have our youth and education services department, our family services department, and my department, which is community development.

    Youth services goes from kindergarten to high school; it involves academic support, such as tutoring, cultural programming, recreation and sports services. Education services also include our high school, the NAYA Early College Academy. Family services are everything from domestic violence and foster care support, to early childhood services and senior services—that all is family services.

    And the third department is community development. My vision for the department is capacity to serve Portland's urban Native community with an integrated comprehensive poverty reduction continuum of support. It includes everything from emergency housing to energy assistance to financial wellness and financial education skill building, including personal finance. It includes household budgeting and credit repair as well. We also are a financial

"The Portland Native community has many challenges reflected in traditional socioeconomic indicators.... But the culture is strong. **Our approach says that communities can overcome their challenges once they become stable**."

fiduciary organization and have individual development accounts for post-secondary education, microenterprise development, and homeownership. We have career skills, job search training, job readiness activities and services for both youth and adults. Our Homeownership program helps individuals prepare to buy homes and become first-time homeowners. We undertake a range of support activities from homeless prevention, to stable tenancy, to support to buy a home. We also have very active microenterprise and small business support program services and social enterprise programs. We also are very active in sustainable economic development planning and neighborhood-focused economic development community initiatives and innovative housing development.

SD: *What are NAYA's main values and principles in its work?*
RE: At NAYA we have a clear mission to work in partnership with the community and promote cultural identity and education. The organization prides itself in incorporating traditional Native values of respect, community, generosity, and kindness. We pride ourselves at NAYA at having that understanding and creating an organization that allows us to work with people wherever they are at. We have a model of service delivery based on an indigenous worldview for all services delivered by agency staff.

The Portland Native community has many challenges reflected in traditional socioeconomic indicators, including having a high poverty rate, poor educational success, high unemployment, high rate of homelessness, poor health indices, high-risk behaviors, substance abuse, and violence. But the culture is strong. Our approach says that communities can overcome their challenges once they become stable. It's about healing themselves, making good choices, having the ability to plan and do the necessary work to take advantage of available resources and build the skills, knowledge, and abilities to improve their life situations.

My experience—I am guided by a vision for social justice, equity, and creating economic opportunity for communities of color. We try to validate that vision daily. It is about planning actions that have a basic understanding and foundation that honors and respects the community's collective and personal assets, talents, and strengths, and provides services in a culturally appropriate manner. We work with staff to have a common vision and approach to service. Ultimately, for NAYA community development, it's about promoting housing, economic, and financial security. Visions, values, and action—that is the approach that has guided my work. This is true specifically with my experience serving the Latino community and for the last—almost eleven—years with the Native community in Portland.

SD: *What led you to work with the Native community in Portland? What would you say are some common challenges among Latinos and Native Americans and what are some unique challenges that Native communities face?*

RE: I grew up in East Los Angeles, California in a Latino or Mexican household. My indigenous side comes from my dad's side. He comes from Yaqui people in northern Mexico. So I have that connection to my indigenous family roots through him. I say that because it is part of my personal family experience and development and support. I grew up with a strong Mexican culture. My folks were bilingual (English-Spanish) and some of our cultural practices were a mixture of Latino and Indigenous/Native cultures.

How I relate to this is that I identify as a Chicano, which is a Mexican-American *and* indigenous worldview. That was my initial orientation that motivated my early social justice work—for the Latino community, but also for other communities of color, I have a rich multi-racial, multi-cultural connectedness from my living and working in Los Angeles, Long Beach, and Orange County. This also includes my working relationship with Southeast Asian refugee "boat people." In short, I've enjoyed the blessing of working and serving a lot of different tribal organizations and communities. I have a sense and perspective that we are all connected. I have a Mexican-American side and an Indigenous side. That's how I approach my community work. While I work with the Native community in Portland, I see and understand the challenges faced by many communities—Native and non-Native. That's my general approach.

There are similar socio-economic challenges. They include educational success or lack thereof, as well as the high poverty rates and high unemployment, criminal justice involvement of youth and adults, and poor healthcare access. Additionally, the lack of an organized political voice is characteristic of a lot of communities of color. My background propels me to give voice to those who struggle.

Additionally, other challenges include poor health indicators, economic indicators, housing instability. We focus on those kinds of challenges, which are shared by many communities.

A unique pressure for the Native community is that Native Americans continue to really struggle with how to maintain their traditional languages and beliefs. There have been lingering effects of federal policy that had been aimed at literally abolishing Native American people, their traditions and cultures. This life experience is all relatively recent history and fosters the broadly held fear and mistrust of government. In Indian Country, there are two distinct experiences, the Native American reservation experience—and the fact that large numbers of Native people have moved off reservation to urban centers. Portland is one urban center with significant Native population—the ninth largest in the country. You have two real different experiences, the urban Indian experience and the reservation experience. Those are some of the challenges.

For Latinos, while there is always pressure for assimilation, it has been relatively easier to retain the Spanish language. Many Spanish speakers have migrated north to the United States from Mexico and other Central and South American countries. The United States is a destination for many Spanish speakers primarily for economic reasons and pursuit of the "American dream." Language retention is stronger. There is a lot more of a challenge to preserve language in indigenous communities.

SD: **What have been some of the key moments in the historical development of NAYA?**

RE: The NAYA story—it was started in 1974 by concerned parents and community members to maintain cultural identity. The focus was on cultural preservation and positive recreation and sports activities. The idea was to try to be positive for the children. That was a significant community organizing effort.

For the next twenty years, NAYA remained an all-volunteer organization. The community members who were actively involved saw trends where young people were facing challenges. In 1994, NAYA incorporated as 501(c)(3) nonprofit to begin to plan a more comprehensive intervention with a focus on young children and youth.

NAYA recognizes violence as a key challenge in the Native community, especially domestic violence and creating support services in that area was a very strategic direction for the agency to undertake. NAYA began to offer domestic violence safety and support services in the late nineties.

A few years later, staff realized that it was not just young people that needed attention—we needed to work with their families. Around 2001, a name change was filed, changing our agency name to Native American Youth and Family Center in recognition of the work with families, beyond working with young people.

Moving beyond providing academic and tutoring support to Native children toward undertaking a more prominent role in participating in the business of education is another significant moment in agency development. NAYA's work in this area moved quickly when I secured a planning grant [2005] to look at the feasibility of starting a small high school. The NAYA Early College Academy opened in the fall of 2007.

So if you think in stages, it started first as a volunteer organization, then incorporated, then added youth programs, then domestic violence support services, then education. After that, we added workforce and housing. In 2009, we started to develop an affordable housing portfolio. In 2010, we moved in the direction of financial services starting with financial education and individual development accounts, and we're currently pursuing development of a Native Community Development Financial Institution (CDFI) for loan making for NAYA's micro enterprise program and other

"In Indian Country, there are two distinct experiences, the Native American reservation experience—and the fact that large numbers of Native people have moved off reservation to urban centers."

community-focused economic development projects. Our current planning priority is sustainable economic development.

SD: *Could you talk about the development of the NAYA Early College Academy? How did that project come about?*

RE: When I joined NAYA, there was interest in becoming more active in education; we were active advocates concerned with the dismal performance of Native children in Portland public schools, but we were not really involved, we were just concerned.

Our first action was a partnership in 2004 with Portland Opportunity Industrialization Center, a local alternative school. We partnered with them and implemented a classroom that was just for Native students. We did that and had some good results. Our partnership continued for nearly two years and gave us a start in that area. At that time, I became aware of an initiative around high school reform. I went to a presentation and found out there was a Native-focused program in Washington, funded by the Gates Foundation, but it was only focused on and within Washington state.

There was some talk about expanding, which they did. I monitored that situation. When it came time to pursue that, I reached out to their administrator at Antioch University, Seattle, who was their program officer. I secured a planning grant. That led to an early college contract, which became the Early College Academy. We had eighteen months to plan. It was during this period that the Northwest Area Foundation made a significant grant award to NAYA to facilitate securing and developing an educational facility.

We had to secure a facility, which I did in northeast Portland.

In the fall of 2007, we welcomed the first class of 32 young people and we've grown to a current enrollment of 90 or so. I was involved in the initial planning grant, site identification, and hired the first principal. We chose the route of setting up a private high school. We wanted to have as much influence over curriculum and resource control as possible. We have been very happy with that approach. We not only have grown enrollment, but we have graduated up to 94 percent of our students and have great attendance, and our outcomes are closing the educational disparity gap in educational success for Native youth. We have received really good recognition in that our approach has been a judged to be a promising practice and it continues to do well.

SD: *Could you talk about the Kah San Chako Haws (East House) project?*

RE: The Kah San Chako Haws project is a nine-unit multifamily, rental housing complex. What is interesting about this project is the construction technology. It is modular construction and has very positive environmental outcomes. It is rated LEED (Leadership in Energy and Environmental Design) Gold. We wanted to demonstrate that that technology could produce a quality housing unit faster and with more energy-efficient performance than traditional stick-built housing. My background in affordable housing comes from my earlier days in Santa Monica. An architect friend of mine, Stuart Emmons, who I worked with in Santa Monica, helped come up with a project that would test these new ideas.

The Kah San Chako Haws project is the first of its kind in the Northwest—three stories, nine units, modular construction. It was a project that went from site preparation to occupancy in seven months. That is 40 to 50 percent of the time necessary for development of traditional housing. We reduced the time it takes to build an affordable unit by more than half. Our cost per unit was approximately five percent less. We think with this type of design—the cost per unit will be within the $130,000 to $150,000 range—has considerable promise. The cost is about $100,000 less than recent traditional construction projects in the Portland area.

We still have a way to go. The idea is to challenge the local housing industry to produce housing faster and cheaper, but with high quality. There is substantial national interest. The U.S. Department of Housing & Urban Development (HUD) published an article about the project. The HUD Native American Program office in Seattle recently toured the project and also seems very interested. So there seems to be interest. I did it through a development team working with local professionals and bringing in the technical people as required. It was truly a public-private partnership.

Our second project, now in planning, is the NAYA Generations project. That project will be the re-purposing of a former public elementary school (approximately three acres)—convert the grounds to 40 units of housing, a Long House cultural and community service center and an early learning center. The 40 units will be inter-generational housing with 10 units for families and 30 units for elders. We're focused on providing housing for Native foster children—we want to celebrate the children exiting the foster system and moving into permanent families. A social service building, the Long House, will provide health, counseling, and employment services and an early learning center which would have 160 to 180 children from birth to age six. NAYA and its partners will create parent interaction programs—Head Start and other child development programs and services. The early learning center is about preparing children for readiness for public education.

SD: *When do you anticipate this project coming on line?*
RE: We just launched our public community planning process. NAYA has site control. I would estimate it is probably two or two-and-a-half years away from completion. Hopefully, by 2016, we will have both the housing and educational learning facility in place.

SD: *What are the market barriers that are keeping these mechanisms from being used more commonly?*
RE: It is the use of a different technology. We decided to take a different approach. It was a learning process. We had a situation where we had a groundbreaking in June, site prep work in August and September, and the actual installation of the modular housing units occurred over three days in October. From the standpoint of neighborhood impact and noise, there were only three days where we had to divert traffic. The next three months we spent finalizing the

work. By January, seven months after we began, the development was completed and final inspections followed. We went from a vacant lot to nine units of housing. No one has done that in Portland. I can't tell you why. There is a well-established affordable housing industry committed to traditional methods and approaches. We tried to challenge local folks to look hard at this approach. There will be local procurement opportunities for housing in early 2014. We wanted to prove the approach was an effective and efficient methodology. It is still too early to tell if Kah San Chako Haws will have any impact on the industry as a whole, but we're optimistic. There just needs to be courageous leadership in place and the funding available to support the initial investment in innovative housing approaches to expand the opportunity for more projects.

SD: *What led NAYA to adopt sustainability as an area of focus? How does NAYA pursue this?*

RE: Sustainability and environmental stewardship have become more central to our work in recent years. I described earlier the development of the NAYA Early College Academy. My early writings on the school envisioned a school that had a direct tie to the land, an ecologically connected school. We need to honor and take care and live in harmony and balance with our environment and surroundings. Active stewardship can play an important role to both teach and learn from.

We want to demonstrate interest in sustainability practice on our site. At the site, we installed a solar panel roof, which has led to a 15 percent reduction in our energy costs. We wanted to and continue to demonstrate sustainability consciousness. We changed the heating system and updated the electrical system to incorporate more green and sustainable practices. This includes solid waste disposal, too. Our current planning includes looking at our property. We are interested in food production on site, so there are urban farm options we will consider and a number of related sustainability initiative activities that we are trying to implement. I went to the NAYA Board, a year and a half ago, and described the type of sustainable development interests that I was looking for opportunities to explore. The Board endorsed and encouraged our interest in sustainability and building practices. It is simply about doing the right thing and being a good steward.

SD: *Nationally, who does NAYA see as its counterparts? Are there other urban Native American organizations that have had similar growth?*

RE: I'm not as familiar with many of the other urban Native community center programs throughout Indian Country. I do know that Little Earth of United Tribes in Minnesota is very similar in some regards to NAYA. We are trying to explore some of the similarities between NAYA and Little Earth in our housing area. There are groups in Seattle and Denver that may be similar to NAYA. There are certainly similarities but at a different scale.

The feedback I get from visitors is that they see NAYA as quite unique. It's common to hear from visitors that they would like to have something like this back home. That can be anywhere in the nation. Something that NAYA has built up over time is our ability and capacity to engage in comprehensive community development.

SD: *Could you describe the Cully neighborhood and the "Living Cully" movement? What is NAYA's role in this coalition?*

RE: NAYA property is in the Cully neighborhood in Northeast Portland. That neighborhood is a very diverse neighborhood in terms of ethnic and racial makeup. It is mostly low income. It is an area of disinvestment, so there is not a lot of economic development or growth that has occurred over time. It has been a neighborhood in transition for a number of years. Other neighborhoods have had more investment that has created pressures and prompted gentrification and involuntary displacement of large number of communities of color and indigenous community members. There is well-documented evidence and experience in Portland where urban renewal investment has destabilized established neighborhoods. Cully has not experienced that yet, but is now drawing attention as one of the last remaining affordable neighborhoods to live, which could lead to pressures for involuntary displacement.

So here in Portland, there has been an effort to maintain and improve neighborhood environmental performance. The local planning initiatives have been eco-districts. They have been linked to urban renewal areas, of which Cully is not, but is adjacent to them. For the last few years, a few community organizations—including

Verde, Hacienda CDC, Habitat for Humanity, and NAYA—have been actively involved in building a collaboration within Cully and to redefine and use environmental and other capital investments as an anti-poverty strategy. The vision is that Cully residents and communities of color should benefit directly from those investments through job training, employment opportunities, enhancement and development of green space.

And we want to do it from a community-driven, engaged process in Cully: we call it the "Living Cully" eco-district. We are not sanctioned by the city as an eco-district, but we decided to call ourselves that anyway. We use green investment as an anti-poverty strategy— where strong community development can take place. We will promote home repair and weatherization improvements to existing homes and small businesses as an anti-displacement activity. We will promote housing development and create homeownership opportunities with Habitat, and do a lot of green space planning to make sure our communities can actively utilize green space. That's the Living Cully eco-district. Some of the work that we have done on community engagement has received some attention from foundations. We are working with and supported by Surdna, Northwest Area Foundation, and PolicyLink. There is a lot of interest in our community-driven approach to revitalization.

SD: *Could you describe the social enterprises that NAYA runs? What have been your successes? What are the key challenges?*

RE: The first social enterprise effort was with catering. It was an activity initially related to our school. We took an existing unlicensed kitchen facility and developed it into a commercial standard operating kitchen that was not just for institutional meals, but would provide us the capacity to establish a catering enterprise and cater special events and meetings, not just with a Native cuisine. We launched the catering enterprise about three years ago. It developed very slowly over time. What we have learned is that we have the capacity to produce, but we learned the importance of marketing and getting our word out and making sales! The challenge is learning how to manage effectively and efficiently labor costs and food purchases. We think there are better ways to be more efficient and get a better margin of return. We're capable, but we need to learn how to be more profitable. We've learned by practical experience. We have much to learn from others in the industry.

The other enterprise we call NAYA Construction. This is a response to the fact that our community was interested in construction work, but they could not get qualified for participation in standard construction apprenticeship programs. What we decided to do is to develop an introduction to the construction trade activity through a workforce training program aimed at on-the-job work experience and knowledge building. We launched NAYA Construction on a very small scale, with a single trainer and crew of four. We have a person on staff that was a general contractor—his license has been transferred to NAYA and he is our principal trainer. NAYA Construction offers a six-month training program. We seemed to have found a niche in our sales—folks that buy our service are interested in supporting the training program. It may take a little longer, but we're competitive on price and deliver quality service. We have experienced marginal success. It pays for itself. NAYA construction does routine maintenance and repairs and turnovers for the 44 units of multifamily housing that we own and does similar services (including landscaping, etc.) for other community development corporations. We have four graduates who have been placed with other contractors. We plan to hire a second trainer and have a crew of eight in 2014.

SD: *How does NAYA go about working with local public officials?*
RE: Here is where my prior history working with the County directly has impacted NAYA. I became involved in local county government in 1990 and had to establish relationships. At the County, I was a liaison to the City of Portland bureau of housing and community development. I was directly involved with the County government elected commissioners and city commissioners as well. Through my personal history, I have brought that approach to building relationships to NAYA and have been able to introduce NAYA to the City, County and Metro regional governments. It has been and is very important to build solid relationships with government staff to advance ideas and get investments in capital processes and to expand services to vulnerable populations. Our education work has also forced us to develop a relationship with the school board—establishing contracts

with Portland Public Schools requires us to build relationships with administrators and the elected school boards.

SD: *Over the past decade, NAYA has had tremendous growth. How has it managed that growth?*

RE: We have seen really rapid growth and endured growing pains. Even in the last five to six years we have tripled the amount of staff. While we have been very successful in capturing service contracts and affordable housing resources and started the NAYA Academy, we knew we needed to develop the necessary administrative infrastructure to manage and support our rapid growth.

We've been fortunate to have Lynn Ward as chief financial officer, who was the budget director of Portland Public Schools for 24 years—she heads the financial and business operation section at NAYA. Having experienced managers with the scope to manage large staff and budgets has helped us develop the infrastructure. Human Resources and personnel management practices—we've had to develop them on the run. We've gone from 25 to 120 staff over the last seven years. That's really rapid growth—the procedures, practices, business operations and management have been pushed to a larger and more complex scale. The complexity of community development work in terms of risk management and liability exposure has required extensive legal staff work. Our success comes with growing pains. We've experienced that.

We are managing pretty well. NAYA, the organization, is blessed. Our budgets continue to grow. Our good work is acknowledged and supported, so we can continue to meet daily challenges of our community. That's the testament to the hard work our organization has done. Of course, we're always trying to advance investment. We will continue to do that. But yes, rapid growth requires staff training, staff development, bringing other expertise in, updating and improving technology, and system development. We've done it all. We have had to.

SD: *Could you discuss the challenges of succession? Not only did NAYA change executive directors eighteen months ago, but you may retire soon. How does NAYA manage this challenge of ensuring institutional continuity even as key personnel change?*

"What we decided to do is to develop an introduction to the construction trade activity **through a workforce training program aimed at on-the-job work experience and knowledge building**."

RE: That's been a topic of discussion for at least two years. Succession planning centers on trying to bring value-added and complementary skill sets into the organization. We feel strongly that we must support the continuity to manage the NAYA way. That's been on our plate the last couple of years. Matt Morton, our new executive director, is transitioning in very well. He brings a different style and approach. Matt is the first Native community member to be elected to Portland Public School Board. In terms of leadership and vision, he is identified as a passionate leader for Portland's Native community, a strong voice on social equity and especially in education for all children. He is a strategic alliance builder with other communities of color leaders. Our CFO, she is not planning to retire, but we have hired a deputy director to build continuity within her department.

For myself, I hope to identify an assistant and work with them to identify my successor over the next few years. My case is different in that I have served the agency as its "seer." I've been recognized by the board and staff as the visionary. It is an honor and privilege to serve and I feel a deep responsibility to secure an effective successor; this pressure is ever present. We are also looking to manage the process as best we can and provide the continuity and organizational support over time—we are not rushing. We are looking for candidates who have the vision and will be here for the long haul as well.

SD: *Are there specific areas where Native American organizations need to focus their efforts to improve capacity and accomplish their goals?*
RE: NAYA as a model continues to define and build its capacity. Part of the practice is working with the broader community. This includes

marketing and telling the NAYA story, educating funders about the challenges and opportunities for positive change. Also, there is a need for strategic alliances with other communities, which allows us to draw attention to the many individuals, not just Native, who suffer from economic disparities. We can work together to all get there together. We can provide leadership and build alliances and community building to advance a broader agenda. NAYA can be instrumental in providing a different voice, a strong voice; it may be also a missing voice.

Training and capacity for advocacy, social media, and marketing: these are skill sets. All of these are areas that an effective organization needs to be aware of and engaged in. And it is not only about the tremendous needs, we need to reframe investment in terms of outcomes that have a broader appeal to investors to bring about the change we want to see. We need investments that not only address the challenges of the most vulnerable of our community but that seize the opportunities to achieve long-term positive outcomes. We want to share our experience. We've made our share of—I won't call them mistakes—but we've learned a lot along the way. We are happy to share that.

SD: *What role can public policy have to better support Native Americans?*

RE: The policy priority at NAYA has not been just one key one. That said, one policy area that has resonated for us is education and educational disparity. For Native children, education reform is critical. Here in Portland, much of the current work is to get children ready to learn. Yet in public school, they become disengaged in disturbing numbers. Native children are not making it through the publicly funded education system and graduating from high school ready for postsecondary education or a career. This fact is not only true for Native children but for other communities of color as well.

Another policy area of concern and focus is child welfare. Native children are overrepresented in the foster care system in high disparity compared to white children. That is another policy area that is both frustrating and challenging. This has a longstanding matter of concern and advocacy. We have tried to address that through recent state contracts. We are just starting to get more relief and cooperation. Through the NAYA Generations project, we hope to spawn a new era of better relationship with State Human Services. Those are the two biggest areas we are involved on.

Another policy area of interest and concern is housing. I sit on the Portland Housing Commission and have raised the concern of equitable access to housing opportunities. Additionally, cultural specificity—housing and homelessness have not been defined from a culturally specific perspective. It can be eye-opening for officials.

The final policy area I would include is economic development. The level of unemployment in the Native community is significant and Native Americans are underrepresented in the small business ownership community. There are significant challenges and opportunities to promote economic security for Native people.

SD: *If you had to highlight a few key accomplishments of NAYA's work to date that you are most proud of, what would they be?*

RE: I am very proud to have brought a community economic development vision to NAYA and have been successful in implementing my vision.

Of course, starting the NAYA Early College High School is a tremendous personal highlight. To see the school established was a personal goal. It touched me personally. Community members have said to me that they never thought it would happen for the community. Recognizing how important the school has been—that has touched me and has been a profound impact. From the response I get from our elders, our young people, and parents, it is clear that the school has been the biggest thing for the NAYA community in its 40 years in Portland.

Coupled with the planning and development of the NAYA Academy was the financial investment of the Northwest Area Foundation in the mission and work of NAYA. A significant grant was made to NAYA to develop the school facility and provide general operating support to launch community economic development programs and services. We leveraged that grant to move NAYA [2006] from a small inadequate facility to our current location where we co-located all staff and programs. Three years later in 2009 we purchased our entire 10-acre campus from Portland Public Schools, ensuring a permanent home for NAYA. Many skeptics thought it would never happen, but in the NAYA way, we continue to demonstrate our ability to deliver on Native community goals and priorities.

I am very proud to have brought affordable housing to NAYA. Having ownership of a small housing portfolio is significant. I am personally very proud of the Kah San Chako Haws (East House) project—and in our ability to form a public-private partnership and get an innovative housing project implemented. I think our work in developing capacity around micro-enterprise is being rewarded by expanding our contracts and getting more capacity. We are expanding our role in individual development accounts (IDAs), and bringing a Native CDFI forward will be very significant as well. I'm very proud of that. Certainly the work we've done on the NAYA Generations project—that I just launched—is a significant accomplishment for NAYA.

The final area that I feel very comfortable with is promoting social equity at the city, county, and regional level. This includes job creation, business development and improving economic opportunities to address economic disparities for Native community and other communities of color community members. I see that very much in the social justice vision. I am very proud of that work.

SD: *Is there anything else that you would like to add?*

RE: I'm very optimistic and hopeful for 2014 to be a year where we move further on economic development and sustainable development for NAYA. I see it as a critical year. I think it will be a good year for NAYA.

Land Banks & Community Land Trusts

In classical economics, scholars ranging from Adam Smith to Karl Marx agreed that there were three major factors of production: land, labor, and capital. While economics often focuses more on labor and capital, it is hard to overstate the importance of land. Land banks and community land trusts are ways to use land to support community wealth building goals. Land banks are typically set up as publicly owned corporations that seek to control and manage vacant properties and put those properties back into productive use in accordance with public priorities. Land trusts, by contrast, are typically nonprofit-owned (with community representation on the board) and seek to hold land in perpetuity in order to promote long-term neighborhood stability. The three interviews here highlight the challenges of this work. Dan Kildee—at the time Treasurer of Genesee County (Flint, Michigan) and now his region's congressman—talks about the need for public agencies to control land, rather than have people "watching infomercials and speculating on tax-lien foreclosures." Boston-based Rosalind Greenstein, who at the time of the interview directed the Lincoln Institute for Land Policy's community land trust program, talks about community land trusts as "a tool that helps you control the community" by taking a portion of land out of the market and thereby creating permanently affordable housing. John Emmeus Davis—who was housing director for then-Mayor Bernie Sanders in Burlington, Vermont in the 1980s, where he helped start what is now the nation's largest community land trust—highlights the importance of using land trusts to achieve "development without displacement."

Rosalind Greenstein

*Rosalind Greenstein is Director of
Research and Education at the American
Institute of Economic Research (AIER).
Before joining AIER, Greenstein was
a Senior Fellow and founding Chair
of the Department of Economic and
Community Development at the Lincoln
Institute of Land Policy in Cambridge,
Massachusetts.*

Interviewed in 2007

***Steve Dubb: Could you begin by describing how the Lincoln Institute
became involved in community land trusts? Why?***

Rosalind Greenstein: Our mission is to disseminate the ideas of Henry
George as discussed in *Progress and Poverty*. So our interest in community land trusts (CLTs) stems from that. CLTs illustrate some of
Henry George's ideas. As a "radical capitalist," George liked competitive markets and private property; at the same time, he was mor-
ally outraged by inequalities in wealth. Like classical economists
he believed that competitive markets were the best institution for
allocating society's resources. However, he understood land to be a
different sort of "commodity" than others traded in the economy.
He did not have a problem with owners of capital making profits
from their own efforts and investments.

He did, however, take issue when landowners made profits simply because demand increased for the scarce resource of land. He
understood that population increases would naturally increase
the demand for land, thus pushing up prices. So, along with his
belief that private landowners ought not to make profits from general population increases, he did not think that landowners should
make profits from government actions (e.g., giving away land or
receiving increased land values with infrastructure investments such
as railroads: George was writing at a time when the U.S. government was giving away huge amounts of land to private interests).

The Lincoln Institute of Land Policy's research and training
focuses on a wide range of land policies and land-related tax policies. We are especially interested in policies that capture the portion
of land value created by public action. The current property tax is
a fiscal instrument for such capture. Impact fees and benefit assessments are other policy instruments available. To the extent that traditional zoning regulations limit property values, they too can be
seen as a mechanism to capture publicly created land values and use
them for public benefit.

CLTs are another mechanism for capturing publicly created land
value for public benefit. When a residential property increases in
price by eight to 10 percent or more per year, it is the increase in
land values, not in the value of the house or the improvements,
which causes the price to rise. In fact, improvements typically
depreciate in value over time. It is this fact of land economics that

makes the CLT a logical and attractive policy to provide homeownership opportunities for households that have been priced out of the homeownership market. When the ownership between the land and house is split and the land is owned by the CLT, the land does not change hands when the house is sold. Therefore, the land value increases are never realized by the CLT. The household, however, receives the benefits of living in the house (what economists call "housing services"); the security of tenure that comes with homeownership; stability and predictability in the monthly housing payments of typical mortgage financing; the equity invested into the house, and in the case of most CLTs, a portion of the land value increase. The community benefits as it receives the long-term stewardship of a stock of perpetually affordable housing.

SD: *What do you see as the main benefits that community land trusts provide? What are the principal benefits in strong market cities? What benefits do community land trust provide in weak market cities?*

RG: If you are thinking of using a community land trust as part of a community development strategy in the broadest sense of the phrase "community development," in a weak market or a place that has lower land values, it's a lot easier to purchase the land—it's more affordable. In hot real estate markets, CLTs have been used to provide homeownership opportunities to those priced out of the traditional homeownership market. Funders—the public sector, private donors, and foundations that see their mission as providing homeownership opportunities for those who have been priced out of the traditional market—see in the CLT a mechanism to use their funds efficiently. Often, homeownership programs allow the first owner to capture the real estate gain when they sell their house. We understand community land trusts as a way to balance these multiple interests.

SD: *What do you see as the appropriate role of "shared equity" housing in affordable housing strategy? Where are community land trusts more appropriate and how should they relate to rental and fee-simple home ownership housing?*

RG: In a report on Shared Equity Housing, my colleague John Davis talks about the "housing ladder."

"CLTs are another mechanism for capturing **publicly created land value for public benefit**."

There are different rungs on the ladder (say from rental, to shared equity arrangements like CLTs and limited-equity co-ops). However, recently I have heard him talk about housing options as a continuum. I think that's helpful. The former implies to me a hierarchy with fee-simple homeownership at the top. However, it's probably more reflective of people's experience to say that at different points in our lives we have different housing needs. I think the continuum reflects that thinking.

I certainly think from a policy perspective it's reasonable to ask, "What is the appropriate role for home ownership within a larger affordable housing strategy?" I don't think that all of our housing needs can be met with CLTs. But I think the idea that CLTs provide one option that can work for some people, and that it's one of many that people can choose from, is fairly sensible.

SD: *Can you add anything more about the community-building impact of land trusts?*

RG: We do know that the community land trust as an organization, when it's functioning at its best, provides services for the households in different ways than many other housing developers or housing programs. These services include pre-purchase workshops, home maintenance information, and, because the CLT has a moral *and* legal interest in the land, they help homeowners who are having problems meeting their mortgage obligations. My guess is that many of the community land trust leaseholders are first-generation homeowners. So CLTs do a lot of training about homeownership, which requires some skills and knowledge and experience. You're not born knowing how to change the filter on your furnace; you've got to learn it—that sort of thing.

CLT staff and volunteers also report that CLTs play a significant role in community building. At the last CLT national conference in Boulder, Colorado [August 2006] there were over 300 participants.

One senses a large and growing community of practitioners. I think the question of the role of CLTs in community-building would be an important research question to explore.

SD: *How much subsidy is required to make community land trusts work? Where does funding typically come from? How does the subsidy level required to make land trusts work compare with other forms of affordable housing?*

RG: The answer, which is annoying, is: it depends. It depends on the market. How much does the land cost? In Cleveland, for example, land is less expensive than in, say, Boulder. So in Cleveland the CLT needs less money to purchase property. So part of it depends on what the market is. Another reason why 'it depends' is that some CLTs find buying older houses and doing rehab on them is a way to increase their stock of housing at a lower cost. In Duluth, Northern community land trust does a significant amount of rehab. They created a construction firm to help them, so they can probably do things a bit more cost-effectively than others.

The income level that you are targeting is another reason why 'it depends.' There are a number of CLTs that have been able to provide housing for households below 75 percent of area median income (AMI). The lower you go, however, the more subsidies you need.

Where does the money come from? Where it *has* come from and where it is *likely* to come from are probably different. For many years, community land trusts were small grassroots organizations with a few units, and maybe no paid staff. A huge amount of passion and commitment and energy, but they didn't produce hundreds of units a year. Now there are a number of land trusts that are of medium size, with a paid executive director and some staff—they are as skilled housing and community development professionals as you're likely to see in any organization. And, there are a couple of CLTs that are fairly large.

There is a new trend, with cities such as Irvine, Chicago, or a number of cities in Florida, where the city government has made an investment in a community land trust. The city of Irvine has committed $250 million over ten years to build 10,000 units of community land trust housing. That's mind-boggling to me. These municipal CLTs look different in their governance structure than the "classic CLT."

I think you're going to see more cities looking at community land trusts for a number of reasons. The Inclusionary Zoning ordinances—the units created by inclusionary zoning—could be stewarded into a land trust. It's my understanding that subsidized units created by inclusionary zoning can "bleed" back into the market. Some municipalities see that an unintended consequence of these programs is that they might offer real estate windfalls to homeowners in the program. To avoid that, the municipality needs to monitor the refinances and re-sales. In this context, some municipalities see the community land trust as a mechanism to provide that perpetual stewardship of the land and the housing. For many municipalities, an investment in a CLT may be a more efficient use of public money.

Another example is in Rochester, Minnesota: The Mayo Clinic was looking at an employer-assisted housing program. Using the Rochester Area Foundation as the vehicle, Mayo put in $7 million and other area employers matched it with $7 million and together they started the First Homes CLT. I think it's an interesting model. Employers—particularly large institutions like hospitals and universities—understand that their role in the city economy is changing. The need for employer-assisted housing may lead these sorts of institutions to think about community land trusts. So, if the question is where can CLTs get their money, I think a CLT can get its money anywhere it can.

SD: *Are there specific ways that public policy could be changed—at either the local, state, or federal level—to better support community land trusts? What changes would you recommend?*

RG: We're doing some research right now about this. One area that strikes us as quite important has to do with the assessing of the properties at the local level. Imagine two houses, side by side. One is fee-simple and one is a community land trust house. The owner of the fee-simple house owns the land, the house, and the "development potential." That is, in many communities the zoning is such that the homeowner can expand the size of the house. In the case of the CLT house, these various property rights are split. That is, the CLT owns the land; the homeowner owns the house. The development potential is owned by the CLT, but they have entered into a contract that says they won't realize that development potential.

Should the CLT house be assessed as if the owner had the option to realize that development potential? I think working that problem out would be quite helpful.

SD: *Often people start thinking about forming a community land trust in an emerging strong market city where rising property values and taxes are disrupting neighborhoods and beginning to push people out of their homes. Are there cases where weak market cities have actually acted ahead of the speculators to develop a community land trust? If so, how did they do it and where did they find the funding to do it?*

RG: The most famous one that comes to mind is Dudley Street Neighbors, in Boston. They've been around for over a decade. That's what they did. The conundrum, of course, is that you don't know in advance that prices are going to go up and it's hard to raise money to get ahead of the curve. How do communities escape this dilemma? They do it with civic leadership and vision. They do it when civic leaders have enough vision and the political will to understand the value and need to do this.

SD: *For a long time, the community land trust movement has shown great promise, but has remained rather small—roughly 6,000 units nationwide. Yet today land trusts have received new interest both from foundations and from public officials in cities such as Irvine, California and Chicago, Illinois. What has caused this shift?*

RG: Maybe people are beginning to understand. Think about the euphemisms we use, such as "affordable housing." In Europe they call it social housing. Each term we use becomes stigmatized and then we come up with a new term. Now it's going to be workforce housing. If you tell people that we need housing for people who don't look like you, they say no. If you say, "We need housing for people who serve you such as fire fighters, police and teachers," then people are willing to say OK.

  To me that leads us to the question of race. While it's difficult to talk about, I think it should be out in the open. I think there are differences of opinion about this. Some people say CLTs are not a good option for people of color because all you are doing is restricting the capacity for wealth accumulation. Some say this is just a modern day version of sharecropping. Others believe that nobody should make real estate windfalls.

Right now I'm taking a pragmatic view. The reality is that access to real estate gains is unevenly distributed and is systematically structured by race and income. That's a brutal fact. What does that mean here? For me the "housing continuum" that we talked about earlier is relevant. The community land trust may turn out to be a preferable option for some people at some points in their lives. I don't think it's a prescription.

SD: **How, then, do you address the challenge race poses?**

RG: I don't know if we even know how to talk about his. Our limited social safety net, how we fund education and retirement, and who has access to these, all mean that if you forgo your opportunity to make real estate gains it's a very big deal. Once you start unraveling this, everything unravels.

My thinking, though, is if you embed the question in how do we have control of our neighborhoods and community, community land trusts might be a tool that helps you control the community. I'm more inclined to see it as part of a community development strategy than the be-all or end-all. Then if you say we want community land trusts to be part of our community stock of affordable housing in perpetuity, and we also support affordable rental housing, and we are also willing to live with people who make real estate profits, then it becomes one of the many options people have. Then it's not that we're restricting this class of people from making real estate gains. Rather, it is that there are things in our community that you get access to—housing services, access to our community, security of tenure, stability of housing payments. You're getting a lot with it, maybe not a windfall at the end, but you're getting other things. And for some, that might be a good option. I think it is important conversation that we need to have.

SD: **It is not uncommon for community development corporations to participate in a development project that might include a mix of market rate and affordable housing, with earnings from market-rate housing subsidizing the affordable units. Are there**

"If you tell people that we need housing for people who don't look like you, **they say no**."

similar examples of land trusts developing some of their land at market rate to cross-subsidize lower-income housing or to finance expansion of the land trust?

RG: I'm thinking of the Madison Area Community Land Trust. They have developed co-housing on land trust land and I think it is mixed income. I think there is a sense that increasingly there will be more of that because of federal funding programs. First Homes in Rochester provides a somewhat different example. Community land trust housing is often scattered site (disbursed throughout a community). In Rochester, the way the community land trust operated there, they worked in a new subdivision and made a deal with the developer. Say, for example, if the developer was putting in 200 units, they might get twenty—that's what lowered the price for them, buying in bulk essentially. So in a subdivision there is community land trust housing right next to market-rate housing.

SD: *What has been the level of the Lincoln Institute's involvement in the formation and development of the National Community Land Trust Network? Beyond the involvement of the Lincoln Institute, what other factors were important in the formation of the National Community Land Trust Network?*

RG: The Network has been in existence for a while now: five or six years. My understanding is that the Institute for Community Economics (ICE) created the Network with the intent that it spin off as an independent network. We were involved with ICE. We had given them funding for two conferences and had done a research roundtable with them. In addition, we were doing some research and developing some training. We were doing that when in 2005 ICE decided they needed to cancel their conference, so Lincoln came in with some funding for that.

SD: *What do you see as the most important challenges or opportunities facing community land trusts today? Where do you think the National Community Land Trust Network will focus its energies over the next five to ten years?*

RG: I see two challenges—or, perhaps they are just two different aspects of one challenge. If you see if it as one challenge, it is about taking something that is on the fringe and making it mainstream.

If you split the issue in two, one part—I don't know if you call it race or diversity—or maybe it's the cultural issue. Whatever you choose to call it, I'm seeing that there is a potential for community land trusts to model a new kind of political behavior and it is a behavior that involves having to balance competing interests, not how you get a win for my side. I think that is the greater opportunity and challenge. It comes up with race—among the Community Land Trust staff, leaseholders and leadership—there are real differences. There's not a unity yet. There's a lot of consciousness about differences of race and cultural background. There's a lot of good will and interest in trying to figure out how these differences coexist. But I guess we're still figuring it out. I guess we don't have lots of good models for it. I would applaud the fact that people are trying to figure this out.

I think the other issue is the future of the new type of community land trusts that are going to be big municipally sponsored organizations. They are going to bring more of a rationalization or a rational approach for CLT housing. That's going to help going to scale and it remains to be seen how the governance is going to play out.

As for the National Community Land Trust Network, they just did a survey of their membership. In the short term, they will focus on capacity building. I think there are some policy issues that it would be sensible to deal with. For instance, there is the secondary mortgage market of buying up CLT mortgages. There have been long-standing discussions with Fannie Mae, but that's not all resolved. On the education front there is a lot of education we can do, particularly informing local officials about CLTs. There are also needs with program evaluation and with trade association services. I think those are all potential areas.

Dan Kildee

*Dan Kildee served as Genesee County
Treasurer from 1997 to 2009. Kildee initiated
the use of Michigan's new tax foreclosure law
as a tool for community development and
neighborhood stabilization. He founded the
Genesee Land Bank—Michigan's first land
bank—and serves as its Chairman and Chief
Executive Officer. In 2007, the Land Bank
received national recognition as one of seven
$100,000 winners for the Innovations in
American Government Awards of the Ash
Institute for Democratic Governance and
Innovation at Harvard University. Kildee
is also President of the Genesee Institute, a
501(c)(3) nonprofit research and training
organization, created in 2004, that provides
planning and technical assistance for other
communities seeking to develop land bank
authorities of their own.*

*In 2012, Dan Kildee was elected to Congress
as the U.S. Representative for Michigan's 5th
district.*

Interviewed in 2009

Steve Dubb: To begin with, could you explain what a land bank is and what functions it serves?

Dan Kildee: A land bank, by our definition anyway, is a public authority of some type that is charged with acquiring, managing, and ultimately repurposing vacant, abandoned, and under-utilized properties. That takes different forms in different communities, but these are public authorities that take care of the worst, most difficult properties in the real estate market.

SD: How was the Land Bank of Genesee County formed? In particular, given the importance of the 1999 Michigan statute that allowed for the formation of the Land Bank, please discuss also the political history of the legislation that has enabled the formation of land banks like yours in the state.

DK: There were two distinct reforms: the 1999 reform changed the tax foreclosure law—eliminating the sale of tax liens (government's right to collect tax) to speculators. Those liens were sold to investors; the investor could collect on the tax at a high rate of tax and foreclosure if it wasn't paid. We eliminated that. That was the main change. That allowed us to control the land rather than have the land controlled by speculators.

I decided we needed something more. We needed more than a rational method of acquisition. We needed a way to dispose of those properties, which could be achieved by creating a land bank authority. We formed our Land Bank in 2002 and, in 2003, we persuaded the [Michigan State] legislature to take our idea and put it into law. We took those two fundamental reforms together and we got a system that creates a lot of potential. It is a very effective way of gaining control of abandoned property and a much more effective way of disposing of abandoned property.

SD: Could you talk a bit about how your land bank is funded?

DK: It is funded in a couple of ways. One source of funds comes from the fees that delinquent taxpayers pay when they actually pay investors. This is the money that previously had been used to attract investors to purchase tax liens. Now we use a portion of the revenue to support the land bank—this year [2009], $2 million. The second primary source comes from the land sales themselves—many of the properties we get can be redeveloped or sold. Rather than enriching speculators, we use that money to fund what the land bank does.

Beyond that, we have created some mechanisms to help finance land bank activity. We developed the Brownfield refinancing act, to make all land bank-held brownfields eligible for financing. We can use tax increment financing (TIF) or other sources to fund remediation. It allows us to cross-finance the cleanup and redevelopment cost across the whole county. The essential value of that is we can use money to clean up vacant neighborhoods where we otherwise would not have the wherewithal—by connecting abandoned neighborhoods to functioning neighborhoods we can do things we otherwise could never do.

SD: *How do you generate political support in the suburbs and rural areas of the County for a countywide land bank given that not all of Genesee County is as poor as Flint?*

DK: That is a difficult part of this job—most people don't think about it. It's tough. I have to use basically every method of persuasion I can come up with. I generally start by using a rational market-based explanation of our work, which makes the point that suburban and rural communities are affected by conditions in the urban center. The value of their property, the quality of their community, is, to one extent or another, affected.

Second is the fairness and equity argument: for 70 years, the city was the economic engine that delivered wealth to the whole region. We imported money by exporting cars, so that wealth that passed through the city was distributed to the entire area. Now that the shoe has passed to the other foot, the region has some responsibility to help its weakest member.

Another thing to note is that we can't sit around waiting for unanimous approval. I don't let an obsession with unanimous support get in the way of progress. I don't let the perfect be the enemy of the good. We get the political support we need to make progress and then move forward.

SD: *Have you had to make any specific compromises to maintain suburban backing?*

DK: Not so many. I wouldn't call it a compromise, in part we just have to ensure that those suburban communities not only see the benefit by cleaning up the city, but also receive some of the direct benefits. In those suburban and rural communities, we will do some demolition and we will do some rehabilitation. It is not that they are not a priority, although they are not as high of a priority. But just because their problems are not as great doesn't mean they should be ignored. They need to understand that there is some direct benefit for them.

SD: *What role has the land bank played in terms of policy advocacy?*

DK: Quite a bit, I would say. Mainly through my participation on behalf of the Institute and the whole effort, we've been able to improve the Land Bank Act. We've amended the Brownfield Act to allow acquisition of property to be a brownfield fund eligible process. I am working on a couple of changes right now to give me authority to assist folks who are really poor avoid losing their property in the first place.

SD: *At the Reclaiming Vacant Properties conference in June 2009, you noted that Flint has lost 45 percent of its population and that General Motors' employment in Flint had fallen over time from 79,000 at its peak to 6,000 today. With GM's bankruptcy, that number may fall further. How has the land bank in Genesee County been affected by the continuing crisis of the auto industry?*

DK: It has certainly made our job harder mainly because there is a lot of economic uncertainty in our community. It means higher foreclosure rates and a weakened demand for property. It does make our job tougher. It's not so much the bad news—we've been dealing with now in our community for 35 years. But it's this uncertainty, this cloud over the future. It makes it very tough—it makes our job a lot harder.

SD: *Even though you are not an auto expert, since you are from Flint, do you have any thoughts on how the U.S. government, now majority owner of General Motors, should exercise its ownership control in the reshaping of that company?*

DK: There are a lot of people in Flint who are not auto experts, which doesn't prevent us from having opinions. My concern is that the company needs to take a longer-term view of things. They've only focused on next quarter's earnings or next year's earnings—they need to think more about how to position the company for the future. Focus on the product. Where I think GM took a wrong turn some number of years ago was of focusing on profit in the short term rather than product in the long term.

By focusing so much on large trucks, much of the profit came from large trucks. That's fine until people don't want them anymore. Where is the GM hybrid? Where was that when Honda came out with theirs and Toyota came out with theirs? It would make them a more sustainable company when the market shifts—so when things change, they don't fold.

SD: *How does Flint view the Shrinking Cities movement? Do residents envision the future as a shrinking city or something else?*

DK: Part of the challenge is that this city has already shrunk. It is not a concept that—gee, these cities should become smaller. It's about us admitting that we are smaller. We've lost half of our population. Our city is designed for twice the population we have and we cannot sustain this. We have a job to do. We have had 30 years of politicians telling us that they can get us back to the good old days. It's just pandering to the public and grotesquely unfair. We need to acknowledge that we are smaller—and then become better. I think we have a long way to go on this subject.

There are some fundamental principles: One, we are not advocating making our city smaller, we just accept the fact that we are smaller; two, the focus should be on the people, what is life like for the people who live in the neighborhoods of Flint—if we keep our focus on that, everything will make more sense; three, we need to focus on market factors—make the point that this is not a socialistic ideological concept, this is a market concept—we have an oversupply of housing. The only way we can adjust to that is to reduce the supply and increase the quality; if we do those things, we'll essentially be following a shrinking cities model; and four, the decision to redesign the city must be inclusive and voluntary—people have to be involved and movement out of sections that will receive less city investment has to be entirely done on a voluntary basis—so residents have a choice to relocate from a blighted to a more vibrant neighborhood, or to remain and live in a greener, lower density part of the city.

"A land bank, by our definition anyway, is a public authority of some type that is charged with **acquiring, managing, and ultimately repurposing vacant, abandoned, and under-utilized properties**."

SD: *What would you say have been the primary achievements of the land bank in Genesee County? How would Flint and Genesee County look different if the land bank did not exist?*

DK: We would have a lot more abandoned houses. That's the most significant immediate benefit. We've been able to demolish 1,000 abandoned houses and wipe them off the landscape. These are properties that diminish the quality of neighborhoods and cost the government a lot of money. Empty, abandoned houses cost more than occupied houses. There is more cost for fire prevention, police protection, and building inspectors. The first effect by tearing down these structures has been to reduce these costs and rid the neighborhoods of blight.

We've also redeveloped some really old buildings that have essentially been forgotten. In the long term, that will have greater value. Restoring old buildings that have architectural value and connect our past to our future is valuable. Those are more intangible benefits, but really significant values we've been able to deliver.

SD: *Could you talk about the evolution of the land bank? What changes have you had to make over time during its seven years of operation?*

DK: We are in a constant state of evolution. We've learned a lot and the conditions have also changed, especially in the last couple of years with the housing crisis. We've had to develop new capacities that we didn't expect to need to have. The most significant is managing rental properties. We have a goal of stabilizing those properties and not just selling those to the first buyer. In order to do that, we have had to develop in-house capacity to be a benevolent, "good guy" landlord. We put the proceeds from the rentals right back into improving the housing. That's been a big part of what we've had to develop as we've grown. Another thing we didn't expect initially is that we would become a developer. We thought the market would soak the properties right up directly. But we've had to become a catalytic developer. We've done several buildings that have spurred other private development. We didn't expect to have to do that, but I'm glad we did.

SD: *Has the land bank been involved with urban agriculture or deconstruction? If not, are these areas you anticipate expanding into in the future?*

DK: There has been some deconstruction—we make our properties available for deconstruction. But first of all, with the kind of property we acquire there has already been a tremendous amount of "informal deconstruction" (stripping). So most of the property that we get is ready for demolition or potentially rehabilitation. There are not as many properties ripe for deconstruction as many people may expect. Another issue: without more attention to the market for deconstruction material, it's going to be hard to bring it to scale. We are very much in favor of it and have worked with Habitat for Humanity and even some for-profit firms.

As for urban agriculture, there is a lot of that. I got up at four o'clock this morning to be in the field with a television crew from a local TV station to get in front of one of our urban agriculture projects—to show that this really does work. Urban agriculture to me is one of those important alternatives. It is intentional use of land that has value but doesn't require a house on top of it to be part of the neighborhood. I imagine a city of Flint that has large and small gardens and even larger scale agriculture scattered across the city. It is beautiful, replaces blight, and helps reshape the city without having to rebuild houses on every lot. Plus it feeds people and provides a source of fresh food. I think this is a very important initiative especially in poor neighborhoods. We're actually doing some exploration on hoop houses (large greenhouse structures) combined with geothermal systems, which once developed could provide a low cost way to extend the growing season by several months.

SD: *Could you talk about the land bank's efforts in the area of brownfield remediation?*

DK: A lot of our sites are contaminated when we get them. We've been able to do a significant amount of environmental cleanup. What distinguishes our effort from most is we can cross-collateralize all of our property, so if the cost of cleanup cannot be covered by federal Environmental Protection Agency (EPA) or state funds, we can essentially borrow or rely on another party—we have a different bottom line than a typical developer. For us, we get paid when we see good things happen. We don't have to make money—we just can't lose money. By using internal subsidy, we are able to take the traditional brownfield tools and add that cross-financing to those tools. It has allowed us to clean up a lot of property that would otherwise sit dirty and abandoned.

SD: *How does the land bank link with community groups like community development corporations (CDCs)?*

DK: We do work with CDCs. We will very often become the land assembly vehicle for a nonprofit. We sometimes will become a partner. It all depends on the nonprofit's capacity. The issue we have here with CDCs is they have historically not been strongly supported. Our role is to bring our substantial capacity in partnership with a CDC to help that organization do more. The relationship can be as simple as supplying marketable land right up to us being a majority partner—we've done everything in between. We have a relationship with Local Initiatives Support Corporation (LISC) to help us create that relationship. LISC helps us in evaluating the capacities of the CDCs to help us determine what role we should play in a potential development project.

I personally thought there would be more capacity, but I think this is a problem across the country—nonprofits have not been sufficiently supported and struggle with issues of capacity.

SD: *How does the land bank involve the public in land use planning?*

DK: Well, we have a few different ways: 1) we hold neighborhood meetings annually; 2) we have a very active citizens advisory committee with 30 to 40 members—they meet monthly and give us very important input, generally meeting the week before the board meeting; and 3) we are very much deferential to local planning and zoning decisions. Land bank properties are subject to local zoning. My own planning staff gets engaged with city and township development staff to work out what we're going to do with property. Right now, we are involved in encouraging and supporting a new Master Plan for the City of Flint.

SD: *Could you talk about the Neighborhood Stabilization Program (NSP) and its 2008 and 2009 variants? What has worked and not worked with the 2008 program? Has the 2009 variant fixed these problems?*

DK: We don't know what has worked yet, because very little has been spent. The 2008 money is just now getting into the field. The 2009 program did correct some of the problems—being more explicit that communities can use money to support the operation of land banks—that's really important to us. NSP 1 (the 2008 allocation) was based on some assumptions about the viability of markets that I don't think are correct. NSP 2 (the 2009 allocation) fixed some of these. There are still some changes that I am pushing for. NSP should really be structured so the money coming in can be used as leverage for public and private sources. It is not so much how NSP is written that is a problem, but the way Housing and Urban Development (HUD) is interpreting it. If HUD becomes overly regulatory in its approach, then the localities will take the shortest path to spend the money and not be creative—not use it as a source of leverage. A good use of NSP would be for subsidies or credit enhancement to help potential purchasers get mortgages. A fund that could be used as a risk pool or provide a credit enhancement to potential buyers. NSP 2 could be a step forward—the grants will be larger, and because they are more competitive, I think they will result in more creativity.

SD: *Even though very little money has been spent on the ground so far, what has been the impact to date of the passage Neighborhood Stabilization Program legislation on land banking?*

DK: It has certainly brought a lot of attention to the concept. It is the first time the federal government has recognized the role of land banks. That's a big open door for those of us who have been advocating urban land reform.

Here's my concern: while that's a big step in the right direction, I want to make sure that the NSP program, whether it relates to land banks or anything else, is a catalyst for fundamental reforms of

"Our city is designed for twice the population we have and we cannot sustain this. **We need to acknowledge that we are smaller—and then become better.**"

---

urban land practices and not just a short-term infusion of capital. That would be a big mistake and a really big lost opportunity.

SD: *Could you talk a bit about the work of the Genesee Institute—how far has the land bank model spread since you formed the Institute five years ago?*

DK: It has certainly grown a lot in Michigan. It started with just us and now we have twenty-one—in virtually every type of market—strong and weak, large and small.

Plus, we're doing a lot of work around the country—Baltimore; Cleveland; Little Rock, Arkansas; New Orleans (helping with post-Katrina); and Palm Bay, Florida (land assembly)—maybe a dozen states. That's all good. The shift the Institute is working on now is to focus on state policy changes. Most of the barriers to addressing abandonment are embedded in antiquated state policy. Over the next year, the Institute will focus its attention in fifteen cities in several states where there is a potential to create land banks and change state policy. That effort is funded by the Ford Foundation through a grant we just got notice for last week. The Institute is the brain and teaching vehicle for this land bank concept that we've developed.

SD: *Do different cities and counties need to adopt different models? If so, what are the types of factors you think that need to be considered in developing land bank authorities in other communities? Are there any particular examples of innovation in other communities that you would like to highlight?*

DK: I think Cuyahoga County (Cleveland) is going to be the next big innovation. It's not so much innovation as replication of our principles, but they're getting it—they are really connecting the economics with land disposition.

Many communities don't see that connection. They want one of these shining land banks, but they don't want to go upstream and deal with the antiquated system of tax foreclosure liens. But Cuyahoga County really "gets it."

Every community needs to adapt it to their own conditions. We've assisted with twenty-one in Michigan and others across the country and no two of them are alike because the markets are different, and the community capacity is different, and the political will to bring this to the public sector varies from one community to the next. We advocate for a very aggressive use of these tools, but not every community is either willing or able to do that.

SD: *A task force you chaired addressing the incoming Secretary of HUD noted the historic success of the community development corporation industry, but cautioned that the foreclosure crisis is "now undermining thirty years of locally sponsored accomplishments and investments." What measures do you advise to stop the undermining of past community development achievements and bring community development back on track?*

DK: Number one, the federal government needs to have a stake in this game and not just put money out on the stump. For the past eight years, the role of the federal government has been to say, "Here's a bunch of money, and don't steal it." And if you do good things with the money, that's great, but we really don't care so much about your plan. So the first thing to do is to put the UD back in HUD.

Second part: the design of the urban form really matters. There has been almost an abdication of the federal government role on that question. They are agnostic on the issue of urban design and sustainability of the urban environment. As we see more federal investment, while there has been some progress made, the current meltdown is erasing even that modest gain.

Let's not make the mistakes of the past. Let's think more carefully—how can we use the federal, state, and local roles, all in concert, to invest in more sustainable communities?

These all sound like platitudes, but these words mean something. We've been so obsessed with growth and expansion that we've undermined our urban areas. I was happy to see [then-HUD Secretary Shaun] Donovan announce that he and others will be working on a sustainable development initiative, including HUD, Transportation, and the Environmental Protection Agency (EPA)—hopefully, the U.S. Treasury and other departments will get involved as well. The goal is to look more holistically, look collectively at investment in transportation and housing—those are really important connections that haven't been made recently.

SD: *At the Reclaiming Vacant Property conference in June 2009, you suggested that the crisis has created "an opportunity to make fundamental changes regarding development, communities, the whole business." Could you outline what the opportunity is and how you think it could be seized?*

DK: The big opportunity is to use the federal money to create fundamental change. This is potentially a big investment by the federal government. It could go a lot further if it is used to create some fundamental change.

The first Neighborhood Stabilization Program (NSP)—the $3.9 billion passed in 2008—delivered to Flint and Genesee County a total of $11 million, which is good, but $11 million doesn't go very far. But if that money was used to create incentives for fundamental reforms of state and local systems of urban development, we could generate a lot more than $11 million.

My land bank concept has generated almost twice that amount of money in the past seven years, just by redesigning the tax foreclosure system. The idea that the infusion of federal capital is going to make a big difference is mistaken if it fails to drive local and state policy changes.

Redesigning these antiquated tax foreclosures systems to get the money out of them and into neighborhoods, instead of the folks watching infomercials and speculating on tax-lien foreclosures, is critical. We need to move the money in this direction.

The simple way to put it is that the redesign of state foreclosure tax systems would create local "NSP machines" right at home—with a lot more flexibility in the money's use, if we think about it that way.

SD: *What is the status of the land banking and vacant property reclamation movement today?*

"Let's not make the mistakes of the past.

Let's think more carefully—how can we use the federal, state, and local roles, all in concert, to invest in more sustainable communities?"

DK: We're sort of at a pivot point. The current crisis has given us a lot more attention. And it is up to us to switch gears a bit. Even for National Vacant Properties Coalition (NVPC)—we have to go from being a campaign to actually being a movement. The campaign is over—we won. People are now paying attention. We need to step up and really function in the way we should. The growing body of knowledge of how to rebuild cities has to become a discipline, not just a campaign. It's going to be hard, but we have to do it.

SD: *Is there anything else that you would like to add?*

DK: The most important point that I keep making over and over again is that these seemingly sleepy systems of local government really do matter. We cannot just pat ourselves on the back for having good intentions. Sometimes inadvertently in the name of trying to improve things we can make things worse. We need to take a close look at how we do business.

John Emmeus Davis

*John Emmeus Davis has been involved in the
development of community land trusts since
the early 1980s. He was one of the founding
partners in Burlington Associates in Community
Development in 1993, a consulting cooperative
providing assistance to nonprofit organizations
and municipal governments in designing and
evaluating policies, programs, and projects
promoting permanently affordable housing. He
previously served as the housing director and
Enterprise Community coordinator for the City of
Burlington, Vermont.*

*He has also worked as a community organizer and
nonprofit executive director in the Appalachian
region of East Tennessee. He is on the faculty
and board of the National CLT Academy and
currently serves as the Academy's dean. He is the
author of many books, articles, and training
manuals focused on community land trusts and
other forms of resale-restricted, owner-occupied
housing. In 2010, he edited* The Community
Land Trust Reader, *published by the Lincoln
Institute of Land Policy.*

Interviewed in 2011

Steve Dubb: How did you become involved with community land trusts (CLTs)?

John Emmeus Davis: I was a graduate student at Cornell. My studies were focused on community development and city and regional planning. I had come to graduate school as an older student. I had been out of school for six years working as a community organizer in East Tennessee. Living in Appalachia, I had become sensitive to what happened when communities did not control the land, since most of it was absentee-owned, with coal companies and timber companies controlling most of the landed resources. By the time I got to Cornell, therefore, I already had an interest in the connection between land tenure and community development. Or, as Appalachia demonstrated, the connection between the lack of local control over land and the lack of local development.

While I was in planning school, I had a U.S. Housing and Urban Development (HUD) internship, which allowed me to work at a housing services organization that was rehabilitating dilapidated housing and promoting homeownership in a lower-income, African American neighborhood on the edge of downtown. I watched this nonprofit organization transform a disinvested neighborhood. By every measure, this was a community development success—improving the quality of the buildings, lowering the crime rate, increasing private investment. But another part of this transformation was less successful, for we also helped to gentrify the neighborhood and to displace people who had lived in that neighborhood for a long time.

I tied that experience in an urban neighborhood to my work in rural Appalachia and said to myself, there has to be a better way to do community development. I began looking for alternative models of land and housing tenure that might promote development without displacement. At Cornell, they organize the graduate school by fields, not by departments. I was in Development Sociology, a field that straddles the boundaries among sociology, planning, economic development, and political science. The chair of my doctoral committee was a professor named Chuck Geisler. He is a sociologist with a special interest in land use planning and community development. Chuck Geisler introduced me to Chuck Matthei, the former executive director of the Institute for Community Economics (ICE). That is how I was exposed to the community land trust as a possible solution to the problems of land tenure I was wrestling with.

After I finished my doctoral work, I went to work for ICE. I was ICE's field representative in Cincinnati and ended up writing my dissertation on the history and transformation of the African-American neighborhood in the West End of Cincinnati. That became the basis for my first book, *Contested Ground*, which examined gentrification, disinvestment, reinvestment, and grassroots efforts to gain community control of land and housing in an African American neighborhood.

SD: *What do you see as the main benefits that community land trusts provide? What are the principal benefits in strong market cities? What benefits do community land trusts provide in weak market cities?*

JED: For years people believed the principal benefit of CLTs was to preserve affordability in hot markets. The model had proven its effectiveness in locking public investment into affordable housing, commercial space, or office space in any area where public monies were being invested to create affordable housing or to create jobs. If you invest public money, the problem is: How do you preserve the affordability of the housing you've subsidized? Or, how do you maintain affordable access to commercial space? The answer provided by the CLT is that you lock those subsidies in place. In a hot market, there are always pressures to remove affordability and to privatize the public's investment. CLTs keep that from happening. They prevent the loss of affordability when real estate markets are hot.

Since the bust of the housing market in 2006, however, we have also discovered that community land trusts and other forms of shared equity homeownership are equally effective in cold markets. The principal benefits of the CLT in cold markets are to protect the condition, the quality, and the upkeep of the buildings on the leased land and to intervene in cases of mortgage delinquency to protect security of tenure and prevent foreclosure.

The shorthand phrase that we sometimes use in the community land trust movement is "countercyclical stewardship"—providing special protection during those turbulent times in the business cycle when homes and homeowners are at greatest risk. Most housing and community development programs in the United States have been designed as if there is no business cycle. What community land trusts are particularly good at is preventing the loss of homes, homeowners, and public investment at both the top and the bottom of the business cycle. We run counter to the threats and dangers that a fluctuating economy imposes on low- and moderate-income people.

SD: *A term that you have helped popularize to describe how land trusts work is "shared equity homeownership." What is meant by the term and how does this form of housing affect the average homebuyer?*

JED: Shared equity homeownership was a term that was coined in 2006 as part of a research project sponsored by the National Housing Institute. This project was mounted to examine the prevalence and performance of various forms of resale-restricted, owner-occupied housing—the principal examples being community land trusts, deed-restricted houses and condos, and limited equity cooperatives. The advisory committee that NHI pulled together to oversee this project wanted a generic term that would describe these models and mechanisms of resale-restricted, owner-occupied housing as a single sector, where organizational and operational features that are common to all of these alternative forms of homeownership are more important than those features that distinguish one model from the other.

Our working definition has evolved somewhat since 2006, the year that the NHI published the results of its research in a book-length manual entitled *Shared Equity Homeownership*. There is more of an emphasis today on how these models perform, especially in the period after a home is sold, as opposed to an earlier focus on how these models are structured. My own definition, recently put forward in an article published in the *ABA Journal of Affordable Housing and Community Development Law*, is that shared equity homeownership is "a generic term for various forms of resale-restricted, owner-occupied housing in which the rights, responsibilities, risks, and rewards of ownership are shared between an income-eligible household who buys the home for a below-market price and an organizational steward who protects the affordability, quality, and security of that home long after it is purchased."

The sharing of equity, therefore, is more than merely sharing the backend proceeds on the resale of the home. You are also sharing many of the sticks in the bundle of rights. In a conventional market-rate home, a single owner holds all (or nearly all) of the rights, responsibilities, risks and rewards. In a shared-equity home, we untie that bundle and reallocate those sticks between the individual homeowner and an organization that stays in that picture for many years. In the case of the community land trust, that organizational steward is a nonprofit corporation with a community membership and popularly elected board. Some of the responsibilities and many of the risks of homeownership are carried by the community land trust rather than by the homeowner alone.

SD: **In terms of dividing up the back-end proceeds, however, how does this work?**

JED: In every case, there is a ceiling as to how much equity a CLT homeowner can remove at resale. This allows the community land trust to repurchase the home at a below-market price. The CLT then turns around and resells that same home for a price that another low-income or moderate-income family can afford. CLTs across the country use many different resale formulas to set that ceiling and to determine how much equity a homeowner will earn when moving out of her CLT home. At a minimum, under most formulas, the homeowner is going to get back her down payment, the amortized portion of her mortgage, and a credit for any capital improvements she made after purchasing the home—plus a return on her original investment, which can be a little or a lot, depending on the formula.

In Burlington, Vermont, where I live, the Champlain Housing Trust (CHT) uses a resale formula where homeowners get back their down payment and whatever principle they have paid down on their mortgage. They receive a credit for any capital improvements they may have made and they earn 25 percent of any appreciation that has occurred in their home between the time of purchase and the time of resale. On average, after five-and-a-half years, a homeowner is going to resell a CHT home and walk away with an additional $12,000 to $15,000, beyond the down payment she originally brought to the deal—at least that is what has happened in Burlington over the past 27 years.

If you look at buying a CHT home purely as an investment vehicle, we can say for sure that it is a better investment than putting your money in a savings account or even in the stock market. In

Burlington, the 233 homeowners who have resold a CHT home have realized, on average, a 31 percent annualized Internal Rate of Return (IRR), according to a recent study by the Urban Institute, entitled *Balancing Affordability and Opportunity.* That same study found an IRR of 39 percent at a CLT program in Duluth, Minnesota and an IRR of 22 percent at a CLT program in Boulder, Colorado.

As a straight financial investment, therefore, buying a CLT home is a pretty good deal. It is not as good a deal, of course, as you could get if you have the wherewithal to buy a market-rate home without the restrictions—and you happen to be in a strong real estate market. A CLT home is a tenure option in between being a renter, where you get no return, and a market-rate home where you get all of the windfall that a rising market might award.

SD: *One of the roles you have played in the community land trust movement is that of an informal historian. For those not familiar with the origins of the CLT, can you highlight some of the key forces behind the movement's emergence?*

JED: The roots of the movement are old and deep, even though the modern-day model is relatively new. The first community land trust in the United States, New Communities Inc., was created in 1969. The roots of the model go back much further, however. The way that community land trusts treat ownership, with one party owning the land and another party owning the structural improvements on the land, is an approach to land tenure that is rooted in the Garden Cities of England, the agricultural co-ops in Israel (*kibbutzim, moshavim*) that are located on land leased from the Jewish National Fund, and the Gramdan Movement in India. All are examples of planned residential and commercial communities on leased land.

The roots of the community land trust's commitment to being an open membership organization, with a governing board on which many interests are represented, are to be found in the American civil rights movement. The leaders of the first community land trust all came out of the civil rights movement. Slater King, a first cousin of Martin Luther King, was president of the Albany Movement. He also became the first president of New Communities, Inc. When he was tragically killed in an automobile accident, the presidency of New Communities passed to Charles Sherrod. Rev. Sherrod had been a field organizer for SNCC (Student Nonviolent Coordinating Committee) and later founded the Southwest Georgia Project.

Another important piece of the history of the first CLT was the connection to Koinonia Farms, located just outside of Albany, Georgia. At the height of the civil rights movement, this community was an oasis of racial harmony, where you had whites and blacks running a cooperative farm that was under attack by the KKK. They had a hard time buying farm equipment or selling their agricultural products to local businesses. Slater King and Charles Sherrod were certainly aware and supportive of the work going on at Koinonia. Bob Swann, someone else involved in the creation of New Communities and a man who went on to become one of the founders of the community land trust movement, was the chair of Friends of Koinonia, a national organization that helped to raise money for the farm and to sell its pecans and other agricultural products. Swann was also on hand when Clarence Jordan and Millard Fuller began laying the foundation for Habitat for Humanity. Indeed, it is fair to point to Koinonia Farms as a seedbed for both the community land trust movement and Habitat for Humanity.

SD: *Can you talk about the impact of community land trusts on foreclosure rates?*

JED: The National Community Land Trust Network has been closely watching and measuring foreclosures over the last few years. The Network now has very solid research, documenting a delinquency rate and foreclosure rate among the owners of community land trust homes that is miniscule; indeed, the foreclosure rate among CLT homeowners is many times lower than the national foreclosure rate reported by the Mortgage Bankers Association (MBA) for market-rate homes. In the Network's latest survey, CLTs across the country reported a foreclosure rate of only 0.56 percent at the end of 2009. This compared to foreclosure rates reported by the MBA of 3.31 percent among homeowners holding prime mortgages and 15.58 percent among homeowners holding subprime mortgages. What makes the superior performance documented by the National CLT Network even more impressive is that CLTs are serving households who are much poorer than most of the mortgage holders in the MBA's foreclosure study.

In Burlington, the community land trust here has boosted nearly 650 low-income households into homeownership over the past 27 years, while having only nine foreclosures. And the Champlain Housing Trust has never lost any lands or homes because of a foreclosure. Even in those nine cases where the land trust was unable to prevent foreclosure, CHT was able to protect the assets and to keep both the land and the homes in its portfolio. That's a pattern of success repeated by CLTs throughout the country.

SD: *Why are community land trust foreclosure rates lower?*

JED: It begins before we ever sell the home. We do a lot of preparation and education with prospective homebuyers so that people only buy homes they can afford. The community land trust also imposes a screen on prospective mortgages to prevent predatory lending and to prevent people from entering into financial arrangements that put them in risk. Community land trusts also build three important rights into the mortgages on CLT homes. First, the community land trust wants to be notified if there is a mortgage delinquency. Second, the community land trust wants the right to step into a default situation and to cure the default on the homeowner's behalf if the homeowner cannot do so herself. Third, if despite this intervention, the community land trust is unable to prevent foreclosure, the community land trust wants the first right to buy the home out of foreclosure, making the lender whole while preventing the loss of the land and the home from the CLT's portfolio. Finally, most community land trusts, after they sell a home, maintain a continuing relationship with the homeowner. We don't just sell a home, take the homeowner's picture, shake the homeowner's hand, and say good luck. In the worlds of Connie Chavez, executive director of the Sawmill Community Land Trust in Albuquerque, "we are the developer that doesn't go away."

Because the community land trust does not go away, while also maintaining a relationship with its homeowners and reserving a third of the seats on its governing board for people who live on its land, homeowners are more likely to notify the CLT when they get in trouble. They don't hide it. They come to us, so we know if they are getting behind in their finances. Then too, CLTs charge a lease fee for the use of their land. Typically, the first thing a homeowner

"If you look at buying a CHT home purely as an investment vehicle, **we can say for sure that it is a better investment than putting your money in a savings account or even in the stock market**."

does who is in financial trouble is to stop paying the CLT's lease fee. We have a built-in early warning system that tells us when a homeowner is in distress. That allows a CLT to work with homeowners before they get more deeply in debt, more seriously behind in their payments. That allows a CLT to intervene at an early stage to ensure that short-term trouble doesn't lead to foreclosure. Put all of that together and that's why I believe CLTs have much lower foreclosure rates than are experienced by borrowers in the regular homeownership market.

SD: *You've been with Burlington Associates since 1993, during which time you and your partners have assisted more than one hundred community land trusts nationwide. What trends have you seen in the CLT movement?*

JED: The first trend is steep growth. There were only a dozen or so community land trusts in the early 1980s; today, there are over 240. The proliferation of community land trusts is quite striking, along with their dispersion across the United States. We now have CLTs in forty-five states and the District of Columbia. There are also community land trusts in Puerto Rico. So the first trend that I've seen is growth: more CLTs, scattered more widely across the landscape, along with an increasing number of CLTs with a substantial portfolio of lands and buildings under their stewardship.

Second, community land trusts are diversifying their lines of business. In the early days, most CLTs concentrated on housing, focusing on owner-occupied housing in particular. Now community land trusts are developing and stewarding many different types and tenures of housing—including limited equity cooperatives, condominiums, rental housing, mobile home parks, single room occupancies (SROs), and homeless shelters. Also, some community land trusts are doing much more than housing—or doing no housing at all. There are CLTs that focus on urban agriculture, neighborhood parks, transit oriented development, job creation, office space, or service facilities for inner-city neighborhoods. They are also diversifying their strategic partnerships, working more closely than ever before with community development corporations, churches, NeighborWorks organizations, Habitat for Humanity affiliates, and both urban gardeners and rural conservationists.

A third trend is regionalization. Thirty years ago—even twenty years ago—almost all community land trusts worked in a single neighborhood or in a single small town. Today, we have community land trusts that span multiple neighborhoods, an entire city, or an entire county or metropolitan region. In a couple of smaller states, such as Delaware and Rhode Island, we have CLTs that span the entire state. We are seeing a trend, therefore, of CLTs that are carving out much larger service areas than occurred in the movement's earlier years.

Another trend that we are seeing might be described as municipalization. There are an increasing number of community land trusts that were initiated by or supported by city or county governments. Twenty or thirty years ago, almost every CLT was created as a grassroots, bottom-up organization that emerged out of local struggles to promote development, to prevent gentrification, to prevent displacement, to empower a low-income neighborhood. There are still a number of community land trusts that get started like that today. But there are an increasing number of CLTs where the local government has helped to plan it, to create it. If you look at new community land trusts today, many have a municipal connection.

SD: *One trend that you have highlighted is the growing role of city governments in supporting the development of community land trusts? Why is there that interest and how are they working out?*

JED: City and county governments have become interested in community land trusts, first and foremost, because municipalities are putting ever-higher per-unit subsidies into helping lower-income people to become homeowners. Prudent public officials don't want to see those subsidies lost in a time of fiscal scarcity. Whether a city's politics tilt toward left or right, there is a desire to make sure that any public investment stays in a project and is not lost. The principal interest in CLTs on the part of cities and counties has come from a newfound concern for subsidy retention—a priority for locking the public's investment in place.

Second, there is interest from municipal officials in making sure that affordable homes produced as a result of inclusionary zoning, incentive zoning, and similar programs are not lost. When government gives a developer a regulatory concession or requires the provision of affordable housing as a condition of zoning approval, cities want to see that those housing units remain affordable for longer than five, ten, or twenty years. Community land trusts are an effective way to do that, whether the housing is rental or ownership.

Recently, a growing municipal interest in transit-oriented development (TOD) has drawn a whole new set of public officials to the community land trust model. If you are truly interested in preserving a mix of uses and a mix of incomes in a redevelopment area surrounding a new transit stop, the only way to accomplish that is to have some sort of long-term controls on the land and the buildings. Otherwise, in a very short time, only the highest uses and highest incomes will come to dominate that area, displacing everything else. Community land trusts are a perfect complement to TOD—a vehicle for perpetuating a social equity commitment alongside a sizable public investment in light rail, smart growth, public parks, and other infrastructure.

SD: *Are the city-sponsored land trusts working? Do we have enough data yet to know?*

JED: We have a lot of information about CLTs in small and mid-sized cities. There, we have a track record of success and sustainability. Some of the efforts in larger cities are either too new or untested to say for sure. Chicago, Irvine (California), Atlanta, Sarasota (Florida)—are all examples of cities that are putting significant resources into creating community land trusts—it is just too early to say what their long-term success is going to be. The scale is so different. In Chicago, if you add 200 units of permanently affordable housing you have far less effect than in a smaller city like

"The leaders of the first community land trust all came out of the civil rights movement. Slater King, a first cousin of Martin Luther King, was president of the Albany Movement. He also became the first president of New Communities, Inc."

Duluth, Minnesota. So it is just hard to measure the impact and success as yet.

The most interesting case that is unfolding right now is in Atlanta, where the largest urban redevelopment project in the United States is underway. The Atlanta Beltline made a commitment from its early days to prevent displacement as part of this massive TOD. The Beltline Partnership, under the leadership of a dynamic, socially conscious woman named Valarie Wilson, has played a starring role in supporting the development of a "central server," the Atlanta Land Trust Collaborative, that will seed and support the development of a number of neighborhood-based community land trusts along the 22-mile light-rail corridor of the Beltline. The Collaborative and local CLTs are being put in place to ensure that low-income and moderate-income residents get to share in the benefits of the city's investment in TOD and don't suffer the burdens of displacement. It is too soon to say how it will pan out, but it is noteworthy and very impressive that people in Atlanta have planned for success. They have tried to anticipate the negative externalities and social inequities that often result from a massive public investment in "urban renewal." They have built social equity into their planning from day one.

SD: *Can you talk a bit about efforts in New Orleans to create local networks of interlinked community land trusts?*

JED: There is a dual effort in New Orleans. In the Lower Ninth Ward, there is a focus on using a CLT to do housing, where an existing organization, the Neighborhood Empowerment Network Association (NENA), is sponsoring a land trust program. There is also a citywide effort, the Crescent City Community Land Trust, which was set up to support NENA but also to support community land trusts in neighborhoods across New Orleans. The Crescent City CLT has a focus not only on the production and preservation of affordable housing, but also on the redevelopment of commercial corridors and commercial districts in less affluent neighborhoods.

SD: ***Can you describe the effort in Cleveland, Ohio to develop cooperatives on community land trust property?***

JED: We shouldn't forget that there are two CLT efforts in Cleveland. The Community Land Trust of Greater Cleveland, formerly the Cuyahoga CLT, has been around for ten years, developing and stewarding resale-restricted, owner-occupied housing. A second CLT effort has arisen more recently in conjunction with comprehensive planning for redevelopment of Greater University Circle. In the latter case, the decision has been made to create a community land trust as a subsidiary corporation that is nested within the Evergreen Cooperative Corporation. The CLT is not going to be a freestanding, autonomous corporation.

I think this idea of nesting a community land trust within a cooperative structure holds potential for being replicated in other places. The three elements in Cleveland that I find most interesting and innovative are: 1) the CLT's integration into a cluster of cooperative enterprises, 2) the CLT's connection to the Greater University Circle redevelopment planning, and 3) the CLT's emphasis on job creation and workforce issues as its first priority. It may branch out into housing down the road, but the Evergreen CLT's initial focus will be on assembling and holding land for enterprises that are cooperatively owned and managed, enterprises that create jobs for residents of a low-income neighborhood. I think that is going to push the boundaries of the CLT and provide new models and best practices that will be replicable and inspiring for community land trusts across the country. That's a pretty amazing trio: a community land trust in a nested structure of cooperatives, tied explicitly to a very large urban redevelopment plan, focused on job creation. Those are leading-edge innovations that community land trusts around the country can learn from, so I am pretty excited about that.

SD: *There has been a growing movement in recent years for cities and counties to create land banks to publicly plan for the productive reuse of vacant land. How do community land trusts relate to these publicly owned entities?*

JED: There are some things that municipal land banks do very well: acquiring abandoned properties, contaminated land, and derelict buildings; clearing title; remediating toxins in the soil; demolishing derelict buildings; and getting those sites ready for redevelopment. What they do less well is maintaining accountability for residents of the local neighborhoods in which they are acquiring land; figuring out what should happen to the land after title has been cleared and problems have been mitigated; and preserving the affordability, condition, and security of housing and other buildings that are erected on remediated lands after they leave the land bank. These latter activities are what a CLT does especially well. There would seem to be the potential here for a partnership, where the public land bank acquires, holds, and improves land and then conveys that land to a community land trust, with the latter serving as the long-term steward of the land and any buildings that are constructed on the land.

Our record in the United States with urban renewal agencies, redevelopment authorities, and public land banks is not very good when it comes to the question of what happens to land after it leaves the land banks' inventory. Most land banks are designed to hold land for no more than five years and to put that land back onto the market. In most land banks, that land is sold at the highest price; therefore much of that land is lost for affordable housing, community enterprises, and equitable development. To build both accountability and long-term stewardship into the system, a land bank is not enough.

What is happening in Atlanta is an evolving partnership between the City of Atlanta-Fulton County Land Bank and the Atlanta Land Trust Collaborative. I know in Cleveland there have been discussions of something similar being negotiated there for the Evergreen CLT, but I don't think that conversation is as far along as it is in Atlanta.

SD: *How much subsidy is required to make community land trusts work on a sustainable basis?*

JED: You have to distinguish between outside support for stewardship and outside support for development. Community land trusts set a goal for themselves of building a portfolio of sufficient size to generate internally enough revenue to cover the cost of stewardship—that is, to pay for their staff and to cover their operating costs of overseeing the affordability, condition, and security of the buildings on land trust land. Until a community land trust reaches the point of having built that sizable portfolio, they are entirely dependent on public and private subsidies to help pay their operating costs. Even when a larger community land trust with a 100-unit, 200-unit, or 300-unit portfolio is able to cover the cost of stewardship, however, it will never reach a point where it can build a surplus sufficient to develop its next project. CLTs will always be dependent on public equity and private contributions to bring land into their portfolios and to bring the price of housing down to a price that low- and moderate-income people can afford. So there is the potential for sustainability and self-sufficiency on the stewardship side, but this is impossible on the development side.

There is nothing about the community land trust that makes it any less expensive for a CLT to assemble land and to develop affordable housing than for anyone else. Land costs what it costs and a two-by-four for construction costs what it costs. And low-income people are always going to be too poor to buy a home without a lot of help. That is the way the world works. If low- and moderate-income people could become homeowners without public assistance, there would be no need for publicly funded homeownership assistance programs. At the start of the Great Depression the homeownership rate in the United States was 45 percent. Without the intervention of government, our homeownership rate would still be 45 percent, instead of being close to 67 percent.

There is no such thing as "affordable" housing. There is only subsidized housing, where public dollars, public powers, or public tax expenditures have helped to bring an expensive commodity into the reach of people priced out of the marketplace. That's true if you're a middle-class person taking advantage of low-interest loans from a state housing finance agency and tax policy favoring homeowners or a low-income household getting rental assistance. There is subsidized housing for three quarters of the population. It is just that some public subsidies are more obvious and politically vulnerable than others.

The largest public subsidy we have in the United States is the deductibility of mortgage interest. That is a $130 billion-a-year federal subsidy for homeowners, most of which is pocketed by the wealthiest homeowners, dwarfing the total amount of money that HUD (U.S. Department of Housing and Urban Development) distributes every year for all other affordable housing and community development programs combined.

SD: *Are there specific ways that public policy could be changed—at either the local, state, or federal level—to better support community land trusts? What changes would you recommend?*

JED: A lot of the money that community land trusts have depended on for their growth comes from federal programs, such as Community Development Block Grants (CDBG), Home Investment Partnerships Program (HOME), Neighborhood Stabilization Program (NSP), weatherization programs, and the secondary market—Fannie Mae and Freddie Mac. All of those programs are presently on the GOP's chopping block.

What do community land trusts need? They need the public funding they have relied on to grow and survive. There is nothing magical about community land trusts. They need equity if they are to provide affordable housing and community facilities for persons too poor to do it for themselves. CLTs can get debt on the private market. But the equity comes primarily from the public sector. Once we bring land and homes into our portfolios, we don't need as many additional subsidies down the road. But you have to get the property into the system in the first place. The big need is equity.

The second concern right now for community land trusts or for any affordable housing developer is affordable mortgages with underwriting criteria that don't preclude you from serving the low-income homebuyers you are trying to serve. With the bursting of the housing bubble, lenders have tightened up on their underwriting and made it harder for our people to get loans—even though we have evidence that our homebuyers seldom default; and when they do, we are there to back them up and prevent foreclosure. Nevertheless, CLTs are still looking at constrained lending through state housing finance agencies and bank consolidations. Many lenders who have lent to community land trusts in the past have merged with larger banks that don't know as much about the model.

The third area we are going to have to tackle is local property taxes, so that taxes align with the resale-restricted value of the home. It is difficult to go into much detail here, because it is a problem that is such a patchwork quilt, differing state-by-state and city-by-city.

A fourth problem area for us is the Federal Housing Administration (FHA). The community land trust movement has been negotiating with FHA through five presidential administrations, trying to get some changes to FHA rules to make it easier for lenders to use FHA insurance and products for financing resale-restricted CLT homes. We're still trying to get these changes, although I think we're close to cracking the nut at long last. I think this administration is finally going to change the FHA program to make it easier to get FHA loans for resale-restricted homes, removing a major barrier that has been plaguing CLTs for many years.

SD: *Can you talk about the role played by the National Community Land Trust Network in expanding the movement?*

JED: Well, the National Community Land Trust Network functions as something of a trade association for CLTs in the United States. It is a membership organization that is governed by the CLTs themselves. It is designed to provide advocacy and support, technical assistance, and training for its members. The Network has taken the lead in negotiating with HUD and FHA, seeking to amend the latter's rules. The Network has also helped to build the CLT movement by forging strategic alliances with other national intermediaries like NeighborWorks America, Habitat for Humanity International, and the Cornerstone Partnership.

One of the Network's oldest and largest programs is the CLT Academy. The Academy is a chartered program under the Network's umbrella with a semi-autonomous status and its own board. The Academy is the Network's training and research arm. It has two departments—one that focuses on developing courses, seminars, trainings, and webinars to raise the standard of practice throughout the field and another department that focuses on research and publications. The latter department oversees the annual foreclosure study

"There is no such thing as 'affordable' housing. There is only subsidized housing, where public dollars, public powers, or public tax expenditures have helped to bring an expensive commodity into the reach of people priced out of the marketplace."

and has recently produced a new technical manual and model ground lease. It is also involved in collecting best practices, evaluating what works well and what doesn't work so well in the world of CLTs. Those "best practices" are then thrown over the fence to the curriculum department, eventually becoming the content for future trainings.

SD: *What do you see as the most important challenges or opportunities facing community land trusts today as the movement expands and becomes more diverse?*

JED: A strength of the CLT model is its versatility in the ways that CLTs are structured, operated, and applied. But a model that plastic and that malleable runs the risk of becoming all things to all people. There is a temptation to lop off key elements of the model that you find politically messy. There is a risk of diluting the model's core values to the point where it may no longer be fair to call it a community land trust at all. There is strength in versatility, but there is always the risk of dilution: you modify or remove so many essential features and values that the pieces no longer fit together to achieve the social justice and economic development aims that you set out to achieve.

There has always been a tension in the evolution of this model. You don't want to be so purist that you don't allow flexibility and variation. At the same time, you don't want to be so lax, so laissez faire as to call anything a community land trust just because it happens to contain a tiny piece or two of the whole package. It's not uncommon these days to find people who come from the worlds of government or banking or business who say, "I really like land leasing, subsidy retention, and permanent affordability, but these democratic elements that come with the CLT are a little too messy." What they are saying, of course, is that democracy slows things down. Democracy gets in the way. Why don't you remove the "C" from community land trust?

But in this movement we believe there are practical, moral, and political reasons for the way in which the "classic" CLT is structured. You can modify that structure. You can tailor it to fit local conditions, priorities, and needs. But you can't simply lop off essential organizational, ownership, or operational elements without doing serious damage to the model itself.

SD: *What do see as the highest priorities for the moving going forward in the next five to ten years? What do you hope to see?*

JED: I would like to see an increase in the number of community land trusts. I would like to see an increase in the scale of individual community land trusts. And I would like to see more progress made toward ensuring the sustainability of the organizations that we have created. Any goals for the CLT movement would have to include these three: number, scale, sustainability.

That is an aspirational goal not only for CLTs in the United States but for CLTs in other countries as well. There are vigorous CLT movements currently underway in Australia and England. There are CLTs being started in Belgium and Canada. I have been invited to all of these countries in the last few years, conferring with very smart CLT organizers who are applying the model and modifying the model in wonderful ways. The CLT movement in the Unites States may soon be learning as much from them as they are learning from us.

Another hope that I have for the CLT movement here in the United States is that we will continue to pay particular attention to racial diversity, making sure that communities of color are included in everything we do. In the governance of the movement, in the trainings that we do, in the priority we give to allocating the Network's resources, we must ensure that communities of color are not bypassed. Both the Academy and the Network are presently giving special attention to the application of community land trusts to what we refer to as Heritage Lands—land-based assets in communities of color where the future of that community in that place depends on who controls the land. If low-income and moderate-income people of color are removed from increasingly valuable land then, as a movement, we will have missed the opportunity to deliver this powerful tool to communities who are most at risk. We will have missed the chance to help people of color to "take a stand and own the land," in the words of the Dudley Street Neighborhood Initiative in Roxbury, Massachusetts.

When you have college towns, suburban communities, and resort communities increasingly interested in community land trusts, there is a temptation to shift resources in their direction. These are places where it is somewhat easier doing development, places where you have the backing of the powers-that-be. Doing workforce housing for hospital workers or inclusionary housing for cops and firefighters in an affluent community are perfect examples. There is nothing wrong with that; indeed, community land trusts are having great success in opening up affluent enclaves to people who could not otherwise live there. But, at the same time, we cannot overlook people and places that need a community land trust as a bulwark against the powers-that-be, a bulwark against economic forces that tend to displace low-income people, especially low-income people of color, whenever real estate markets get very hot—or very cold. We are trying to make sure these communities are not neglected.

The CLT emerged out of the civil rights movement. If we are to remain true to our roots and values, we must continue to give priority to people who are outside of the political and economic mainstream. We must continue to embrace what the liberation theology of an earlier day referred to as "a preferential option for the poor." That commitment has to be intentional. It has to be directed. It has to be conscious. It is the moral ground on which CLTs must stand—and from which CLTs must continue to draw their purpose and vitality—in good times and bad.

Community Organizing & Education

Educate, Agitate, Organize *may be an anarchist slogan from the early twentieth century, but it is also an accurate description of the reality of most movements for social change in American history from abolitionism to women's suffrage to the movements of today. The five interviews in this section highlight some of the more creative methods that have been employed to build community and empower the disempowered. John Taylor, who grew up in the housing projects of Boston, now heads a national organization led by a 26-member board that has balanced bank regulatory interventions with community-based activism. Caroline Murray in Massachusetts and Rev. Barry Randolph in Detroit have both used community organizing as a means to build up locally-owned co-ops and social enterprises that can economically empower their communities. San Francisco-based Raquel Pinderhughes has developed an educational curriculum that has helped thousands of people who face barriers to employment obtain good paying green jobs; a key element of her approach is to bring issues of equity and justice to the fore within the training curriculum, which helps turn students "on to learning instead of off." Ai-jen Poo, executive director of the National Domestic Workers Alliance, has used organizing among immigrant workers to redefine domestic work as work meriting labor protection and, more fundamentally, is working to build an entire economy based on the idea of "Caring Across Generations."*

John Taylor

*John Taylor is the founding president
and CEO of the National Community
Reinvestment Coalition (NCRC), which
he has led since 1991. Today, NCRC
brings together 600 national, regional,
and local organizations from across the
country that work together to increase the
flow of private capital into traditionally
underserved communities. A key focus of
NCRC's work has been to strengthen and
enforce the Community Reinvestment
Act (CRA). Passed by Congress in 1977
to end "redlining" (a practice in which
banks would draw a red line around
low-income and minority neighborhoods
and subsequently refuse to make loans in
those areas), CRA creates an "affirmative
obligation" for banks to lend money
and invest capital in a safe manner in
moderate and low-income communities.*

Interviewed in 2010

Steve Dubb: *Could you explain how you came to be involved with community reinvestment and what inspired you to focus on that sector?*

John Taylor: I grew up in the public housing projects in Boston. My father was a union organizer and frequently unemployed because of it, so we always had a sense of responsibility to our fellow man. My father was strong about that. I was one of six kids, and the first one in our family to go to college. When I got out of college, I went to law school at Northeastern University and decided to focus my career less on the law and more on helping to end poverty in America.

I spent the first half of my career working on community development activities and running social service programs in the Boston area, including food banks and mediation projects. There was really an emerging community development movement in Boston at that time. When I worked on housing development, I began to see that some banks would regularly work with us and others would never even meet with us. So occasionally I'd fire off a letter to bank regulators, not giving much thought or hope that the letters would make a difference. But I ended up getting in this major battle in 1985 with the biggest bank in the city of Somerville. Long story short, after meeting with the Federal Reserve Bank of Boston and raising concerns, I procured a $20 million lending and investment commitment from that bank. At the time, in the mid-1980s, it was the single largest commitment in the country by a bank to an individual community group. This experience taught me about the power and promise that CRA held for low-wealth neighborhoods.

Next, a group of us, led by the Massachusetts Association of Community Development Corporations, which I chaired, and the Massachusetts Affordable Housing Alliance, focused our efforts on challenging the eight largest Boston banks to do more Community Reinvestment Act related lending. That effort led to an astounding (at least at that time) $1 billion commitment. The money funded a number of community programs; it also got me noticed in Washington, where Congressman Joe Kennedy and sixteen national groups were in the process of forming the National Community Reinvestment Coalition. These included the National Low Income Housing Coalition, Local Initiatives Support Corporation (LISC), the Association of Community Organizers for Reform Now (ACORN), the

Center for Community Change (CCC), the National Congress for Community Economic Development, the McCauley Institute, the Enterprise Foundation, the NAACP, and other groups. He called those groups together and said, "Look, you're going to lose CRA if nothing is done." In particular, he was worried that some of the Democrats in Congress were willing to trade it away.

The effectiveness of CRA at that point was due almost solely to efforts by Gail Cincotta at National People's Action, but the organization's geographic footprint was too limited to influence the government and ensure that banks across the country adhered to CRA's requirements. What I did in Boston brought me into Washington circles, and eventually they hired me as the first staff person for the National Community Reinvestment Coalition. The Center for Community Change gave me office space to begin organizing the coalition. Because of my community development background, I knew a lot of groups that were doing affordable housing development, most of whom had limited or no involvement with CRA. I got their attention and showed them why CRA was important. Within a year, we expanded the coalition from sixteen groups to one hundred.

Our first order of business was to preserve CRA, because it really was under attack. We got together the 16 initial groups and several dozen others, and we managed to stop the Democrats (with the blessing of nearly all Republicans) from trading it away. That effort brought us together.

So we had won a victory, and the next question was how to make CRA more relevant. Most people in neighborhood revitalization and community development had a very narrow view of CRA, or no view whatsoever. So we started by working to improve the quality of Home Mortgage Disclosure Act (HMDA) data that comes out of every transaction. We've always said that data drives our movement: the more you can point to what lenders are doing, or not doing, in underserved neighborhoods and compare that to what they are doing in wealthier neighborhoods, the more leverage you have.

The Community Reinvestment Act is very simple. It is only one-and-a-half pages long. But it doesn't mince words. A bank doesn't just have an obligation—it has an affirmative obligation to meet the credit needs of communities. That means the bank must actively pursue opportunities to investment in those neighborhoods. And, just in case there was any doubt, Congress added the words "including low- and moderate-income neighborhoods." It was a great law on paper, but it wasn't being enforced. Our idea was to get more information into the hands of community groups so they could really use the law, and to ratchet up its enforcement.

I saw this in Somerville. If you were a working class truck driver and you tried to get a lender to give you a mortgage for a "triple-decker" home—and there are many of these three-level row homes in Boston—then the bank would say no, you couldn't afford it. But if you were a doctor from Boston and you said, "I want to buy properties in these neighborhoods and convert them into luxury condos," they would give you a loan. So there was a financial access gap along income and class lines. And the banks were actively participating in gentrification. I saw that early on.

SD: *How has NCRC's work evolved over time?*

JT: After stopping CRA from being gutted, we got HMDA information changed. I remember meeting frequently with Alan Greenspan during the 1990s and insisting that since Congress had mandated that home mortgage data be made available, the Federal Reserve needed to make it available in a more user-friendly form. You shouldn't have to be at a university to be able to use that information, I argued. Because of our work, today, for a few hundred dollars, you can buy two CD-ROMs that include data on every single mortgage listing the race, income, gender, geographic distribution, and census tract data on loans made that year. That really opened up a plethora of opportunities and empowered community groups across the country.

Then we had another victory. Following on the heels of that effort, President George H.W. Bush's Justice Department brought the very first fair lending case against a bank that included a violation of CRA as part of the complaint. To this day, it bewilders me that this happened under Bush, but it did, and it happened in Atlanta. They filed in the morning, and the bank settled in the afternoon. It was a shot heard around the financial services world.

We built on that example to show the need for strong enforcement of CRA. We were very critical of the regulatory agencies. The law says "an affirmative obligation," not just a responsibility, to serve low-income communities. And yet pawnshops were opening

"We've always said that **data drives our movement**."

in low-income neighborhoods while banks were closing. How was this possible?

In 1992, Bill Clinton was elected president. He announced plans to rewrite the enforcement of CRA and to create the Community Development Financial Institutions Fund (CDFI) on the same day. That day, the NCRC Board Chairman, Irv Henderson, spoke on the south lawn of the White House along with President Clinton and Vice President Gore, calling for CRA reform and a new CDFI fund. The Federal Reserve responded by saying they would send out a request to the field for comment regarding bank regulation under CRA.

This became the next great battle for our newly formed coalition. For the first time in the history of the Federal Reserve, people from the community out-commented the financial industry. After the new CRA reforms were announced, the Fed began their next meeting by recognizing the work that NCRC did in making sure the rules were reflective of community concerns. We had actually provided twice as many comments about what the CRA rules should look like as the banks.

One of the key reforms announced at that time was a change to CRA examination rules, which shifted the process for evaluating banks under the law. We transitioned from what was an almost exclusively process-oriented exam to one that based the banks' CRA grade on their performance. So in the past, a bank simply had to have a CRA file somewhere—literally a folder entitled "CRA"—and they needed to have signs in the bank lobby noting that they adhered to fair lending laws. Nothing more. Because of the reforms at that time, we moved from that ineffective system to a results-oriented evaluation that required each bank to pass three tests measuring its levels of lending, servicing, and investments in low-income communities. As a result of this new system of grading banks, the universe began to shift for community development corporations (CDCs) and CDFIs, and for low and moderate-income communities.

Many CDCs and CDFIs don't even know this history. Their ability to get support from these institutions is directly related to the work NCRC did to improve CRA's effectiveness in the 1990s.

At that point, NCRC had 400 members. Today, it is closer to 550 or 600. Over time, you could see an uptick in the amount of business being done by financial institutions in low-income areas. Not only did President Clinton change the rules, he also brought in someone devoted to CRA to head the Office of Comptroller of the Currency (OCC). Finally, in Eugene Ludwig we had someone as head of the national banking system who actually cared and spoke about CRA. That was important. In the first year under Clinton, 10 percent of banks failed their CRA exam, which was unheard of.

But the banks responded. 120 banks changed their charters from being regulated by the OCC to be regulated by the Federal Reserve, because banks can choose how they are structured and who regulates them. Well, grade inflation was alive and well at the Federal Reserve, and today 98 percent of all banks pass their CRA exams. This happened at a time when banks were abandoning low-income neighborhoods, closing branches and leaving town.

Since then, and especially under President George W. Bush, there has been regulatory malaise. Banks simply have to be in existence and they're already three-quarters of the way to a satisfactory grade. In effect, there were incentives to leave the banks alone. Some of Bush's appointees, like Don Powell and James Gilleran, were outright opposed to CRA. Gilleran, who ran the Office of Thrift Supervision (OTS), actually said at an NCRC conference that he wasn't "a fan of CRA, but since I am in charge of the OTS I guess I need to enforce it."

It's still a real problem: having a strong sheriff matters a great deal, and we haven't seen one in recent years. We're hopeful that we'll get one to head the newly forming Consumer Financial Protection Bureau (CFPB).

We've done a lot of other things. NCRC played a key role in financial reform over the past year, working with Americans for Financial Reform to get the legislation passed. We tried to get CRA covered under the CFPB, but the banks' lobbyists didn't want a consumer protection agency with the authority to enforce CRA. They successfully removed coverage of CRA by the CFPB from the original bank reform proposal from President Obama.

SD: *What is the status of the community reinvestment movement in the United States today? In what ways have NCRC members been impacted by the Great Recession?*

JT: CRA is still an important tool in the effort to address poverty and financial injustice in low-wealth neighborhoods, one that could help ensure that pawnshops and check cashers aren't serving as the banking services of choice. But like any law, it's only as good as the sheriff enforcing it, and before the financial crisis, there was no real commitment on the part of the government to enforce the letter of the law. How could regulators give passing CRA grades to banks that had abandoned low-wealth neighborhoods where the only source of mortgage loans were subprime and high-cost mortgage lenders? All of this was allowed to happen. CRA took it on the chin.

A CRA agreement, which outlines a bank's commitment to make loans and investments in underserved neighborhoods, comes out of negotiations between a bank and community groups; it documents the bank's commitment to the community. Those written commitments added up to over $6 trillion through the present day! But when the sheriff was told to hold back, what we saw was the demise of the enforcement of those commitments. Regulators under Bush wouldn't even consider those agreements when evaluating a bank's CRA compliance. That's absurd: nothing gives more insight into a bank's activities and plans than their CRA agreement.

Bank branching—the opening and closing of branches—is another key component to low-income communities' ability to access credit. But regulators under Bush would tell me that a branch is not a "credit need," which the law examines, and therefore its presence in low-income neighborhoods was irrelevant to a bank's CRA rating. Is access to a place to bank your money safely not a basic need of most people? We asked, "If banks don't have vehicles like branches, how do they meet the credit needs?" Fortunately, today, the regulators have changed this practice. But banks are not rushing in to reopen their branches in low-wealth communities, at least not without some serious community organizing.

SD: *How does NCRC support itself financially?*
JT: Our revenue sources are very diverse. We receive support from foundations, member dues, and individuals. We have contracts with the Department of Housing and Urban Development and a number of state agencies to provide direct assistance to homebuyers and homeowners experiencing foreclosure. While we do not accept

funding from banks and other corporations for operating support, some do help underwrite our national conference, which helps keep registration fees low for our attendees. This diverse portfolio has allowed NCRC to weather the storm currently faced by many organizations. In fact, NCRC has grown to 55 staff members, an all time high for the coalition.

As we have not relied upon banks for operating support, we have not been appreciably damaged by the decline in the banking industry. Support for our conference has gone down, but because we have a very diverse funding base, we've done reasonably well. We also own our own office building, called the National Center for Economic Justice, which generates some income. So we've managed to weather the storm in pretty good shape. Fortunately, foundations have generously recognized the importance of what we do.

SD: *It would appear that there has been some decline in community reinvestment due to the Great Recession. What do you see as the key problems that need to be addressed to restore community investment?*

JT: You're right. There has been a decline. There is no greater way to reverse that than by strengthening CRA and ensuring that it is fully enforced. Not only was there lax enforcement during the George W. Bush years, but the administration also changed the frequency of exams. They created a small bank exam and a large bank exam, and kept inching up the criteria for a small bank, with the end result being that fewer banks had fewer exams. They also allowed banks to take subsidiaries, such as mortgage and finance companies, and let the banks decide whether or not to count the performance of those institutions on the bank's CRA exam. That's like allowing someone to decide their GPA without counting certain classes or grades. NCRC called attention to this, but the regulators ignored us. This all needs to be changed. Credit unions, insurance companies, and independent mortgage companies should have a CRA obligation. And to not have a public hearing when one large financial institution is buying another doesn't make any sense.

Congress just passed a financial reform bill. It does make some headway in protecting citizens against bad loans. What it doesn't do is create better access to credit for people, particularly those in low-income and minority communities. This is the unfinished business of the 111th Congress and [House Financial Services Chair] Barney Frank. I'm very confident that we will see Congressman Frank address this issue before this Congress expires. After all, what is the likelihood of CRA being expanded and strengthened if it doesn't happen this year?

CRA is a fabulous law, but it was only very briefly under Gene Ludwig in the mid-1990s that it really began to deliver on the promise that it offers, which is to make capitalism work for everyone. The uptick in sustainable lending in the 1990s was tremendous. This was all prime lending, all sustainable loans. These loans performed very well until the unregulated segments of the industry began to provide significant numbers of subprime, high-cost loans to low-income people.

The Federal Reserve has done a study that shows that less than six percent of subprime loans were made through CRA-regulated institutions. Had the independent mortgage companies been covered under CRA, they would have had their records dinged by the regulators.

SD: *Can you talk more specifically about the Community Reinvestment Modernization Act and how passage of the NCRC-sponsored legislation would impact communities?*

JT: The most significant thing is that it would expand the act to cover other segments of the financial services sector, such as credit unions, investment banks, independent mortgage companies and insurance companies. They would not all be treated the same, but they would all be covered, and it would ensure that credit-worthy customers have access to credit. This is the biggest complaint that we hear from consumers today—that banks simply won't lend. If we are to improve our economy and create more jobs, this has to change immediately.

If banks had not been allowed to close their branches, far fewer low-income people would have been driven to the subprime market. Indeed, we have found that every time we have successfully pressured banks to keep their branches open in low-income neighborhoods, they become viable. People think there are no resources to support banking in low-income communities. This is not true at all. Income is much denser in poor, urban neighborhoods: there may be less average income, but the total income is greater. That's

"If banks had not been allowed to close their branches, **far fewer low-income people would have been driven to the subprime market.**"

what these banks have found, whether they're in Watts in Los Angeles, Boston's Roxbury, Chicago's Southside, or Harlem: branches in these neighborhoods can be viable. There is nothing more important as an economic anchor than the presence of a bank in a community: it draws business into the area.

SD: *What impact has consolidation had on community lending? For example, the big four banks (Bank of America, Citi, JP Morgan Chase, and Wells Fargo) now hold 39 percent of all deposits.*

JT: Consolidation is important, but it is also important to note that we still have 9,000 other financial institutions. A lot of the big banks have assets that are never available to most communities anyway. Citibank, for example, which has a presence in one hundred countries, may look like a huge bank, but 1) not all of their assets are in America, and 2) not all of their assets are in retail banking. But retail banking is still very important. The independent mortgage companies ate the lunch of the banks by selling bad lending products. They said, "Fine, if banks won't lend in low-income communities, we will." And they made a huge number of subprime loans. It is important to note that this lending wasn't about expanding homeownership; less than 10 percent of loans went to new homeowners. This whole debacle was actually about refinancing, buying a bigger house, or expanding the house.

Consolidation still needs to be dealt with. Competition is good and healthy, and I'd rather see more financial institutions than less. I don't want to see our financial services sector evolve into a "drugstore world" where there is only CVS, Walgreen's, and Wal-Mart. With consolidation, decisions are made centrally and banks become less connected to communities. And fewer quality jobs become available. So I say, the more the merrier.

We love the idea of having banks with boards of directors who actually live in the community; when you have a board made up of members who live three states over, you're going to have more difficulties ensuring that local community needs are considered in the corporate boardroom.

That's the key role of community reinvestment activism: to make sure the credit needs of communities without access are met: It's not just an abstract matter of justice; it's also the law. Even some people in community development don't realize what a debt of gratitude so many owe to this kind of activism. Without it, not many community investments would have been made. The regulators went to sleep on this; they took a long nod. But they're awake now. Lo and behold, they're finally learning that banks and companies that do bad community loans really affect the safety and soundness of the system. Who knew? We did. We told them and they didn't listen.

SD: *NCRC is a fairly rare organization in Washington in that it does a lot of policy work while maintaining a vibrant grassroots organization constituted by over 600 groups across the country. How do you manage the challenge?*

JT: It's true; it is rare. The way you do it is you make a commitment to it. You have to respond to the power and interests of your grassroots members. We have a board of 26 men and women—all of who are community activists—and that's the core source of our success, more than any person on our staff, including me. You also have to be in constant contact with the membership and never take their involvement with you for granted. I remember, as someone who spent years running local organizations, how busy and often short staffed we were, and how challenging it was. You have to be there for the leaders of local organizations.

The membership elects a third of the board of directors every year. This insures that our members have direct input into the paths the coalition takes. I work for that board, and I never forget that.

We cover board members' expenses to travel and participate in NCRC activities. This allows us to attract not only the well-heeled organizations, but also smaller groups. And we spend a lot of time every couple of years deciding key questions related to our mission and programs; every three years, we develop a new strategic plan, from soup to nuts. We constantly reexamine our mission: is it current, is it as relevant as it needs to be?

As a coalition, we are frequently called on to perform direct services, such as job development and foreclosure prevention. We've helped tens of thousands of people facing foreclosure to keep their homes. We've provided assistance to hundreds of minority and women-owned businesses, and trained 5,000 financial literacy experts.

NCRC performs numerous direct services because we recognize that doing it is necessary to fulfill our mission; it also informs our policy work. But we never allow ourselves to get too far from our core mission of advocacy and organizing, being the voice of the people, in order to make capitalism more democratic and ensure that the financial services sector works for underserved people.

SD: *What is the status of the Global Fair Banking initiative? Do you see specific lessons from abroad that might inform community investment practices in the United States?*

JT: The Global Fair Banking initiative is alive and well, in spite of never having been highly funded. We've received funding for it from the Ford Foundation in the past, but for the most part we piece together the budget. In spite of that, we have seen some remarkable successes. We've created a European counterpart, the European Committee for Responsible Credit (ECRC). They're now celebrating their sixth year; I just went to Hamburg to speak at their conference.

It's composed of non-governmental organizations (NGOs) from 29 European countries that work on financial laws in Europe to keep out abusive subprime lending.

We have also created a Global Fair Banking website, thanks to the work of NCRC board member Maryellen Lewis. This allows us to remain in constant contact with NGOs from around the world to share ideas, strategies, laws, regulations, and other information relating to financial inclusion and the prevention of abusive lending.

We've also worked in Central America, South America, India, Australia, and South Africa. South Africa now has CRA- and HMDA-like legislation. We've had a great deal of success in building this global communication about mechanisms that can increase wealth and investment in underserved areas. It is intriguing that the private sector in the United States has an affirmative obligation to be engaged in this; in most countries, affordable housing started out as a social enterprise, but they are heading towards a private sector model because the governments cannot afford to maintain it.

What I learned more than anything from our international work is that regulation matters and consumer protection matters. The consumer protections they have in many parts of Europe just don't allow for predatory lending. They punish the lender severely. In one case that I learned about, the courts forgave not only the penalties on a high-cost loan, but also the principal. They did this as a signal to show financial firms that it's not permitted. It really matters when courts are allowed to protect consumers from abuse.

They are really interested in CRA over there. Several countries— France, Germany, and England—are seeking to pass CRA-like legislation. Just like us, they're trying to create a more democratic capitalism. You can't just lend money to the well heeled; there has to be a way for the system to invest in anyone who is credit-worthy.

SD: *Can you talk a little about NCRC's effort to create regional organizer positions? How far along is the effort? What do you see as the challenges and successes to date?*

JT: We've filled six new organizer positions, all aimed at strengthening NCRC's relationship with member organizations and other nonprofits. Currently, they're all focused on ensuring that this congressional session doesn't end before a real effort has been made to increase people's access to credit, which means expanding and modernizing CRA. Eventually, our organizers will work more directly in the field in different regions. For the time being, they are being trained and immersed in NCRC's diverse programs and projects, as well as our mission and goals.

SD: *Could you discuss NCRC's Generating Real Opportunities for Work (GROW) initiative? What is its current level of development?*

JT: The idea is that in seeking to stabilize and develop neighborhoods, you can't just concentrate on the housing side of the sector; you have to create jobs. A lot of these neighborhoods will need to be rebuilt, and there is a tremendous need for infrastructure, so why not train people from these neighborhoods so that they can be directly employed to regenerate their own communities? It's a concept that's getting attention within some government agencies, HUD in particular.

SD: How does NCRC work with community organizing networks, such as the Center for Community Change? How does it relate to community development financial institution (CDFI) networks, such as the Opportunity Finance Network or community development corporation (CDC) groups? What can be done to improve coordination?

JT: One of the key reasons NCRC has been successful is because we have representatives from all of those groups as members of the organization. When we get together, whether on a listserv or at conference or regional setting, there is always a diversity of perspectives presented. It isn't an either-or situation: we can always find common ground, mainly because as diverse as we are, we all want to ensure communities' access to capital and credit. Certainly, you'll have people in advocacy who don't think community development is at the heart of the matter, or vice versa. Of course, both of them are wrong. Those who are seasoned realize that the most powerful community development and advocacy efforts bring in groups with connections to all of the elements that make up a neighborhood.

To revitalize neighborhoods, do you need CDCs? Absolutely. Do you need CDFIs? Absolutely. Do you need advocacy groups? Very much so. These organizations need to work together: that's when we're the most powerful and can affect the most change. For us, this attitude relates back to having a board of directors with a connection to underserved communities. We never get away from our core mission because my board wouldn't stand for it. It is about really understanding that we are all foot soldiers in a very large battle. We need to work together, or we won't win. We don't need to spend a minute babbling about differences.

SD: What are NCRC's priorities within the green economy?

JT: Fifteen years ago, we were writing to regulators complaining that low-income neighborhoods were being targeted for the production, storage, or disposal of toxic products, and that banks were financing this. Now we are thinking more strategically. I think there is a real opportunity for environmental groups, community development organizations, and advocacy groups to work together strategically to develop both quality, clean, green jobs and housing. NCRC's vision of a community is one that is diverse, healthy, and vibrant.

It is important for each to learn more about the other. Creating sustainable communities must involve green thinking and practices throughout the process of development. We need appropriate technology, greater efficiencies, and less toxicity. All of that relates to development—and developers and environmentalists are beginning to work together on both sides of that ledger. That's certainly what we're promoting.

Civil rights activists, faith-based groups, and community organizers need to understand why their different fields of interest (such as the environment, health care, or education) need to complement each other, and why we need to spend time integrating our area of expertise with others. You can't just build a nice house in a polluted zone with no health care. Our efforts have to evolve into a more holistic approach.

For those of us working on legislative issues, eventually all roads will lead to campaign finance reform. Until we fix that, not much can change. I actually ran once for Congress, so I learned firsthand the role that money plays in an election. If you can't get on TV, if you can't get on the radio, you can't get heard. So millions of dollars are spent on elections, and that influences who winds up representing us. This country has a lot of very bright and dedicated people who really care about its future. But that isn't the first criteria for getting elected; the first of the criteria is the ability to raise money. Anyone in the business of community reinvestment and neighborhood revitalization has to be engaged in making sure people get registered and vote, so that politicians are forced to see that they need to put people first and campaign financing and reelections second. We have the best Congress that money can buy—Senator Durbin (D-IL) said that in this session. And he's absolutely right.

SD: *What are NCRC's main priorities going forward?*

JT: Our main priority is CRA modernization and continuing to build a local grassroots movement that influences regulatory agencies and elected officials, so that our system of capitalism can be genuinely

"You can't just build a nice house in a polluted zone with no health care. **Our efforts have to evolve into a more holistic approach.**"

democratic. So people who pay their taxes have an equal opportunity to borrow money—as long as they can pay it back—as anyone else. Within that, we have a lot of priorities related to job development and ending the foreclosure crisis.

SD: *We still have an ongoing foreclosure crisis? What solutions is NCRC advocating for?*

JT: Yes, it's still continuing. There are another three to four million homes that are on a path to foreclosure in the next year or so. We've been advocating for a more aggressive solution since the very beginning, first to Secretary Paulson and then to President Bush back in 2008. We proposed a program called the Homeowners Emergency Loan Program (or HELP Now). The program was a broad-scale loan purchase and modification program that would have bought loans at a discount and passed the discount along to the homeowner, making the loan affordable. Once the loan was performing, it could be refinanced or sold to the private market, with a guarantee, if necessary.

You cannot have a federal foreclosure program that relies on voluntary compliance by the industry. The government has to mandate participation in the modification, and they have to mandate principal reductions. At one time, it looked like the government would actually take up something like HELP Now—that is, buy loans at a discount and pass the discount on to the borrower. We know it's possible, and profitable, because this is what Lew Ranieri, the inventor of the mortgage-backed security while at Salomon Brothers, is now doing with his own fund. He's buying the loans at a substantial discount, making them sustainable for homeowners, and then getting FHA [Federal Housing Administration] to refinance and receiving double-digit returns for his investors. This is what the government should be doing.

Every few months the Obama administration comes up with something new. The government should be buying loans in bulk and modifying them to be good, sustainable loans. These bright guys in Washington keep coming up with one voluntary program after another, no matter how many months go by with data showing that it isn't working.

SD: *If you had to choose three accomplishments that you are most proud of at NCRC, what would they be?*

JT: First, preventing CRA from being repealed. Second, changing the way that banks are examined under CRA. Third, building a grassroots movement focused on economic justice and financial inclusion that is an outgrowth of the civil rights movement. I'm most proud of the last part.

SD: *Is there anything else that you would like to add?*

JT: One further thing that I should mention about my background is my education. I came from a family where my mother and father never went to college. I had three brothers—all went into military service—and two sisters. In high school, I was going to an all-boys public school in inner city Boston, which was 80 percent black. To put it politely, not a lot of educating was going on in that building. Then through the Catholic Church, a family from a well-to-do suburb invited me to live with them and finish my last two years of high school in this suburban community. The quality of education was such a complete contrast. Without a doubt, I wouldn't have gone to university were it not for those last two years of high school. Most people in this country don't know what it's like to be poor in a community that has very little economic opportunity and not a lot of role models. Your options are limited; when I was young, they amounted to joining a union or the service, or you just didn't think about it. Ensuring the success of the least privileged among us comes down to developing sustainable, healthy neighborhoods.

Capitalism appears to be one of the better economic systems that have been developed, but it still doesn't work well for low-income neighborhoods. It needs to be more democratic, and there has to be fairness and ethics in the process. Clearly, in my view, CRA holds the main key in the effort to build wealth and revitalize poor neighborhoods. This is my mission and why I work for NCRC.

COMMUNITY
ORGANIZING &
EDUCATION

Caroline Murray

Caroline Murray was Executive Director of the Alliance to Develop Power (ADP) from 1993 to 2011. Headquartered in Springfield, Massachusetts, ADP created $80 million in community-owned enterprises, which employed 125 people in living wage jobs. In 2011, Murray left ADP to become Organizing Director of Rebuild the Dream. Murray currently works as a strategic campaign consultant.

Interviewed in 2012

Steve Dubb: Could you explain how you came to be involved with community organizing and what inspired you to become a community organizer?

Caroline Murray: I grew up in the 1970s and graduated from high school in 1983. My family experienced an interesting dynamic where our class identity shifted a number of times, due to marriage, divorce, foreclosure, and bankruptcy. I went from hanging out at the country club pool to relying on food stamps and living with extended family. But my mother was a strong-willed entrepreneur with a keen sense for business that got us through. So I grew up knowing that something was very, very wrong with how our economy worked. I understood from a very young age how fragile the middle class was.

When I graduated from high school, I went to the University of Massachusetts at Amherst, this of course was when an education at a state university was still relatively affordable and Pell Grants were readily available for low-income students like me. I became involved in student organizing, the anti-apartheid movement, and was elected to student government. And there I learned there was a career called "community organizing." For me, working in organizing and community economic development—people power and economic power—is the continuation of my life and my life's work and has become my calling.

SD: Could you talk about how you got involved in ADP and how it has developed as an organization over time?

CM: After working in electoral politics for a number of years and organizing with the welfare reform movement, I went to work as the Executive Director of ADP in 1993. At that time, it was a very small nonprofit advocacy organization, but I had a vision of creating a new kind of membership-based organization that was rooted in building power. At that time, ADP was a single-issue organization and was part of an incredibly important national fight to save hundreds of thousands of families from displacement because of laws that allowed private developers to convert their publicly-financed affordable apartment complexes to market rate, or condos, or tear them down and put up a strip mall and make windfall profits. ADP was a project of the National Low Income Housing Coalition and part of a national campaign to win new federal legislation that would stop these landlords from profiting off the backs of low- and moderate-income tenants and the taxpayer, while at the same time create new financing mechanisms to keep the housing permanently affordable.

While most of our allies around the country went on to find nonprofit housing developers to purchase the apartment complexes—we latched upon a novel idea that was actually being touted by Jack Kemp, Secretary of HUD—why not buy them ourselves as membership-based, democratically governed corporations? Here was an opportunity to convert ownership of the housing to the people who lived there and develop long-lasting leadership. We could keep it permanently affordable for generations to come. We could stop capital flight by controlling the money that flows in and out. And we could alter the relations of power between landlord and tenant.

I believed then, and I still believe today, that we need to think big—we need to stake our flag way out ahead—and be aspirational in our goals as we work towards truly transformational change. We need to do this among ourselves, with our neighbors, and in our society as a whole. Changing the dynamics of ownership and decision-making really became the foundation of my work.

SD: *Could you discuss the origins of how the first housing cooperative came about?*

CM: The first buyout campaign took seven years to win and the others took about four. We also lost a few, including the apartment complex where I lived. My rent for a two-bedroom apartment went from $568 a month to $1,400 a month overnight. It was an intense period, and we bought out about 1,200 units of housing, making it the largest block of tenant-controlled housing in the United States. ADP members also saved about 4,000 more apartments as affordable by working with the existing landlord when we couldn't convince them to sell. It is far too complicated to get into the details of how a campaign like this works. But the most important thing to take away is the understanding that everyday people do extraordinary things every day. Of course, you also need resources, a strategic plan, tactics that make sense, a number-cruncher but nothing gets done without community leaders and community organizers who understand power.

You see the same thing at Occupy today. It is one thing to win policies and that of course is critically important. But what we really need to be thinking about is fundamental restructuring of the systems that perpetuate inequity. We need to be talking and taking action in order to reshape and change the dynamics of power.

We have an opportunity to create a new economy movement that is based on our values and bring economic power back into the hands of the people and community. Every day there are new cooperatives and community-owned businesses being created, expansions in the shareable and gifting economy, collaborative consumption, and more socially responsible entrepreneurs—everyday people know that the economy is out of whack, and we are fixing it one business and one neighborhood at a time.

In my work, we did that with affordable housing complexes, worker-owned businesses, food cooperatives, community centers, sharing, gifting, and training. All of these economic institutions came out of organizing campaigns and represented concrete improvements in the lives of the people and their communities and society as a whole. And they came out of the hearts and minds of people who were fighting everyday to create the world, as it should be. We want to own stuff too, not just fight people who own stuff.

And the beautiful thing is the work continues and will reflect the hearts and minds of a new generation of leaders. ADP continues to do amazing things, including addressing food insecurity and predatory lending with the creation of a community-owned bodega that will sell fresh food grown by the community and provide non-predatory financial services like check cashing. That is revolutionary.

SD: *How did ADP manage to forge the community economy it has helped create? Could you break down how ADP achieved some of its key objectives?*

CM: The essence of community organizing is to work with people at the grassroots level to build power, identify the problems, and win solutions. There are methodologies for doing that, outreach and listen to the community, develop leaders, identify a campaign, do a power analysis, identify the decision maker, issue demands, wield power, negotiate, and so on.

"It is one thing to win policies and that of course is critically important. **But what we really need to be thinking about is fundamental restructuring of the systems that perpetuate inequity.**"

We created a model that takes that one step further. In other words, we wanted one outcome of a campaign to be the creation of a membership-controlled alternative economic institution that would control wealth and assets. So when we organized tenants, rather than simply try to keep the rents affordable or fix the broken toilets, we would seek to purchase the property so the toilets would never break again and the rents would remain affordable for generations. And by converting major properties into tenant ownership, then the community would control millions of dollars of real estate. You can use the surplus funds you control to benefit the commons. I always say, "The way you ask a question determines the answer." And so, we started asking different questions. How do you meet an unmet need in the community? How do you capture a surplus and expand the commons?

I remember one of our first budgeting meetings after a successful buyout. We were reviewing the operating budget and got down to the landscaping line item. One of the members said, "Why don't we pay ourselves to mow the lawn?" And it was like a lightening bolt hit. In that moment, all the questions changed and an infinite number of possibilities became clear. And so we decided to create a landscaping business. Then we added up all of the money the community now controlled through these large apartment complexes, and met with the president of a local bank who we knew because he was a former political appointee of then-Governor Weld, a strong supporter of our work at that time. We told him we would move our money, millions of dollars in cash flow, into his bank if he financed the startup of our company. And we were off to the races.

At some point, we realized that we had a captive market and we could create a new "community economy" that served this captive market, filled unmet needs in the community—both in terms of the services provided, but also in terms of creating living wage jobs—and generated a surplus that could fund organizing. And so we created and expanded the businesses that served captive markets: for example, landscaping, snow removal, painting, cleaning, and construction. But it is important to note that these businesses also came out of or supported organizing campaigns. And so we organized workers on construction sites who were experiencing wage theft, created a worker center that filed wage-and-hour claims and won back millions of dollars that had been stolen from workers. At the same time, those workers founded the worker center and became leaders in the construction arm of the business.

Another great example is the work in the green economy. ADP joined a statewide campaign with the Green Justice Coalition to increase investments in energy efficiency, lower our dependence on fossil fuel, and ensure resources made it to the communities of color and low-income communities that bear the brunt of environmental injustice and were suffering from the economic crisis long before the banks crashed. And so, groups all over Massachusetts went door-knocking and created a new market for energy efficiency services, while at the same time building power to win new policies. However, many energy efficiency jobs are low wage and have very high rates of on-the-job injury. So the campaign partnered with the carpenters and the painters unions, in order to ensure the work was creating living wage jobs and to drive up wages in the overall market and improve the sector. But at ADP of course, a new business was created in the energy efficiency sector. And so a whole new base of leaders came into the organization, new relationships were built with partners, major policies were won at the state level, and a new business was created that filled an unmet need and benefited the commons.

The bottom line is to build people power and economic power. I think of this work as creating the world as it should be and modeling what sustainability really is. It is living out what people call the "triple bottom line" and actually understanding that our actions can drive the economy, rather than having the economy control us. And, as my mentor Julie Graham taught me, it means striving to achieve equilibrium—balance—in a community economy that is ever-expanding and interconnected.

SD: *One area that has always been a challenge for co-ops has been the issue of scale. Scale can boost organizational capacity, but can also create larger organizations that may become disconnected from the communities they serve. How did ADP seek to negotiate these tensions?*

CM: One of the challenges in the movement as a whole is the issue of moving from opposition to governance. If you look at any social movement—people are protesting, but the goal is to govern. Governance is a different skill set, and acting in a way that is in opposition to our existing free market economy and rugged individualism is not easy. It requires constant attention. Creating a worldview, acting on principles, engaging in training, and recognizing the interconnections among people are all important.

It is a constant process. There are challenges in all movements to do that. If I were to critique the existing co-op movement, I would say two things: One, they are often in silos, not focused on the larger structural inequities of society; and two, they are somewhat apolitical and focused very much on their own workplace. We have to push ourselves to think and act bigger. For anyone who is participating in a co-op, we have to constantly challenge each other on how to build beyond that.

It is a constant struggle. The cooperative movement is acting in opposition to the existing worldview. It is very challenging, both personally and organizationally. If you don't focus on your worldview work or true vision of an equitable society, you can become very inwardly focused, which doesn't address the larger issues.

SD: *Could you talk a bit more about the board structure?*

CM: Like all cooperatives, each entity has its own board and its own governance structure. And they all connect to each other via representatives who serve on the ADP board, so there is accountability throughout all levels. And there are a set of principles that guide decision making. One of the key factors of the success of ADP is flexibility and being able to make pragmatic decisions and mid-course corrections. People learn as they go. It is a stretching exercise to challenge oneself to think outside of the box and not get stuck in one structure or one idea. Don't be rigid and respond to the needs of the community, which change over time. We learned from studying Mondragón—they call it "developing new habits of the mind." Adapt and move towards a vision. So governance also changes, as the organizations and people involved grow and change. The key to any success is that it is rooted in principles.

SD: *A few years ago, ADP changed its name from "Anti-Displacement Project" to the "Alliance to Develop Power"? Could you discuss the reasons for this change?*

CM: When I started in 1993, it was an advocacy organization whose mission was to stop the displacement of low-income tenants from their housing. As we grew and expanded our mission and our constituency, we kept the name for years knowing it wasn't really the right name for us and so we really just used ADP. And the rallying cry became, "Who are we? ADP!"

Changing a name is a really big deal when the identities of people are wrapped up in it. Finally, the organization went through a year long strategic planning and renaming process many years ago that engaged hundreds of people. Out of it, three camps emerged: some wanted us to keep the name because the brand ADP was so strong for them, others said let's keep the letters ADP but change what they stand for, and some wanted an entirely new name: out with the old and in with the new. The option to change the words, but keep the letters "ADP" won out. Turns out there are a lot of words that begin with the letters A, D, and P that are relevant to our work, but few that work well in multiple languages. And so, Alliance to Develop Power was chosen. The new name was unveiled along with a new logo when the ADP Worker Center had its public opening about five years ago.

SD: *Many organizations have difficulty maintaining community organizing and community development under one organizational umbrella. How has ADP managed this tension?*

CM: For me, during my time at ADP, the focus was on community organizing first, developing leaders, and winning real improvements in people's lives and in society. That meant building people power first and economic power second. The institutions that were created came out of community organizing campaigns. They came out of experiences of real people. It wasn't an outside entity that said we want to start a business or that wrote a study and decided how to create jobs. It was a

"If you don't focus on your worldview work or true vision of an equitable society, you can become very inwardly focused, **which doesn't address the larger issues**."

group of folks in the community who said, "We have these skills. There is a need for jobs. There is a need for food. Let's match our skills and make something new." So it was rooted in the experiences of ordinary people in achieving power that kept ADP honest, so to speak.

SD: *What do you feel has been the ripple effect of ADP?*

CM: For many years, we were toiling alone as a community organization in the new economy sphere, and it got pretty lonely out there. Now there is a growing movement and interest in the new economy that is across all sectors. Thankfully, organizers and activists and thinkers who are fighting against radical free market fundamentalism aren't just looking at policy fixes, they are now envisioning how we can create an economy from the ground up that reflects our values, puts people first, and brings balance into this crazy world. It is a really exciting time where people are willing to ask those hard questions and experiment in the new economy, and ADP is a wonderful example of what is possible.

I want to also stress that ADP has known its cadre of powerful leaders who speak truth to power and who engage in smart, strategic, and successful campaigns. They have won major campaigns on affordable housing, immigration reform, financial reform, and have built strong relationships of accountability with elected officials from mayors to senators. Last year, ADP got Senator Scott Brown (R-MA) to support the financial reform bill, bringing in the deciding vote that got that legislation passed. And that is a testament to direct action and the power of people to make change.

SD: *Could you talk about some other community organizing groups that have done similar community economic development work?*

CM: Just in the sector of community organizing I'm most familiar with, there are a number of groups that are looking to organize housing co-ops or worker co-ops. Of course there is Evergreen in Ohio and the partnership between Mondragón and the Steelworkers. Other examples include PCUN (*Pineros y Campesinos Unidos del Noroeste* or Northwest Treeplanters and Farmworkers United) in Oregon, where they have a community-owned radio station and other enterprises. There is the Green Workers Cooperatives in the Bronx. There is an effort in Missouri led by GRO—Grass Roots Organizing—where they are organizing folks in manufactured housing, where so many families are suffering with predatory mortgages, and they are looking to cooperatively purchase their manufactured housing park. The Filipino Workers Center is leading the way in creating new worker-owned businesses and financial services led by immigrant women. In San Francisco, there is a group of Occupy folks who are putting together the "People's Credit Union." And as more and more people look for alternatives to the big banks, they are saying, "Hey, we want to do more than move our money, we want to control how it is used and invest it in our communities." I believe alternative financial institutions and products that enable people to truly wield economic power—that are just and values-based—will be the next big wave.

There is also an explosion of new ideas and enterprises in the shareable economy—groups like Kiva, Kickstarter, Ride Share—these are not quite the same as building alternative economic institutions, but they are very much about people taking control of their own economic activity and using it intentionally to benefit the commons.

Community ownership, collaborative consumption, cooperative enterprises—there is a new economic movement blooming right now that is very exciting and it takes all different forms. The definition of community economic development is that it happens locally and is based on context, place, time, and people. The challenge is how to get some of these efforts to scale, but we can never create cookie-cutter models because then they won't be rooted in the experiences of everyday people. We can share models, tactics and methodologies, but each experiment will be unique.

SD: *ADP, like most nonprofits, has been the recipient of foundation support. Famously, Andrea Smith edited a volume a few years* *ago titled* **The Revolution Will Not Be Funded.** *How did ADP seek to negotiate the challenges of what Smith has labeled the "nonprofit industrial complex?"*

CM: That is a very important question. I would say a few things. Foundations are crucially important to our work. There are a lot of good people and amazing family foundations out there that are committed to fundamental change—change that is equitable and rooted in the dignity of the human spirit.

However, we've got to find ways to fund our own work. One of the things that I am most proud of from my time at ADP, and that I now evangelize, was our ability to create a permanent stream of internally generated revenue. A substantial portion of the organization's revenue has been generated internally through membership dues and subsidiary businesses. The surplus generated from the businesses was invested back into the organizing work, which gave the organization a tremendous amount of freedom and allowed it to take some risks that maybe it couldn't if we were 100 percent foundation dependent.

The structure of nonprofits is actually quite limiting to organizations in our movement. It is quite difficult as a nonprofit public charity to create income-generating streams or subsidiary cooperative businesses. There are all kinds of regulations about which way the money flows that can easily trip up good people doing good work. We found that nonprofit competitive bidding requirements actually harmed our ability to use our own companies because we paid living wages and were not typically the lowest bidder. So we were competing against companies that submitted lower bids because they abused and underpaid their workers.

Another problem is that nonprofits are not eligible for SBA [Small Business Administration] guaranteed loans and are excluded from many traditional financing mechanisms because they lack the ability to provide guarantees for the loans. We really need to find new models—whether it is benefit corporations that expand corporate accountability so they are required to make decisions that are good for society, not just their shareholders—or co-ops, or even traditional limited liability companies governed by structures that balance the needs of the individual, the community, business and the environment. In addition to building economic power and creating

"There is a new economic movement blooming right now that is very exciting and **it takes all different forms**."

our own structures, we really need to think about throwing off the nonprofit yoke that is on all of us. This doesn't mean becoming a purely for-profit entity; it means running socially responsible businesses that invest in the commons.

In my work now, I'm organizing young people who are between the ages of 20 and 35. There is some amazing creativity. I just visited Hawaii where a group of tech-savvy entrepreneurs created an innovators' hub. They share workspace, ideas, social, and intellectual capital. They've created their own community economy. It is truly innovative.

The millennial generation is faced with a whole new paradigm—the traditional dream of our children having a better life than we did is no longer true. Student debt, which is now higher than credit card debt, has a stranglehold on young people and the unemployment rate for young people coming out of college is very high, so they have no choice but to come up with new ideas. I think this young generation is going to forge a new path for all of us. They are entrepreneurial and innovative and keep in mind issues of equity and social justice in new ways, but not the traditional ways that I was raised in.

SD: *What made you decide to leave ADP and go work for Rebuild the Dream? Presumably it has something to do with wanting to work at the national level?*

CM: It all goes back to that issue of scale. How can we take these amazing ideas at the grassroots level and scale them up? I am excited to have the opportunity to identify great important work and new ideas, spread them around, share them, and amplify them. And I also can share my experience at the local level with other folks.

It is so important that our movement engage in passing the baton, in paying it forward. I hope to learn from and share experiences and knowledge with a whole new group of people who are engaging in this work. And at the same time, ADP is led by a talented group of leaders, including Tim Fisk, the Executive Director, and William Cano, the Deputy Director, who are truly visionary and who will forge new paths in creating the world as it should be. I can't wait to see what is next for them.

SD: *Rebuild the Dream often appears to be focused on advocacy. But as you have noted, it also aims to build a new economy. Could you talk about these new economy efforts?*

CM: Rebuild the Dream is about building grassroots people-powered innovations to create an equitable and sustainable economy. We have over 600,000 members and are growing every day.

First, we are running important campaigns that will have an immediate impact on the lives of everyday people and on our economy. Right now we are zeroing in on preventing the interest rates on student loans from doubling and on getting relief for the 11 million homeowners who are underwater. And we are creating smart new technologies to amplify our organizing and advocacy so more people can engage with each other and with decision makers.

Second, we are expanding our work on the ground and in the community, especially with young people who hold the key to a whole new future. We are going deep into key states like Wisconsin and Florida and lifting up art, culture, innovation, and smart ideas from the folks on the ground in order to build real power. We just came back from an amazing event in Hawaii, where there is a movement to truly build a sustainable economy and where they are on the verge of winning legislation to create a state bank, making it only the second in the country and the first in nearly one hundred years.

And third, we are meeting with and learning from people like you who are innovating in the new economy, what we call American Dream 2.0. And we hope to evangelize this movement and help people in the community really build economic power that is balanced and just.

SD: *Could you provide an example?*

CM: Right now, we have kicked off the "Rebuild the Dream" revivals. We are working with partner groups in key states—bringing together artists, cultural creators, young people, activists in the new economy—to really envision what the dream is. We need to dream big about what society could and should look like. The 99% Spring mass training and actions are moving hundreds of thousands of people to take action and are exposing the role big banks played in crashing our economy and the stranglehold that money has over our democracy. We are so excited to be a part of that, but we also have to lift up solutions.

So Rebuild the Dream is investing in solution-oriented policy campaigns, like the state bank legislation that is moving in Hawaii and is also going deep with groups that are working in the new economy. In Hawaii, 700 people took over the state capitol in a beautiful expression of our values with poetry, art, music, movement-building trainings and small group discussions. We also met with a group of young entrepreneurs who have never considered themselves politically active but want to be part of re-envisioning and rebuilding the dream. These are smart people who have a lot to offer the movement. And Rebuild the Dream is creating this big tent to identify what the dream should look like and to take action in creating it.

As we travel around and learn from folks and meet people who are really forging the way, we want to be a vehicle to expand the message and share the amazing ideas around the country. We see ourselves as seeding future work—spreading the campaign to create state banks in other places, amplifying the campaign to cap interest rates on predatory loans in Missouri, and so on. How does that translate at the personal level? It may mean moving your money to a community bank or perhaps getting together and creating a credit union. We are really look at the micro economy and macro economy and seeding efforts to create a dream anew.

SD: *Thinking nationally, co-ops are enjoying new visibility in the United States, in part due to growing frustration with what might be called "American business as usual." This new interest can be seen in many venues, such as with the protestors of the Occupy movement. What do you see as steps that the co-op movement needs to take nationally to build on this new visibility and take advantage of the moment?*

CM: From my experience, and I think the co-op movement is growing and expanding as we speak, but it is a pretty insular movement and it is somewhat inaccessible. Making sure it is inclusive of low-income

"I would say a third thing is that we need to de-mystify business creation. We are the experts. **People can figure things out if they have the tools.**"

people and to people of color is crucially important. And addressing issues of equity is crucially important. The economic crisis is nothing new to low-income people and communities of color. We need to make sure these institutions in the new economy are not only inclusive of people who have been hurt most, but also led by them. That would be one thing.

Sometimes folks become very focused on their own co-op business, and we really need to politicize the cooperative movement and get folks who are committed to changing the relationship between worker and owner to also engage in broader worldview work and engage in politics. Get out of the silo of their business. Get out of the silo of their own workplace or business and thinking of themselves as just working with co-ops and thinking of themselves as a part of a broader new economy movement.

I would say a third thing is that we need to de-mystify business creation. *We* are the experts. People can figure things out if they have the tools. That is one of the goals of Rebuild, to really expand this notion of what is possible and reinforce this idea that everyday people can create new enterprises that are just, and forge ahead in the new economy.

SD: *What do you see as the top priorities of the U.S. community organizing movement going forward?*

CM: It is impossible to pick one or two. When I think about my work, I think about making sure that it is transformational for the people who are involved in the community and for society as a whole. We need to be organizing for structural change, really changing the institutions that perpetuate inequity.

And we should be thinking big. Certainly we need to achieve small victories in that long march, but we have to be aspirational.

And right now in this moment we have that opportunity to get out of our issue silos or traditional constituencies and build a real movement that makes our economy work for everyone.

Along those lines, we need to figure out ways to rein in the stranglehold that money and lobbyists have over our democracy. We have to change the dynamics of the power that the big banks and corporations have in our government and our economy and really get into the hearts and minds of everyday people, so that we can take back our democracy and put people before profits.

I think everyone would agree that corporations are not people. And we have to solve the immigration crisis that has tremendous impact on our economy by passing thoughtful immigration reform that reflects our values and honors the dignity of the human spirit.

What is the dream of America? It is certainly not hate and fear. The folks I talk to say it is about values, equity, and being able to envision a future for your children—and your children's children—that is sustainable.

How much is enough? How much is too much? I think all of that is on the table as we work out what is this new economy looks like.

Raquel Pinderhughes

Dr. Raquel Pinderhughes is Founder and Executive Director of the Environmental Literacy Curriculum Project, which manages Roots of Success, and Professor of Urban Studies and Planning at San Francisco State University, where she teaches courses on urban environmental planning and policy, sustainable urban development, and environmental justice.

Interviewed in 2012

Steve Dubb: Could you talk about your background and how you got involved in work related to prisoner reentry and environmental justice?

Raquel Pinderhughes: For the past 35 years, my work has been focused on how we can improve quality of life for people in underserved urban communities. I spent the first part of my career documenting environmental injustices in low-income communities and communities of color and working in the environmental justice movement to improve environmental conditions in these communities. Many of our efforts in the environmental justice movement focused on remediating polluting facilities or shutting them down entirely. Unfortunately, as we won, many of these same polluting facilities moved to the South and then overseas. So we began to think about how people can produce, consume, and dispose of goods differently so that everyone can live in a safe environment. That moved me into the the emerging field of sustainable development. where I turned my attention to understanding questions related to environmental planning and policy and began to explore how we can manage cities in ways that are more environmentally and socially responsible. My focus has always been on cities. I started by looking at environmental issues in underserved communities and moved into work that focuses on how everybody can be protected from environmental harm. That moved me into the field of environmental sustainability. I spent more than a decade working in cities around the world—Cuba, Spain, India, and Brazil—working with people who manage programs that improve environmental quality and reduce poverty.

That first part of my career was focused almost entirely on teaching and research. The second part has been focused on teaching and research but also on developing and implementing programs that improve environmental quality, break the cycle of poverty, help people achieve their personal goals for success, and inspire them to work to improve conditions in their community. Mid-career I was asked to develop and direct the Delancey Street College Program, where I had the opportunity to teach ex-offenders about urban environmental policy and planning issues. Delancey Street was important to my development as a teacher and a person because I had to present these issues in a way that was relevant and meaningful for a population with multiple barriers to education and employment. Working at Delancey Street deeply informed my understanding of the needs of incarcerated and reentry populations and strengthened my commitment to improving the quality of life for disenfranchised populations. Later on, I became the director of the Willie Brown Internship Program, which supports the professional development of students who face barriers getting to and through college by placing them in prestigious San Francisco city government internships and mentoring them as they work in these agencies and pursue their career goals.

In 2004, I wrote a textbook that summarized much of what I had learned from working in cities around the world, called *Alternative Urban Futures: Planning for Sustainable Development in Cities Throughout the World*. It focused on how we can manage urban infrastructures related to water, waste, energy, transportation, and food systems in ways that are more environmentally and socially responsible. At the end of that period, I had a very well developed understanding of urban infrastructures and the jobs that come on line as we move from a pollution-based approach, to a more sustainable approach, to delivering goods and services in these five areas.

One of the things that became clear is that, as we transition to a more sustainable economy and society, we need to think about who this new sector of the economy will include and exclude. We could easily green our infrastructure while reproducing the exact same inequalities and injustices that exist in the traditional labor market and pollution-based economy—locking people with less education and skills into low-wage, dead-end jobs or keeping them out of the labor market entirely. I am committed to working to ensure that the people who are most impacted by the problems that stem from a pollution-based economy—the people who need jobs most—receive the training and support they need to access good jobs and careers in the green economy and are empowered and positioned to help us figure out how to address the problems we are facing.

I spent 2005 to 2007 studying the green economy, dividing it into 22 sectors, and interviewing employers in 21 of these sectors. I wanted to know what it would take for employers to hire workers with barriers to employment for green jobs in their firms. I asked employers what are the qualifications you look for. How do you make decisions about who to hire? What is the worker's trajectory

"I am committed to working to ensure that the people who are most impacted by the problems that stem from a pollution-based economy—**the people who need jobs most**—receive the training and support they need to access good jobs and careers in the green economy."

over time? I asked other questions about the mission of the firm. I found out about a lot of interesting things, including the importance of public policies and industrial zoning.

At the end of this study, I really understood the green jobs landscape. I broke down the jobs that required no college education and used the term "green collar jobs" to describe jobs that are available to people with lower levels of education and skills. I learned that employers typically hire college graduates for these jobs because they want employees who are academically strong and understand the environmental mission of their firm. More than hard skills or relevant experience, it is passion and commitment to the mission of a firm that makes job applicants most attractive to employers. As a result of that study, I developed the first green jobs training model, which is colloquially called "the Pinderhughes model," from which I later developed the Roots of Success educational curriculum.

This model was first used by the Oakland Apollo Alliance and the Ella Baker Center, which Van Jones founded and directed at the time, to create the Oakland Green Jobs Corps. We received a lot of attention from the press and policymakers interested in green jobs training. What made the model unique was that, in addition to focusing on soft skills (academic skills), hard skills (the job you do), and job readiness (labor market skills), it included environmental literacy training, a paid internship, and a Green Employer Council that is structured to deepen the relationship between job training programs and employers. Later, the model influenced the development of the federal government's Pathways out of Poverty program funded with stimulus [American Recovery and Reinvestment Act] dollars and the Pinderhughes model took off fairly quickly.

I found myself consulting with staff in training programs throughout the country, where I quickly learned that there were no environmental education curriculums specifically designed for the youth and adults who have been failed by traditional academic settings and who live in the neighborhoods most heavily impacted by environmental and public health problems. That's why I created *Roots of Success*, an educational program that prepares youth and adults with barriers to employment for good green jobs and to improve conditions in their communities. The curriculum is a direct result of my professional and personal experiences up to now—my teaching and academic research in the United States and abroad, my work with low-income youth and adults who have barriers to employment, my work with job training programs, and my work on the green economy and green jobs.

SD: *How do you define green jobs?*

RP: Green jobs are jobs that directly improve environmental quality. They should also provide workers with living wages, safe and healthy working conditions, benefits, opportunities for continual training and career development, and the right to organize. Since we are rolling out a new term and idea, it is important to include the conditions that people labor under into the definition.

I'm interested in green jobs because they have the potential to fight poverty and pollution simultaneously. To reinvigorate our economy, we need to do at least three things—raise the minimum wage (so consumers can spend more), put more people to work, and repair and green the infrastructure. If we did this, we would have good, well paying, green jobs that cannot be outsourced.

SD: *Could you discuss the origins of the "green jobs" movement? How has it evolved over time?*

RP: I would trace the green jobs movement to the environmental justice movement, which early on in its history focused on the fact that the people most impacted by environmental hazards should be trained and paid to remediate them. This gave rise to job-training programs such as the Chicago Green Corps, which initially focused on Hazardous Waste Operations and Emergency Response standard (HAZWOPER) training—that is, training that prepares people to do jobs such as lead and asbestos abatement.

In the mid-1980s, as mayors began to address local environmental problems—such as traffic congestion, running out of landfill space and community opposition to incineration—they expanded mass transit and created recycling programs, which expanded and created green jobs. Since the 1990s, the focus has expanded to energy efficiency, alternative energy, urban agriculture, sustainable agriculture, and many more areas. These jobs grow as public officials and managers deal with local and regional environmental challenges.

SD: *It seemed that there was a big boost of support for green jobs in 2009, but that has dissipated? Where are green jobs today?*

RP: To understand where green jobs are located, you need to look at the decisions that city managers and their colleagues are making as they deal with a wide range of environmental challenges. In rural areas, you have problems with cattle breeding, factory farming, waste pools. In suburban areas, you have problems associated with suburban sprawl and growth. In urban areas, you have problems related to air quality, waste management, automobile dependency, food deserts, and mass consumption. Many of these challenges get dealt with by the city managers, who do not talk in terms of "green." They simply say we are running out of landfill, what are we going to do? Well, we are going to improve recycling. We are having huge problems of air contamination, how will we address it? We will use carpool lanes and mass transit. Problems related to fuel prices and climate change promote energy efficiency and solar installations. Every major institution is trying to increase energy, water, and waste efficiency in order to cut costs—HUD [U.S. Department of Housing & Urban Development], the military, public schools, prisons, and jails. You find green jobs being created in the places where environmental problems are being solved. If you understand this, you can see that green jobs are one of the fastest growing sectors of the economy, even in the recession.

SD: *What is the federal role?*

RP: The federal government has a huge role to play in the transition to a green economy. In addition to passing and supporting environmental policies, the federal government has always paid for infrastructure. The ARRA [American Reinvestment and Recovery Act or "stimulus bill"] dollars were also very important. Most of our first clients came from these dollars. *Roots of Success* is a really good marker of the degree to which ARRA supported new programs, allowed existing programs to expand, and how, after the stimulus funding ended, these programs were ending or retracting. ARRA made a huge difference and was a huge shot in the arm for low-income people seeking employment. The Pathways Out of Poverty grant supported programs that prepared thousands of low-income youth and adults to work in the green jobs labor market. These programs have to scale back significantly now that the stimulus dollars have run out.

We collect extensive data on the programs that use our curriculum. In 2011, the average job placement rate of these programs was 51 percent. That's an incredibly high success rate considering the barriers the populations we are working with face in the labor market and in this recession.

We are now focusing our attention on the $7.2 million that the Obama Administration has allocated to train veterans for green jobs, as well as the interest the private sector has in training and hiring vets for jobs in the clean energy sector. We see this as a perfect market for *Roots of Success* since 74 percent of veterans don't have a BA degree and 51 percent of veterans participate in some form of job training each year.

SD: *Could you discuss the origins and development of Roots of Success? Could you describe what your training approach is?*

RP: *Roots of Success* is designed to prepare people who come from communities that are heavily impacted by environmental and public health problems for the green jobs and careers that emerge as we put solutions to these problems into place. Without programs like *Roots of Success*, people who come from underserved communities, and people who have been failed by traditional educational institutions will not be able to compete with college-educated graduates for these jobs. *Roots of Success* provides people who have multiple barriers to employment with the academic skills and environmental knowledge they need to get to the point where an employer will take them seriously. As important, since we have a captive audience in a job-training program, we use this opportunity to strengthen the skills people need to improve conditions in their community. This is why one of the nine modules in *Roots of Success* focuses on community organizing and leadership. We want people to improve their life circumstances through green jobs and careers, but we also want them to be able to deal with the economic and social forces—such as gentrification—that profoundly impact low-income communities.

Roots of Success is a basic skills curriculum (reading, writing, math, critical thinking, problem solving) and job readiness curriculum (understand the difference between jobs, career, career pathway, introducing them to unions and apprenticeships, developing a resume, cover letter, going through mock interviews) that focuses on environmental issues. The curriculum is divided into nine modules (Water, Waste, Transportation, Energy, Building, Health, Food and Agriculture) bookended by introductory and concluding segments. Eight modules focus on environmental sectors and one module focuses on community organizing. We help people understand the root causes of environmental problems and how we can address them from multiple perspectives—planning, policy, technology, organizing, etc.

We describe *Roots of Success* as a college education for people without a high school degree. Although most of the people we work with are considered "not ready" for college, none of the information we present is dumbed down. Students are systematically presented with the knowledge and skills they need to understand the root causes of environmental problems and the range of approaches that can be used to address these problems. By the end of the course, students understand scientific processes that help to explain water cycles, nutrient cycles, incineration, bioaccumulation, fossils fuels, climate change, etc., as well as social and political processes that help to explain environmental decision-making, cost-benefit analysis, the precautionary principle, environmental injustice, climate injustice, etc.

SD: *Can you say more about what a module looks like?*

RP: Each module has the same basic structure: introduction, problems,

"74 percent of veterans don't have a BA degree and 51 percent of veterans participate in some form of job training each year."

solutions, an overview of green jobs and career pathways, a quiz, reflection questions, and an application and practice section where students can take what they learned in the module and apply it in their lives.

To develop *Roots of Success*, I interviewed job-training directors around the country who told me that they have no extra time for additional training. That's why each *Roots of Success* module can be delivered in four to five hours and why programs can teach as many or as few of the nine modules as they like. It's a very efficient and flexible curriculum. The way we cover so much content and so many objectives is by using an Instructor's Manual that every single instructor is trained and licensed to use, and by using a multi-media approach that uses videos and visuals to introduce students to complex issues and systems like electricity, climate change, water and nutrient cycles, green building techniques, etc. For example, we can help students understand a range of issues related to fossil fuels, coal, electricity and greenhouse gas emissions using a four-minute video. Once we incorporated multimedia, we had all sorts of opportunities. We don't just use video. We also use visuals on slides. This approach allows us to simultaneously teach to visual, auditory and kinesthetic learners. We get auditory learning from the teacher, who reviews the concepts. Kinesthetic learning uses team-based activities to introduce students to all of these ideas. As we tried to address the challenges programs face as they prepare people with barriers to employment for jobs and the challenges of students who have been failed by traditional learning settings, the curriculum evolved into a deeper and more effective experience for both instructors and students. There's very little time that the teacher is just talking to the students. The way it typically works is that the teacher throws out an idea and students respond. I've been talking about it as a "call-and-response pedagogy."

SD: *Could you tell us a bit about the demographics of the groups you serve?*

RP: All of our instructors fill out a survey on the demographics of each class they teach. In 2011, 98 percent of the students in our classes were living in poverty, 93 percent were unemployed at the time they took the class, and 42 percent had been incarcerated as children and/or adults. Fifty-one percent were men and 49 percent women. The median reading level was seventh-grade proficiency; the median math level was fourth-grade proficiency. The overwhelming majority of our students are low-income students of color from groups underrepresented in higher education (82 percent in 2011)—47 percent African American and more than 35 percent Latino in 2011.

SD: *In a short period of time, you have partnered with groups in 34 states, Puerto Rico, and the United Kingdom, trained 500 instructors, and certified 3,000 graduates. Talk about how you managed that growth.*

RP: When people see those numbers, people think it's a lot of growth. We think it is small because the need is so great. We are a very tiny organization. We have two full-time staff people. I work pro bono. The only way people learn about us right now is through word-of-mouth, by hearing me at a conference, or through the Green For All website.

There are very few, if any, other environmental curriculums out there designed for adults with lower levels of education. Program staff members know that if they want to keep the attention of the youth and adults they are training, they have to keep them interested. Our pedagogical approach doesn't just provide information on the environment, we connect that information to people's concerns and hopes and we try to inspire people to become activists—the justice aspect is very important to our organization. The fact that it focuses on issues of justice is important. People working with our student population deeply care about justice. They don't want a curriculum that is just about global warming. They want a curriculum that focuses on equity and justice. They know that will be more relevant for their participants. The fact that we do this is important.

Roots of Success meets the needs of a wide range of programs for three or four reasons: 1) the content is what people need (environmental knowledge plus academic skills); 2) the curriculum is flexible—you don't have to teach all nine modules; 3) It is very affordable. It costs $600 per instructor for a one-day training and then instructors order student workbooks for $50 for each student; and 4) the Instructor's Manual is critical—because it allows people who don't have expertise to teach the course. The people teaching *Roots of Success* often teach or work in a wholly different subject like hard skills or counseling. The Instructor's Manual is very important to our success because it allows people from many different areas of expertise to teach the curriculum. Our teachers are welding teachers, math counselors, job training staff, prisoners serving long-term sentences, parole officers, etc. The Instructor's Manual allows people to come up to speed quickly and to teach the curriculum effectively. I just did a training session with 20 teachers. Of these twenty, about five had a horticultural teaching background and one was a GED teacher. The rest had less than that.

Youth and adults that have failed in traditional academic settings enjoy *Roots of Success* because it makes learning relevant, focuses on success, connecting education to employment, and inspires individuals to change their own personal behaviors and conditions in the environments.

Instructors really appreciate that the curriculum is extremely organized and user friendly. Everything you do is carefully designed and well laid out. It's a turnkey curriculum. Instructors love that—even people who know the content will appreciate having everything in one place and knowing exactly what the student learning outcomes for each module are.

Because our curriculum is affordable, easy to use and deals with scientific and social issues, our content is really relevant to the people whom programs are serving. It turns them on to learning instead of off. People also appreciate that the curriculum presents a balanced view on most issues. Some of the people we train are Republicans or Libertarians. They feel comfortable teaching *Roots of Success* because we allow them to present both sides of the nuclear issue or fossil fuel issues. Upon completion of the curriculum, we provide students with a certificate at the end of the course that is increasingly recognized by employers and educational institutions. This is critical for students when they finish their programs. Instructors really like the training. We've been able to get continuing education credits for people who are trained.

The *Roots of Success* curriculum was designed with a lot of intention. I did a lot of research on the needs of the programs that we work with and created the structure with these needs in mind. The price-point is critical. It has to be affordable. Instructors who aren't experts in the content need to be able to teach the course since many programs don't have environmentalists on their staff. Every module has a huge amount of content on green jobs and careers in that sector. I'm always thinking about how it's going to be used and by whom. Each module was reviewed by a panel of experts, then piloted in six different programs, then changed and improved over the first three years we piloted it. We are always listening to our users and improving it to meet their needs.

SD: *On your website, you mention that you work with organizations in a number of sectors (green jobs training, advocacy groups, government, community colleges, historically black colleges, high schools, and prisons). Could you describe how your work differs from sector to sector and how you accommodate the different needs of these populations?*

RP: Because our pedagogical approach is based on the information in our class being directly relevant to each student, we've created customized versions of *Roots of Success* for different audiences. This is very important. The *Roots of Success* experience allows each student to build on past knowledge and experiences. Our secret sauce is that students feel that the content is relevant and meaningful to them.

The first curriculum was for adults in green jobs programs. The second was translation in Spanish. We found all new videos produced in Spanish-speaking countries. We wanted people to see themselves and hear their language. We had a team of Puerto Ricans, Chicanos, Argentinians, and Mexicans working on the translation since different Spanish-speaking countries use different terms to describe similar things. We produced what we call a universal translation and all of the videos we use were produced in Spanish-speaking countries. Then we realized that we needed a version for youth in high schools and youth programs—so we created a youth version. Then, as it started to be used in prisons, we learned that they didn't have access to computers. So we adjusted our curriculum and we added content on the greening of prisons.

And, most recently, we created a new version for low-income social entrepreneurs that want to or currently own and operate green enterprises. And we're hoping to develop a curriculum for worker-owned cooperatives. About 80 percent of the content in a customized version is the same, but where things change is in the activities, exercises, and examples. You have to give people opportunities to apply what they are learning through a lens that is more similar than different to their own. For the United Kingdom, we worked with colleagues in England to flip out all of the content that was U.S.-focused and make it U.K.-focused. And we're now talking with colleagues about developing a version of the curriculum for South Africa. It is the same fundamentals, but all of the examples change. Customized versions are critical because they make the material directly relevant for participants.

Organizationally, we are small and underfunded, but we have found that problem helps us to be incredibly nimble. It allows us to respond quickly to what programs and people need. For example, we were able to quickly take out all of the computer content to create a version for prisons, jails and juvenile justice facilities.

SD: *Why did you set it up as a nonprofit social enterprise? Did you consider being a for-profit?*

RP: Being a for-profit was never an option. It's not my style and that has never been a goal. What I wanted to do was reach as many people as possible. Originally I thought that I would create a curriculum and teachers would download it as an open-source document. As I began to understand that there needed to be an Instructor's Manual, the need for people to be licensed became apparent. The pedagogical approach is critical to our success. The reason people are trained and licensed is to ensure that no matter the program, location, instructor, or students, *Roots of Success* is communicated in the most impactful way. The only ongoing cost to programs interested in using *Roots of Success* is purchasing student workbooks for each student in their classes. This investment from programs is the principle means the *Roots of Success* organization grows. With every new instructor and every new program, the organization can turn around and build a better curriculum, staff our

"People working with our student population deeply care about justice. They don't want a curriculum that is just about global warming. **They want a curriculum that focuses on equity and justice**."

support team, and continue to outreach to new programs across the country. The best way we can grow in reach is to build the best curriculum for the people we aim to serve. Our growth as an organization is a direct result of programs seeing the curriculum's impact on their community, then making the decision to make *Roots of Success* the go-to curriculum for environmental literacy and job readiness skills.

SD: *What are your main priorities going forward?*

RP: Our main priority going forward is that we would like to serve more programs and people. There is a huge need for *Roots of Success*, not simply because of its green jobs focus, but because of its transformative impact. The experience helps people who've been failed by the educational system feel more competent and more connected. People need to know more about us, and we would like to get more revenue into the organization, so we can hire more staff and reach more people.

Roots of Success is a nonprofit social enterprise, which allows us to focus on developing the best curriculum and supporting teachers and programs to provide the most effective and transformative educational experience for the people we serve.

I am also excited about the impact of my work on job training more generally. The focus on environmental literacy has changed the way green jobs training is moving forward. People now understand that it is not just about hard skills training. When people are training to be health care aides, they learn nothing about the health care system. Job training has been primarily about getting people off the welfare rolls into low-wage, not very autonomous jobs. Bringing the idea of literacy—connecting people to the issues—is transformative for the job-training world. I don't want to take too much credit for that, but it's an important shift—it's not just hard skills and soft skills, it's helping people understand the arena in which they will be working.

I am proud that we have helped people. Our graduates talk about the fact that this training has made a huge difference in how they see themselves and the world around them. A lot of students talk about how they talk with their children about what they learned in the class when they would not have before, and that they are now behaving differently with their kids and families—recycling, buying less toxic products, consuming differently, eating foods that are healthier for them, going to community meetings.

SD: *If you had to highlight a few key accomplishments of Roots for Success' work to date that you are proudest of, what would they be?*

RP: One of the things I am proudest of and that is most fulfilling to me is that I produced and manage *Roots of Success* primarily with young people who come from the communities that we serve. I am very proud of the workplace that we have set up together—we work collaboratively, as a team, minimal hierarchy, decent salaries and benefits for paid staff, good working conditions. *Roots of Success* has become a place where young people of color can be mentored, paid well, launch their careers, and give back to their communities. I didn't know I would be doing that when I started, but I am really proud of that—that young people can be mentored here, that I can learn from them, and we all benefit.

I am also excited about the fact that we produced a curriculum that can be taught by instructors who don't have expertise in the content. People who are not experts in the content and/or who don't have teaching experience can become instructors and teach using our teaching materials. Many of our instructors have never taught before, and the experience of teaching *Roots of Success* has transformed them. In one of the prisons we work with in Ohio, we have men who are serving life sentences in prison teaching men who are serving shorter sentences, so they can get jobs in the green economy when they re-enter society. I like the idea that people who don't have the expertise can communicate complex environmental justice and social justice issues effectively to others. That's a success of the curriculum. This has put us in a position where lots of people are now teaching *Roots of Success*—job counselors, probation officers, people in prison, welding instructors, GED instructors, graduates of community-based green social enterprise programs. These are people teaching *Roots of Success*, along with more experienced teachers.

I am excited that *Roots of Success* accomplishes much more than we intended. We thought it would primarily help people understand the environment and acquire academic skills that would put them in a better position to find work in the green economy—but the curriculum clearly inspires people to get involved in their community. It's also clear that the curriculum makes people feel more connected to larger issues in society and in their neighborhoods. I have had students tell me that they felt completely disconnected from these issues before they took the course and now this is what they really care about. It's clear that people are integrating the information into their lives—that it has changed them—that they have become environmentally aware and engaged in ways that are meaningful for them. I am very proud of the transformative impact of the curriculum on both instructors and students.

SD: *Anything else you would like to add?*

RP: A lot of people contributed to the development of *Roots of Success*. I was the creator of the curriculum. I developed the content and the pedagogy, but a lot of people helped—students, staff, evaluators, and pro bono consultants. The program staff members we work with constantly tell us what we need to do to make it better. We also have a phenomenal in-house staff—Chad Flores (deputy director, director of operations) and Shamar Theus (contributed to the curriculum and program director). Right now the three of us are *Roots of Success*— we're the worker bees, but multiple hands have gone into this work.

We also have great partners. Our partnerships with Green for All and the Center for Working Educators in New York City have been very important. Working with organizations doing green jobs training and advocacy work has been really important. The work we are doing with people in the prisons is incredibly important, and we've met amazing people through our work there.

Reverend Barry Randolph

*Reverend Barry Randolph is pastor
of Church of the Messiah, a Detroit
church that has developed four social
enterprises to date, one of which is a
private community-based business and
three of which are owned by the Church
directly. The Church has also sponsored a
CDC for the past 35 years. In addition
to being a pastor, Rev. Randolph is also a
leader in the community, having joined
other groups in coalitions, including
church consortia and a public safety
group. Barry is also on the board of the
Center for Community Based Enterprises
(C2BE). [Note: the interviewer is also
on the Board of C2BE]. The Church,
founded more than a century ago, found
itself on hard times a decade ago, but
under Rev. Randolph's leadership, the
Church has grown rapidly, becoming
a leading community group in Detroit
revitalization work.*

Interviewed in 2013

Steve Dubb: Could you talk about your background in small business and how you came to be pastor of the Church of the Messiah?

Barry Randolph: I was born and raised in Detroit. I was already interested in business. That was actually my career goal, to do that. I did that. It was working. Let's just say, what got me to Messiah was that I was interested in the community work that the Church of the Messiah was doing, so I wound up coming here. I had no intention of becoming a priest or pastor. In 2002, I became pastor of Church of the Messiah. The problem was the church then had 40 people showing up on Sundays, no money, and the building was too big. So I came up with a plan to rebuild the community and the church. It worked. Currently, we have between 250 to 300 people showing up on Sunday. Now the building is so full of activity that it is too small. So the plan worked. So my business is bringing the good news of the gospel to the community while building the community. Primarily, the congregation is young people. Sixty percent are African-American males under the age of thirty. The vast majority of the congregation is under thirty, which is unusual.

SD: Could you talk about the process of rebuilding the church and the community?

BR: Messiah has a long history of working in the community. Because the church was in decline, few people realized how much it did. Part of what I did was let the community know that the church was alive and kicking. We became more political, working with Metropolitan Organizing Strategy Enabling Strength (MOSES) and the city. We started a crime and safety group, Citizens United for Safety. That made us more politically active. That started us working with young people with anti-crime measures. Often the young are the victims, but they are also often the perpetrators of the crimes. We started working with young people for conflict resolution. That also led to job training, working with the judicial system, working with the police, and working with families rebuilding the community. It also led to working on more housing projects, doing a feeding program and a community garden. It also led to nutrition projects. Oddly enough, it also led to entrepreneurship. There are four viable businesses started by people inside the church. We worked on changing the mindset. Let people know we were alive and kicking and a force to be reckoned with. It also gave us the opportunity to evangelize at the same time.

SD: *Could you talk about the concept of ministry and how it informs the Church's community wealth building work?*

BR: Ministry is community building. The Gospels mean the Good News. We are to go out and spread Good News. But we are also to *be* good news. The way we are good news is supporting, rebuilding the community, and changing the mindset of the community by making the world a better place. That is what ministry is to us. Ministry is not a religious concept as much as it is about changing mindsets.

SD: *Could you describe the four social enterprises of the Church of the Messiah?*

BR: The biggest is Nikki's Ginger Tea. It was started by a single mother in the church who was raising her daughter and decided that she didn't want to be on general assistance of any type. She decided instead to be a business owner. She came up with a concept that she loved experimenting with the herb ginger. She came up with an incredible concept for her business. She has six flavors of teas and is in 40 stores across the state of Michigan. All of her employees, 10 people, are young people from the community. The tea is made in the church's commercial kitchen. It was founded 17 years ago, but it has really taken off in the last seven or eight years. Some of the stores that she is in are Whole Foods, Schiller's Market, Public Town Market, and a whole bunch of other independent stores, like health food stores.

Another one is called Basic Black. That is a t-shirt and design company. That was started last year. That is a community-based business inside the church: It is run by people who are in the community, who have an interest in manufacturing clothing and who are interested in art design. It employs about seven people right now.

Lawn King is a landscaping company, started earlier this spring. It is a community-based enterprise run by people in the church. It employs seven people right now.

The fourth one is called the Repeat Boutique. It is a thrift store, which is run by the people in the church. It is also a community-based business. The proceeds go back into the ministry of the church and it is used primarily for job training. It employs six people right now.

They contribute earned income to the church and are used for job training. They are open to anybody. We use them for people who are usually unemployable or hard to employ—a convicted felon who wants to start their life over or a single mom with limited job education and training. They can use the job as a stepping stone, so they can get back to the workforce.

SD: *Who owns the businesses?*

BR: Monique owns Nikki's Ginger Tea. The other three were started through the efforts of people in the church and are owned by the church.

SD: *Could you talk about the Mount Elliott Makerspace project? How did it develop?*

BR: Mt. Elliott Makerspace started about two years ago. They have a connection to Massachusetts Institute of Technology (MIT) and the Kresge Foundation. The Mt. Elliott Makerspace was created to allow people in the community to get hands-on training at reinvention, learning about technology, computers, and alternative transportation. It is because of the Mt. Elliott Makerspace that the t-shirt business came to be. It is through the Mt. Elliott Makerspace that the entrepreneurship happened. It provides a space for creativity, hands-on training for different things. It is also linked to our woodshop. We have a fully functional woodshop that is going to be concentrated on making furniture.

Right now, they have four employees. They've hired interns throughout the summer to work on different projects. They've done that for the past two years. Most of these people are from the community or from the Church.

The other asset of the Makerspace, because of the type of things they do—they do a lot pertaining to education at so many different levels. A lot has to do with a Maker Fair in Dearborn—they help bring people from outside of our community into our community, because everybody is interested in the type of programming that takes place at the Makerspace. The Makerspace operates inside of the Church. It started the t-shirt business and woodshop.

SD: *What has been the history of the Church of the Messiah Housing Corporation?*

BR: The Housing Corporation was started 36 years ago. It is one of the oldest CDCs in the country. It was started by members of the Church who were alarmed about the decline of the neighborhood and who wanted to do something to rebuild it. They started with one apartment building that was across the street from the Church—that was in 1978. Now, we have 213 units of property and through our partners we have invested about $48 million in the neighborhood. Some are renovated properties and some are from the ground up. And all of them are rental properties. The Housing Corporation is a separate 501(c)(3) from the Church. It has its own executive director and employees. It is also located inside the church. At one point, our building was gigantic—now we are running out of space.

SD: *You mentioned once that the Church owns 123 vacant lots in a city with more than 70,000 vacant lots. What is the strategy for using them?*

BR: We have fewer lots today, but we still own a large number of vacant lots. We intend to build on those lots. Right now, the economy is bad. We can't get financing. One of the things that we are looking at is partnering with other organizations in our area to come up with ideas of what do we do with the land once the economy recovers. Do we want to put something on that land? Do more community farming? Some degree of land repurposing that may not necessarily be housing? Possibly put in a greenhouse or hoop house—feed more people and use that as a possible business that also serves for job training.

It is interesting because the city of Detroit is a hot commodity right now. They are running out of land in midtown and downtown. We know that they will come this way. We intend to be a major stakeholder in our community when that happens.

SD: *Could you discuss some of the major challenges that you face and how you address them?*

BR: This work is not for the timid or the weak. It takes guts and vision and heart in order to do it. You don't do it for ambition, fame, or money. You have got to do it because it is the right thing to do.

I grew up here. I like it here. There are a lot of good people here. When you love your community and you watch it fall from its glory days almost to its demise, it is hard to sit back and watch that without doing something. My motivation—if we don't do it, if the people who live here don't do it, no one else will. We have to rescue ourselves.

"Ministry is community building. The Gospels mean the Good News. We are to go out and spread Good News. But we are also to *be* good news. The way we are good news is **supporting, rebuilding the community, and changing the mindset of the community by making the world a better place.**"

As a stakeholder, I have a vested interest. I want to see it prosper. We don't need to look back to the "Big Three" [General Motors, Ford Motor Company, and Chrysler]. But we can be better than we were.

We need innovation and collaboration. That's why we are interested in community-based enterprises. These are community-based businesses. General Motors (GM) and the big corporations—all of that is gone. There has to be a new way of thinking and living. Doing it from the point of view of the community—that's my motivation.

SD: *Do you see other churches in Detroit emulating the Church of the Messiah?*

BR: Yes. This last Friday [September 27, 2013], I was in a closed-door meeting with clergy of Detroit talking to members of the White House.

When President Obama came, I was in one of those meetings. I was talking about community development from the point of view of place-based—redevelop the community, it wasn't just about faith-based—but they wanted faith-based leaders who were doing things in their community. That was a good meeting.

There are other churches that are trying to rebuild their community. A lot of them are not on the scale of the Church of the Messiah. We're on the forefront. There are groups that are working together. We are part of the Riverfront East Congregational Initiative (RECI). It is a group of 18 churches in the Riverpark area, District 5, near downtown Detroit. We are working together as a collaborative to try to rebuild the community.

SD: ***Has the city's filing for bankruptcy affected the church or church members? If so, how?***

BR: The only impact is psychological. You stop and think about what's going to happen to the future of Detroit. As a church, we concentrate on the good news. We don't deny the bad news. We do defy it. We use it to motivate us.

SD: ***Could you talk about the role of foundations? How would you describe their present approach to Detroit? Are they addressing the right problems? If not, how should they be adapting their approach?***

BR: Let me say this: I can get a little angry when I think about it—and also a little motivated. All of the work that the Church of the Messiah does to rebuild the community—whether housing, entrepreneurship, growing our own food, educating our own people, teaching people about the political process and why they should be a part of that—we don't get a lot of foundation support.

Our support comes from individuals who believe in what the Church of the Messiah is doing and they help make that happen. We have done some things that have been funded, like Kresge funding the Makerspace. We have had some degree of support from the Community Foundation, which was helping us as we were creating the "villages," but for the most part we have not had a lot of foundation support.

Let me combine that with what I was telling the Obama administration when we were talking about getting funds to projects that need to be funded. Cut out the bureaucracy and red tape of getting the funds. All of the funneling through city government takes too long. If there were some kind of process that would fund it directly without going through the red tape, that would be wonderful. It should not be that hard when you have results.

We do a lot more than that. We have a harder time getting this money, a lot of times too with a lot of foundations. I like what they do, but sometimes they don't fund important things that we are doing. A lot of times they want money to go into programming, when what we really need it for is operations. When you look at the Church of the Messiah, with the exception of things like entrepreneurship—the money generated helps to pay the people. The church is an all-volunteer operation, including me. The Church doesn't pay me. And the Church staff members are all volunteers. We are all volunteers working to make it happen.

SD: *What organizations do you ally with? Since you're on the board of the Center of Community-Based Enterprises (C2BE), could you comment on what role you see C2BE playing in Detroit?*

BR: One of the major organizations that we work with right now is MOSES. MOSES is an organization that primarily works through religious organizations that help the community—they are helping us with getting the word out about the upcoming election and helping galvanize people to become active in their communities to make it a better place to be. It is primarily through community organizing. We are working with the Riverside Congregation Alliance through the Michigan Roundtable. We also work with the villages, which came about through the Community Foundation. We work with Genesis Hope, which is another CDC that does some of the same things we are working on. A lot of good things are happening right now.

As for C2BE, I became involved about two years ago. I was interested in that organization because of the fact that it helps to build the community, creating a new community economy, which is something that is totally different, especially for Detroit—we are known for manufacturing, automobiles, working for corporations. This is a different concept—it is community-based. It is about the community taking ownership of the economy and business. That's why I am interested in it. That's why I believe C2BE is going to be a major part of the future of the city of Detroit. I really do believe that.

SD: *Are there specific areas where Detroit community organizations need to focus their efforts to improve their capacity to accomplish their goals?*

BR: All community organizations should be working toward helping to change the mindset. Until we change the mindset of the people

"This work is not for the timid or the weak. It takes guts and vision and heart in order to do it. You don't do it for ambition, fame, or money. **You have got to do it because it is the right thing to do.**"

of the city of Detroit, you can forget everybody else. You have to change the mindset. People of Detroit feel like second-class citizens—they feel neglected, dejected, rejected. You can bring in all of the business and money, but the mindset has to be changed—that people feel they are worthy of being a first-class city.

There is such a breakdown of the community—you don't just become violent. You take out the tax base, decimate the schools—you can't just build and expect the mindset to change overnight.

The mindset needs to be changed. Forty-seven percent of Detroit is illiterate. When you look at 47-percent illiteracy, you don't have an educated workforce ready to take jobs. So it has to be worked at in the community—job readiness, literacy, rebuild the neighborhoods.

We focus so much at the top, we've forgotten about the bottom. There are two cities of Detroit—it is seen as "us and them"—we've got to get rid of that mindset too. The capacity-building has to be to bring up the people at the bottom, change the mindset and school system.

There are so many things that need to change. In order to do this, the groups need to look from the bottom up, not the top down. New resources. They need to be brought up to that. Until that happens, the problems will persist in Detroit. People want parks, trees planted, bike trails. But what happens is that when these things are done, the way it is done makes it seems like none of this is for them. You have to change that mindset. That's why you need organizations like Church of the Messiah. We don't ignore the fact that there are people who are unemployable. Until you make them employable, you can't change the community.

We are a church. We are about reconciliation. We can do that. We can work to do that. That's why we have the Makerspace, affordable housing, and grow our food. We do that so the people's mindset can be changed. We don't have an ulterior motive. We are here. We are not going anywhere. The resources are here. We are a safe place. Come. We will raise your mindset. You will vote. You will be part of this process. You need to know what's happening with the emergency manager and the election. You do have a voice and you do have a place. That's why we do this.

The money is out there. They don't get to us. Maybe we don't try hard enough. Sometimes, when the funding is not there, we do it anyway. A lot of times we are the pretty girl who can't get to the prom; everyone thinks someone else already ask you because you're so beautiful.

They see the workshops, they see the housing, they see the businesses, they think we have money and we don't.

SD: *As you know, there has been a long-standing debate regarding how to balance development and organizing and these goals are often seen as contradictory. How does Church of the Messiah achieve this balance?*

BR: Part of it is that we don't compromise in terms of what we believe, in terms of the gospel. We don't think about leaving our community or abandoning things. We refuse to sell out. It is a degree of freedom to say it as it is. We're not in anybody's pocket. No one can tell us what to say because they funded certain things. We don't have to do that. We say it is. We hope if the organizations and funders are right, we do it. We're going to do the right thing. We do have a pretty good relationship with city government. We do have a good relationship with the community groups. We take our money and put it back into the community for us to be able to do what we do. With our housing, so many times the church has a little money—sometimes money is not there. It's a catch-22. Because the economy is bad, people don't pay their rent.

We too have to do our stuff based on deficits, and we do it the best we can. Funding is extremely difficult and hard to find. We help to change the mindset of the people in the neighborhood. That's one of the reasons to change the mindset. You're not trying to get anything out of it, except to rebuild the community to be the place it would be. I wish the funders and foundations would see this. I hope they are in this work for the right reasons. It is community-based.

"We know we can't do business as usual. The days of working for the corporation are limited and gone. We know those days are gone. **Co-op brings together the opportunity for community development, employment, and entrepreneurship.**"

We all have a vested interest in how the neighborhood looks, that lights are on, and that our neighborhoods are clean and safe.

We have town halls on a regular basis. We don't bitch about the lights, about where are the police. We understand that the city has no money. The majority of the population is gone. We know that there are certain things that we need to do. We will do our own garbage. We have our community groups. We get our own lawn mowers and cut the lawn ourselves. We keep the community looking better. When your neighbors see you out there, they will be out there. And then they know that we can count on each other. Sometimes you have to do what you're going to do.

SD: *If you had to highlight a few key accomplishments of the Church of the Messiah's work to date that you are proudest of, what would they be?*

BR: We have a church that is filled with young people. The majority of our congregation is African-American male under thirty. We are changing the mindset of some of the most vulnerable. These were the gang bangers, car thieves. Now they are working in landscaping, ginger tea, thinking they can be entrepreneurs. They have been given a second chance.

Teach the greatness inside of you—you were not created to steal cars. Who are you? We have an opportunity to teach them who they are. The same ones who were stealing the cars are watching the parking lot. They have legitimate jobs. Their mindset has changed. They have a place in the future of Detroit. That is our greatest accomplishment.

Some of the same ones who used to destroy the neighborhood are now community organizers working with MOSES. Change the community and mindset. They are changing the mindset of people who thought they didn't deserve to benefit. They are becoming community organizers; they are now owning their own businesses. That's incredible.

SD: *How do you support yourself?*

BR: My family—my brothers and sisters contribute—it is what it is. There is a two-bedroom apartment. When I decided to do this full time, I left my house and came here.

The theory—I remember telling God—if this doesn't work, I'll be unemployed, homeless, and churchless. I believe in it as long as I have the necessities of life. I'm trying to be effective. It is about being effective and changing the mindset.

SD: *Where do you see the potential for cooperatives in Detroit?*

BR: It is incredible. We know that we can't do business as usual. The days of working for the corporation are limited and gone. We know those days are gone. Co-op brings together the opportunity for community development, employment, and entrepreneurship. It creates the type of community where every individual has a stake and a voice. It gives the average person a voice.

That's why cooperatives are so important to the city of Detroit. It is also about changing the mindset—people are cynical—when you create opportunity in a co-op, everyone has a stake and vested interest. That's so important in a city that is neglected. It actually brings about empowerment. It makes everybody equal.

SD: *You've referred at times to Detroit as being a blank slate. What do you see as the potential for Detroit?*

BR: I see Detroit being the model for the rest of the country. Because we've been at the bottom, we had to reinvent ourselves out of necessity. We now know what doesn't work. The whole world is watching to see what happens in the city of Detroit. We're not afraid to experiment.

It is like someone who has a terminal illness and all of the conventional treatments didn't work. You don't have anything to lose. You'll die anyway.

It is an opportunity to experiment and see what works and people can learn from Detroit what will work. This is a wonderful time to live in the city of Detroit. You have the option to try something new and different. Everybody knows what didn't work.

SD: *Is there anything else that you would like to add?*

BR: Let me just say this. I look at the city of Detroit—recreated similar to the church. In 2008, we almost closed. We had no members, no money, and the building was too big.

Since we were on the verge of closing, it made sense to try something different. We are a part of the Episcopal Church. The Episcopal Church, like the Catholic Church, is steeped in tradition.

When we were on the verge of closing, we knew we had to try something else. We kept our beliefs, but we experimented, got out in the community, brought in young people, and started some businesses. We took a chance, and it worked. Now we are being looked at as a beacon of hope within the church. We took a chance at doing something different. And it worked.

Rebuild the community. Change the mindset. The same thing can happen for the city of Detroit—you have to have the courage. Just do it. Stop waiting for something to save you. Just do it. That's our work. And that's the part that I like.

Ai-jen Poo

*Ai-jen Poo has been organizing
immigrant women workers since 1996. In
2000, she co-founded Domestic Workers
United, the New York organization that
spearheaded the successful passage of the
state's historic Domestic Workers Bill of
Rights in 2010. In 2007, DWU helped
organize the first national domestic
workers convening, where the National
Domestic Workers Alliance (NDWA) was
formed. Ai-jen has served as Director
of NDWA since 2009 and works on
elevating women of color and domestic
worker rights issues at a national level.*

Interviewed in 2014

Steve Dubb: *Could you talk about your background? How did you become involved in organizing domestic workers?*

Ai-jen Poo: Very early on, I was interested in women's issues, probably because I am very much influenced by my mother and my grandmother. Starting in high school, I was involved in the women's forum and issues that affect low-income women. In New York City, while I was in college, I started to volunteer for the Committee Against Anti-Asian Violence. We were just starting a project to organize Asian immigrant women who were working in low-wage service jobs. At the time, a lot of the garment factories were starting to close down in New York City, and the women who worked in those jobs started to move into service work, particularly care work—home care if they had their immigration documents; domestic work, restaurant women, and beauty parlor work if they were undocumented.

So we saw a huge increase of Asian women working in poverty wage service jobs. These are highly vulnerable jobs where women were working twelve-hour days and still earning below poverty wages. So we decided to reach out to women and explore different possibilities for organizing. It was always the domestic workers who wanted to come together and break out of the isolation of their work, support each other, and ultimately wanted to organize. The project started organizing with Filipina domestic workers. From there, we began to organize domestic workers of all nationalities. It started out as an Asian worker organizing project, but quickly grew to be a citywide, multi-racial organizing project.

SD: *Could you talk about your work at Domestic Workers United? How was the organization formed and how did it develop over time?*

AP: In the early years, it was members of the Women Workers Project, primarily Filipina domestic workers, who came together with other domestic workers. Some of them had worked in Hong Kong where the domestic workers' movement had been organizing for years and years. They have an incredible organization and they have achieved strong legal standards for domestic workers. Many of the Filipina workers were accustomed to such standards and a set contract and established paid days off and such. When they came here, they were taken aback by the lack of protections and standards. And the lack of respect and recognition that this work was real work. They immediately asked the question: the rest of the workforce isn't organized either. We need to organize together. So they began to organize Latina and Caribbean workers. That was the origins of Domestic Workers United.

Those domestic workers who had experienced a different level of worker standards, protection and power basically knew that they had to work industry-wide to establish the same power here. So Domestic Workers United was launched in 2000 to bring Caribbean, Latina and Asian workers together to establish basic protections and build recognition that this domestic work is real work and that this workforce really is a part of the real economy and should be valued as such.

SD: *What are some achievements of Domestic Workers United to date and what are the continuing challenges?*

AP: We decided to use legislative strategies to lift up the visibility of the workforce and test whether legislative campaigns would help us organize both workers and supporters. We started with a campaign in the City Council that would compel the agencies that place domestic workers to notify workers of their rights and employers of their legal obligations. Roughly 15 percent of the workforce is placed by an agency. These agencies are licensed by the City Department of Consumer Affairs. That bill was introduced in 2001 and came into effect in 2003. Hundreds of domestic workers went to City Hall to tell their stories, and that resulted in the passage of legislation, known as the Nanny Bill. Its political champion was Gale A. Brewer, who is now the Manhattan Borough president.

After we passed the city bill, we were ready for the next step. We knew it wasn't sufficient to have workers know their rights because legally domestic workers are excluded from many basic rights and protections. So we set out to change labor law, and in order to do so, we had to go statewide. We actually held a convention in November 2003 called the Having Your Say convention where we gathered over 200 domestic workers from all over the city. We had simultaneous interpretation in six different languages. They participated in small group discussions about what would it mean to have respect at work. It was an all-day convention.

We came out of that convention with a long list of priorities—health care, living wage of $14 an hour, notice of termination—a lot of things that you might find in a good union contract. We then worked with the New York University (NYU) Immigrant Rights Law Clinic, who helped us turn these priorities into actual draft language for state legislation that we introduced in 2004. That was the beginning of the campaign for a New York State Domestic Workers Bill of Rights, the state campaign to win rights and respect for domestic workers in New York, which, after it passed in 2010, became the flagship for us nationally.

SD: *Could you briefly outline what a Domestic Bill of Rights looks like?*

AP: They range from state to state, but it could entail everything from overtime and paid days off, to protection from discrimination harassment, a day of rest per week, written contracts are in some of the bills—in short, basic workplace protections and standards.

SD: *As you mentioned, in New York State, the Domestic Workers Bill of Rights passed in 2010. What has worked and what are some of the continuing challenges?*

AP: The visibility of the workforce was dramatically increased. There is much greater awareness among both workers and employers of basic rights. The Department of Labor gets calls from employers quite often. We've heard from companies like Breedlove and Associates, which helps employers comply with tax laws, that after the law passed, New York went from ninth to second among states when it came to employer compliance with tax laws, second after California. There is a strong correlation between compliance with tax laws and labor laws.

We believe that a real cultural change has occurred, which occurred not only because of the passage of legislation but because of everything that made the legislation possible, like the media work, outreach and alliance building, all of the work that went into the seven-year organizing campaign. That, in conjunction with the partnership with the New York Department of Labor, elected officials who championed the bill, and the media visibility it got once the governor signed it, really catalyzed a change in culture. It is much more recognized that this is a real job, one that plays an important role in our economy, supporting other working professionals. The idea that domestic work is the work that makes all other work possible is something that broke through in the public imagination in New York.

When the first domestic workers bill was passed in City Hall, City Council members—one after the other, particularly members of color as they announced their votes, talked about their mothers and grandmothers who did this work. Their vote for this bill was paying tribute to the unrecognized work the members of their families did. For them, it was about lifting up that untold history, righting an historic wrong, and supporting a 21st century workforce that was growing because of the growing needs. And we saw a very similar dynamic at the state level. There were many state legislators of color—of all nationalities—including many Irish immigrants and others whose personal stories are tied to this workforce.

SD: *What led to the transition from working at the local level to the national level? What do you see as the relationship between national and local advocacy?*

AP: Organizing among domestic workers in New York was growing. But parallel to New York, there were workers coming together in church basements, community centers, and workers centers in California; Washington, D.C.; and Seattle, among other places. Most of that organizing was very slow and incremental, step-by-step, worker-by-worker. In the early 2000s, it was still a challenge to gather eight women in a room together. But slowly through real, on-the-ground outreach at bus stops, train stations, and word-of-mouth, we started to reach more workers, and then reach out across the cities. Having a very visible campaign in New York helped catalyze that process, as it provided a visible example that this work was possible.

SD: *You personally went from working on the New York City effort to working nationally. What led you to make that switch?*

AP: I was part of a cohort of 50 domestic workers and organizers from six cities in 2007 to gather in Atlanta to share lessons and strategies. Just the idea that we could lean on each other and learn from each other was a huge incentive to come together. When we did, it was so clear and palpable how powerful it would be to have a national vehicle and voice, both for mutual support, but also to raise respect and recognition of this work across cities and states. We started to imagine bigger and bigger, even globally. At that time, I was still working for the New York organization. A year or so after the founding of the national alliance in 2007, we were able to raise the resources to staff the national alliance. A year into that, we decided to hire a national director, and I was hired.

SD: *When did the National Domestic Workers Alliance begin to hire staff?*

AP: We hired our first staff person in 2008. I came on in 2009. Jill Shenker, our current Field Director, was the first person hired by NDWA.

SD: *How has the organization evolved? What are the NDWA main program areas?*

AP: It went from a mutual support and capacity building network where we primarily focused on strengthening the impact of our affiliates locally to starting to think about national campaigns and state-by-state coordinated strategies, and now building our own chapters. In the first few years, we focused on supporting our affiliates in their state campaigns, which we still do. New York, California, and Hawai'i have all passed domestic workers state legislation. Then, in 2010, we built the capacity to launch national campaigns of our own. We launched a campaign around Immigration: "We Belong Together." In 2011, we worked with Jobs with Justice to launch "Caring Across Generations."

SD: *Could you elaborate on what the Caring Across Generations campaign is about?*

AP: It came about because in 2009 there was increased demand for training among our members, specifically for elder care. Even for people hired as nannies, they increasingly were being compelled to take on responsibility for home-based care for the aging and for people with disabilities or chronic illnesses. It was such a pattern that we decided to take a step back and figure out what was going on. And what we learned is that domestic workers are on the front lines of a tremendous shift in our generational demographics. The Baby Boom generation is reaching retirement age, and people are

"We believe that a real cultural change has occurred ... not only because of the passage of legislation but because of everything that made the legislation possible, like the media work, outreach and alliance building."

living longer than ever … we are going to have the largest elder population we have ever had and we have no infrastructure to support that. The "Sandwich" generation—the millions of Americans who are struggling to manage care for both their children and their aging parents and grandparents—are under tremendous pressure. There is very little support. If you are very poor, you might qualify for Medicaid. If you are very rich, you might be able to afford long-term care insurance. But even those supports are precarious in this current economic environment, and most are caught in the middle without any support at all.

Between the struggles of families and the vulnerability of this workforce there has to be a win-win scenario, where we could lift everyone up. We as a country should be prioritizing the caring for each other across generations. Bringing families, workers, seniors and people with disabilities together to create a more caring economy seemed like a powerful proposition in light of this age wave. That's why we launched Caring Across Generations in 2011. It is a multi-generational movement of millions to embrace multi-generational relationships and caregiving.

SD: *What impact has the Caring Across Generations movement had to date?*

AP: We worked with a broad coalition of groups to move a regulatory change at the Department of Labor that extended minimum wage and overtime protections to over 1.8 million home care workers who were previously excluded from coverage. This change will come into effect in 2015. In Ohio, where there is a rapid rate of aging in the state, we were able to move $169 million in Medicaid funding to support home- and community-based care.

SD: *The Affordable Care Act creates a new legal requirement for nonprofit hospitals to conduct community health needs assessments every three years, forcing them to think about health beyond the hospital walls. Also, now, if patients are readmitted within thirty days of discharge, in many cases hospitals must meet the expense of repeat care. All of this makes quality home health care more valuable to hospitals. To date, what impact, if any, have you seen the Affordable Care Act have on your work?*

AP: The ACA expands access to health insurance for low-wage workers under the expansion of Medicaid, in states where that expansion has been adopted. Many domestic workers and home care providers will have access to health insurance as a result. Many states, like Georgia have yet to adopt Medicaid expansion, so this potential has not been fully realized.

Ultimately, however, we believe strongly that home care workers and domestic workers can play a critical role in preventative health care, and transforming the health care delivery system to create new efficiencies. With the appropriate support and training, care workers can help manage chronic illnesses, prevent unnecessary emergency room visits and much, much more to both support a better quality of life for the families and individuals that they support and save our healthcare system money.

SD: *Recently your organization had a joint conference with a community-organizing network known as National People's Action. What led you to build this alliance?*

AP: We believe very strongly that a new economy is coming into being, and that the people whose experiences are the most invisible in this current economy must have a voice in shaping the future. That means small family farmers in the heartland, it means undocumented workers in urban areas, families that are facing deportation, and people coming out of incarceration. It means reaching all of those people and human potential that we want to be truly included in the new economy. We think it is possible. This is a country that has done incredible things, solved profound problems—built the transcontinental railroad, built the highways, brought the internet into all of our homes. This country has invested in that infrastructure. We believe that it is important to involve as many people as we can in designing the 21st century infrastructure that we need to invest in—it's both access to quality care, policies like paid family leave to support working families to do the work that they do, in addition to innovation, technology, and energy. It is not an *either-or*; it's a *both-and*, and we have historically been able to do those things.

Innovation and technology are essential to progress. The question is the values and priorities driving that innovation—if there are robots that are being built, they should enable domestic workers to improve the quality and increase the impact of the work they are doing. They should improve the quality of life for the workforce and the quality of care for the consumer, rather than replacing the workforce.

SD: *As you know, Cooperative Home Care Associates (CHCA) in the Bronx is the nation's largest worker cooperative, with more than 2,000 employees. Have you thought about worker cooperatives as a path to reforming the field? If so, what steps do you see as necessary to move this forward?*

AP: I think that worker cooperatives and social benefit corporations and other innovative models for both employment and opportunity should all be explored, especially a project like CHCA, an incredibly important endeavor. I know that if you talk to folks at Cooperative Home Care Associates, they are not sure how replicable their model is. It took more than 10 years to build. There was a very specific set of conditions that allowed for their model to succeed. Wherever it is possible, it is definitely worth pursuing.

I think of it in terms of different forms of power to create social change. There is political power, organizing and voter engagement are part of it. There is also narrative power—the ability to tell the story of why things are the way they are and shape the public narrative. There is also market power and modeling power. It allows us to shape what is possible and open people's imaginations to a new way of being that we want to move forward.

What cooperatives offer is both modeling power and economic power, offering us a model for a different type of employment

"We as a country should be prioritizing the caring for each other across generations. Bringing families, workers, seniors and people with disabilities together to create a more caring economy seemed like a powerful proposition in light of this age wave."

and economic relationship. I believe it is most effective when it is alongside a strategy of building political and narrative power, but it is also powerful in and of itself. We are exploring enterprise models, and we have a lot of affiliates that are worker-owned cooperatives.

For example, in Boston, Vida Verde is a Brazilian women's green cleaning cooperative; they make their green cleaning products themselves. The National Alliance is working on developing a social enterprise model that can create high-road jobs for domestic workers, promote higher standards, and generate revenue to support our organizing. We're launching several pilots this year to that end.

SD: *What do you see as the role of policy in breaking down some of the barriers to cooperatives in the care sector?*

AP: We are trying to figure that out. Once we figure out the viable business models, then we can figure out the structural reforms that would make that model more successful. Policies that support social benefit corporations at the state and federal level are helpful. We should incentivize high-road development. We give millions of dollars to corporations in tax breaks that are questionable. Why wouldn't we incentivize the high-road employers? In some ways, it is about leveling the playing field. We should transform our economy into one where it pays to be a good employer rather than an economy where good employers lose out.

Caring Across Generations is our movement to change the care industry into a model industry for an economy where workers and consumers work in partnership to shape the future of the industry—rooted in values of connection, care, support, and practical needs of families and workers.

Obviously, the economy is a vast place. We see our contribution as helping build this vision. If we can figure it out in care, we hope it will be a model for retail, restaurants, and other sectors. It is a movement. We are working at the state, federal, and municipal levels. Through the Caring Across Generations movement, we are working on policy; we're engaged in advocacy, community and worker organizing, narrative and culture change strategies to expand access to quality care for individuals and families, while creating and transforming care jobs into jobs that you can really take pride in. At the same time, NDWA is working on strengthening labor standards and building alternatives to support dignity and opportunity for the domestic workforce.

SD: ***Over the past decade, NDWA and the domestic workers movement has had tremendous growth. How has it managed that growth?***

AP: A mentor of mine said that you are going to have problems no matter what. There are two kinds of problems—problems of growth and problems of decay. You generally want the problems of growth. They are great challenges to have—sustainability, and how to get to real scale, and the kind of impact where every domestic worker in the nation knows that there is a movement they can connect to. There is a lot of work to do to organize, build, finance, and sustain the movement. Most of these questions are not unique to us, so we work closely with other organizations to both learn and share as we experiment and build.

SD: ***Could you elaborate on what you have learned?***

AP: We have to continue to do what we do best—support our members. Leaning into your strengths is key. Whatever you already do well, that has to continue. But clearly what we know how to do isn't sufficient, so I do believe that you also have to break off a certain amount of resources to experiment, take risks, and consistent with the notion of a "lean startup model"—be willing to fail, fail often, fail cheaply, and learn.

Evaluation, reflection, and sharing out the reflections across the movement—nine times out of ten there are local versions of the challenges we run into in national work, and the other way around. Working and learning across all of those levels is key.

SD: *Are there specific areas where the domestic workers' movement needs to focus their efforts to improve capacity and accomplish their goals?*

AP: We're working on a new generation of state-level policy campaigns. We are calling it "Domestic Workers Bill of Rights 2.0." We have now won a Domestic Workers Bill of Rights in three states—New York, Hawaii, and California. And we thought to ourselves, "Okay, so what can we be doing differently to take this work to the next level, rather than just doing what we know how to do?" So we are pulling together our best policy expert partners and organizers to help us conceptualize some more experimental state-level policy to expand our ability to build power long-term for the movement. Hopefully, some of those bills will be introduced in 2015 and 2016.

SD: *If you had to highlight a few key accomplishments of NDWA's work to date that you are most proud of, what would they be?*

AP: One is that we have this beautiful movement with 42 local organizations of domestic workers who are organizing and bringing women together locally to bring dignity and respect to this work, while envisioning a different future for our entire economy and democracy. We are growing movements. Our members are a huge source of inspiration and power.

We are also proud of having launched Caring Across Generations with our sister organization Jobs with Justice, bringing together interests that have historically been pitted against each other, to create a movement and set of solutions from the point where our interests come together. I think we're modeling the kind of 21st-century American democracy effort that will strengthen opportunity for everyone.

And we are proud of having won protections for domestic workers, by domestic workers in many of the states where they are most concentrated.

Cooperatives

Cooperatives form the oldest and most pervasive form of community wealth building. Co-ops can be new or old, small or large. Regardless, all are governed according to the principle of one-member-one-vote. Co-ops are also among the most internationalized forms of community wealth building. More than one billion people worldwide are member-owners of cooperatives. A few years ago, the United Nations recognized the economic importance of the co-op model, declaring 2012 to be the "International Year of the Cooperative," so it is appropriate that the interviews in this section have a more international bent. Ramon León is working in Minneapolis, but he adopted the mercado model of having a large number of vendors operating in a common space from his native Mexico and adapted it to the Minneapolis community. In Minneapolis, León helped organize 45 vendors into a vendor-owned cooperative that together came to own their common Mercado Central marketplace. Paul Hazen, who now heads the Overseas Cooperative Development Council, talks about the National Cooperative Business Association's international development work (which forms more than 80 percent of the organization's budget) and considers how one might applies lessons learned in cooperative development abroad to the U.S. context. The Seikatsu Club Consumer Co-op Union interview came about precisely because during the International Year of the Cooperative, the group decided to tour co-ops outside of Japan. Started by a group of 200 housewives in Tokyo in the late 1960s, Seikatsu has grown to having 340,000 members located in communities across Japan.

Ramón León

Ramón León is the founding Executive Director of Latino Economic Development Center (LEDC), a nonprofit membership organization serving over 300 businesses in South Minneapolis and which has expanded to operate statewide. León also serves as the chair of the economic development committee of the National Association for Latino Community Asset Builders. Prior to joining LEDC, Mr. León was the founding President of Cooperative Mercado Central, a co-op marketplace that houses 45 small businesses and has sparked the revitalization of Lake Street in Minneapolis. LEDC is perhaps best known for its work in helping develop the Midtown Global Market, a multi-ethnic marketplace that opened in 2006 and brings together Latino, Somali, and other immigrant vendors in nonprofit owned public marketplace under one roof.

Interviewed in 2009

Steve Dubb: *Tell me a little bit about your background and how you came into community development work.*

Ramón León: When I came to the United States, I came from Mexico and from a business family. My family owned a business in Mexico for generations. When I came to the United States in 1987 in California, I started my own business. I did the same when I came to Minnesota; I started getting involved in social justice issues. I realized that a lot of people who didn't speak English suffered the consequences of not speaking it well and not knowing the system or understanding the laws. I began to work to find ways to overcome these challenges.

In 1991, when I came to the state of Minnesota, we started to push the religious leadership of the Archdiocese to give services in Spanish in Minneapolis. That's how the Church of Sagrada Corazón was founded. People started to complain about several issues. Because of my business background, people would ask me questions of how I got set up. So I used to guide people. The most important reason I became involved is I realized we were talking about social justice issues that were easily solved when economic power is built and exercised. When I started listening to particular people, they started complaining.

After services, we would meet in the basement of the church for coffee, *tamales, atoles*. We would talk about police harassment, INS (Immigration and Naturalization Service, now Immigration and Customs Enforcement, or ICE) issues, and education issues. We would talk about how their children were segregated into a corner because they don't speak English well and there were not enough bilingual teachers.

The newcomers in the 1990s didn't speak English. Most of them did not. Because of their undocumented status, they didn't have access to higher education. But a number of them used to operate businesses in Mexico. They would say, "I had a business that was fairly successful. If I could open my business and be successful, I would give back." All of the people started talking about forming a Latino bank. We need business opportunities. Back then there was not a single Latino business in Minneapolis. I understood that. I came from a business family. Social responsibility is taken seriously.

We formed several teams to attack those problems: education, health, immigration, and economic development. We formed a joint committee on immigration and the economic development team of which I was the founding president, which ended up with Mercado Central, which now has 45 businesses.

We asked CDCs to provide help. We formed a partnership with Interfaith Action (which provided leadership training). We formed a partnership with Neighborhood Development Center for micro-enterprise trainings. We worked with a Community Development Corporation. Another organization, called Project for Pride in Living, offered to buy an existing building that was in bad shape, renovate it, and give it to us. So we had community organizing, real estate organization, and community development come together.

SD: *What were the origins of the Latino Economic Development Center? How has the organization's relationship to the community from which it emerged evolved over time?*

RL: From the experience with creating the Mercado Central, we decided Latinos needed to face their own issues, take responsibility for our own growth, and develop that capacity. So that was why we formed LEDC; there was not a formal organization. The organization was born and the vision was ambitious: we wanted to have a Latino credit union or bank, we wanted scholarships regardless of documented statues, we wanted to have other economic opportunities (whether buying a home or starting a business). We also wanted to form an organization that supported a socially responsible business community. It is easy to forget that social injustices exist. Sometimes we are our own victimizers. When we have employees, we treat them in a way that we don't want them to be treated.

Mercado Central took four years to develop. Back then no one believed in us, not even our own people. I belonged to Interfaith Action, a faith-based social action organization. I invited people to join. They asked me what it would take. "You're going to open what? How much will it cost? Are you crazy? I don't even have documents. Why open a business? So I can lose it?"

The Mercado Central had $800,000 in sales in its first three months. After five years, it had annual turnover of $7 million. At least three of the businesses that first started in the Mercado now have combined sales of $3 million each: Tortilla la Perla, Taqueria la Hacienda, and Cafetería La Loma; Cafetería La Loma now makes *tamales* all over the state of Minnesota. One business has 60 employees.

"In Mexico, you have a Mercado where the people who shop there and work there live in the neighborhood. The money that moves and is spent stays in the neighborhood. **That to me is strong community development.**"

Latino people started coming to us. How can I access our opportunities? Lake Street stretches 4.8 miles. It was full of criminal activity, empty storefronts, shooting, drugs, trafficking, and prostitution. Immigrants started renting those places; they were almost for free. The Latino community started to exercise buying power. In less than 10 years, more than 300 businesses had opened on Lake Street. We started orientating the opportunities in those communities. Started integrating the businesses into LEDC, which serves as a kind of Latino chamber of commerce.

SD: *What is the membership and size of LEDC?*

RL: We have 350 businesses. We also decided to limit the membership. Members acquire not only rights but also responsibilities. They get the right to 20 hours of technical assistance, but we have only so many staff that can provide that assistance. We decided to focus the membership in the Twin Cities. We also made it a little more difficult to become a member. If you take a training session, then you can make a decision to become a member.

SD: *What are the obligations of membership?*

RL: You have to name a representative to the organization, but the most critical one is to commit to being a socially responsible business owner. This can mean different things at different times. Sometimes it means treating your employees well, sometimes it means providing incentives to employees, and sometimes it means getting involved in your community. Each year, we provide an award to the most socially responsible business.

SD: *Describe in a little more detail the Mercado Central project and why was it set up as a cooperative?*

RL: When we started talking about business opportunities in 1992, people asked, "Why don't we form the Mercado similar to what we had in Mexico? In Mexico, you have a Mercado where the people who shop there and work there live in the neighborhood. The money that moves and is spent stays in the neighborhood. That to me is strong community development.

There are also business advantages of being together. When you have those kinds of businesses all in the same place, you have more traffic. They can do marketing together. They can share earnings or losses. The co-op, which owns the building and elects the board, reinforces this.

The way this worked is the sponsoring team started to recruit members of the co-ops. A business could buy a share of the Mercado for $1,000. One additional criterion would be taking the entrepreneurial trainings. We also decided that nobody would own a piece of the Mercado Central. When they leave, they can take the business itself—they own the name, but they can't sell their share. If you leave, you can only sell your share back to the co-op.

SD: *Describe the Midtown Global Market project. As I understand it, the project was a four-way partnership in which LEDC owns a 25 percent share. What challenges did working in this partnership entail and how were those challenges overcome?*

RL: It wasn't easy, but it was not extremely difficult. We got involved in that particular project when LEDC did not have any capacity. At the time, the staff was just myself, and I was part time, when we learned that a 40,000-square-foot store was going to come into our community and wipe out our local businesses. We felt that we had at least the obligation to let the Latino community know what was going on and work on an alternative. We had been working with Mike Temali at the Neighborhood Development Center. I knew that they had capacity, and I came to them and told them that we need to get involved. We met and talked more about it. Mike started conducting his own exploration and decided to get involved. We then invited the African Development Center and the Phillips Cultural Wellness Center. We formed several teams. One worked on the legal part—ownership. One worked with the overall general contractor. One worked on architecture. One worked on tenant recruitment. One worked on financial assistance for start-up businesses. One worked on fundraising for the entire project. One worked on historic tax credits.

Honestly, I don't know how we overcame all of the challenges. But one of the most important traits is that we were willing to listen to each other and accept mistakes and respect each other.

SD: *As part owners of the global market, does LEDC earn any income?*

RL: Not yet. It was a $19 million project. Most of the financing is from New Markets Tax Credits and similar sources. When the investors get out, then we (the four partner nonprofits) will get 100 percent. In the meantime, we collect rent to pay the master lease and common expenses. So the businesses are basically being subsidized. Eventually, they'll be able to pay normal rental fees. Then we'll have earnings. In the meantime, we don't.

One thing to note: We bought the first floor from the City for a dollar, but we still have to pay real estate taxes. In Mexico, the *municipio* (local government) is the partner, so it doesn't charge real estate taxes, which also helps a lot for the businesses being incubated there because that money can be used for something else.

SD: *Any lessons that you think others can learn from your experiences?*

RL: From all of the markets we're engaged in, we learned a lot. One thing that has been forgotten in much of the United States is that public markets are community development tools. They are a very important part of the community. There are many aspects to this work: real estate, loans, community organizing, training, business incubation, facility development, business development, and market management. We have started to write a curriculum with money from the Annie E. Casey Foundation. Theme public markets are very effective business incubators and tools for strong community development. There are many lessons to be learned.

Right after it opened, I started getting calls from different parts of the country, asking us to assist. We didn't have any money, so we cannot take on the work. But I tell them, "Just come." It's not only sharing, but also advising them on other issues. I always highlight the immigrant community. There is a strong determination to succeed. I also say that we are wasting skills. We should put our efforts with the people we know are more likely to persevere and are determined to succeed. These happen to be immigrant communities. If others want to do this, that's good too. But you need to focus on the assets. Don't focus on the weaknesses.

In 1994, there was not a single Latino who owned a building on Lake Street, and the buildings that were there were nearly worthless. Now there are over 300 Latino business owners. Now the buildings cost more than a million dollars. Enrique Garcia started at $7 an hour as a dishwasher. Now he owns a business worth $3 million a year. That is wealth creation. Family ownership. Something you pass to the next generation, if the next generation is advised and educated to take over.

I also tell the folks in Mercado Central: the 45 businesses that are there own the building. I tell them, "You could use the equity to buy another building and give these opportunities to other people."

SD: *Describe the scope of your organization's work. You began in the Lake Street area of South Minneapolis. How far have you expanded beyond the initial area?*

RL: We now are a statewide organization. We go to any community. Latinos outside of the Twin Cities also need economic opportunities. We have a lot of energy.

Rural communities of Minnesota approached us. For instance, we were asked to come to Eden Prairie. They asked us to come. We went. And we saw that they were making a mistake if they bought the building—it was not viable. So we told them that it was not a good idea to buy it, but we can help you work on individual businesses. Our general approach is that we have decided, instead of providing direct technical assistance, to focus instead on building the capacity of local organizations to assist bilingual Latinos. We implemented a "train the trainer" program—we train people as community organizers and business-related technical assistance providers.

SD: *Unlike many community development organizations, LEDC has chosen not to focus on housing. Why is that?*

RL: We know there are a lot of needs in terms of housing opportunities. But we decided to form a partnership with an existing organization that did that. Eventually, I know we will do it, but it is not the right moment right now.

"You know the difference between an economic development lender and a loan officer? **A loan officer only sees numbers, but an economic development lender sees people and takes risk.**"

SD: *According to the Census, between 1990 and 2007, the Latino population in Minneapolis expanded from two percent of the city's population to nine percent. What factors are behind this rapid growth?*

RL: In some neighborhoods, the percentage of Latinos is even higher: some are 25 percent. There are several reasons. Economic opportunity is one of them. Second, the State of Minnesota became a portal area not only because of this, but because people here are more open to providing opportunities than denying opportunities to newcomers. If you look at some other states, they have much worse anti-immigrant issues. There is a huge difference between putting up blocks and helping you access the opportunities. The Latino community here is seen as a contributor, not as a burden to the community.

SD: *Does working in the Twin Cities present any unique challenges or opportunities compared to other areas, such as California?*

RL: When I was in California, I was more dedicated to the success of my business than doing social justice work. But there is a huge difference. In California, the Latino business community has been there for hundreds of years. In the Twin Cities, it's only been around 15 years. That's an advantage and a disadvantage. The disadvantage is that we didn't have anything. The advantage is that we could start anew. In this particular case, we decided to have socially responsible business—we are very intentional. Of the 300 Latino businesses in our area, a third are socially responsible— that's a very large percentage. In California, they were not intentional when they started their business development. The challenges and opportunities are different. In California, if you were

Latino, it would be more difficult to succeed. In 1991, I planned to move to Chicago. But a cousin of mine from Minnesota said to me, "Why are you are going to Chicago? It is the same as California. There are a million Mexicans there. A business will have a better chance to succeed here." I came and I never left. Why? We have a better chance to succeed—not only in the Latino community but also in our whole community.

SD: *How has South Minneapolis and the community that LEDC serves been affected by the credit crisis?*

RL: In part because of the language barrier, we tend to ignore what is happening. But actually the bigger problem has been anti-immigrant sentiment. I'm an American citizen, but in most Latino immigrant families there is at least one person who is not documented—that makes us cautious. With a number of thriving Latino businesses, once raids happen, those businesses fail. It is hard to run a business when you rely on a buying power that might not be here tomorrow or workers who might not be here tomorrow.

SD: *You serve on the board of the National Association for Latino Community Asset Builders. What role does it play in asset building for Latino organizations?*

RL: For me, it is an organization that is critical that it exists. When we began, we didn't have any experience in community development. I was really impressed in 2003, because I saw all of these people who have been involved in community development for 30 to 40 years. I observed all who are in Texas, California, New Mexico, and Colorado. I said: "You are very fortunate. You have a lot of capacity. We don't." But we have some advantages. All of our people are seen as diamonds. Why? It is because we are not many.

I rely on the association to find economic development lenders. You know the difference between an economic development lender and a loan officer? A loan officer only sees numbers, but an economic development lender sees people and takes risk. In the Latino community, we don't trust people who don't understand the legal and cultural barriers that we face. I felt more comfortable when I knew there was an organization that served our community.

We also benefit the more experienced members. Those

organizations that have existed forever need to know that there are growing Latino communities up here. We need to be a strong part of the whole body.

SD: *How do you see race impacting asset building?*

RL: If you pay attention, on the issue of racial difference, there are policies that benefit white communities. The reason why Native Americans don't have anything is because everything was taken. Blacks were slaves for 200 years, but even after slaves were freed there was a huge barrier that was put up that has separated many blacks from opportunity. Same thing with the Asians; they were brought in to work on the railroads; when they were finished, many of them were sent back. We need to reduce the racial wealth gap that exists. We need to force the government to generate policies to reduce the gap. In Minnesota, there is a campaign to work to end poverty by 2020. If we don't adopt aggressive policies, we won't achieve that goal.

SD: *What about LEDC's work are you most proud of?*

RL: For the Latino community, they know they have a place to go. They didn't go to others. Why? We are the same people. They consider us, them. As a whole, thanks to the work we have done and because the organization works to make a contribution to the community, the whole community sees us as a contribution, not as a burden. It is really difficult to top that. Making the people aware that we exist here, it's not just for our own benefit, the Latino community benefit, but also for the community as a whole.

Everyone learns from everyone whether we have a good or a bad experience. Sometimes we tend to be forgotten. Why? Probably it is because white people are still in power and are still making most of the decisions. They don't always acknowledge minority achievement. When we opened Mercado Central, I said to the foundations and others present, "Now you can see your money is not wasted." Our achievements are not always acknowledged in the way they should be.

Paul Hazen

*Paul W. Hazen was formerly the President
and Chief Executive Officer of the National
Cooperative Business Association (NCBA),
the leading national cooperative membership
association in the United States. In the fall
of 2011, Hazen announced that he would
be stepping down as CEO, after working 25
years at the organization, 13 of which he
spent as leader. As CEO, Hazen led several
important NCBA initiatives, including the
creation of the "dot-coop" Internet domain
name for cooperatives. Also, under Hazen's
direction, NCBA's international cooperative
development program grew to more than $32
million in annual funding, with 30 projects
in 18 countries.*

*Since leaving NCBA, Hazen has become
the CEO of the Overseas Cooperative
Development Council, where he continues
to support international cooperative
development.*

Interviewed in 2012

Steve Dubb: Could you explain how you came to be involved with cooperatives and what inspired you to focus so much of your life's work on that sector?

Paul Hazen: I became involved with co-ops in a formal way when, in 1984, I became the executive director of Rural Housing, Inc. in Wisconsin. That is a nonprofit organization that was founded by the electric co-ops to promote and build cooperative housing in rural areas of the state. Prior to that, growing up in Wisconsin, I had been exposed to many cooperatives. My parents were members of the electric co-op. And many agricultural co-ops held their annual meetings as public events—with picnics that brought together the whole community. So even though my parents weren't farmers, I also attended those.

I first became really interested in working for co-ops, though, when I worked in the 1970s for Representative Al Baldus. He was on the House Agriculture Committee and Chair of the Dairy Subcommittee, so I would go to many co-op meetings with him. Really, co-ops were his political base. Attending these meetings, for the first time, I began to understand these were economic businesses that were striving for the success for their members, but that they also had a social purpose. It was so logical and made so much perfect sense. From then on, I knew I wanted to get involved with co-ops. Later on, I was able to do just that—first, with the housing cooperatives and then in 1987 when I became director of consumer cooperatives at NCBA.

SD: *You hail from Wisconsin, where co-ops play a significantly larger role in the overall economy than they do nationally. Could you discuss how your experiences in Wisconsin have informed the way you look at the role of cooperatives nationally?*

PH: There is a very strong cooperative movement in Wisconsin. The greatest lesson I can take away from that, I think, is that the cooperative movement was able to build an infrastructure that supports existing co-ops and makes it easier to form new cooperatives.

Part of this was a strong extension service through the Department of Agriculture. There was also a lot of cross-sector work ensuring that there were good laws. Because there was a critical mass, the environment there is so correct for the development of cooperatives that it has become a model for the rest of the country. That level of infrastructure does occur in some other places, but certainly the Upper Midwest has developed a co-op environment and culture to the extent that there is a continuous growing co-op movement in those upper Midwest states.

SD: *When you first came to work for NCBA in 1987, NCBA was already a mature organization with 71 years of history behind it, but surely the past two-dozen years have brought considerable changes. Could you discuss how NCBA has changed over this period and also what has stayed constant?*

PH: What has stayed constant is a commitment to the cooperative principles and values. We always keep those out in front. We see ourselves as the protectors of those principles and values. While they need to evolve and be flexible, those basic fundamentals stay in place. A commitment to cooperative development, both domestically and internationally, that has been constant. I think one thing that we have added is a commitment to being a common table that brings all of the cooperatives together. That has changed. We have had a real focus on making sure that all co-op sectors are involved. Back in 1987, purchasing, worker, and daycare co-ops were not at the table.

A real concerted effort was made to make sure that everyone has the opportunity to participate. That's a real positive change. Another change is that in the 1980s we had perhaps one woman on the board of directors. Now at some points we've had up to 40 percent of the directors be women. So that's a real positive change. The global view that we have a responsibility to participate with cooperatives in the world, not only in our development work, but engaging with our colleagues, that has also been a constant.

SD: *Could you talk also a bit about how the nature of the co-op movement in the United States has shifted over the past couple of decades? What sectors or market segments are seeing a growing co-op presence? Are there any sectors that have been declining?*

PH: As an overall issue, I am seeing much more focus on cooperative identity in various sectors. In the electrical cooperative sector, they have done a tremendous job. The credit union movement is coming up behind that. Of course, we see that strong sense of co-op identity with worker and food co-ops. Overall, there has been a generally positive shift, with more cooperatives and larger cooperatives embracing their co-op identity.

Where we are seeing real development occurring is with worker and food co-ops. The recent recession is a big driver, but also people's attitudes are changing. People are asking, "What is the role of business in community?" People are expressing a desire to have a greater say in that. We are continuing to see fewer credit unions but more memberships. In order to compete, credit unions have to get larger, and one way they are doing that is with mergers. But there has been a great spike in growth in the past one to two years in response to the financial collapse and the ongoing shift of the concentration of wealth to fewer people. Credit union expansion is a natural response to that.

We do see fewer farmer co-ops because we have fewer farmers. So there are fewer cooperatives, but the percentage of the market that cooperatives are engaged in continues to grow. One area that is going to be really tough is with telephone cooperatives. It is a very competitive marketplace, and the technologies make it difficult to compete. That is an area where we are not seeing growth. We are seeing growth with electrical co-ops where suburbs expand into what were formerly rural areas, bringing new members. Purchasing co-ops—independent businesses compete in a global marketplace—there too we are seeing continuing growth.

SD: *In recent years, NCBA has placed a greater emphasis on generating research regarding the economic impact of cooperatives. Can you discuss some of the findings of this research work to date and what you see as research priorities for the field going forward?*

PH: In the United States, there has been a tremendous amount of research on cooperatives in particular sectors, such as agriculture or finance. But there has been little comprehensive research about the sector in general and little hard research about the competitive advantages of cooperatives. So NCBA a number of years ago initiated a program to get that basic data. We are looking for data regarding such matters as the number of members, number of cooperatives, economic turnover, job creation—in the hope that academics would take that basic data on the impact co-ops have and apply that data, not only nationally but regionally. And then dive deeper into the secondary benefits—does a cooperative provide competition to other businesses and drive down prices for people who are not even members? Is there a further economic benefit? That's the kind of hard data and research we would like to have. Similarly with the tremendous amount of training and education for members—are they better citizens? Do they vote in a higher proportion? Are institutions with cooperatively trained leaders more effective? We see this anecdotally, but we would hope to demonstrate that. That's the real goal. We're part way there. We need research in that area—over a period of time, rather than just a snapshot—to demonstrate the real benefits of co-ops.

SD: *Since a large part of NCBA's work concerns international co-op development, could you explain some of the challenges in the international co-op development process and how NCBA has been able to meet those challenges over the course of the past decades?*

PH: NCBA was the first U.S. cooperative organization to do international development work. A real legacy is that we have gotten many other cooperative organizations engaged in that work, such as Land O'Lakes and Co-op Resources International. We also helped start the World Council of Credit Unions and Agricultural Cooperative Development International and Volunteers in Overseas Cooperative Assistance (ACDI-VOCA).

The impact that we collectively have around the world is significant. On the International Cooperative Alliance (ICA) board, I've come to appreciate that here in the United States we really do have the greatest capacity to do this cooperative development work in developing countries. We have a good funding source from the federal government and from our members, but also the intellectual and human capacity to work in very difficult situations. We have helped develop over decades some very substantial cooperatives serving hundreds of millions of people—raising people out of poverty. Often the co-ops that we develop provide people with their very first opportunity to have a say in their lives when they can vote for the board of directors. The challenges we face are that these days many donors and organizations don't want to fund co-op development. Well, that's a bit strong—let's just say that it is not their

"We have an attitude in the United States that very low-income people don't have the capacity to run cooperatives. **That's not our experience**. It is our belief that everybody has the capacity to do this if they have the right tools."

priority. They are looking to achieve such goals as wealth creation, democracy building, and the empowerment of women. We do all of those things through developing co-ops. But we need to change the dialogue. We need to say that co-ops are about those things. We need to ask: How do we get those goals completed by developing and expanding cooperatives? If we can turn the debate around, then we can get policymakers and donors to think of co-ops as the first option of how to change people's lives for the better.

SD: *What lessons do you see that NCBA has learned from its international cooperative development work that might be applicable in the U.S. economic context?*

PH: The approach that we take is a very bottom-up approach. Starting at the local level, we help people address their own problems. In the United States, we have had too much of a top-down mindset where folks come in and say, there is a need over here. And a bunch of professionals will get together and try to recruit members. Bringing people together in the community and asking them what are the problems they want to address. Empowering them. We need to be much more attuned to that. We have an attitude in the United States that very low-income people don't have the capacity to run cooperatives. That's not our experience. Many of the people we are working with in Africa don't have writing and reading skills, so we teach them literacy and numeracy skills. It is our belief that everybody has the capacity to do this if they have the right tools.

SD: *One area that has always been a challenge for co-ops has been the issue of scale. Scale can boost organizational capacity, but can also mean larger organizations that may become disconnected from the communities they serve. Of course, NCBA itself is made up of a large number of cooperatives—some large, some small. Could you discuss some ways that NCBA member cooperatives seek to negotiate this balance?*

PH: Those co-ops that have a very strong Board of Directors can install into their cooperatives the culture that it is their responsibility to be the interface between the members and management. Where we find a disconnect is when management has too much say and doesn't see the involvement and empowerment of the members as part of its business operations. A key question with any co-op, large or small, is whether the Board of Directors is creating opportunities for member engagement.

Health Partners, a Twin Cities-area consumer healthcare cooperative, has over 500,000 members. But they work at engaging their members. They do so by having open board meetings, and they also do it by engaging with local councils. They really have a governance plan to drive down to ensure that the members are engaged. To me, that is the key: Have a governance structure where you don't have a disconnect between the large co-op and the membership.

SD: *What is the level of presence of cooperatives in the green economy? To what extent is the green economy a focus of NCBA's current work?*

PH: We can hope that we can step back and say in a couple of decades that we really own the green economy. We as a co-op movement missed an opportunity with fair trade. Almost all fair-trade products are from co-ops, but we are not seen as part of the fair-trade movement. The co-op movement is integral to the success of the green economy. Whether worker or consumer owned—there is a role for both. This should be our top priority. We have promoted green co-ops for a number of years. I don't think we have done the job we could have, but the green economy is tailor-made for our domestic development initiatives and policy initiatives.

SD: *Thinking nationally, co-ops are enjoying new visibility in the United States, in part due to growing frustration with what might be called "American business as usual." This new interest can be seen in many venues—among policymakers in Washington and the protestors of the Occupy movement, to name just two. What do you see as steps that the co-op movement needs to take nationally to build on this new visibility?*

PH: A common theme here is to ensure that there is the infrastructure and tools in place so that when people want to organize themselves into a user-owned business, they can accomplish that. Make sure there are good laws, educational materials, and technical assistance. This time we have a better chance of seizing on the renewed interest in co-ops. We do have a network of cooperative development centers. We have the financial institutions that help. And for worker co-ops, while we don't have a lot of resources, we have many more than we had a couple of decades ago. It is the infrastructure that is the key, and we just have to keep building upon that.

SD: *What are the co-op movement's primary goals in the areas of legislation and infrastructure?*

PH: From a public policy standpoint, the action is going to be primarily at the municipal and state level, where co-ops can serve as incubators to fulfill the desire that there needs to be a different way to organize businesses that provide services to community. That's better done at the municipal and state level. What the federal government can do is provide regulations and resources that make it easier for states and local municipalities to empower people. That's going to mean money and that's going to be difficult in the current economic situation. But if we are looking at jobs and economic development, we have results that we can demonstrate that co-ops bring long-term community and economic benefits.

SD: *Many within the co-op movement strive to be apolitical, while others see co-ops as a means to not only deliver business value for member-owners, but also as a mechanism to achieve a more just economy. What is your view of the relationship of cooperatives to such broader social economic justice goals?*

"To me, that is the key: **Have a governance structure where you don't have a disconnect between the large co-op and the membership**."

PH: One of the foundations is that our businesses aim to create communities where there is social and economic justice. I recently was at the People's Food Co-op in La Crosse, Wisconsin. Their mission statement is to create a cooperative economy in their region of Wisconsin. That was the vision of the people who started co-ops, both in urban and rural areas—to have opportunity, fairness, and businesses that provide competition and choice. At times we may have lost our way around that, but that's what differentiates our businesses from pure investor-owner business—we have that double- and triple-bottom line in mind.

That can take many different forms. It doesn't have to be one size fits all. I see that sense of vision in the credit union movement. It's not just about getting people good financial services, but financial literacy—making sure their money works for them—and that members have access to all of the services they need and deserve.

SD: *The United Nations has declared 2012 to be the International Year of the Cooperative, an effort that, of course, NCBA helped promote. What do you see as the importance of these international developments for the co-op movement in the United States?*

PH: The greatest importance is that we have recognition from a global body of the cooperative business model. The United Nations has created a tagline—"cooperative enterprises build a better world." Can you imagine if they said, "capitalist businesses build a better world?" They would be laughed out of New York City.

This is significant. So to be included as a part of that—it is very positive. Many people around the world look to the model of U.S. cooperatives and say that is the model we need. That's an important thing for U.S. cooperatives.

We've already seen the benefit from a public policy standpoint. From Congress and the federal government—there is already a higher recognition. I think we can expect a broader profile with policymakers around the country. Hopefully that will spur many more units of government to promote co-ops in their particular areas.

Seikatsu Club Consumers' Co-operative Union

In August 2012, a delegation of the Seikatsu Club Consumers' Co-operative Union of Japan toured co-ops in Cleveland, Ohio; Iowa; and Washington, D.C. (where this interview was conducted). Founded in 1965 as a buying club by 200 housewives in Tokyo, today the Seikatsu ("lifestyle" or "living") co-ops have over 340,000 members. Together, network enterprises have an annual turnover of U.S. $1 billion. The Seikatsu network also includes over 600 worker co-ops that employ over 17,000 people in such businesses as food distribution, food preparation, catering, recycling, childcare, and education.

Interviewed in 2012

Delegation Members

- **Takayuki Watanabe**, Chief Managing Director, Seikatsu Club Consumers' Cooperative Union
- **Kyoko Okamoto**, Board Member, Seikatsu Club Consumers' Cooperative Union
- **Hitomi Igarashi**, Board Member, Seikatsu Club Insurance Cooperative Union
- **Junji Asou**, Executive Director, Seikatsu Club Insurance Cooperative Union
- **Momoko Toda**, Seikatsu Club Liaison Committee on GMOs, Board Member, Seikatsu Club Consumers' Cooperative Ibaraki
- **Ryoko Shimizu**, Planning Division, Seikatsu Club Consumers Cooperative Union
- **Ichiro Kishi**, Deputy General Manager, Grain Section, Feed & Livestock Production Division, Zen-noh (National Federation of Agricultural Cooperative Associations)
- **Yosuke Ota**, WTO and EPA Office, Agricultural Policy Department, Central Union of Agricultural Cooperatives (Ja-Zenchu)

Steve Dubb: How did the Seikatsu Club begin?

Kyoko Okamoto: In 1965, in Setagaya Ward in Tokyo, a group of housewives formed a buying club to be able to collectively purchase milk. In 1968, the Seikatsu Club became a consumers' cooperative. When we started, we worked in groups that are called *han*—so those groups started to act as collective buying clubs. At the beginning, their main focus was on reducing the price of goods. By buying in a group, the buying club can have greater purchasing power to reduce the price. Later on, they began to notice that conventional products are contaminated in chemicals, so they started to buy chemical-free products. They also started an initiative to oppose chemically harmful detergents. And regarding milk, the collective purchasing of milk, our members launched a company to produce milk. So now we have a milk company, which produces milk.

SD: *What inspired the creation of the Seikatsu Club? Any key individuals who led the effort?*

Kyoko Okamoto: There was a lady who was named Shizuko Iwane. Initially, the Seikatsu Club was a club exclusively for women. But then soon after that, men could also join Seikatsu.

The group of women—those women wanted to have a community that is independently governed by those women at the local level. So that was the start of the Seikatsu Club. There were about 200 women at the beginning.

SD: *Could you comment on the role of women in leadership in the cooperative movement in Japan? Is female leadership common in the co-op movement in Japan or is it a contribution of Seikatsu?*

Kyoko Okamoto: In the 1970s, many cooperatives in Japan that were run by women disappeared or merged. At that time, there were many small co-ops that were run by women, but many of them disappeared or merged into larger cooperatives. So there are many cooperatives that are led by men instead of women, but I think the Seikatsu Club is a very successful example that is still run by women and very successful.

SD: *Could you talk about the process of expansion? Were there key stages in Seikatsu's development? How did it grow from 200 members to hundreds of thousands?*

Momoko Toda: From the beginning, there were very active women in the Seikatsu Club. They were highly educated. They were Baby Boomers. Many graduated from university, but they stayed at home and they were housewives. They wanted to have a place where they can be very active and play a key role in society. Seikatsu Club played as a stage to be active. From the beginning, the numbers increased very rapidly.

SD: *Who is attracted to join Seikatsu Club co-ops? Why do people join?*

Kyoko Okamoto: We have challenges to attract more people. We have problems with that. People who join the Seikatsu Club want to eat safe food. In order to get safe food, it helps to have scale. So existing members work to recruit more members to participate in the Seikatsu Club.

Momoko Toda: For example, in the case of milk, women members found a lot of problems with the commercial milk supply. That's why members wanted to start our own milk factory and company in order to address the problems and issues in the commercial market. In order to have our own product, we have to have more members.

So that is the starting point of the cooperative. Still there are people who join in order to buy safer goods, safer food products.

SD: *For the milk factory, did the capital come from the members or were there other sources of financing?*

Takayuki Watanabe: Our member cooperatives are in 21 prefectures in Japan. The capital is coming from six member cooperatives: Tokyo, Kanagawa, Osaka, Chiba, Saitama, and Nagano. All have shares in the milk company. Those shares are financed from the members' equity in each cooperative. These cooperatives have shares in the milk company, but the Seikatsu Consumer Cooperative Union is the purchasing cooperative for all of the Seikatsu Club.

SD: *What is the value of the member share investment in that business?*

Takayuki Watanabe: There is about $6 million capitalization from all members in the milk company. There are six producer groups. Three organizations out of those six are dairy farmer groups and the other three organizations—two of them are farmers and one is an affiliated company in charge of logistics. That company is called Taiyo Shokuhin Hanbai, and it distributes goods nationally.

SD: *What persuaded each of you to join Seikatsu? How did each of you become involved individually?*

Hitomi Igarashi: It was quite common—it is still common—for Japanese consumers to buy synthetic detergent. It was difficult to find a place to buy natural soap instead of synthetic detergent. So being able to buy natural soap was important to me. More broadly, the most important reason that motivates me to work as a leader of the Seikatsu Club is that I understand that one individual person cannot do much, but if we get together in a group and cooperate, we can do a lot of things. We can be stronger together. That is the most important reason to work as a leader. One single person cannot change the world, but if we can work in larger numbers in solidarity, in cooperation, we can change the world, such as—for example—when we started a milk company. We can't do that as individuals.

Momoko Toda: First of all, I wanted to get reliable food products for children.

Kyoko Okamoto: The reason I joined was that I wanted to buy good milk and good eggs because I have allergies. So the reason why I became a leader was because I worked on social activities, including networking—which is a political movement in the Seikatsu Club. I got more and more interested in the Seikatsu Club. It became more attractive to me.

Junji Asou: In 1978, I was first hired by the Seikatsu Club Tokyo. I am an employee of the Seikatsu Club. At the same time, I am a board member of the Seikatsu Club. I was a board member of the Seikatsu Club Tokyo, and after that I joined the Seikatsu Club Consumer Cooperative Union as a board member as well. I now work as a member of the board of directors of the Seikatsu Club insurance company, which began as a project of the Seikatsu Club Consumer Cooperative.

Takayuki Watanabe: Seikatsu Club Saitama first hired me in 1975. My case is similar to Mr. Asou. I was an employee at the Seikatsu Club Seitama. At the same time I was on the board of directors of Seitama. Six years ago, I began to work at SCCU as one of the board of directors.

Ryoko Shimizu: I am also employed by Seikatsu Club Tokyo. I am now dispatched at Seikatsu Consumer Cooperative Union's national office to work as full-time staff. I first became interested in Seikatsu because of my interest in consumer issues. A woman who was named Katsuko Nonura came to my university. She made a speech, and I got interested in consumer issues. She also taught me to speak English. She was a mentor to me. As a student, I became interested in consumer issues. Someone asked me to join. He was a friend of my mentor. That was the start of my career. I've been working at the Seikatsu for thirty years.

SD: *Can you discuss the broader cooperative movement in Japan? How does Seikatsu interact with the broader cooperative movement in Japan, which has more than 20 million member-owners?*

Junji Asou: There is an umbrella body for consumer co-ops in Japan called the Japanese Consumer Cooperative Union (JCCU). The Seikatsu Club is a member of JCCU. So we sometimes work with other consumer co-ops in Japan under the aegis of the JCCU, depending on the issues. In some areas, we work with other co-ops. But JCCU has its own private brand of their products, which is called "Co-op Brand." We do not sell Co-op Brand. We have our own products.

There is a very big difference between JCCU and Seikatsu Club regarding commitment to the local community and also a big difference in the business management and governance model. JCCU has a business model that is based on competition, so they want to compete with conventional supermarket chains. Many cooperatives that work closely with JCCU tend to merge with other cooperatives to become bigger.

So when you ask us about the cooperative movement, we try to tell you how many cooperatives there are in Japan, but we are not sure of the exact number because many cooperatives get merged. There are fewer and fewer cooperatives in Japan at this moment.

Another important point of distinction regards our commitment to the local community. In order to be more community based, Seikatsu Club has been divided into prefecture [Japanese equivalent of "state"] units and some prefectures are divided into smaller Seikatsu Clubs. And each cooperative has its own legal status at the local level. In the case of Tokyo, there are four local Seikatsu Clubs. And Kanagawa has been divided into five local Seikatsu Clubs. All of them have got their own legal status as cooperatives. Each cooperative is member governed by residents of that locality. The decision-making structure is divided into the local areas, but we supply the same product line to all of our member cooperatives.

SD: *Could you talk about the Seikatsu Club's "han" or branch structure—how does this function?*

Junji Asou: Before we introduced delivery service to individual members, the *han* worked as a basic unit for our activities and businesses. So regarding *han*, our products were delivered to a group and people in this group would divide those products into the orders of the individual members. By doing that, we can reduce the cost of the delivery, but at the same time, the *han*—the group—also functions as the base unit in the decision-making process. Each *han* sends a representative to a branch in its area and the branch sends a representative to the individual co-ops. That used to be the decision-making structure.

SD: *What is the decision making structure today?*

Junji Asou: The branch structure remains, but you no longer have to be a member of a *han*. In 1980, we introduced a new system to deliver our products to individual households instead of the *han*. We now have more individual members than group members.

Momoko Toda: It depends on the prefecture [state]. In Ibaraki, half of the members still belong a *han*. Nationally roughly 30 percent of our members belong to a *han*. A majority, 54 percent, are individual members. *Han* remain a key venue for members to share information.

SD: *Many supermarkets often stock tens or even hundreds of thousands of items. Famously the Seikatsu Club carries only about 2,000 products (the majority of which are staple foods like milk, rice, and vegetables) and only one or two types of each product. Could you talk about why your stores are structured that way?*

Junji Asou: There is a background behind this policy. We decided to not have many product lines, but it is also true for us to say that we couldn't afford to have so many product lines. We only have one line of milk. There are not any other milk products. We don't work with other milk companies. That is the same for other products. We only have one variety of soya sauce, one variety of ketchup, mayo, or anything. In doing so, we can have closer relations with those food companies from which we buy. With milk, it is our own company, but even when it is not our own company, we have closer relationships with those food companies and we can have more say, we can influence those companies, and we can tell them what we want because of this close relationship.

SD: *In the 1990s, you began to also form a network of worker-owned cooperatives. How did this occur? What are the areas of business where you have had the most success with that approach?*

Hitomi Igarashi: In Kanaga prefecture, in 1992, co-op members began a shop. They needed to have workers who'd work there. They did not want to have employees at that shop. They learned from European countries about worker collectives where members are not employed by anyone but are owners of the worker collective, they invest in the worker collective, and they are engaged in the management and governance of the cooperative. A workers' collective was started to run the business of the shop. But now they have businesses in many other areas of services, which include providing for the welfare of the elderly or kids. There are many kinds of activities that worker collectives are doing now.

SD: *Can you discuss Seikatsu's work in the area of genetically modified organisms (GMOs)?*

Momoko Toda: In 1997, the Seikatsu Club declared that we would not use any GMO ingredients in our food products, which was just after the Japanese government decided to introduce GMOs at the end of 1996. So since then members of the Seikatsu Club worked hard with producers to eliminate GMO ingredients from our food products. As members of the Seikatsu Club, we learned about GMOs, and it is very important to know—members worked very hard to learn what a genetically modified organism is. We also worked to share information about GMOs. And we worked to build public awareness of GMOs and to draw public attention to this issue.

SD: *Have there been any public policy achievements that resulted from this effort in Japan?*

Hitomi Igarashi: We circulated a petition to ask the government to label GMOs. When GMOs were first introduced to Japan, there was no mandatory labeling. That's why we circulated a petition and gathered more than one million signatures. After that, the Japanese government introduced a law to have mandatory labeling of GMOs. That law was enacted in 2000.

But that law is not enough. It is not very good. They introduced mandatory labeling—the government introduced a law—but that law is not good enough for consumers because if the altered DNA or protein is not detected in the final product, then there is no mandatory labeling on that product. For example, in the case of soya sauce or edible oil, there is no labeling, even though it is from GMOs, because in the final product we cannot detect altered DNA. So that is why we don't believe we have adequate labeling. In relation to that, we have a very high threshold for GMO contamination, so even though the product, like corn or canola, is contaminated, if it is less than five percent, then there is no labeling requirement. That is why we don't think it is enough. Because we think the law is not enough, we are working very hard to change the law and improve the law. We urge the government to do so.

SD: *What are your impressions of your tour of the United States? In what ways are co-ops in the United States similar to Japanese co-ops? What are some of the key differences?*

Hitomi Igarashi: I can tell you one key difference. The key players in the United States are workers, as far as we have seen. In Japan, the key players are members: consumer-members.

SD: *Your tour may be mostly with worker co-ops, but consumer co-ops are the norm in the United States.*

Hitomi Igarashi: Even in the case of U.S. food co-ops, which are similar to Japanese consumer co-ops, I felt that in those food co-ops the focus is more on employees at those food co-ops rather than members. The food co-op we visited in Iowa has its own pension program and health care programs for the employees. We thought that even though they are consumer food co-ops, they are working and focusing on the workers. In the case of the Seikatsu Club, the focus is more on the consumer members.

SD: *Do you have any other observations regarding your visit to the United States so far?*

Hitomi Igarashi: The thing that I found familiar is that cooperatives are based on the same principles. We are both based on International Cooperative Alliance (ICA) cooperative principles. So our missions are very similar to each other.

In Japan also, like the United States, there is a widening gap between the rich and the poor. When I went to Cleveland to visit the Evergreen Cooperatives, I saw that cooperatives could work toward closing that economic gap.

SD: *As you know, 2012 has been designated by the United Nations as the International Year of the Cooperative. Can you talk a bit about your work in support of the International Year of Cooperatives? What activities are occurring in Japan around this event?*

"In a sense, we don't care what kind of government policy they have—we do— **but we try to keep vocal about the importance of building an alternative society**. That's why we are doing our activities."

Ryoko Shimizu: This tour is an example of our activities to celebrate the international year of cooperatives. This tour is one of our activities for the year.

Hitomi Igarashi: There is a national committee organized by stakeholders, which is named the Japan National Planning Committee for the International Year of the Cooperative 2012. The Seikatsu is one of the active members on the national committee.

SD: What are activities that Seikatsu is engaged with regarding the International Year of the Cooperative within Japan?

Momoko Toda: Mainstream cooperatives in Japan are more like supermarkets at this moment. The Seikatsu Club identifies itself as a genuine cooperative. We are based on cooperative principles. We are telling our members that it is our unique characteristics that work to make us a true cooperative. That is a part of the activities that we are doing in the International Year of Cooperatives.

Kyoko Okamoto: Regarding this tour, we are going to share information about our trip on the Internet. We also have many publications of our member cooperatives, so we are going to use those publications to disseminate information about our trips, including here and other parts of the world.

Hitomi Igarashi: We will also do two other tours. One is to Australia and one is to Italy and Spain, including visiting the Mondragón cooperatives in Spain. Those are the series of our trips. At home, we also are working to organize symposiums. We have had already one symposium by working with another co-op on green co-ops. We will have another meeting in September and, as the culmination of the year in Kyushu, we will hold an international conference on cooperatives. Speakers will include Paul Hazen (Executive Director of the U.S. Overseas Cooperative Development Council) and Dr. Ian McPherson (former Director of the Centre for Co-operatives and Community-Based Economy at the University of Victoria) from Canada.

Junji Asou: We put the logo of the international year of the cooperative on our cards. And on our website. We use that logo in various publications.

SD: *Is there anything else that you would like to add?*

Momoko Toda: The most important thing for our members is to know what the products they buy really are. Information disclosure is the most important thing for the members of the Seikatsu Club.

Hitomi Igarashi: The paradigmatic product is milk. The reason why we wanted to start our own milk company is that we wanted to know what milk really is. We wanted to know the cost structure, the distribution structure, and everything else about the way milk was produced. That would be a foundational point of the Seikatsu Club.

In a sense, we don't care what kind of government policy they have—we do—but we try to keep vocal about the importance of building an alternative society. That's why we are doing our activities.

Another thing that after coming here I came to know: I came to be more aware of incubator organizations and intermediaries. In order to start an activity or movement, it is important to have an incubator organization to support many groups, which work for various kinds of change. Intermediary or incubator organizations are very important.

Worker Cooperatives & Employee Ownership

Our last and most extensive section of interviews is on employee ownership. In large measure because of The Democracy Collaborative's work with the Evergreen Cooperatives in Cleveland, we have come across many leaders who are beginning to convert worker cooperatives into a leading community wealth building strategy that has been adopted by a growing number of cities, including Cleveland, Ohio; New York City; Madison, Wisconsin; Rochester, New York; and Richmond, Virginia; among others. Those interviewed here talk about the challenges of incubating worker co-ops (a theme covered in the interviews of Hilary Abell, Melissa Hoover, Molly Hemstreet, and Emily Kawano), as well as the challenges of governance (a theme covered in the interviews of Rodney North, Blake Jones, and Rob Witherell).

The interview of John Logue deserves special mention. John Logue founded and helped build the nation's most successful state employee ownership center. Most of his work focused on employee stock ownership plan (ESOP) companies and to date, OEOC has helped convert 15,000 jobs to employee ownership, a number that worker co-op activists in the United States can only dream of. Logue also played an outsized role in the development of the first of the Evergreen Cooperatives, the Evergreen Cooperative Laundry, which launched in October 2009. Tragically, two months after the co-op's founding, Logue died of pancreatic cancer. But his vision lives on in the growing employee ownership movement.

John Logue

John Logue was the Founding Executive Director of the Ohio Employee Ownership Center, based at Kent State University in Kent, Ohio. The Center began in 1987 with grants from the Cleveland and Gund foundations and the Ohio Department of Development to provide information and preliminary technical assistance for Ohioans exploring employee ownership. Over its first 20 years, the group, on an annual budget which in 2007 totaled just over $600,000, worked with 566 employee groups and retiring owners to determine whether employee ownership made sense in their cases. Eighty-one of them became partly or wholly employee owned, creating 14,685 new employee owners. Follow-up research on data through 2003 for forty-nine of these eight-one companies found that these firms had created $349 million in equity for their employee owners.

Nationwide, according to the December 2015 of the National Center of Employee Ownership, there are more than 10.5 million owners at 6,795 companies. Total value of employee ownership in these companies is $1.23 trillion.

On December 9, 2009, John Logue passed away, about one week after being diagnosed with cancer.

Interviewed in 2008

Steve Dubb: Briefly, what were the origins of the Ohio Employee Ownership Center?

John Logue: The Center developed out of our experience with the efforts to use employee and community ownership to avert the steel shutdowns in Youngstown in the late 1970s and early 1980s. We did three years' worth of research on the utility of employee ownership as an economic development strategy in Ohio before starting the Center in 1987.

SD: Could you explain employee ownership and the advantages it poses for business development?

JL: It has some obvious advantages. It anchors capital and jobs in the local community. Employee owners reinvest in the businesses they own out of their own self-interest for jobs and benefits in the future. Additionally, there is a lot of evidence that participatory employee-owned companies outperform those that are authoritarian and certainly outperform their conventionally-owned business competitors. So from an economic development standpoint, employee ownership looks like an excellent bet.

SD: Are there any particular disadvantages?

JL: I don't think there are any disadvantages from the point of view of the employees or the communities from which the business are located. If the employees buy a business that is bound for shutdown, they may be making a bad investment of their time, energy, and money unless they can turn it around. But conventional business wisdom is to shut the business anyway. So the fundamental questions for employees trying to avert shutdown is "Do you think the business can be saved?" If you were buying a profitable business, the issue is much simpler.

There is a school of theory in economics that says that employee-owners will eat their seed corn—they will not re-invest. I know of no empirical evidence that supports this economic theory, but economists who ought to know better continue to maintain it.

SD: You first got involved in Youngstown in 1977, in a heroic—albeit ultimately unsuccessful—attempt to save a steel mill by converting the plant to employee-ownership. Could you talk about what happened?

JL: "Heroic" is right. The effort to save the Youngstown steel plants—there were ultimately four major mills that shut down—brought together the community, the churches, civic leaders, and the union locals. It failed. It failed because we didn't know enough about how to do large employee-ownership deals—and also because the Steelworkers didn't know how to do them. Subsequently, the Steelworkers reworked their entire approach to employee ownership and that's one of the major changes that Youngstown caused and the Steelworkers saved hundreds of thousands—probably millions—of man-hours of work in the steel industry through employee ownership.

The Youngstown effort was ultimately unsuccessful, although part of one of the mills was bought by managers and local investors and subsequently sold partly to employees. That's MacDonald Steel and it is still running today—30 years later. They just made a major investment in replacing their heat-treat furnaces with energy-efficient ones.

Though it failed, the Youngstown effort was an education to the whole country on employee ownership. The genesis of the Ohio Employee Ownership Center was in Youngstown.

In retrospect, it's worth thinking about whether that effort could have succeeded. There is no question that there was the core of a viable steel business in Youngstown, especially had the employees succeeded in buying the Campbell Works, the first of the mills to shut down. You could certainly create an easy scenario for the continued existence of a significant steel company in Youngstown.

Four Youngstown steel mills were shut between 1977 and 1982. Knowing what we know today, we could have consolidated and modernized them under employee ownership. At the time of shutdown, there were probably 12,000 to 14,000 working in those four mills. If the employees had bought them, you would probably have 4,000 working today, and a fair portion of the remainder would have drawn their pensions with ten or fifteen additional years of work. Employment would have been downsized as the mills modernized. Youngstown would be a much more vibrant community.

SD: *Today, Youngstown has been widely touted for its "Youngstown 2010" planning process that seeks to acknowledge its smaller size, but build a sustainable model. However, employee ownership does not play a significant role in that model. What potential does employee ownership have to play a positive role in places like Youngstown, Dayton, Erie, Scranton, or other similar mid-sized "Rust Belt" cities today?*

JL: Fundamentally, the best potential is to use employee ownership in family-business transition when there is no heir. It's a small-scale strategy but a highly successful one.

Sixty percent of ESOP deals that are done in Ohio are family-owned businesses to create liquidity for departing business owners. The average employment per company is 100 to 125. So in Youngstown, we've done about six out of the eighty-five that we've done statewide. Brainard Rivet is one: It's the only one done in a shutdown situation. The other five are all retiring owner situations: Falcon Foundry, a steel industry supplier; Fireline, another steel industry supplier; McDonald Steel, discussed above, and two service companies. If you look at the group, it is clearly focused on steel industry suppliers. They have all had a hard time, because of the decline of the steel industry. With the exception of Brainard, every single one of them was a family business. Brainard belonged to Textron. It was the only unionized facility they had left in the United States. It was also ironically their most profitable facility. Management thought they could run Brainard's work more profitably at a nonunion facility in Virginia. Turned out they couldn't.

SD: *This sounds important, but the scale is small. Is it possible for a weak market city to employ an economic strategy that places employee ownership front and center in its work?*

JL: Yes, it is, but it would require that a city say, "This is what we want to do." There aren't a whole lot of cities that are saying, "We want our businesses to be locally owned. And we prefer the ownership be broadly shared with employees." If they said that, we know how to do it. We're currently trying very hard in Cleveland to learn how to start employee-owned businesses building on existing institutional business. That's a very viable strategy in Youngstown. It requires the kind of forward thinking that very few American cities have committed themselves to. It requires that progressives stop seeing the state as the only way to handle issues of income inequality and start thinking about how to generate more economic equality in the market. Progressives today look like the proverbial squirrel on

"Progressives today look like the proverbial squirrel on the treadmill: **they keep having to run faster and faster to stay in the same place.**"

the treadmill: they keep having to run faster and faster to stay in the same place. This won't change unless they get to the source, which is within the market economy.

What you're asking for is a city to say: "We want to build an economy that is inclusive of working people in our community." You're asking a Chamber of Commerce to say, "We are more interested in developing businesses at home than in chasing smokestacks from major publicly traded corporations." You're asking for the press to say, "We celebrate the success of locally owned businesses not just when they sell themselves, but in their rootedness to the community and their contributions to the local United Way."

Absentee-owned corporations contribute to charity only about a fourth of what local companies do, if you adjust for size. Employee ownership is one component of a local economic strategy. It is not a be-all and end-all. You can't wave a wand, chant "employee ownership," and conjure up a different vision of the future. It takes hard work, company by company.

SD: *From the beginning of your Center's operations, one of the key features of your work has been to do studies on whether employee ownership would be feasible. Could you explain in more detail how this process works?*

JL: We start with a big outreach program. We have 18,000 subscribers to our magazine, *Owners at Work*, and an annual conference that more than 400 people attend; we will speak whenever two or more people come together who are interested in employee ownership. We get a lot of media. So the requests for feasibility studies don't end up on our doorstep by chance. The first thing we do is to provide generic information about employee ownership. The second thing we do is talk with them about their specific situation. Does employee ownership make any sense in their specific circumstances and, if it does, how would you do the transaction? In the case of a family-owned business where the owner is fifty-eight and wants to be out of business by sixty-five, the answer is a multi-step transaction that avoids over-leveraging the business. Those transactions are very easy to do if you have five to ten years to do it, and our success rate is close to 100 percent.

On the other hand, there are those cases where someone comes up to us and tells us that their plant is up for sale and that if they are not sold they are in danger of being shut down or—worse—they've got a "Warning" shutdown notice and ask us "What do we do?" Those are much tougher to do. Usually the business is troubled in some manner. Otherwise, there wouldn't be a shutdown threat. In those cases, we administer the Rapid Response Unit of the Ohio Department of Job and Family Services Grant fund to hire professional consultants. We can't save all of these, but we do succeed in perhaps 20 percent of these cases.

SD: *Another facet of your organization's work is the Ohio Employee Owned Network, which aims to provide continuing support for existing Ohio employee-owned businesses. Could you discuss how that network was formed, how large it has grown to be now, and what impact it has had on its members?*

JL: The origins of the network lie in a conversation I that had with Tom Moyer who was the local Steelworker union president at Bliss in Salem, Ohio. The employees had bought the plant under Tom's leadership. "John, I know how to bargain a contract," Tom said. "I can file and resolve grievances, I can lead a walk-out, and I can lead a wild-cat if I have to, but I haven't the foggiest notion of how to read the financial statements that I am getting now that I'm on the board of directors. *You* need a course on that." So we brought in an accounting professor. He taught a course that our staff benefited from immensely, but the target audience was baffled: so we thought the Center had a role to convert technical business information into something employee-owners could understand and use. About the same time, we had a panel of several managers from employee-owned companies talking about what they thought we needed to do to be more useful to their companies. There was a confluence of pressure from below and pressure from CEOs to do something for training and organizational development.

We had a naïve belief when we started the OEOC that employee ownership was the goal and, once we achieved that, our role was over. What we found was that employee ownership wasn't the end of the road. Rather, it was simply the start of a new road. What do you do the day after you're employee-owned? You still had the same boss, the same customers, and the same line of business. To the average employee, it didn't look any different. But it needed to be different: there needed to be more employee involvement, more communication about the business, open books, training to underpin the employee participation and involvement, and information about the business. That was a pretty tall order. This required a serious company makeover. That is what the Network is really about. It is a joint company network. There are now 80 companies in it with 16,000 to 17,000 employee-owners. The Network runs a program or two every month. This month we're running a program in Cincinnati on ESOP administration and another for ESOP company CEOs and CFOs in Columbus. Most programs are for non-managerial employees. We'll have 400 to 500 employee-owners go through our training every year.

SD: *A newer OEOC effort is your Succession Planning Program. What are the origins of that effort and what are your goals with that program?*

JL: It has always been clear that the best time for employees to buy companies is when family owners put them up for sale, when they are viable companies. There is even a tax break to encourage family owners to sell their businesses to the employees, but it is not known about as widely as it should be. So we got into business ownership succession to encourage employee ownership when you didn't have a family member who could take over the business. The further we got into this, the more we realized that succession planning, business ownership, and management succession planning ought to be part of every economic development professional's tool kit.

One hundred years ago, business ownership succession was a slam dunk. When you had families with seven or eight kids, there had to be at least one of them who would be competent to take over the business. Fifty years ago, the average family size was three or four kids, the percentage of the kids going on to college was

"What we found was that employee ownership wasn't the end of the road. Rather, **it was simply the start of a new road**."

---

still pretty low and, when business owners' kids went to college, they typically got a degree in something like industrial engineering and went back into the family business. Today, your family size is down to 1.8 kids, the odds that they are going to college is close to 100 percent, and once you've seen the attraction of college and the professions you most often don't want to go back and run a thirty-person foundry working 60 hours a week like your dad did. Go and be a merger-and-acquisition specialist instead: You make a lot more money, the hours are better, and you get to travel. In the 1980s, studies suggested that maybe one in three family businesses still made it from the first to the second generation and maybe one in six made it to a third generation. In 2004, there was a study by the Small Business Administration that showed that only one in six was passing from the first to second generation and one in twenty to the third generation.

So this means that in 20 to 25 years, you have halved—or more than halved—family business succession. The failure to plan for business succession is the number-one cause of *preventable* job loss in this country. So there ought to be a major role here for economic development professionals, for the Chambers of Commerce, for cities, for counties.

So we've developed an outreach program on business ownership succession. We've been running a Cleveland program for the last 10 years. About two years ago we expanded the program to Akron. In the next three years we will be expanding statewide. We want to be running similar programs in smaller industrial towns. We're doing webinars. We're building a website that will have a tremendous amount of material. There's a DVD—the production is almost finished—which will be available in streaming video on the website as well as in DVD format.

SD: *In your* Owners at Work, *you have run a series on sustainability in the ESOP movement, including a recent article on YSI [originally Yellow Springs, Incorporated] in Yellow Springs, Ohio. How are ESOPs incorporating green principles into their businesses?*

JL: YSI is really impressive. They are in the business where they have to be ecologically minded—they make environmental monitoring devices. YSI takes their green principles very seriously. They have minding the planet as one of their three bottom lines. But they are a great sustainable business in many other ways as well.

In employee-owned companies, we think of environmental sustainability as part and parcel of social and economic "double bottom" line thinking. It's not just green principles: it's health and safety, employee education, money to go back to school and college, training, and workplace issues. It's what being put back into the community. It's general community sustainability—not just putting solar panels on the roof. It is sustainability much more broadly defined.

Sustainability makes a lot of sense in employee-owned businesses. A lot of businesses say employees are their most important resource, but you wouldn't believe it from their financial statements. Employee-owned business does better with that. Investment in health and safety makes intuitive sense. Training makes intuitive sense. Green principles make intuitive sense for employee-owners, too. They particularly do when there are ways to reduce costs and reduce your carbon footprint or waste of energy simultaneously. The biggest opportunities come when you are making new investments.

There is a lot of economic low-hanging fruit—especially given high energy prices. There are a lot of opportunities to develop new products, which will make implementing green principles more economically feasible. For example, we have an employee-owned network company that is developing hybrid drives for small trucks and buses that can be used to retrofit an existing fleet. That kind of thing is potentially dynamite.

SD: *You've mentioned in many cases that you viewed the Mondragón model of worker cooperative businesses in Spain, which employs tens of thousands, as a model that could be spread to a weak market city like Cleveland, Ohio. OEOC is* *now currently doing some work to develop what you're calling an "Evergreen" network of worker cooperatives in Cleveland, including an employee-owned business that would provide clean linen laundry service to area hospitals. Could you discuss the Cleveland effort and, more broadly, what you see as the potential for developing over time an Evergreen network of businesses?*

JL: The effort in Cleveland rests upon using the purchasing power of the anchor institutions to buy goods and services from local and employee-owned companies. The advantage of buying from employee-owned companies as opposed to merely buying locally is that you have a broader ownership of wealth that is created, somewhat higher wages, notably higher benefits, greater investment in the employees in training and otherwise. There is a range of services that anchor institutions in Cleveland need that can be provided by employee-owned businesses, so the hope of starting a network of employee-owned companies to provide goods and services to anchor institutions seems reasonable. Certainly the feasibility study done on the first of these businesses—Evergreen Cooperative Laundry—is very promising. This work has been supported by the Cleveland Foundation, which has dual commitment to economic inclusion and to sustainability. [Editor's note: With the help of OEOC, The Democracy Collaborative, and the Cleveland Foundation, The Evergreen Cooperatives project successfully launched in 2009, and today is a network of three worker-owned cooperative green businesses.]

In the Cleveland model that we are attempting to implement, a central role is to be played by the Evergreen Cooperative Development Fund, which would be the equity investor in starting new employee-owned businesses.

SD: *How would the Fund work?*

JL: All of this is hypothetical at this point, but our model currently calls for the fund to invest in preferred shares in the new co-ops. Those shares would be redeemed over time as the co-ops capitalize themselves financially through retained earnings, which will be credited to member accounts. After they pay down the bank debt, they'll redeem the Fund's preferred shares, freeing those funds for the next startup.

SD: *At your conference this past April you mentioned that if Ohio's manufacturing sector as a whole had matched the employment record of manufacturing sector ESOPs within the Ohio Employee Owned Network, there would be 306,000 more manufacturing jobs in the state of Ohio than there are now. A few years before, in 2003, Steve Clem testified to Congress: "Every year, in our technical assistance at the OEOC, we have lost at least one otherwise viable employee buyout because of the lack of timely, friendly capital. To put it bluntly, almost every year for the last fifteen, we have seen at least one viable employee buyout effort fail with the loss of 100 to 200 jobs because no one could round up financing in a timely fashion." Discuss briefly a few of these missed opportunities.*

JL: There are too many examples: Massillon Stainless—a decent sized equity fund could have saved that plant and 200 jobs rather than shipping all the equipment to China. Cold Metal Products in Youngstown is a steel finishing facility that could have been saved. CSC Steel in Warren is the big one: 1,300 jobs. The Amanda stove plant in Delaware, Ohio, could have been saved. The most recent plant we lost was Hoover, the vacuum manufacturer, in North Canton. 800 hourly jobs and about 200 salaried jobs were lost when it shut down, but it had been up at 2,500 employees. The Chinese outfit that bought the firm shut down the North Canton facility. They kept the nonunion facility in El Paso and one in Ciudad Juarez and contracted out the rest of the work to China. That is an example of a facility of an iconic employer where jobs were needlessly lost.

I should mention that in every one of those cases, it would have been better to get in sooner. I am not sure about Cold Metal Products, but the other three had been bought and sold several times over the last several years and it would have been easier to intervene earlier.

One other thing: Employee-owned companies tend to reinvest at higher rates than their competitors, so it's not that they are avoiding shutdown, although they do, but the strategy is that every day you are working for the long-term survival of the company. That's a different strategy than focusing on what the next quarter's bottom line is going to look like.

SD: *What would need to be done on the policy side to keep such jobs from continuing to be lost?*

JL: On the policy side, we need a long-term, patient, equity capital fund that can be invested at less than venture capital rates. There aren't many manufacturing businesses that can sustain a rate of return that venture capital funds want. So you need to create more patient equity. The most likely place to look for it is in the Taft-Hartley funds [pension funds that are managed by a joint union-management board of trustees] and the public employee funds. The public employee funds in particular have a vested interest in retaining a strong tax base in our communities.

SD: *When the OEOC testified to Congress in 2003, the legislation proposed was an employee ownership bank. How would that have worked if the legislation had passed?*

JL: It was set up to be a new lending institution: a special purpose bank for employee-owned companies. Currently, we have a range of special lending institutions that focus on different sectors. For instance, there is a special lending facility for rural electric cooperatives. Of course, the whole Farm Credit system, which has existed since the Great Depression, is set up as a specialized lending model.

Another example is from the Carter Administration, which set up the National Cooperative Bank. Reagan privatized it and expected it to fail, but the National Cooperative Bank has done well on its own. It is effectively a credit union for consumer cooperatives. It does a little bit of employee-ownership lending as well. The thought behind the proposal of Bernie Sanders (I-VT), who sponsored the employee ownership bank bill, was to have a bank that was a specialist in employee-ownership lending. It also would allow the bank to extend loan guarantees. When used judiciously, loan guarantees are a highly effective way to enhance the creditworthiness of employee-ownership deals.

One of the problems with employee-ownership deals is that if you are going to do 100-percent leveraged buyout, there is no one who can personally guarantee the loan. You need some sort of a credit enhancement. We are working on one deal on right now where a credit enhancement would be quite useful. It is a retiring owner situation. Usually you do that through a multi-step process.

For instance, the first step would be for 30 percent, so that the retiring owner gets the ESOP tax benefit, but the retiring owner still owns 70 percent initially, so the bank is comfortable with the deal. Then you do another 19 percent. When you get to the last piece, the employees have 49 percent, which they have paid for, so the bank feels pretty comfortable. The problem with a 100-percent leveraged deal is that it is hard to get a bank to be willing to finance it, and here is where a guarantee would be quite useful. One of the great benefits of the Sanders bill was the loan-guarantee provision.

SD: *ESOPs have recently begun to attract a higher level of opposition. The President's Commission on Tax Reform, for instance, advocated eliminating federal tax breaks for employee ownership. Also, the ESOP buy-out of the Tribune received a high degree of criticism. Are the criticisms justified? If not, what should be done to counter the criticism?*

JL: I think that it is problematic to have public policy on employee ownership rest primarily on tax expenditures. By and large, tax expenditures go to the well-to-do. There are not a whole lot of them which benefit working people. I think you can name them on the fingers of one hand: the mortgage interest deduction on your house, employer-provided medical insurance and pension contributions, the deductibility of union dues, and, for the people who work for ESOPs, the ESOP tax benefit. It is hard to drive good public policy with tax expenditures, without some of those tax expenditures being used for other purposes than Congress intended.

Why are ESOPs encountering more opposition? I don't know. The ESOP tax benefit doesn't cost much, certainly not by comparison with what you get. Think of that number for ESOP assets you cited at the beginning: there is almost $1 trillion in employee equity, triggered by $80 billion or so in tax expenditures over the last 34 years. Generally, it is believed that ESOP tax breaks cost about $2 billion a year. That wouldn't finance a week of the Iraq war, would it?

If one were to look farther down the pike, maybe what there should be is general legislation that businesses that come up for sale would be offered first to employees, so employees would have a right of first refusal.

Certainly, if one were concerned with job flight, it might make sense to write legislation that if a company is closing down production in the United States, it would have to give the employees the right of first refusal on the plant, property, and equipment. The only corporations that would scream are those that are intending to move their jobs abroad. Workers and communities would cheer.

SD: *What do you see as the most important challenges or opportunities facing ESOPs today? Where should the employee ownership movement be focusing its energies over the next five to ten years?*

JL: First, it is hard to say that there is an employee-ownership movement. I wish there were. Employee ownership has a lot of support in Congress. It is very broad, but quite shallow. In the American population in general, surveys show repeatedly that Americans think employee ownership is a good thing. They would prefer to buy from employee-owned companies. They would prefer to work for employee-owned companies. Most do not have the opportunity to do either. It would be nice to have a movement.

Employee-owned companies have tended to be islands among themselves, rather than seeing themselves as part of a movement.

If I were to look forward optimistically, I would look to those islands building bridges among them and becoming archipelagos, with more communication, more collaboration, and more economies of scale. The median employee-owned company has 100 to 125 employees with $12-15 million in annual sales. Those companies have a lot to gain by collaborating with each other and creating some economies of scale. Imagine the advantages they would get from joint research and development or an export co-op. You could set up an export co-op for employee-owned companies in whatever trade or industry you would like. There are models of that elsewhere—you see some of that in northern Italy, in Spain, and a bit of that in France. We could do it here.

The truth of the matter is that cooperation among small companies even in the same industry is not going to trigger antitrust inquiries—look at the huge mergers that get approved by the Justice Department today. If you look at the American agricultural cooperative sector, which has sustained family farming in big areas of the United States, these co-ops create secondary co-ops to provide

"The failure to plan for business succession is **the number-one cause of preventable job loss in this country**."

what the primary co-ops need to serve their farmer-members. It would make a tremendous amount of sense for this to happen in the employee-ownership sector.

Think for a second about the structure of federal support for agriculture and agricultural cooperatives. The Department of Agriculture has a network of agricultural extension agents that work with the land grant colleges to provide direct assistance to family farmers. It is one of the reasons that the agricultural sector has modernized so thoroughly. The Department of Agriculture has co-op development experts who are in every state, who assist farmers and value-added cooperatives. The Department of Agriculture funds nearly 20 co-op development centers at the state or regional level, which provide grants to help folks set up co-ops in rural areas.

We need some of that in the employee-owned sector. Farmers aren't the only source of good ideas. Why can we not have some of the same kind support in the employee-ownership sector? If you did you that, you would have much more rapid development of employee-owned firms. I guess the natural home would be the Department of Commerce.

One could imagine more states setting up programs like ours. If you allocated every cent of state money we have spent over the last twenty years to our job retention function, the cost per job is less than $400. Compare that with $225,000 per job to lure Mercedes to Alabama. Or $60,000 plus per job to keep Jeep in Ohio. If you allocated 100 percent of our costs-to-asset creation, the ratio between employee equity in forty-nine of the eighty-five companies for which we have data as of 2003 is about $60 in equity for every dollar in cost.

So there are a lot of things of that sort that could make a lot of difference going forward. They are cheap by comparison to tax expenditures, and they have a high degree of leverage. So one could imagine the development of an employee-owned sector where there is a lot of collaboration between employee-owned companies, where they create the joint services they need. One thing we notice is that employee-owned companies are very thinly managed; it is always good to minimize your overhead, but you get in trouble when you need assistance. In Spain, with the Mondragón network of worker cooperatives, they have a management intervention team to support cooperatives that get into trouble. That would be a good thing in our system as well. There are a lot of ideas that would pool resources in employee-owned companies and that would make a lot of sense. And if employee-owned companies looked to where they could be in ten to twenty years, they would find a lot of models within the United States, particularly in our agriculture sector, which they could build on.

If one were to look abroad, the best place to look is the province of Quebec, which has a major cooperative development effort around start-ups. They are creating fifty to one hundred worker co-ops annually, which combined employ between 1,000 and 1,500 people, particularly in outlying areas of the province. So you don't have to go all the way to Spain and Italy to find models that are worth emulating. You can just drive north of the border and see some pretty impressive things going on.

SD: *Is there anything else you would like to add?*

JL: I think that it is worth mentioning the role of The Democracy Collaborative in stimulating thinking about employee ownership. There have really been two new sources of thinking on integrating employee ownership into the broader economic context. One is Bill Greider and the other is the work of the folks at The Democracy Collaborative. In both cases, what you're doing is trying to put employee ownership into a broader reform strategy for the United States. It is interesting to me that this is coming from people who are basically outside the employee-ownership sector.

Another interesting thing is that employee ownership is very much a market-based solution to some of the ills of economic inequality in American society. It rests on the belief that ownership matters. This is something that most economists seem to want to argue doesn't matter. That doesn't mean, of course, that economists want to give away their property to the poor, so ownership does

"If I were to look forward optimistically, I would look to those islands building bridges among them and becoming archipelagos, with **more communication, more collaboration, and more economies of scale**."

seem to matter for them personally. But they seem to believe that the concentration of ownership isn't material in the economic system. But it does matter. It matters because employee ownership creates serious financial assets for working people. It does so because of the way the capitalist system multiplies the value of productive assets. And ownership matters because we associate ownership and control. It matters in a market economy, particularly if it is tied to productive assets. If one developed a system in which far more Americans had ownership of productive assets through their work, you would have a very different economy.

Let's say that every American corporation had to contribute five percent of their wage sum to an employee-ownership fund in that company. You would generate, over a period of relatively few years, substantial value, because the value of those assets multiplies, at least in companies that don't go bankrupt. So the fund would produce more wealth, more productive assets, as you share in the retained earnings of your company. If we believe in a capitalism-based market economy, there is a powerful argument for far greater employee ownership in order to build equality into ownership and influence for working people. Thereby you build greater equality into the results.

If you think seriously about employee ownership, the appropriate comparison is to the Homestead Act of 1862. The Homestead Act put productive assets—then largely land—in the hands of the men and women who worked that land, and, of course, that made all of the difference in American democracy, creating millions of new family farms over the next 50 years. Agriculture consequently remains the one sector of the American economy where ownership and productive labor go hand in hand.

That's how ESOPs are set up. You buy with borrowed money and pay off the loan with the results of your labor. You could imagine a large sector of the economy covered by mandatory employee-ownership funds. That would be a very different society in terms of distribution of wealth and income and influence over economic decisions.

It would be interesting to see what would happen in publicly-traded companies. If employee-ownership funds were able to vote a significant number of shares at shareholders' meetings, it would probably help cap the extraordinary rise in executive compensation and significantly slow the movement of jobs overseas. In any event, in a market-based system, it would obviously have an impact on the economy. So there are some interesting questions. There must be some graduate students somewhere in need of dissertation topics.

Hilary Abell

Hilary Abell served as Executive Director of WAGES (now known as Prospera), a position she held from 2003 until 2011. WAGES is a co-op business incubator that presently supports a network of five eco-friendly house cleaning worker cooperatives in the San Francisco Bay Area. For fifteen years, WAGES has worked with low-income immigrant Latinas to launch green business cooperatives. WAGES-affiliated co-ops presently have 85 worker-owners, who earn above-industry wages ($14 to $15 an hour plus benefits) as well as having an ownership stake where they work. In 2010, approximately 2,000 Bay Area households were customers of WAGES cooperatives.

Since leaving WAGES, Abell has continued working in the employee ownership field. In 2014, Abell authored a report for the Democracy Collaborative titled Worker Cooperatives: Pathways to Scale. *In 2014, Abell also co-founded Project Equity, a nonprofit based in Oakland, California that provides technical assistance for worker co-op start-ups and existing businesses seeking to convert to worker ownership.*

Interviewed in 2010

Steve Dubb: *What were the origins of WAGES?*

Hilary Abell: I came to WAGES many years after its founding, but I have met the founders and can share the story. There were three women who were community workers of different kinds, ranging from community health to social work, who came together to start WAGES in 1994 and incorporate it in 1995. They had worked with immigrant women, mostly from Mexico, in East Palo Alto on the San Francisco peninsula through a Catholic Charities-affiliated nonprofit. They were running support groups of women and working on domestic violence and other issues. A common theme voiced by the women in the groups was the need for economic stability as a foundation for becoming more empowered in their lives.

Some of the women had founded an informal cleaning cooperative. The women involved in forming WAGES were assisting that cooperative, and it was making a real difference for the women involved. As I understand it, the program's funding ran out, and, at that point, the founders of WAGES decided to start another nonprofit with the purpose of helping low-income women form cooperative businesses.

SD: *Could you discuss the organization's early development and explain how the organization has changed since you became executive director seven years ago?*

HA: I think of WAGES' history and development in four stages. In the initial stage, WAGES worked with three groups of women—one was English-speaking and two were Spanish-speaking. The approach at that time was business planning education and cooperative education. They worked with groups for nine to fifteen months—the women themselves would identify a business sector, and the education process was very intensive. One lesson of that first phase was that the co-op model is not for everybody, but it is very powerful for those who want to do it. The English-speaking group didn't want to do it, but the two Spanish-speaking groups did open businesses. One group formed a nontoxic housecleaning co-op. The other group founded a store called Fantastic Fiesta—Party Supplies and More. It was an actual retail store in Redwood City; it lasted eighteen months, but wasn't viable. But the cleaning business was viable and set the direction for WAGES from there on out.

The second phase was to focus on developing that niche for eco-friendly housecleaning. WAGES did this because it was a relatively high margin business with low barriers to entry, it was healthy for the women, and it was profitable if done right. The second phase involved replicating these green-cleaning co-ops for the first time—late 1990s to 2002. During this period, the two oldest of our five existing co-ops got started. Both were successful but they had a hard time growing beyond fifteen worker-owners.

So we had encountered some challenges around scale and structure of the co-ops. WAGES had begun to move into the third phase when I came into the picture in 2003. The board and the previous director had made some good decisions to have more impact by moving towards a more streamlined, "representative democracy" model and away from a collective model. They had also decided to address the mixed relationship toward management that the co-ops and WAGES had had thus far.

Our co-ops operate with a general manager position and an operations manager position. The latter involves customer service and scheduling jobs, while the General Manager deals with performance issues, marketing, planning, and financial management. During WAGES' second phase, the general manager position was considered transitional, and the operations manager position, while permanent, was envisioned as a learning position for co-op members. We had beneficiaries of the project who served as office staff, and they were learning computer and English skills on the job. The idea was that operations positions would rotate among the cleaning staff so everyone could learn those skills.

We learned a lot of lessons during this time about successful management and administration in a cleaning business. The people who work in the operations management position, that's a very skilled position. When you talk with some of the operations staff, many will immediately know the clients' voices when they pick up the phone. They provide a high level of customer service.

In other words, we recognized that a different skill set is required in scheduling than in cleaning. We wanted our workers to not only be paid well, but also get health benefits and the other things that we have developed over time. The stability and effectiveness of the office was primary, so we decided office positions would not rotate.

That's one of the downsides of our industry—housecleaning companies have a very flat structure. If you have 15 cleaning staff, maybe you have two or three staff in the office. If you have 30 cleaners, maybe four staff are in the office. So you're looking for people with the right kind of experience and preparation to do those key office jobs. We still prioritize skills development for the worker-owners, but in other ways.

Our larger co-ops serve up to one hundred clients a day. You're entrusted with keys and may have to manage 15 or more teams that each are cleaning five houses a day. Operating an efficient and profitable housecleaning business is a lot more sophisticated than WAGES realized when we first got into the field. That's why both the operations manager and general manager positions emerged at this stage as key elements of success for our model.

In this period, WAGES focused on addressing the challenges we had previously experienced by improving the management model and our approach to governance. We developed a more stream-lined board, which is a hybrid board that has WAGES representatives who bring their expertise in business development and help guide the businesses. We also embraced professional management and operational efficiency as ways to build bigger cooperatives. As a result, we got the co-op we were focused on in Oakland up to scale. It has four people working in the office and thirty co-owners who do cleaning, and they have health benefits, paid vacation, and a documented increase in their members' family incomes of 50 to 70 percent. We were able to get that co-op to a larger size relatively more quickly. And now, we are doing it even more quickly with our newest co-op, which is in San Francisco and started last year as part of our fourth phase.

The fourth phase started in 2008—we did a three-year plan for 2008 to 2010, and we are about to start on another phase of strategic planning that is oriented toward even more rapid expansion. We are now building for a somewhat faster incubation process and multiple incubations at the same time to scale up the model so we can benefit more women.

This is one of the most powerful opportunities for economic stability that we know of for the community we serve. What we have created is a program that helps them build wealth and create a dignified job out of these cleaning jobs. It is professional work that these women can do and do well.

We've got something good here, but we recognize it is still pretty modest in scale. We are looking to learn from social enterprise and other scaling models. Our focus now is both on completing our current vision for growth—what I call saturating the Bay Area (and we are now working in almost every part of the Bay Area)—and also to take the model to other parts of the country.

SD: *Prior to becoming Executive Director at WAGES, you previously did what I think is fair to call movement-based work in fair trade, environmental health, women's health, and immigrant rights. The work at WAGES obviously is related to these issues, but has much more of an economic development focus. What inspired you to make this switch?*

HA: It has been a shift. It was two things. One is that I had been working for many years on international issues but always from the United States. My passion had always been the fair trade farmers, the co-ops and the community organizations we supported in other countries. When I worked on women's health, we were providing $1,000 grants to communities where no grant money had ever gone before. In fair trade, we were creating direct relationships with co-ops that had never exported their own products before. I loved that work, but I got to the point where I wanted to work locally because I wanted to have more contact with the people on whose behalf I was working. That was one of the things.

The other was incredible serendipity or providence. I had been living in the Bay Area for some time and was taking time off between jobs and I did not know about WAGES. When I heard about WAGES, I saw it as an application of fair trade principles to the local service economy. I had been a sales person of fair trade coffee for Equal Exchange and got to know some things about the application of business strategy to social justice issues. Fair trade is an economic development strategy, but the work is done very differently than the job creation work we do at WAGES. WAGES touches on many issues close to my heart and it gave me the opportunity to work on all of them while building something very innovative and exciting. So my shift to WAGES was a combination of intention and good luck.

In the process of doing this, I have become very passionate about cooperative development and community economic development.

SD: *How does WAGES incubate a co-op? Could you explain the process of creating a new co-op, from capital formation to finding qualified management to the recruitment and training of co-op worker owners?*

HA: Our co-op incubation process has four parts. One is recruitment and training of the worker-owners and a second is finding qualified management, which is an important piece of our model. A third piece is technical assistance. We help our partners get a loan through Opportunity Fund in San Jose. Thanks to our partnership with Opportunity Fund, the procurement of capital hasn't been a time-consuming part, but it is part of the technical assistance we provide, along with business planning and legal and financial modeling. And a fourth piece is what we call our governance piece.

To the degree that there is an entrepreneur that is moving the incubation effort forward, it is WAGES as an organization. We bring a lot of knowledge of what works well and what doesn't from the 15 years we have under our belt. We take a strong role in governance and management because we've found that we can achieve our mission more effectively by having more of a decision-making role, especially in the incubation period. We think about it as, on average, a three-year business incubation period.

Part of what we are now trying to do is layer on a social franchising model. We are looking to standardize as much as possible. In 2009, we launched our co-op network. It has five member co-ops right now. It is the vehicle for putting in place and achieving everyone's mutual agreement to business strategies that will make each co-op and the whole effort more successful. The network can deal with issues such as complementary service areas—that is, avoiding competing for the same clients. It can also help ensure that we maintain our high environmental standards. The network is already doing joint branding and joint purchasing of supplies. We hope it will eventually help us do joint purchasing of insurance, but we aren't there yet. We also ensure that WAGES maintains an ongoing relationship with the mature co-ops even after the incubation period and link them to the new co-ops through this network.

"WAGES has always been a learning organization, but we took it to a more sophisticated level by figuring out the management model and developing the toolkit. **Better management makes a difference**."

SD: *How does management at a WAGES worker co-op function? How are managers hired, supervised, and (if necessary) replaced?*

HA: The relationship of management shifts depending on whether the co-op is a mature or new co-op. With new co-ops, during the incubation period, WAGES subsidizes the manager's salary and works closely with the manager. Over time, the co-ops pay a development fee to help cover some of the costs for the incubation. One of the key criteria for when incubation ends is when the co-op is generating enough profit to fully cover their own management costs.

With everything else, the co-op is covering all of its operations, but we do cover the key role of the manager until the incubation period ends. Related to that, WAGES does the hiring and firing of the manager during that period. After the incubation period the co-op board takes over.

SD: *When the co-op board takes over, how does the Board-manager relationship work?*

HA: It is similar to most boards. We train the co-op boards to be governing boards and focus on policy issues and key strategic tasks like approving the annual budget and year-end profit, evaluating the general manager, and hiring and firing her if necessary. The General Manager will do most human relations functions, but because of the co-op nature of membership there are some things that would come to the Board. For a full member to leave the co-op, that would be a Board decision, not a manager decision.

SD: *How often do full membership meetings occur?*

HA: Mature co-ops meet once a month. We may be recommending for future co-ops that they make these meetings either less frequent and/or more structured. Membership meetings provide training, information, and cover items where the Board wishes for the full membership to provide input. Additionally, the co-ops' operating agreements spell out some decisions that must be made by the membership alone or which require approval from both the Board and the membership.

SD: *How does one become a member of the co-op?*

HA: It's a little different when they are mature or in incubation. WAGES' incubation model includes an in-depth training program for new co-op members. Women get three weeks of training before they become members—they learn our green cleaning technique, what it means to be a co-op, basic business training, and basic financial literacy training. With our newest co-op, we are enrolling new members in individual development accounts (IDAs) as well. Then they join as provisional members for six months. Then, if they pass their evaluation, they become full members and get voting rights, an increase in their hourly pay, and access to health insurance.

SD: *How does the "worker ownership" piece work financially? In other words, what does a worker share cost, how do workers pay for their share, and what kind of business equity can a worker at a WAGES network cooperative expect to build up over time?*

HA: The membership fee is $400—each member has to put $150 when she joins as a provisional member, and the additional $250 is paid over six months through payroll deduction. The $150 has never been a barrier; there is usually some kind of training stipend that they can apply toward the $150.

With our new model, which we have piloted with the new start-up in San Francisco, the co-op has an IDA (matched savings) component relating to the membership fee. The individual has to qualify, but if she does, then the membership fee is $1,200, with the worker contributing $400 and getting an $800 match. That's something we are excited about. It generates more working capital for the co-op and increases the value of the worker's internal capital account.

This is the first instance I am aware of in which IDAs are used in a shared ownership framework, and we hope it will be the first of many. Because co-ops refund the membership fee when a member leaves, we developed a vesting situation, where a departing member's access to the matched savings increases year-by-year. If the worker leaves the co-op after only one year, she gets 25 percent of the match and the rest stays with the co-op to support its mission; after four years, the worker gets 100 percent of the match.

SD: *How does profit distribution work?*

HA: According to international co-op principles, year-end profits are allocated to individual members according to their hours worked during the year. The board of the co-op will make a decision after each fiscal year to look at how much profit there was and how much will be distributed to members in cash or retained in their internal capital amounts. There is a minimum amount we distribute to cover everybody's tax burden. Other than that, there is no standard practice, although moving forward we will be reviewing this. One of the things in every case is that we limit payouts until a reserve fund is established. In terms of internal capital accounts, in the newer co-ops we have used a three-year revolving system, in which retained earnings will get routinely paid out three years after they are generated. In our most successful co-op, there are two kinds of special distributions—year-end and three-year retained-earning distributions.

As for how much is distributed, one school of thought is that the retained earnings will contribute more to members' economic security over time than more frequent payouts would, since the retained earnings function as a sort of obligatory savings. Then there is another philosophy to pay out as much as you can to members during the year as part of their regular pay and benefits, leaving little or no year-end profits.

From an asset building perspective, one other thing is worth pointing out: our co-ops offer emergency loans at no interest to their members. The loans get repaid through a payroll deduction. In spite of earning more than they earned before, our co-op families still live pretty close to the margins and most don't have emergency savings. So about 60 percent of members take advantage of these emergency loans at one time or another, and this helps them steer clear of predatory lending.

"I'm really excited that the co-op movement is at a point where **more players outside our movement are taking co-ops seriously**."

Down the road, we would like to move in the direction of long-term stability, such as providing vehicles for retirement savings, like Cooperative Home Care Associates does in New York City.

SD: *How much is the profit distribution worth to the average worker?*

HA: It can range anywhere from a few hundred dollars to a few thousand in a given year. The few-thousand level is the exception; that is not at all the norm. Four thousand dollars would probably be the maximum as a combination of payout for year-end profit distribution and the retained earnings payment. The minimum would be a few hundred bucks between the retained earnings payout and profit distribution. Still, this is an important benefit for families who have little or no savings or access to capital.

SD: *Anything else you would like to add about WAGES' use of IDAs?*

HA: The reason we made this innovation is that the people we were working with would meet the income qualifications for IDA programs, but they were not strong candidates for the specific savings goals that are typical for IDAs: starting your own business, buying a home, financing college education. By and large, they weren't in a situation to be an entrepreneur. Buying a home, that's a story we don't need to tell; homeownership is out of reach for most working people in the Bay Area, and many who did buy in recent years did so on unfavorable terms. And few of our co-op members had kids who were about to go to college.

But this new application of the IDA works really well for co-ops. Over time, we hope it will also serve as a gateway to help the members take advantage of IDAs for other purposes, such as education, retirement savings, or home ownership, if it becomes more viable.

SD: *As you know, WAGES developed two co-ops in the 1990s, one in 2003, and then added two more to the network in 2009, one of which was a WAGES start-up and one of which involved a partnership with a nearby nonprofit group. What facilitated expansion in 2009 and what made expansion prior to 2009 more difficult?*

HA: The reason there was only one new co-op between 2003 and 2008 was due to our decision to focus on developing a model to allow for a single co-op to be larger. We were working with the older co-ops on other projects as well. But the ball we were keeping our eye on was to get a co-op up to 30 members that would be sustainable. Out of that effort came the development model and the toolkit we have developed for use in our own replication efforts and to share with others across the country.

Since 2008, we have expanded staff but we also have a lot to work with that we didn't have before. WAGES has always been a learning organization, but we took it to a more sophisticated level by figuring out the management model and developing the toolkit. Better management makes a difference. The Oakland co-op took off when a more professional manager came in. The San Francisco co-op has grown 30 percent faster than the Oakland one, and that's because of the manager we brought in and the improved operational model we developed in Oakland, which includes software that allows you to be more efficient on a day-to-day basis.

SD: *As of the year 2010, WAGES cooperatives include about 85 worker-owners. It is my understanding that you hope to expand that number over time to 200. Could you discuss WAGES' strategic plan for expansion and how you plan to carry it out?*

HA: We're still shooting for 200 or more, but we've adjusted the timeline because of the economy. Up until the second half of 2008, we were the leaders in green cleaning and we could be confident that the housecleaning niche would continue to grow. Customers were coming to us and the limitations on growth were mainly internal. But in the meantime the economy crashed. Marketing became a new challenge, which put a wrench in our growth plan. We can't add members unless we know that business will grow to give them reasonably full schedules in a reasonable period of time.

In spite of the economy, we did grow last year by more than 15 percent in both co-op sales and membership. We felt pretty good about that—even though it is far short of what we had initially aimed for. Our hope had been to get to 200 members by the end of 2010. Now we're projecting 100 members, which still represents 15 percent annual growth for both 2009 and 2010—the worst economy in eighty years.

But we're still holding a vision of 200 or more members in the years ahead. Initial scenarios for our next strategic plan suggest that we can do five co-op start-ups over a three-year period and add one hundred new worker-owners for a total of 200. That could involve a mix of local co-ops and co-ops outside the SF Bay Area. We aim to continue to get more economies of scale by incubating multiple co-ops simultaneously.

SD: *WAGES mentions on its website that it provides advice and information to dozens of organizations, including three community partners that are developing green cleaning cooperatives inspired by WAGES' model. What has this consulting work entailed? How successful have these efforts been to reproduce the model outside of the Bay Area?*

HA: Our first consulting project was with SEED Winnipeg in Canada. In 2002, we trained their staff in green cleaning, and they formed a co-op that survived and became a green janitorial service. In 2005, we provided technical assistance to another housecleaning co-op, in Los Angeles, working with a day labor center. This co-op is called Magic Cleaners. They are still around, although I don't think they are on a steady growth path.

The new co-op in Concord (California), Green and Clean, is a more intensive year-long effort, and this co-op has become an affiliate member of our network with a slightly different status. We're not incubating them, but we are providing a high level of support. It will be great to see how that goes over time. The other nonprofit, the Michael Chavez Center, is definitely the lead partner but we are more closely involved than in our previous consulting projects.

We have also provided our toolkit and assistance to several other groups this past year, including groups in Denver, Washington, D.C., New York and North Carolina. In North Carolina, there are two green cleaning co-ops that have sought our advice, and one, which is supported by The Center for Participatory Change, has used our co-op development toolkit. I'm providing consulting to the CPC cleaning co-op, and they are doing quite well. CPC is working with a cluster of small co-ops in different industries.

Consulting is an experimental part of our work. I've always wanted to give others access to the model and help people to not reinvent the wheel. WAGES has incubated seven co-ops—and all but the early ones have survived in the long run. We see certain patterns over time, and we bring a strong perspective to these consulting relationships on what has worked, as well as what hasn't worked.

WAGES' main focus is to scale up using a social franchising approach—that is, by focusing our efforts on the co-ops we incubate ourselves. But we want to keep a foot in that other area of providing technical assistance to other organizations, in order to explore other ways to achieve impact and to keep learning. I'm really excited that the co-op movement is at a point where more players outside our movement are taking co-ops seriously. We look forward to helping make the co-op model accessible to more people.

SD: *Are there any changes that you have had to make to your consulting work over time?*

HA: It's been different in every case and it's a fairly small sample. What I have observed is that the sooner we can get involved or the group can have access to our model, the better. What's really hard is when you have a group of people who work on a co-op project for years without a strong sense of where they are going or a viable business plan. When that happens, you don't gain that much and you lose people along the way. One of the things I encourage groups to do is to look at their business plans really earlier on. A lot of the groups that are involved in community organizing or social justice are drawn to the idea of a co-op, but they have never built a business before. I encourage groups to put the business planning piece front and center, because worker co-ops need to be successful businesses to generate and sustain jobs for their members. It helps to get people to focus on the business side early on, instead of dwelling on the structure side, which is where many co-op enthusiasts tend to start.

In thinking about decision-making and business structures, you really want to think about why you want a certain structure and how a structure will help you achieve your business goals, as well as other kinds of goals. Our lawyer always tells us that we have to figure out what we want before she can tell us how to best reflect that in our legal documents, and that's what I tell the groups I advise as well.

SD: *To date, WAGES has worked primarily with low-income Hispanic women. Why has WAGES focused on this community? Do you see any likelihood of expanding the model into other low-income communities?*

HA: WAGES' mission is to empower low-income women, and the mission is not specific to Latinas. Our focus on Latinas is more about our history and where we feel we can have the most impact. In WAGES' first phase, we worked with one English-speaking group and two Spanish-speaking groups, but the Spanish-speaking groups were the only ones to pursue co-ops. Today, our competency in working with the Latino population and our chosen business sector go hand-in-hand. In the Bay Area, the cleaning industry is mostly Latina. In the near future, we will maintain a strong sector focus with Latinas in the cleaning business. If we start developing co-ops in other parts of the country, that may open things up, but even nationally this sector is largely Latina. Plus, the demographics of our state and country have shifted, so that Latino and immigrant populations are a stronger presence in our communities, so we are serving a growing market on many levels.

SD: *WAGES has partnered with Seventh Generation, an eco-friendly cleaning products producer. How has that partnership functioned? Can you describe any other corporate partnerships you've developed? How effective have they been?*

HA: The partnership with Seventh Generation is the main corporate partnership that we have. There are some banks that have given us grants and we've worked pretty closely with Levi Strauss Foundation, which has involved the company to some extent. But Seventh Generation is our most significant partnership.

This relationship is very unique. The WAGES co-ops have always

"Some of what the most successful social enterprises have done is to combine case management with job training and job placement, and this could be extended to support people in the worker-owner role as well."

used Seventh Generation products. Over time, we had opportunities to meet people in the company. There was a time they were looking to do more for social justice, and they reached out to us in 2006 to 2007, and we were also interested in looking for new partners. Through a year-and-half of conversations, we agreed to a significant strategic partnership. That started with a product-testing project we did together. That was a really neat professional development opportunity for the women in our co-ops. Now we are negotiating a bulk purchasing arrangement as part of improving our eco-friendly cleaning technique and developing our co-op network services.

The main focus of the partnership, though, has been the launch of our newest co-op, Home Green Home Natural Cleaning in San Francisco. Seventh Generation's role has focused largely on marketing. Seventh Generation actually hired a PR firm that did branding for that co-op—and the logo has some echoes of Seventh Generation's logo while remaining distinctive. We didn't want to joint brand it, since we are separate organizations and our roles in the project are very different. But Seventh Generation really wanted to offer the power of their brand, which is very well trusted with our target customer base, to enhance the co-op's marketing efforts. And one of the reasons for the faster growth of this newest co-op is that we did more marketing and media work with the help of Seventh Generation.

Our trainer is one of the founders of the Fantastic Fiesta cooperative I mentioned earlier. When that store closed, she joined WAGES' staff. At this moment, she is in New York doing interviews with Oprah's magazine and with several national parenting magazines on green cleaning. The Seventh Generation team made that happen. Their co-founder, Jeffrey Hollender, also co-hosted a fundraising party for WAGES. They've been very generous in helping us expand our donor base and build visibility for our efforts.

SD: *Internationally, worker co-ops are often seen as a primary vehicle for social enterprise, but this is not so in the United States. Is there anything you think that worker co-ops in the United States can learn from the social enterprise model?*

HA: WAGES has always been pretty squarely focused in the co-op movement and women's development. Moving forward we are trying to learn about the social enterprise world.

The scaling issue is something I think all co-ops could learn about from the social enterprise world. With co-ops, there is often a natural resistance to growth. In the social enterprise world, if you look at the initiatives sponsored by Ashoka and others, taking social projects to scale is what sets them apart. Although we have a few examples of large worker co-ops in the U.S., I don't know of many examples where a co-op has done that in this country. In Northern Italy, on the other hand, I saw a lot of examples of co-ops that were also social enterprises.

I'd like to see more people involved in building the co-op sector for the most disadvantaged workers. The core focus for us is improving the income, benefits, and assets of low-income people. Most co-ops don't focus on reducing poverty in that way. Some, like Cooperative Home Care Associates in New York City and Child Space Cooperatives in Philadelphia, do, and like us, they see co-ops and community development as linked.

Co-ops could also learn from the social enterprise field about case management with worker-owners. In a typical worker co-op, you wouldn't do that and wouldn't need to. But there are specific needs in low-income communities around job preparedness, financial literacy and life skills. Some of what the most successful social enterprises have done is to combine case management with job training and job placement, and this could be extended to support people in the worker-owner role as well. WAGES has always done this informally, but we don't call it case management. This helps the business managers to focus on the business side. The key is how to combine the social supports and the holistic needs of the women, along with the business development and job training pieces.

SD: *WAGES, of course, in addition to being a worker cooperative is also a "green" business. How has the elevation of "green business" in the national political discussion affected WAGES? What do you see as WAGES' role in building a "greener" economy?*

HA: I think WAGES' particular contribution, especially right now, is that we can bring a woman's voice and a woman's experience to the green jobs movement and the green economy. A lot of green jobs programs tend to serve men. They tend to be in construction trades, such as weatherization and solar installation. Of course, women can do these jobs: I'm very enthusiastic about getting women into non-traditional sectors and about creating green jobs for men. But we are improving and greening jobs in the traditional female sectors and that's where the majority of low-income women are working. This is an important dialogue for the green jobs movement. It's happening, but we need to have it in a more explicit way.

The other contribution that we try to make is around developing a holistic definition of green jobs, including the toxics reduction piece. The national attention on green jobs does provide a new lens in which to view what we are doing. But we haven't gotten any stimulus dollars. It is all focused around energy efficiency, which is very important. But toxics reduction is also important. Also bringing in the health piece—everyone knows that health and the environment are connected, but when you look at toxins on the job, the health angle is front and center. That's part of why WAGES was started in the first place. We were working with women who were in cleaning and were getting ill as a result. The fact is that you don't need toxic chemicals to clean!

SD: *Could you talk about the sustainability of WAGES itself? How does it successfully raise funds to maintain its operations? To what degree does earned income help WAGES?*

HA: We're committed to enhancing our earned income, but it's not a big percentage of our budget yet—probably on average 8 to 10 percent. The problem has been that the co-ops would pay a development fee when they were in incubation and after that, nothing. The idea of starting the network is that co-ops will always be part of the network, and there is an annual fee that co-ops are paying. It is pretty modest. We hope the network services will pay for themselves over time. We've also established a sub-corporation that is a member of Home Green Home, our newest cooperative. In doing that, our sub-corporation put in some equity and will have the possibility of getting returns over time. That's brand new. We think it's a really important strategy for building sustainability for WAGES and the whole effort over time.

We have very strong data to show impact, and the foundation sector that supports economic development has been pretty receptive. We have shown steady growth over time, even though we are still working on the scaling question. Also, the retention of people in our co-ops is much longer than at typical cleaning jobs. WAGES is in a fairly strong position, in spite of the economy, because new funders have come on even in the past year. It was definitely difficult to be in a growth plan and add staff at the start of the recession, but we have been pretty happy with the response of the foundation sector.

We are definitely focused on increasing earned income and our individual donor base. A nonprofit is supposed to have a three-legged stool—earned income, individual donor income, and foundation income. We do have the three, but it is a lopsided stool that relies heavily on foundation support. We're also looking into program-related investments and other kinds of funding vehicles as we scale up.

SD: *Shifting gears and thinking nationally, obviously worker co-ops are enjoying new visibility in the United States, including recent articles in Time.com, The Economist, and the Christian Science Monitor. What do you see as steps that the worker co-op movement needs to take nationally to build on this new visibility?*

HA: Strengthening the United States Federation of Worker Cooperatives is really important. [Executive Director] Melissa Hoover and everyone else have done a great job of building that in its early years. There is no substitute for infrastructure. That needs to include sharing of resources and technical assistance—whether peer-to-peer or helping worker co-ops get other forms of technical assistance.

Also, the co-op model needs to be better documented. The kind of study that the University of Wisconsin, Madison did last year—that needs to continue. We have to do evaluation and documentation of impact. Also, I'd like to see more co-ops use data to improve their businesses and to understand the impact they are having on themselves and their communities.

There is great potential to expand the model. Worker co-ops should think about growth for themselves and how that can meet social and community needs. Serving the low-income community—I think it is something that co-op people care a lot about, but it is a good challenge to consider further. I should also mention financing: the availability of funding for cooperatives is important too—both on the foundation side and the capital side. We're still kind of in the dark ages in terms of financial institutions and funders understanding what co-ops are and that they are legitimate vehicles to invest in.

I'm not very involved in the policy side, but when you look at Italy and look at government policies and how they supported co-op development, the role of the state is critical. A strong case can be made for our government to invest in worker cooperatives, for example, because of their profound value for asset building and job creation.

SD: *What are WAGES' main priorities going forward?*
HA: I think the main priority is figuring out to how to scale up the model and what an appropriate definition of scale would be for us so we can give more low-income women access to the benefits of what we are doing.

SD: *If you had to highlight a few key accomplishments of WAGES work to date that you are most proud of, what would they be?*
HA: One is very broad, and that is not letting go of this dream that hundreds of women have shared of having truly dignified work. WAGES and the women in the co-ops have stuck with this, and I am proud that we have continued to improve the model over time and held out a vision for growth. When we launched our Co-op Network, we had 70 women there and we spent an afternoon and an evening together celebrating and learning. The pride in every

one of those women's faces was wonderful to witness, and they loved sharing both the challenges and the successes they have had. These are 70 women who are proud and professional cleaners—they work so hard and are so proud of what they do. They do an amazing job in their clients' homes and also participate as worker-owners and provide for their families.

I am definitely proud of increasing the pace of our work over time. The San Francisco co-op has grown 30 percent faster than the previous one, and we now have a network of five co-ops. We're learning to get it done faster and increase our impact.

And the last, but most important, accomplishment in my mind is the impact the co-ops have on families' economic well being. We've seen a 70 percent increase in family income for the average worker at the Oakland co-op, for example. That is something that few programs can claim. We've been able to fine-tune a model that delivers very powerful benefits. The combination of income, health benefits, and asset building—I am very proud that we've been able to address all three. And these women deserve it.

Melissa Hoover

Melissa Hoover is the founding Executive Director of the United States Federation of Worker Cooperatives (USFWC), where she worked from 2004 to 2014. The Federation is a national trade association for the worker cooperative movement. In 2014, Hoover left her trade association post to become the founding executive director of a newly created USFWC-affiliated nonprofit, the Democracy at Work Institute (DAWI), an organization that conducts research and provides technical assistance resources to worker cooperatives.

Interviewed in 2010

Steve Dubb: Could you explain how you came to be involved with worker cooperatives and what inspired you to focus on that sector?

Melissa Hoover: Like a lot of us, I got involved by working in a worker co-op. I was a bookkeeper on the management team of Inkworks, a print shop in Berkeley. To back up a little bit, I studied cooperatives in college—I studied the cooperative movement, particularly women's roles in consumer cooperatives in the upper Midwest in the 1930s, the way cooperatives supported political action. My parents were cooperative organizers when I was a kid. It goes way back.

I was lucky enough to be working at a co-op at a time when there was a lot of activity. The Network of Bay Area Worker Cooperatives and the western conference had been going for a while and the eastern conference was inspired by the western conference. That started a discussion of whether it was time to have a national organization. The momentum had gotten to such a point—it wasn't an "if" question but a "how-to" question. I was at that founding meeting. I went on a lark and was so inspired—a staff position opened up six months after that and I applied for it and was hired. I always had an interest in larger movement-building work, rather than just working in my own co-op, and so I moved in that direction.

SD: Worker cooperatives have been around for a long time, so what new push led to the formation of a national trade association this past decade?

MH: It's a pretty multi-layered story. There was local organizing and regional organizing and this national group came out of that. There were a few people pushing it forward, but when they decided to push there was a lot of interest. There is actually a generational seeding of growth that is happening. There was an explosion of worker co-ops in the 1970s and before that in the 1930s and a little bit of growth in the 1980s, but most didn't last. The worker co-ops that survived from the 1970s, they didn't just survive—they thrived, particularly in the San Francisco Bay Area. By the 1990s, they were in a position where they had some resources: Arizmendi was founded, Rainbow Grocery had an institutional program of technical assistance. So there was a pretty conscious effort to take those resources and use them to seed that growth.

At the same time, the anti-corporate, anti-globalization movement was coming to fruition nationally in the late 1990s and people were looking for positive alternatives. These folks brought maybe a more outward-looking energy. Some of the 1970s worker co-ops were motivated by utopian tendencies. By the 1990s, that was largely gone and the people who were interested in worker co-ops were much less utopian and much more willing to engage with the market and other institutions. If you take those different strands you can see why by 2004 there was pretty strong support for organizing a national group.

SD: *Could you discuss the trade association's early development and explain how the organization has changed since you became executive director six years ago?*

MH: Well, despite our progress, I would say that we continue to be in our phase of early development. We have come a long way. We started with $7,000 in the bank and an agenda to do everything. We've since refined our focus a little bit. One of our key principles when we were founded: we wanted to be member-supported and accountable to our members. The bulk of our funding comes from member funding. The nonprofit organization that we are founding is supposed to be subordinated to that member will. Several of us had been exposed to the conversations about the problems of non-profit funding and wanted to stay away from foundation funding. We weren't sure if that would actually work, but we're able to support staffing and projects. There is a limit—there aren't that many worker co-ops and they don't pay that much in dues. We're sustainable on a low level. The question of growth is vexing right now.

For the first five years, the question was: "Can we do this?" The answer is yes. Now the question is: "Can we take it to scale? Can we be a player in terms of policy? We need to figure out how to put the final piece in place. We need to move to full-time staffing—maybe even have more than one staffer. I don't equate the federation with the worker co-op movement, but more and more we are asked to speak for the movement and corral it together. So I think in the six years that we've been around, we've been able to catalyze a little more dialogue and be there when someone asks what are worker co-ops and why do they matter. That capacity wasn't there before in terms of a central point of contact.

In the last six years, the movement has gotten bigger and more diverse. The worker co-op community is one of the most diverse communities that I have been a part of. There is a vibrant tension within our movement about what our politics are, what our culture is, what our scope and scale is, and where we are going.

SD: *Could you talk a bit more about the scope of the diversity of the movement?*

MH: The vast majority of worker co-ops are small businesses and even very small business—typically a worker co-op has less than fifty employees. There are a couple of large worker co-ops and a couple of large worker co-op projects in development. We seem to be headed to a larger scale. But our members are primarily small businesses. Management is everything from a collective with no hierarchy to a manager who hires and fires. Governance is everything from completely decentralized to a board of directors with outside directors. In the last 10 to 15 years, there has been more interest in worker cooperatives from low-income communities and communities of color. There is a whole new strand of Spanish-speaking worker cooperatives. It is a given that we will offer interpretation at our conferences, which wasn't the case when we started. On the whole, people involved in worker co-ops tend to be younger than other areas of the cooperative world. One of our board members says that when he goes to other co-op sector conferences he's among the youngest people in the room and when he goes to the worker co-op conferences he's one of the oldest.

SD: *Since you also do worker co-op development, could you explain some of the challenges of the process of creating a new co-op, from capital formation to finding qualified management to the recruitment and training of co-op worker-owners?*

MH: I am in the thick of two co-op developments right now. One thing that I have noticed in people who call the federation—typically, co-op developers and business owners looking to sell to their employees—the thing they are most concerned about is capital formation. And rightly so—it's hard to get financing for worker co-ops, although it has gotten a little better. Community banks are opening up—successful projects have paved the way. Financing is opening up a little bit. We are working to get the member business cap increased so that credit unions can make loans to worker co-ops.

Still, while financing is important, I think it would be wrong to identify that as the main issue. It is what developers think about the most because they are used to thinking about this. And I'm a finance person. I am well aware of it. But what I think the real issue in worker co-op development is the question of creating and building democratic capacity in the workplace. It is not easy. It doesn't happen naturally at all. We have very little practice balancing individual needs with the common good.

One of the things that animated the founding of the federation was that there was a lot of practice and tools for building democratic capacity within existing worker co-ops and no one knew about those. New co-op developers were consistently reinventing the wheel. What we really wanted to do was create a venue for sharing those best practices. There is still a crying need for effective successful democratic practices to be shared—and refining those— let's share what doesn't work so we can learn from that too. I think that's the largest challenge—I think it is a larger challenge than in any other form of co-op development.

The idea is not just building democratic capacity within the business, but building participatory capacity within people. Democratic management has to be not-frustrating—people have to feel heard and have some power within their business. There is a lot of thought and effort to figure out what system is best for what workplace. There are no off-the-shelf models—it varies by industry, population, and size. We are under-theorized and under-modeled in that area. At the same time, worker co-ops are effectively doing their thing and no one is asking them how they are doing it.

SD: *How does the "worker ownership" piece work for rank-and-file workers financially? Obviously, this differs by sector, but can you give some broad numbers of what worker shares tend to cost, how workers pay for their share(s), and what kind of business equity can a worker-owner build up over time?*

MH: I think again—of course, it varies by industry and sector, but it also varies by age and generation. I think as we build a more professional infrastructure, there has been a bigger emphasis on this in newer co-ops. It is a focus of a lot of new co-op development. Consequently, they may have larger buy-ins and larger member capital accounts. This idea of building member equity in the co-op may not have been as present. The amount of capital required to buy-in ranges from $1 to $5,000. I don't know of anyone that is more than $5,000. For the most part, you're talking about working class jobs. Anything above $5,000 represents a pretty significant barrier.

Well established worker cooperatives can build substantial member equity. For example, in Rainbow Grocery, members have requested to withdraw their shares to put a down payment on their house. That's an asset-builder's dream. And I know Rainbow retains patronage for a very long time and they pay a significant interest rate—when people leave they often want to leave their money in because it earns a better rate than is available at a bank or credit union.

On the other end of the spectrum, others have very low patronage. That's because members need the compensation sooner rather than later. Those tend to be the smaller co-ops that don't have the same kind of technical assistance resources or capital needs.

I was working with a co-op just yesterday, which asked: "Why would we retain our patronage for longer? We're not trying to grow." That's still at the end of the spectrum. This is what co-op developers often see as a barrier to growth: those co-ops that say, we don't want to grow, we don't need capital. I don't think it is necessarily a barrier. It's just a different kind of worker co-op.

SD: *How is the worker co-op movement affected by growing participation by people of color?*

MH: We are just starting to see the effect on the movement as a whole. The founding conference was an incredibly racially and class diverse group of people. There was an effortless coming together to elect a lot of people of color to the board. Since then, our board composition has changed and our member involvement—the more established co-ops, which tend to be whiter, have gotten more involved in the Federation. There is a push within the Federation that the changing demographics need to be reflected in the organization. So we plan to address that intentionally and make sure that co-op development connects to a movement.

"I think the real issue in worker co-op development is the question of creating and building democratic capacity in the workplace. It is not easy. **It doesn't happen naturally at all.**"

Part of that is our responsibility and part of that is the responsibility of co-op developers. There have been informal conversations for years—we do have an equity and inclusion circle—a group of members who talk about these issues. That circle and our future initiatives are predicated on the idea that co-ops are a way to build equity in society—not just financial equity but societal equity, for people who have traditionally been left out of the economic mainstream. It's not just that the movement got more diverse and we need to account for that, but that worker co-ops are intended to be an economic mechanism to benefit excluded groups. The realization of that vision is both exciting and challenges us as an organization to realize our deepest commitments to equity.

SD: *One area that has generated significant discussion among worker co-ops, as in most community building movements, has been the issue of scale. Scale can boost organizational capacity, but can also mean larger organizations that may become disconnected from the communities they serve. Could you discuss some ways that co-op federation members seek to negotiate this balance?*

MH: I think, to be frank, many co-ops have sought to dodge the question. To me, this is one of the central tensions in worker co-ops. When faced with the opportunity to grow, there is little incentive to grow, you are going to sacrifice some return the more members you have. Faced with a decision, when it is optional, the choice is often to stay small. There are exceptions to that. One is when market forces dictate that you have to grow to survive—Equal Exchange and Rainbow Grocery are two examples. In both cases, they sat down and said how do we create a structure that scales.

There is also a new wave of worker development where the push for scale has been built into the projects by developers. Cooperative Home Care Associates in the Bronx is one key example. The Cleveland project as well is an example—the idea is to reach scale.[4] I think it can be very helpful. It may be helpful to have an outside push to reach growth and scale. My sense of worker-owned cooperatives is that on their own in many cases they will choose to stay the size they are.

Arizmendi in San Francisco sought to deal with scale in a different way. We said, "We are going to develop co-ops that are not going to be more than 25 members. So we are going to grow by growing small." We will have a bunch of small businesses that feed back into a central organization—they feed back money into the organization and have a seat on the board. The businesses themselves are relieved of the pressure for growth. We honor that impulse to maintain small scale, yet harvest the energy and resources generated to do co-op development. The idea behind Arizmendi is exponential growth. The more co-op bakeries there are, the more development you can do. Fifteen years in, we are evaluating the results against our expectations.

There have been a few approaches to scale—it continues to be one of the larger questions that we face. The more innovative ideas for reaching scale come from partnerships that include worker co-ops but also other sectors. The Cleveland project is one of the more exciting things that I see. It comes from workers' co-ops but also from completely other perspectives. It's a really rich dialogue there.

SD: *What is the level of presence of worker cooperatives in the green economy? Is this a focus of the worker co-op federation's current work?*

MH: It is sort of an unknown area for me. Worker co-ops have tended historically to be in green industries to some extent, such as the natural foods movement, bikes and alternative transportation, solar and alternative energy. I think that before there was the notion of

---

4. Editor's Note: The "Cleveland project" refers to the Evergreen Cooperative Initiative, which is leveraging the procurement and investment power of Cleveland's anchor institutions to create green living wage jobs and worker cooperatives in the city's low-income neighborhoods. Melissa Hoover served briefly as a consultant on this project, producing a paper that summarized best practices in co-op governance and worker training and education.

a green economy, there were worker co-ops doing that work. And worker co-ops always tended to implement green practices long before it became a buzzword.

The other angle is more strategic… If we see green development taking off and a lot of funding for green economic development, worker co-ops have to be part of that conversation. What's going on with the Cleveland project is a great model. This is a part of the market we could be serving. We are just starting to talk about that and we don't have any plans or strategies around it. I would be interested in engaging those of our members who are working in the green economy. As a federation, our capacity is fairly limited, but I would think it would be a partnership—beginning of a policy initiative or dialogue with a group that is already doing co-op development. I think it is a hugely exciting area and a direction we need to be going.

SD: *Thinking nationally, worker co-ops are enjoying new visibility in the United States, including a recent article you co-authored in the* Christian Science Monitor. *What do you see as steps that the worker co-op movement needs to take nationally to build on this new visibility?*

MH: I think there are a couple of things we can do. Our members need to—and are interested in—joining up with the larger co-op movement and one another in economic relationships, which we don't have a lot of. The only way to build the power of our movement is to build those linkages—when we do that, we will be able to generate resources for other goals—for example, more public education. Our goal is to make the co-op form as visible as any form—so that co-ops are on the table as an option. Until we link up with one another and generate more resources and support for the form, it won't be normalized as an option.

Worker co-ops are this inspiring thing—they get deployed in policy discussions and movies—they are a really holistic form. One of the challenges is to take that inspiration and help people figure out on a larger scale how to implement this. To take it beyond being an amazing model, to be an amazing model that is available. It is a combination of creating the linkages, adequate technical assistance, and, adequate financing—it is such a struggle now to create a co-op. You need 10 experts and incredible fortitude and resilience and savvy and a lot of patience; we need to move the development process beyond the difficulties and barriers people face now. That requires a lot of not-so-glamorous infrastructure work. The visibility isn't a problem—from the public, journalists, even policy makers, the response we get is "This is a great idea, but [it's not pragmatic]." We need to get beyond that… this is a great idea and a possible idea.

SD: *What are the worker co-op federation's primary goals in the areas of legislation and movement infrastructure?*

MH: We are just beginning to form a policy agenda. The main goals in movement infrastructure are to build a library of models, do a critical evaluation—we would like to be able to have that—develop a literature on what works and doesn't work and then train the people to implement that. Train the next generation of co-op developers who are rooted in practice—not to replace existing developers but supplement their work. Via our peer advisor training program, we take motivated smart worker co-operators who are interested in co-op development and train them to be useful in that way. That was one of the founding principles of the federation—to get our knowledge out there.

Other infrastructural stuff—obviously, there is the money piece. Create relationships with financial institutions that lead to access to financing. People are doing that in an ad hoc way—Evergreen in Cleveland is the most successful example of that. Several of our members are working within community banks and community loan funds to get them to lend to worker co-ops. We also need to crack the outside investor piece—that's another piece of the puzzle. Outside investment for worker co-ops—it hasn't been done very much, but where it has been done, it has allowed co-ops to grow. Equal Exchange is one example. And we have to also work to increase the economic relationships among co-ops.

Legislatively, one of the projects that we have worked on this year is the legislation to fund state employee ownership centers. The employee ownership bank seems like a very long shot. The state employee ownership centers have a better chance. To the extent we can link up with the employee stock ownership plan (ESOP) company movement, which has greater resources, to find points of common interest—that would be great.

"Because when you are talking about running a business, you are dealing with a myriad of compromises.... **To me that's where it gets interesting, where the rubber hits the road and your principles are tested**."

We've been advocating with the National Cooperative Business Association to change the Small Business Administration's loan guarantees to include worker co-ops. If we can unlock that, it would be a first step to access greater financing. Then we have also been advocating for the member business-lending cap to be raised for credit unions, which is another part of the cooperative-to-cooperative linkages we need. Credit unions are financial co-ops. If we can get that cap raised, that would make it more possible. I think that could be a very powerful connection.

I have to append all of that with the caveat that we are six years old and people have barely begun to listen to us. We haven't had a sense of our own voice until very recently. In August, our board will present a legislative agenda to the membership for the first time.

I'm not a policy person. I bring myself up to speed by reading a lot and trying to figure out what the policy landscape is. The Community-Wealth.org website is instructive and a meeting that we had at the Annie E. Casey Foundation has helped. We are working to listen to what the larger conversation is and figure out where we stand.

SD: *What is the role of the newly formed Democracy at Work Institute?*
MH: That's our training mechanism. It is a grant-funded 501(c)(3). We've gotten a little bit of funding from cooperative foundations to do some analysis about governance and democratic processes that exist in worker co-ops, and develop a models-based curriculum. It is also the venue for doing training programs.

SD: *Worker co-ops were often seen at the U.S. Social Forum, a*
        gathering of 15,000 activists held this June in Detroit, as
        playing a key role in the development of a solidarity economy?
        What is your view of the relationship of worker cooperatives to
        such broader social justice goals?

MH: I think it fits squarely in there. Part of the attraction of our form is that
     it is a practical form—it can be used whether you share broader social
     justice goals or not. But the co-op principles are intended to be a
     social justice mechanism. So I think there is an inherent relationship.

     In some cases, social justice movements see worker co-ops as
     an economic engine to fund other social justice work and address
     the problem of grant funding. In other cases, worker co-ops have
     been a mechanism for the realization of social justice goals—greater
     equity, participation, job creation and wealth-building for people
     who have traditionally not had access to those things. We have an
     institutional connection with the Solidarity Economy Network. To
     the extent there is a recognizable part of the solidarity economy in
     the United States, you could consider it the co-op part. So to me it
     is a natural connection.

     It is also potentially an area of tension. Because when you are
     talking about running a business, you are dealing with a myriad of
     compromises that you have to make to be in the marketplace. To
     me, that's where it gets interesting, where the rubber hits the road
     and your principles are tested. But I've seen a lot of nonprofits that
     are developing worker co-ops that struggle with that question. It's a
     compromising form—I don't think of that as a bad thing—but it's
     not pure. You are operating on principles that contravene the prin-
     ciples of business as usual and there's a struggle there. Organizations
     pursuing social justice goals would do well to take that in mind.

SD: *In October 2011, the first North American worker conference is*
        scheduled to take place in Quebec City. And the United Nations
        has declared 2012 to be the International Year of the Coopera-
        tive. What do you see as the importance of these international
        developments for the worker co-op movement in the United
        States?

MH: I think the International Year of the Cooperative designation is
     huge actually. One of the organizations leading the charge was the

National Cooperative Business Association (NCBA), the U.S. co-op apex organization. We live in a much more globally connected society now—and it's significant. The Quebec worker co-op meeting comes out of a recognition that the North and South American regions are very different. Central and South American co-ops have a long history. The conference in Quebec will bring together co-ops from Canada, the United States, and Mexico to hopefully have some more meaningful connections and create economic and social linkages with one another. That's an incredibly positive development and that's very exciting. For the American co-op movement to be engaged in that is nothing but positive.

With the International Year of the Cooperative, we have to be able to seize on that. Not just with public relations, but with building the infrastructure that is necessary for us to grow. It is a huge opportunity and our members have a lot of energy around that.

It is important for worker co-ops in the United States to make those connections, since there is such a dearth of models here. There are a few, but there are not enough. So we look abroad. Many have been inspired by Mondragón. So it is important that we know Mondragón and understand it. And the same is true with understanding worker co-ops in Emilia Romagna in Italy—and also the worker co-ops of Latin America. We need to study their successes and learn from their failures. It has to be a learning opportunity for us.

SD: *What are the worker co-op federation's main priorities going forward?*

MH: I think the development of the training infrastructure is probably the top priority. This idea is that we need to share our resources with others who are interested in worker co-ops. To the extent that we can collect our models and train others, we can have a big impact.

I think other priorities are to continue to increase the visibility of worker co-ops. We made a commitment a year-and-a-half ago to get out in the media and we have had more success than I would have imagined. There is the *Christian Science Monitor* article and *The New York Times* blog entry, the *Time.com* and *CNNmoney.com* articles. The Cleveland project has gotten such amazing coverage. Another priority is to build on that visibility and go beyond the initial excitement to identify what are our issues and what we can do on financing. A fourth issue is to develop a legislative agenda. These things are all connected. You can't advocate for legislation until you have visibility. There is an interplay between these things.

The other thing is we're also dealing with defending our very form. A couple of our members are undergoing audits by the Internal Revenue System, which would potentially endanger the member equity part of the worker co-op form. There is nothing more boring than tax law, so I won't go into the details here. But in addition to these forward looking and visibility measures, we also have to think about how we defend and justify ourselves to bureaucrats who don't understand the form. We need to explain why what we do is legitimate and why we deserve the same treatment as other cooperatives.

SD: *If you had to choose three accomplishments of the worker co-op federation's work to date that you are proudest of, what would they be?*

MH: The first I think is to continue to exist, which was not a foregone conclusion after our founding. The fact that we have managed to build an organization that has a consistent and dedicated board, staffing, and a membership that is deeply involved, while maintaining a democratic structure, is no small feat.

The second is the training of these peer advisors and the development of a training infrastructure. At our founding meeting, I recall that one member said, "We don't have a movement yet, we are a bunch of worker co-ops." The point was that until we had adequate financial and technical assistance we're not a true movement. For me, getting this developed is a really huge thing.

The third is micro-level but really meaningful. When we had our conference two years ago in New Orleans, we did a volunteer work-week. We worked with seven projects—both to provide manual labor but also technical assistance and advice for projects that want to rebuild a city using the co-op model. For us, it was the first time that we had reached out as a movement. It's a small accomplishment, but it shows how worker co-ops do things, with direct one-to-one consulting and assistance, and it was the start of our sense that we had something to offer other areas.

SD: ***Anything you would like to add?***

MH: Well, maybe some statistics. We started with maybe 20 workplaces and now we have over 100 members. The total workers in those workplaces are between 1,400 and 1,500 workers. The gross revenue of those workplaces is $180 million. We still don't really know how many worker co-ops there are, we think, between 300 and 400 co-ops and between 3,000 and 4,000 workers.

We are growing to represent a significant share of the whole. These are all modest accomplishments. We are very young. We have a shoestring budget. While we are very proud and invested in them, we recognize that we are but a tiny drop in the ocean right now. So we're small, but we get a lot of buzz because the idea—the form—is powerful and hopeful.

Rodney North

Rodney North was a worker-owner at Equal Exchange for 19 years from 1996 to 2015. For many years, North served as Equal Exchange's "Answer Man," responsible for public relations. At the time of the interview, North was one of six worker-owners to serve on the board and held the position of vice chair. Equal Exchange, the Massachusetts-based worker cooperative has, as of 2015, an estimated 120 worker-owners. In 2014, Equal Exchange posted a record $61 million in annual sales. In 2015, North left Equal Exchange to become Director of Marketing and External Relations for Fairtrade America.

Interviewed in 2012

Steve Dubb: What were the origins of Equal Exchange?

Rodney North: The three founders—Rink, Jonathan, and Michael—met while working for Northeast, a food distributor co-op. They valued the co-op model—Northeast was owned by its customers, which were food co-op retailers, independent grocers and buying clubs—but in their work they also realized that as they sought to get better prices for their co-op members, that put downward pressure on farmers. Northeast had already started to think about how to balance the co-op members' needs and the farmers' needs, but they didn't have a way to do this for international products, like coffee or cocoa.

Also, the model didn't explicitly address the needs of the workers. So they wanted to create their own business, with a new model, built on cooperative economics that addressed everybody's needs—the farmers, the workers, and the end purchasers—and which applied ecological principles and cooperative economics as the capital model. At best, the project, which coupled a private business model with a nonprofit mission, was viewed as utopian. At worst, it was regarded as foolish. But it worked and here we are 22 years later. To meet the needs of the farmers, they adopted Fair Trade practices. To protect the workers, they adopted a worker cooperative model. The mission is entrusted to the worker-owners.

From the beginning, they were interested in sourcing or providing organic foods or at last sustainable foods. In the mid-1980s, there was not a lot of organic tea or coffee to be had, but as soon it became available (around 1990), it became a focus for Equal Exchange. And now over 95 percent of our product line, from coffee to almonds, is certified organic. A lot of the most innovative work at Equal Exchange lies in the structure of the worker cooperative and the way we capitalize the company.

SD: In the lead-up to the creation of Equal Exchange, the co-founders considered structuring Equal Exchange as a nonprofit social enterprise, but ultimately chose to be a for-profit worker cooperative. What were seen as the pros and cons of each model and why was the decision made to become a for-profit worker cooperative?

RN: Had the founders adopted a nonprofit model that they knew, they could probably still benefit farmers, have a decent workplace, etc., but there would be little innovation in creating one more well-meaning nonprofit. But if you could do this as a business, *that* might shake things up. So one goal was to show the viability of this new kind of for-profit model, to show that you could run a for-profit business on other terms. With the typical for-profit/nonprofit split, there is deep down the perception that you're either in it for yourself or for somebody else. By creating a for-profit social enterprise, you throw out those assumptions and are compelled to *internalize* a lot of the trade-offs that are normally externalized in the for-profit economy. By choosing a for-profit social enterprise model, we have to explicitly balance the interests of farmers, workers, investors, customers, and the environment. In short, we have internalized what in the for-profit world is usually externalized and pushed out of the picture. We definitely want to set an example for the for-profit world, and we are. For example, we're regularly asked to speak at business schools and business conferences, and we recently won the Social Capitalist Award from *Fast Company* magazine.

SD: *Could you explain the advantages employee ownership poses for business development?*

RN: Our example isn't just one of worker ownership but of *democratic* worker ownership, which is much more rare. The first benefit of democratic worker ownership is it is an end onto itself. It is a good thing. But it also delivers business benefits, including more informed, engaged employees—employees who are not only financially invested, but also emotionally invested in the success of the company. It is also a powerful recruiting and retention tool. It minimizes turnover. There are also investors and customers who are more enthusiastic about us because we're employee owned. Some of our nonprofit partners, such as in the faith-based community, are more comfortable aligning with us because of our democratic and egalitarian worker ownership, so it's a boost for alliances. Also, as a cooperative, it fosters much stronger ties with our farmer co-op suppliers and consumer co-op customers. It definitely strengthens the Equal Exchange story that we share with the public and media. It's another reason we won the Social Capitalist award.

SD: *One of your challenges has been securing financing on terms that were compatible with both your fair-trade mission and worker-co-op model, especially regarding outside equity. Could you describe Equal Exchange's equity model and how it differs from a conventional worker cooperative?*

RN: Frankly, most worker cooperatives have very little capital. They tend to be much smaller in size or they have very little need of capital. For instance, Cooperative Health Care Associates, which is based in the Bronx, although large in terms of its employee-owner base, has a limited need for equity capital. I can think of only two U.S. worker cooperatives on our scale that have big capital needs—Rainbow Grocery in San Francisco and Union Cab in Madison.

One key to our financing has been the sale of non-voting Class B shares. They have a targeted return of five percent. In some years—like last year, when things are going really well, we'll pay more—we paid six percent last year. The share has a fixed price. It is sold through private placement, so it can be bought only from Equal Exchange and only sold back to Equal Exchange. Because of U.S. Security & Exchange Commission regulations, we cannot have more than 500 investors. Currently, the minimum investment is $5,000. But of course we are trying to maximize the investment for each of those 500 slots. One way we do that is to attract larger investments from socially responsible investors. Trillium Asset Management helps us with that. Currently, we have raised about $5 million that way over the 22 years.

There are three other ways we raise equity. The next most important would be through retained earnings, which now are about $2 million. Until last year, the worker owners would reinvest 80 percent of profits back into the co-op. In co-ops, this is also called the collective account, but it functions the same as retained earnings. Now the model is to reinvest 60 percent of net profits.

Of the remainder—whether it was 20 percent or now 40 percent—that goes to the worker-owners, half of that stream also gets reinvested into internal capital accounts. For example I have an internal capital account myself, into which goes half of my share of each year's profits and it stays on the company books and is available as capital the company can tap. If you add them together we now have $400,000 in the internal capital accounts of our 80-plus worker-owners.

The fourth and least significant would be the Class A shares that are bought by worker owners when they join the co-op. Each worker owner buys one share that now costs $3,100, but which is adjusted each year for inflation. So the two big streams are the class B shares and the retained earnings.

Right now, we have a capital working group, which is investigating options to raise more capital, because we are going to hit that Securities & Exchange Commission limit of 500 investors.

SD: *Do you claim your capital account when you leave the company?*

RN: Yes, aside from borrowing from the account for special circumstances like an illness or buying a house, that is the only way you access the funds. Those accounts do not accumulate interest, but at some point the worker-owners could decide to change that.

SD: *Equal Exchange is participating in an effort by the National Cooperative Business Association, the leading national co-op trade association, to create a new model for raising equity for cooperatives. Could you explain what this new model might look at and how it might work?*

RN: Raising capital is a considerable obstacle for many kinds of co-ops, including worker, food, housing, and purchasing co-ops, and the dearth of it keeps this portion of our economy unnecessarily underdeveloped. So we're working with others like the Co-op Fund of New England as part of the NCBA's Capital Task Force. The Task Force studied all of the ways, old and new, that co-ops around the world raise capital. In the end, the Task Force recommended the creation of a national fund, like a mutual fund, that both private individuals and co-op institutions could invest in, but which would only be used to fund the creation or expansion of cooperatives. This might resemble similar funds used by and for co-ops in the Basque region of Spain or in Northern Italy that handle billions of dollars. The fund (or funds) might also offer investment options with higher or lower risk and returns.

Currently NCBA is studying the feasibility of such a fund. However, in the meantime more modest efforts, like the Co-operative Capital Fund, are already underway, and will soon be providing friendly equity financing for co-ops here in New England.

Besides simply pooling and distributing money, a tool like this could make it much easier to acquaint the larger public with the idea of investing in co-ops, just as they're already comfortable with stocks, bonds, mutual funds and CDs. In turn, that could dramatically increase the pool of capital available to co-ops, and could be an exciting example for others interested in building community wealth.

SD: ***Are there any particular disadvantages of employee ownership?***

RN: Arguably, it takes longer to make decisions, but a caveat is that it is likely that we make better decisions because of the transparency and participatory nature of our decision-making. Because of our worker ownership, we have to be more creative and arguably work harder to raise capital, but once we've done that we enjoy many benefits from our capital model, most of all maintaining our independence.

SD: ***Equal Exchange is known both for its fair-trade practices with small-scale farmers around the world and for its worker cooperative structure for its own operations in the United States. What do you see as the linkage between these two practices?***

RN: The link is that fairness and economic democracy are always good things no matter where it is happening along the supply chain. For us, fair trade is really built upon farmer cooperatives. For the same reasons farmer cooperatives are good and desirable, so are worker cooperatives. To have the cooperatives run for and by farmers introduces economic and often political democracy in these regions. The American workplace itself is more often structured as a feudal system and it, too, sorely needs greater fairness and transparency for the people doing the work everyday. There is no shortage of horror stories of life in the American workplace and worker ownership goes a long way to addressing those problems.

SD: ***Since its inception in 1986, Equal Exchange has helped pioneer fair-trade food and beverages in the United States. What contributions do you see your fair-trade business making to build community wealth?***

RN: Through everyday mundane practices and purchases, it makes people think about their economic connections to people around the world. It has made them ask, "Could this purchase make the world a better and fairer place?" So maybe the greatest contribution fair trade makes to community wealth is to educate and motivate citizens to think

> "One key to our financing has been the sale of non-voting Class B shares.... It is sold through private placement, so it can be bought only from Equal Exchange and only sold back to Equal Exchange."

more about their economic relationships with everybody around them and to realize that new relationships are very possible.

SD: *Equal Exchange exists at the intersection of a number of different co-op models that don't always "play well together." For instance, Equal Exchange is a worker co-op that primarily buys its products from farmer co-ops abroad and markets much of this production through consumer food co-ops.*

RN: Yes, we also get some financing from the National Cooperative Bank and laterally we have business ties to other worker cooperatives; for instance, we collaborate with La Siembra in Ontario for our chocolate and cocoa products, and are co-investors with Equal Exchange (an independent co-op in Scotland with the same name) in a new fair-trade nut enterprise. We also have worker cooperatives as some of our vendors—for example, for our printing (Red Sun). We also were recipients from, and now are an investor in, the Co-op Fund of New England and their new Cooperative Capital Fund.

SD: *What do you see as the relationship between worker and consumer cooperatives? Are there different circumstances when you think it makes more sense to choose one capital model or the other?*

RN: In terms of the relationship, we have had very healthy relationships with consumer co-ops. Probably a big part of that success is how compatible our work is with theirs. We do something they can't do and vice versa: we provide the coffee and they provide the retail storefront.

When to use one model or the other? Some like Weaver Street in Carrboro, North Carolina, for instance, do both and have a hybrid consumer-worker model. But I suppose one key factor in deciding on your model is determining who has the greatest vested interest in the success of the enterprise—the workers or the consumers of the product or service that is produced? Coffee drinkers probably are not going to want to buy shares of their coffee company, but employees of a coffee company are.

Sometimes access to capital is a big issue. In our case, the worker co-op model works for us, because we have access to other forms of capital on acceptable terms. You do have some other consumer co-ops like REI where there is a looser connection between consumer and the store than you do with food co-ops. Did they choose the best model? I don't feel qualified to answer, although obviously it's working, even though their members don't walk in twice a week like food co-op customers do. Trying to determine which model makes most sense, it is probably a combination of who has the strongest interest and what kind of capital is available. I know that for a lot of consumer co-ops all of the capital is raised from the members, which is not the case at all for our worker co-op.

One other thought: When trying to ask which co-op model to pick, ask yourself which co-op model would best protect the integrity of the enterprise. For something like a business providing affordable home heating fuel, a consumer model might make a lot of sense. It is such a big economic purchase that members may be willing to make a long-term investment and get involved. There is a big difference between buying your oil or electricity versus buying coffee.

SD: *Equal Exchange has created an educational curriculum for grade school students about cooperative economics. Could you talk about what information Equal Exchange is trying to convey and how widespread its distribution has been?*

RN: We realize for all of us who work here at Equal Exchange, that we pretty much were not exposed to any of this when we were young. In other parts of the world, they are better at teaching kids about cooperative economics, so that they always know there is another way of organizing business. And that choice is not just either government or private business. For example, in Quebec, it is just presumed that a new café or campus store is probably going to be run as a student co-op business. That is clearly not the presumption in the United States.

Our work in schools started in a fairly obvious way, by offering a fundraising program, where a school can buy wholesale from Equal Exchange, sell the products at retail, and keep the difference. In concept, it is the same as when the students sell a magazine subscription to raise money, but when you sell a fair-trade product, you don't just raise money for your group, you also learn about where your food comes from, the farmers who grew it, about trade, and social justice. At first, the education component was entirely informal. But quickly there were requests for more formal instruction about fair trade and the co-op model, so we created this sixteen-unit curriculum. Schools can use either a single unit or all sixteen. If used in conjunction with the fundraiser, this will really get students' attention, because they're buying and selling the products, probably eating them too, and talking about them. And from then on, kids will know, and as adults they'll know, that there are options. And there are choices we make that can promote these alternatives. We sometimes talk about fair trade as a "gateway" product—first, you buy fair-trade coffee, then its fair-trade tea and fair-trade certificates of deposit and there is no going back.

SD: *How large is the program?*
RN: We just launched this effort a short while ago, but it is growing, and already 59 schools have ordered the curriculum. We are also working with the New York State teachers' union to promote the fundraiser, which indirectly will expose thousands of teachers and administrators across New York to the curriculum.

SD: *There are now thousands of employee stock ownership plans (ESOPs) in the United States with an estimated $928 billion in assets, while there are only a few-hundred worker co-ops, with combined assets of well under $1 billion. In fact Equal Exchange is one of only a small number of U.S. worker co-ops to have more than one hundred employees or surpass $30 million in annual revenue. What are the obstacles that hinder the formation of worker co-ops in the United States and that keep most of them quite small?*
RN: A big one is the lack of familiarity to the idea of a worker cooperative. You're not going to set one up if you've never heard of it.

Almost no one has heard of the model. Of the people who have heard about it, hardly anyone has been exposed to *how* you do it. If you want to start a franchise, there is lot of information on how to become a franchise owner, but you don't have that kind of information for starting a worker co-op.

We were very lucky that Equal Exchange's founders had the ICA Group here in Boston to assist us in the start-up phase. Plus, it is definitely hard to raise capital. The founders had to do a lot of original thinking. If you're going to start a private business, magazines such as *Inc.* and *Entrepreneur* and college business classes will tell you about the capital infrastructure and how to access it. You don't have that capital or educational infrastructure for aspiring worker cooperative entrepreneurs. Also, most of the capital out there is chasing the greatest return and you're not going to get that at a worker cooperative. To redirect capital to building community wealth, people need to think differently about what they get for their investments. In others words: Do they get stable communities? Do they get social justice? Do they get a higher standard of living across the board? Or do they just get the maximum return for this quarter?

One thing that we're doing to address this problem: We've always redistributed ten percent of our profits to other organizations. Before this year, we gave that money away to nonprofits working in Fair Trade. But this year the Board created a new policy. There are hundreds of billions of dollars already flowing through the nonprofit sector ,and there is almost no money available for future Equal Exchanges. So we are now going to invest three percent of our profits in other enterprises like Equal Exchange—other startups (seven percent will still go to nonprofits). This is similar to models used in Europe, such as in Northern Italy. We are very much hoping that other co-ops will adopt this three percent model, to create a bigger pool of equity for co-op start-ups.

SD: *What do you see as the relationship between ESOPs and worker cooperatives? Both involve employee ownership, but they differ significantly in their governance structure. Are there different circumstances when you think it makes more sense to choose one model or the other?*

RN: At a Vermont Employee Ownership conference that I attended recently, they wanted to put Equal Exchange out there as a model of *democratic* employee ownership. I think we (worker co-ops) have some lessons to share. Worker co-ops can encourage ESOPs to take those steps toward greater employee participation and governance. I think we can make it less scary to put an employee representative on the board, to actually pass through voting power to employees. Regarding when to do which (go co-op or ESOP), to my knowledge worker co-ops have a much better chance of success if the business is founded as a worker co-op. You are simply going to hire differently as you're hiring future owners. For all of those existing businesses, an ESOP makes a lot of sense, at least as a first step. There is a lot of work to be done to go from conventional ownership to an ESOP, and there are a lot of steps that you can take to make the ESOP more participatory and democratic. On some occasions, if the stars align, a business might be able to convert to a worker co-op, and there are some examples. For example, I was on a panel with an entrepreneur who converted his conventional construction business (Red House Building, Inc. of Burlington, Vermont) into a worker co-op.

SD: *In 2006 the worker-owners of Equal Exchange approved an ambitious 20-year vision to create "a vibrant mutually co-operative community of two million committed participants, trading fairly one billion dollars a year in a way that trans-forms the world." In that vision, what is the potential role for other community development practitioners such as CDFIs, and publicly or community-owned institutions?*

RN: Where they might be buying standard certificates of deposit, they could invest in Equal Exchange CDs. A community-owned retail development could invite consumers to create a consumer co-op as the anchor grocery store. For that, they could link up with NCB's Co-op 500 Fund. There are also all kinds of conventional activities—school fundraisers, grocery shopping, bank deposits—where communities without spending any extra money can make a co-op choice, instead of a conventional choice. For example, move some of your investment portfolio to the new Cooperative Capital Fund or adopt the three-per-cent model that Equal Exchange is starting. Through a lot of these everyday choices, you can look for fair trade and co-op options. It could be the coffee you serve in the office or place of worship, but it could also be bringing in or supporting a co-op retailer. Could your

"Worker co-ops can encourage ESOPs to take those steps toward greater employee participation and governance.

I think we can make it less scary to put an employee representative on the board, to actually pass through voting power to employees."

affordable housing be affordable *co-op* housing? You can also look to co-op vendors—such as builders, printers, and caterers—for your everyday needs.

SD: *How does Equal Exchange feel about scale? On the one hand, when Equal Exchange grows, it can benefit more farmers and add more worker-owners, but are there any disadvantages you have encountered with growth?*

RN: The one clear challenge posed by growth is maintaining the human ties that make our worker co-op work. At 100-plus people spread over three time zones, you just can't know the people the way you did when it was 30 people in one building. The human ties are essential for the trust that is necessary for the democracy.

SD: *How do you mitigate this problem?*

RN: We have video conferencing to link the Oregon and Minnesota offices to Massachusetts. We have staff meetings every two weeks. Those are imperfect, as the people outside of Massachusetts don't participate, but they do see the minutes of those meetings. We fly people back and forth from the various offices a lot. And the whole company is connected through a private intranet in which we invest a lot. We have a two-day annual retreat that all staff attends. And we have big phone bills.

SD: *In 2004, the United States Federation of Worker Cooperatives was formed. What role has Equal Exchange played in that group? What challenges and opportunities do you see that this nascent national trade association can play?*

RN: We are one of the founding members, and we currently have an employee, Aaron Dawson, on the Federation board. We have presented at every conference. An obvious potential is the sharing of best practices—for worker co-ops, there is such a dearth of information available, so we need to learn from each other and the Federation facilitates that. For instance, it has collected bylaws of many cooperatives and put them online, so we can at least compare that. And the Federation is working to do some fairly obvious things like group purchasing for health insurance, which is really hard for these small businesses. The Federation is also looking at possible joint promotion of the worker co-op model. It's the kind of thing that 100 worker co-ops together might be able to do, but none of them individually can do. Some kinds of marketing do require scale, so this is one area where we can take advantage of the strength of numbers.

SD: *What do you see as the most important challenges or opportunities facing worker co-ops today? Where should the worker cooperative movement be focusing its energies over the next 10 to 20 years?*

RN: One key area is to focus on the continued viability of existing co-ops, because many of them are struggling. If these co-ops don't make it, everything else the worker co-op movement might want to do will be harder—joint promotion, etc. The biggest challenges will be finding suitable capital, professionalization, and promoting the worker co-op example. And the biggest opportunity would be the public's incredibly profound dissatisfaction with the typical workplace and the typical business structure.

SD: *October is Co-op Month. Is there anything Equal Exchange is doing to celebrate this?*

RN: Within the food co-op community, we're running ads in the various co-op newsletters and distributing articles that we've written. And we talk about it in our own newsletters. October is also fair trade month. For it what we are doing is a *Reverse-Trick-or-Treat* campaign. Working with other organizations and volunteer families, and their kids, we are going to help distribute 200,000 *Reverse-Trick-or-Treat* cards with a piece of our fair-trade chocolate. So when children go door-to-door, they can hand out one of these to inform folks of the issue of forced child labor in the cocoa industry and promote the fair-trade alternative. It was so successful last year that we have bumped up the program fivefold for this year.

SD: *Anything else you would like to add?*

RN: We should at least mention the role of the faith-based groups. They now represent 30 percent of our business—that's $10 million in fair-trade goods that they are buying and selling and using. These partnerships with groups like Catholic Relief Services and Lutheran World Relief potentially represent over one hundred million Americans. They are doing incredible work to promote the fair-trade idea. Fair trade is so compatible with the ethos of building community wealth that we shouldn't fail to mention this activity and draw some hope from it.

Blake Jones

*Blake Jones is Co-Founder, President
and CEO of Namasté Solar. Beginning
his career in the oil industry, Jones co-
founded Namasté Solar in late 2004,
which later became an employee-owned
cooperative in 2011. In this interview,
Jones discusses what he learned in the
oil and gas industry, the early stages of
Namasté's development, the future of the
solar industry and the green economy, and
the details of how Namasté functions as a
worker-owned cooperative.*

Interviewed in 2013

Steve Dubb: *What were the origins of Namasté Solar?*

Blake Jones: We started at the end of 2004. There were three of us who wanted to start a solar company. We were really passionate about solar power. We were also really passionate about doing business in a different way. We all intuitively believed that there was a better way to do business than the conventional norm and we wanted to prove it. We felt that the only way to do that was to create a sustainable company that incorporated our ideals. With solar energy really starting to take off, with the public and different governments around the world starting to provide support for solar, and with technological advancements starting to bring the costs down, we felt that the timing was right for us to start the company.

SD: *Could you say a little bit about two other co-founders?*

BJ: Both were friends of friends. One had ten years in solar experience, which was really rare for that time. He is really technically competent. We shared the same values. It was a perfect fit. The other co-founder didn't have solar experience, but understood marketing really well and had worked and lived in the Boulder-Denver area for twenty years. I had just come back from working in Nepal for three years and learning about small businesses. We all worked very well with each other and were closely aligned in our values. It was a great founding trio.

SD: *Prior to helping start Namasté Solar, you worked in the oil and gas industry and then shifted to work on solar, wind, hydro, and electric vehicle technologies in Nepal? What did you learn, positive and negative, from those experiences and how does it inform your work at Namasté Solar?*

BJ: Working in the oil industry, I experienced a lot of its benefits firsthand. There were huge budgets. There were amazing, talented, smart people. There was cutting-edge technology. They were really exciting projects to work on. I learned so much and met so many wonderful people. It is such a big industry and it is so profitable. It is amazing to see the things that it can do.

That is also some of the downside. The margins are so high and the money involved is so great, that money was the number-one priority. Sometimes I saw people mistreated—they were secondary priorities. The environment as well: for example, it was often more cost effective to dump something than it was to properly dispose of it. I also got to see firsthand that oil makes the world go around. It is a source of tremendous power. Only certain countries have oil. Only certain companies control it. And it leads to a lot of economic and power disparity, socioeconomic problems, geopolitical problems. It is the source of a lot of conflict, definitely lots of geopolitical disputes. It is a double-edged sword. There are a lot of bad things that come from oil.

One of the things that inspired me to get into renewable energy is that I want us to have a more balanced energy portfolio. We're too dependent on fossil fuels and I think that overdependence is risky and unhealthy. Right now, renewable energy is highly underutilized relative to the benefits it can provide to the environment, to our society, to our economy, and to public health. I like that you cannot monopolize, embargo, or control the sun.

SD: *You said you want a balanced portfolio. So that means you wouldn't want 100 percent of our energy to come from solar power.*

BJ: No, I wouldn't want it all to be one technology or one source. A well-balanced energy portfolio is important. I would not advocate for replacing our overdependence on oil with an overdependence on solar. I want 20 percent from solar, 20 percent from wind, 20 percent from fossil fuels, etc. There is no silver bullet to our energy challenges, there is only going to be silver buckshot.

SD: *Could you discuss Namasté's early development and explain how the organization has changed since your company's founding in 2004-2005? Were there key stages of development? What were some of the key changes you made along the way?*

BJ: We've gone from three to 100 people. We started with our own version of employee ownership, a very unique form, where we invented our own wheel. It was based on one-person, one-vote. Then two years ago, on January 1, 2011, we officially converted into an employee-owned cooperative, also called a worker cooperative. We started the company thinking we could never bring in external investors because it might compromise the way we run the company. Later, we decided we could bring in external investors if we found the right ones and didn't give up governance or control. So, we recently just started selling a class of non-voting preferred stock to external investors.

We have made a number of changes in governance along the way. When we grew to be 15 to 20 people, we changed from *consensus* (where everyone had to affirm decisions) to *consent* (where there had to be no thumbs down, but people could abstain), When we reached 30 to 40 people, we changed from consent to democratic decision-making by either a simple majority or supermajority, depending on the issue. Those were pretty big evolutions for us. One of the issues that helped initiate a switch from consent to democracy is that we wanted to rebrand. We realized a logo is a very subjective thing, and it is very difficult to reach consensus or even consent.

When we were around 15 to 20 people, we also started to create committees. It is similar to how it works in the Senate or Congress. When a new bill is introduced, it is sent to a committee for analysis and deliberation and then brought back to the group for a vote. We started doing that, and it really increased the effectiveness of our decision-making. For example, not everyone is interesting in marketing, finance, and so on. So you can let the experts and those non-experts who are interested in the issue kick it around and bring back some options for the whole company to vote on.

We also have adopted what we call "empowerment votes." With these, a committee is empowered to decide what to do within a given budget and reports back to the group afterwards—that was another important evolution for us.

We have also changed our compensation practices. We all used to make the same salary. Then we began a process of stratification whereby people with different levels of experience and certifications and levels of responsibility make more or less. We evolved to have a 2:1 cap on highest to lowest. That evolved to 3:1, as we grew larger. Now it is 4:1. So, as we've grown bigger, we have increased that ratio, but we've kept it far lower than the industry norm. For us, those were very big decisions.

Another change we've made is to our charitable giving policy. We used to give one percent of our revenue regardless of profit away to local charities. Now it is 20 percent of our after-tax profit, so that the community, as a stakeholder, couldn't potentially benefit so much more than our other stakeholders if we had a bad year. The good news is that we've been profitable every year since 2005, which was our first year, but we wanted to change that policy before we ran into a potential problem.

One last major change that I'll mention is in our board structure. We used to have an internal board in which the board consisted of five co-owners. Just last year, in 2012, we increased the size of the board to seven people and added two external directors, in addition to the five co-owner directors.

SD: *What is the impact of Namasté Solar in terms of installations and business volume?*

BJ: We range from $15 to $30 million in annual sales. We have installed solar electric systems on more than 2,000 homes, businesses, and institutions throughout Colorado. That's more than any other company has installed in the state. It totals more than twenty megawatts of generation capacity.

SD: *Could you discuss how the solar industry itself has evolved since Namasté was founded?*

BJ: It has really exploded since the early 2000s, both worldwide and in the United States. It has become a multibillion-dollar industry. There are over 120,000 people working in the solar industry in the United States—in some ways, our company's growth is very representative of what happened to the solar industry in the United States and worldwide. The cost of solar has decreased dramatically. The cost of installing a system that has decreased by 60 to 70 percent and this is because of a couple of reasons: One, economies of scale due to mass production volumes; and two, technological improvements with manufacturing and overall process improvements with the actual installation of solar systems.

There has also been greater public awareness of solar among customers and permitting offices and building inspectors. And so the industry has really matured a lot—become more efficient, become more streamlined. And I think we're still scratching the surface. We still have a long runway—a lot more potential to decrease costs, increase efficiency, and improve the technology.

"Right now renewable energy is highly underutilized relative to the benefits it can provide to the environment, to our society, to our economy, and to public health."

I also think that there is a growing movement towards a different type of company. Employee ownership is on the rise. Democratic workplaces are increasing. Multi-stakeholder companies are increasing, like B-corporations. Younger employees are demanding more transparency and democratic workplace practices. That is a great thing as well. We are passionate not just about solar but also about doing business in a different way, in a more healthy way for the economy and society.

I don't think I can say the same thing about worker cooperatives yet. The cooperative economy is huge in all categories, except worker cooperatives. We would like to be a part of growing the community of worker cooperatives, so that more companies start as worker cooperatives or convert to worker cooperatives. Worker cooperatives are just one type of business model. There are lots of different ways to practice employee ownership and practice workplace democracy and transparency. We support them all, but we would like to see the worker cooperative movement grow too.

SD: *What kind of a background in terms of education and training do you need in order to work at Namasté Solar?*

BJ: We have people from all types of backgrounds. It helps if you have skills that are transferable to the solar industry. If you have electrical knowledge—such as an electrical license or engineering degree, for example—that is desirable. We also hire engineers in general. If you have a trade background—carpenters, steel workers, or trades people—they have valuable skills. People who are involved in technical sales are also valuable. People from construction companies tend to have a lot of transferable knowledge.

That is just on the solar side. We have a lot of people who didn't have any solar experience but the industry has been booming—if you have one year of experience, you're a veteran. As for being a cooperative, it helps when people come from collaborative backgrounds. We look for people who measure their happiness holistically, not just in terms of a paycheck.

Our company measures its profit and success not just in terms of our bottom line, but also in terms of our contributions to the community and our impact on environment, the level of employee satisfaction, and so on. We also like employees who think long-term. We prioritize long-term over short-term thinking. We want employees who plan to be with the company long term, so their thinking is aligned with the long-term thinking of the company.

SD: ***What do you do in terms of education and training in the cooperative aspect of the business?***

BJ: Each hired employee goes through a twelve-month candidacy period. They then become eligible to purchase one share of voting common stock. During that candidacy period, they have a candidate curriculum to follow. They have to talk to different people in different teams to learn background information, our history, and how we do things and why. There is a curriculum checklist. They have to check all of those line items. They also have a mentor who helps guide them and helps answer questions. The mentor helps connect them to different resources or people who can answer their questions.

Also, all of our meetings and all of our books are completely open, and we encourage people to attend committee meetings and team meetings. Then every month we have an all-day "big picture" meeting, which we often call "BPM." At each BPM, we review our financial statements together, we review our performance against our goals, we have big picture discussions, and we make big picture decisions. That is a great way for people to learn about our culture and how we democratically engage in discussion and decisions. Then we have two retreats per year, where we get away from the normal daily patterns and we go up in the mountains and talk about highest level, big picture strategy and decision-making. And all of those forums create opportunities for people to interact and engage in and foster a stronger democratic culture.

SD: *At the end of the twelve-month training period, is there a vote to enable an employee to join the co-op?*

BJ: Yes, you have to be approved by owners for us to sell a share. Nobody has been voted down. If a person is still around after twelve months, that means we think they are a good fit. We have had two people who decided they didn't want to make the commitment to be a co-owner. You have to purchase a share, and it costs $5,000. You can get a four-year loan—we want to help people who don't have access to capital, but we also want it to be a significant financial commitment. That is part of sharing the complete experience of being small business owners. You can't just share the decision-making and rewards. You have to share the risk and responsibility. We had two people decide they weren't ready for that yet and that's okay. You're not required to be an owner of the company if that is not right for you.

SD: *How does management at Namasté function? How are managers hired, supervised, and (if necessary) replaced?*

BJ: We don't call it management. We talk a lot about the difference between leadership and management. It is more leadership than management. Most people in teams are self-managed, but we do need leadership. We call it a meritocracy whereby the people who have earned the trust and confidence of their coworkers tend to be democratically empowered with more responsibility. Leadership does not entail an entitlement to authority, but instead is democratically empowered. Teams will designate their team leaders.

SD: *How does this work for you as CEO?*

BJ: I'm empowered by the democracy with certain responsibilities, but it doesn't compare with the authority that a conventional CEO has. Similar to conventional companies, the Board of Directors is technically responsible for holding me accountable. And the co-owners democratically elect the Board of Directors on a one-vote-per-person basis, instead of by stockholders on a one-vote-per-share basis. I also co-chair the strategy team with our vice president. The strategy team basically consists of the team leads—so there is broad representation. The strategy team is not a management team—even though someone from the outside might see it that way. What we are tasked with doing is coming up with our five-year strategic

"We don't call it management. We talk a lot about the difference between leadership and management. **It is more leadership than management.**"

planning and facilitate buy-in by the teams. It is subject to review by the board and by co-owners at our big picture meetings.

SD: *How does decision-making work at Namasté Solar?*

BJ: We have six levels of decision-making. At the lowest level is the individual level. Individuals are empowered to do certain things on their own—I'm empowered in my job role to give a presentation to the public about our company, for example. There are some things that we can't do as individuals, like provide discounts. That second level is "peer review" which requires approval from a group of colleagues. The third level is the team or committee level. There are many teams and committees (finance, strategy, HR, marketing, etc.), which are empowered to address certain issues. The fourth level is the big picture meeting. Above that is the board of directors. And above that, the sixth and final level, are the co-owners—an official stockholder vote by the employee-owners.

Sometimes, when we have a new issue, we have to see which decision-making level it belongs in. Sometimes we will kick an issue back down to a committee or team or, vice versa, sometimes a committee or team will kick an issue up to a big picture meeting. Once it is an issue we are familiar with, it kind of gets added to institutional policy or knowledge. For example, if it's a discount—it belongs at the peer level. And everyone knows that. With a given issue, you can add it to a charter of a committee or team. Sometimes, we'll change policy too. We're doing that right now with our credit card policies. We just got our first full financial audit. We had financial reviews before, but it was our first formal audit. And the auditors gave us recommendations. So with credit cards, we are now changing some policies regarding who is empowered to have one, what they can purchase with it, etc.

SD: ***How does profit distribution work?***

BJ: The default is 20 percent of our profit goes to charity, 20 percent goes to co-owners, and 60 percent is retained. The co-owners can vote to change these numbers. Co-owner dividends are based on time at the company during the applicable year—if you're worked full-time the entire year, then you get the same profit distribution as everyone else. If you were there half the year, you would only get half.

SD: ***What is a typical profit distribution?***

BJ: We're about to close for last year and we'll soon be able to determine our profit level for the year. People are pretty excited. But we think per co-owner it will be pretty high.

SD: ***What were profit payments in past years?***

BJ: We reinvested all of our profits for most of the first seven years. One of the reasons is that we had no other sources of capital. The only source of capital we had was new co-owner purchases of shares and retained earnings. We just added a new source of capital by making it possible to bring on external investors (by selling non-voting preferred stock). Now that we have that new source of capital, we have more flexibility to distribute a portion of profits to ourselves. We could have paid ourselves dividends in the past, but then we wouldn't have been able to grow like we have. The democratic decision was to support the balance sheet and support growth instead of paying dividends. Now that we are bringing in external investors, the default share of profits that will go to employee-owners will be 20 percent. We might have given out $5,000 per person, or something like that, in profit distribution in 2006. But after that we decided to retain all or our earnings because we needed the capital to grow.

SD: ***Shifting gears and thinking nationally, worker co-ops are enjoying new visibility in the United States, in part because of recent films like* We the Owners *and* Shift Change. *What do you see as steps that the worker co-op movement needs to take nationally to build on this new visibility?***

BJ: I think we still need more visibility. The movies help. Business school case studies help. The year 2012 was the International Year of the Cooperative, but it didn't do enough. We do have some good visibility from the recent films though. I hope that people take that viral and encourage folks to watch the films and post links. I hope people host viewing parties.

In terms of building the movement, I think we need to reach entrepreneurs—future entrepreneurs—whether it is in business schools or elsewhere—so that they know cooperatives are an option. When we started, we didn't know about cooperatives. We didn't know it was an option.

We also need to set a positive example. We hope to set a positive example that you can indeed transition to a cooperative and don't necessarily have to start out that way. A lot of people transition to ESOPs. We also want companies to transition to worker cooperatives.

And we need to have more successful cooperatives. In *We the Owners*, we're the only co-op highlighted in that—right now, I can name a bunch of successful employee-owned companies. I think we need more examples of successful worker cooperatives to point to. We need highly visible examples that people consider role models. We want people to think, "Wow. Being a cooperative allowed them to be more successful." We think for ourselves that the cooperative structure is the secret of our success. We hope that other people will see this as well.

Books are also important. We wouldn't have known about South Mountain Company, a successful worker cooperative which has been around for thirty years, if they hadn't written a book. Hopefully, Equal Exchange will write a book. Hopefully we will too, when we have a lengthier track record. Books are very powerful, I think. And they are a great way to provide examples of better ways to do business, as well as provide encouragement and inspiration.

SD: *Namasté, in addition to being a worker cooperative is also a "green" business? What do you see as Namasté's role in building a "greener" economy? How do you define green jobs?*

BJ: I think the business that we do is squarely in the green economy in that we are installing solar systems. But also the way we do business sets a positive example. Our two office buildings are LEED (Leadership and Excellence in Environmental Design) certified. Our main office is LEED Gold. We use plug-in electric vehicles. All of our installation teams use biodiesel fuel. We are committed to a zero-waste program where we recycle 80 to 90 percent of our operational waste.

We also facilitate personal recycling: Employees can bring in things they can't recycle at home to our office. And we also are committed to helping our employee-owners to be green in their individual lives. We provide unlimited bus passes for personal use, for example.

We are very proactively involved in policy advocacy, so we're down at the statehouse a lot. We talk to our state legislators and congressional representatives a lot. We support renewable energy, energy efficiency, renewable portfolio standards, carbon standards, and benefit corporation legislation—things like that. I think that is important to do. We need to engage in advocacy for things that are beyond strictly financial interests. There are now trade associations in renewable energy that are getting stronger, Sierra Club types of organizations. Environment Colorado, Green America—those kinds of organizations are great.

SD: *What do you see as the most important policies that government (be it local, state, or federal) can provide to encourage the adoption of renewable sources of energy like solar?*

BJ: We think more broadly than just the solar energy—we are big supporters of energy efficiency. We are very happy about the CAFE (Corporate Average Fuel Economy or car/truck mileage) standards increase. We like to support general environmental legislation, like green building codes. Those have been really helpful here in Boulder. Water conservation is big here in the West. Renewable portfolio standards have been very effective. Investment tax credits for solar, production tax credits for wind—those have been really important—they have helped level the playing field, since there are so many subsidies for conventional energy.

Insurance liability for nuclear power is an example of current policy that enables conventional energy costs to be externalized. We also advocate stopping the subsidies for conventional energy or that externalize their costs. That's why we support a carbon tax.

The production tax credit for wind—it got extended for one more year, but it needs a longer-term horizon. Renewing the production tax credit for one or two years at a time, that's not enough to optimize the wind industry's growth potential. Investment tax credits for solar, which passed around 2008, lasts until the end of 2016. That was eight years. That was a great policy that allowed the solar industry to do more long-term planning and investing and

"We are very proactively involved in policy advocacy, so we're down at the statehouse a lot. **We talk to our state legislators and congressional representatives a lot**."

---

enabled it to hire the people it needed to grow the market. Public policy wherever possible needs to have a long-term outlook.

SD: *It seemed that there was a big boost in support for green jobs in the 2009 stimulus bill. Has that dissipated? How have political shifts affected Namasté's business?*

BJ: Coming into the economic downturn in 2008, solar was booming. The investment tax credit was strong and there were a lot of state-based renewable energy credits. The ARRA (American Recovery & Reinvestment Act or "stimulus" bill) helped solar and wind to grow by changing the tax credit into a cash grant during the Great Recession. Same amount of subsidy, but in the form of cash instead of tax credits. Overall, the provisions of the stimulus bill really helped. What's a good next step from here? It would be nice to have a national renewable energy portfolio standard.

I think the solar industry in the United States is going to grow in 2013 and 2014. Of course, we would like it to grow faster and do more. More of the action needs to happen at the state level—half of the states have a functioning solar energy market and the other half don't. The federal investment tax credit alone isn't enough. It needs to be complemented with policies at the state or even municipal level. Austin is an example of a municipality that is taking the lead in supporting renewable energy. Solar is thriving in Austin. Not so much in Houston. The difference is because Austin has supportive municipal policy. At the state level, California is number one and New Jersey is number two. The reasons are the combination of high conventional electricity prices and pro-solar policies.

SD: *What do you have in mind when you say "pro-solar policy"?*

BJ: A net metering law is one example. If you own a home and you produce solar electricity during the day, you need to allow for the meter to spin backward and forward at the same rate, at least up to the point where you are producing the same amount as you consume in a given year.

There are other forms of pro-solar policies. Some are types of incentives. They can be state tax credits, cash rebates, renewable energy credits, feed-in-tariffs, and financing. Financing is particularly interesting. The city of Boulder has been a leader in this, as has Berkeley, California. Different cities have provided low-cost financing for people to make energy efficient improvements. These are generally known as "PACE" programs or "Property Assessed Clean Energy." Boulder's was a fantastic program.

Another thing the federal government can do is to address the bottlenecks that slow down the adoption of PACE policies. The idea is simple. If there is a new sewer line that needs to be installed in the neighborhood, a city will put out bonds and they will repay the bond with a property tax assessment.

With energy efficiency, it is the same concept, only it is voluntary and by household. I want to put in more insulation or new windows, so I get a loan that is attached to the house. The homeowner will get a loan with a low-interest rate, amortized for twenty years, which is great, because the cash flow is positive. The homeowner, in other words, saves more in reduced energy costs than the cost of the loan. The homeowner will repay the loan through the property tax system. If they sell the house, the loan is attached to the next homeowner's property tax because the loan is attached to the property. And the city sells bonds to finance it and gets repaid through the property tax assessment, just like it would finance a sewer.

It was fantastic, especially in the economic downturn, because people didn't have equity in their homes. PACE financing really stimulated the industry. But mortgage lien holders got upset— because a property tax lien is higher in the pecking order than the mortgage lien. The way these were designed, they were to have positive cash flow, but there was a lot of confusion at Fannie Mae and Freddie Mac. Banks were upset, because they saw it as competition for providing loans, even though they would never lend to people without equity. There was a lot of pressure to stop PACE programs. Fannie and Freddie put a stop to it. We want to get it back on track.

SD: *If you had to highlight a few key accomplishments of Namaste's work to date that you are proudest of, what would they be?*

BJ: First of all, being number one in the Colorado market. Showing that our business model does have competitive advantages. We needed to prove that we could achieve conventional business success in a conventional way through the strengths of our unique business model. We are really happy that we have eight years of a successful track record of being market share leaders in Colorado. That helps provide credibility to our model. We are also proud of some of the awards and recognition we've gotten, such as best place to work awards or most democratic workplace. They have come from a lot of different third parties. We like those too. It says there is something to pay closer attention to here. It helps get our message out there better than we could do on our own.

We are also proud of scaling our model. People said it would be hard to grow and maintain a democratic workplace. We want to be another example like Equal Exchange or Union Cab [in Madison, Wisconsin]. We have done it—so far, so good. We are also happy to have installed over 2,000 systems. And we have donated over $500,000 to local non-profits. To grow and scale our model without compromising our original values, we had to change our policies and practices, but they are still aligned with our principles. One last thing to mention is that we are a certified B-corporation. One of the neat things about the B-corporation movement is that it forces us to think about how to measure social and environmental impact in a holistic way. We got a really high B score. We were in the top twenty of over 600 B corporations. We're proud of that, but it also means we've still got room for improvement!

Rob Witherell

Rob Witherell works for the United Steelworkers union at its headquarters in Pittsburgh, Pennsylvania. In addition to working on contract negotiations, benefits analysis, research and organizing, Rob has also led the United Steelworkers' efforts on developing union co-ops and is the union's lead liaison with the Mondragón Cooperative Corporation.

Interviewed in 2013

Steve Dubb: Could you tell us a bit about your history in labor organizing and what has led you to dedicate your career to the labor movement?

Rob Witherell: When I was an undergrad at the University of Massachusetts, our tuition and fees doubled in the years that I was there, and so I got involved in student organizing and student government. That experience led me into politics and working on political campaigns, which eventually led to the opportunity to earn my Master's degree in Labor Studies. As a graduate research assistant, I was a UAW member and our union contract allowed me to attend grad school full time with full health insurance for a whopping $300 per semester, and earning the best pay rate that I had ever had. Since my undergrad degree is a Bachelor's in Business Administration. I am probably one of very few people around who has both a business and a labor degree.

SD: **Could you discuss what put co-op organizing on the Steelworker agenda, given that employee-owned cooperatives are not exactly the typical way unions today go about organizing new members?**

RW: In the late eighties and early nineties, we put a lot of effort into employee stock ownership plan (ESOP) owned companies as a way to rescue troubled companies. In some cases, that meant complete worker ownership. For most of them, it meant minority worker ownership.

And what we found is that where things didn't change at all, the ESOP wasn't successful. Where we had some success—and where the ESOPs still exist—the companies are typically 100 percent employee-owned. A key to these successes was that there was a change in the culture of the workplace, so that the ownership of the company means more to the workers than the value of their shares.

SD: **Could you elaborate on the differences between the successful and unsuccessful ESOPs?**

RW: In a lot of the cases, we were dealing with cash-strapped companies. Doing these buyouts were a way of exchanging shares for concessions. So the business stayed open, but nothing really changed in terms of the product, market, business structure or business plan. Eventually those shares got bought out. So while it saved those companies in a lot of cases, our members didn't feel any sense of ownership.

So the ones that have been able to survive as employee-owned companies are the ones that started functioning more like a cooperative—that is, they were companies which had an active union and a company management that listened to its workers. In these companies, there was more of an emphasis on having a partnership with the union and in talking and listening to employees and respecting employees as owners.

SD: *How did the Steelworkers become aware of Mondragón?*

RW: In 2008, I was in Bilbao at an economic development meeting there to convince or help convince suppliers of one of our employers here in Pennsylvania to expand their supply operations into the United States. And while I was there, thanks to Michael Peck, who is Mondragón's North American delegate, I had the opportunity to talk with Jesus Herrasti, who was the President of Mondragón International division at the time. And so it was a good conversation. We found that we had a lot in common. And that led to a lot more conversations with [United Steelworkers President] Leo [Gerard]. And that led to the point when we announced our collaboration in 2009.

SD: *In a recent paper, you write, "people wondered: what, exactly, could labor unions and cooperatives have in common?" But you concluded that they had a lot in common. Could you elaborate on what you see as the commonalities between the two movements?*

RW: What we have in common is that we are trying to accomplish the same things. Why do unions exist? Why do people try to create cooperatives? At the most basic level, in both cases, it is about workers helping each other out to create a better life for themselves.

When you start from that baseline, we can start thinking about worker ownership and cooperatives and unions as part of a broader labor movement. The means for achieving their goals are different, but their goals are very much aligned.

SD: *Over the past three-and-a-half years, the Steelworkers has developed and maintained a partnership with both the Mondragón Cooperative Corporation and the Ohio Employee Ownership Center. Can you discuss how the partnership was first formed and how it has developed over time?*

RW: Initially this collaboration was between the Steelworkers and Mondragón. It developed as a series of conversations between [Steelworker President] Leo [Gerard] and [current President of Mondragón International] Josu Ugarte. So that created this opportunity to collaborate. Based on those conversations, Michael Peck and I have been working a lot together exploring different paths where we can collaborate.

One of those instances is this laundry project in Pittsburgh, which is similar to the Evergreen Cooperative Laundry in Cleveland. So Jim Anderson of the Ohio Employee Ownership Center (OEOC), who helped establish that co-op laundry, has been helpful in getting the Pittsburgh project together. And it is really through this particular project that we have worked pretty closely with OEOC.

Then, in the course of the project, you start thinking through the basic questions of how does this work. Why does a unionized worker cooperative business make sense? It is not only the questions we got from everybody else, but as we tried to think through the questions of what are the mechanisms and why it makes sense, we had to think through the details and that is why we released a paper that described that model in March 2012.[5]

SD: *Could you discuss how the union-co-op model will function?*
RW: The primary idea, the seed of the idea, came out of those very first conversations. And, in addition to the Mondragón model being based on one-member, one-worker shared ownership as a cooperative, one of the institutions that they have is the Social Council. The Social Council, unlike the Board of Directors, has a broader representation because people elect members from their work areas and there are a lot more people who serve on the Social Council than who get elected to the Board. So the Social Council's function includes: one, maintaining the communications between the shop floor workers and management and the board; two, they advise management and the board; and three, they are responsible for allocating 10 percent of the profits back into the community, that is part of their charge.

But in terms of the relationship—not only how this Council is created, but in being the go-between for communications and advising management on a day-to-day basis—that sounds an awful lot like what

---

5. For a copy of that paper, see: http://www.usw.coop.

our local union people do. We have bargaining committees that bargain a contract every few years, but these are the people who are also working things out with management on a day-to-day basis. Where there has been an effort on the part of management and the union to develop a good working relationship in existing traditional workplaces, that relationship has been pretty positive. So if we can take our bargaining committee and swap it in for the Social Council, we think we can successfully adapt the Mondragón model for the United States.

Another point: If we think about what a worker co-op looks like today, most co-ops are fairly small. And so, if you think about a co-op of 10 to 20 worker-owners, is this added level of process really needed? Mondragón itself actually recommends for its own cooperatives the use of the social council structure for any cooperative of 50 people or more.

But if we are talking about scaling up and applying this to a larger workplace, say, of 100 people, how does a cooperative maintain the accountability that is intended? Because voting for directors and having an annual meeting is a good step, but that only happens once a year. How do you maintain that accountability on a day-to-day basis? This is where we see the union structure and collective bargaining making a lot of sense.

SD: *You've written about challenges of "size and perception" in developing worker co-ops. Can you elaborate regarding what these challenges are?*

RW: I think there is a tendency for people to think of worker co-ops as some kind of hippie commune where they've dropped out of society and are trying to create some utopia. And that's obviously not the case. The truth right now is that, despite their successes, worker co-ops in the business world aren't really considered legitimate businesses at this point. And so that inhibits their ability to get financing, to get investment, and to attract workers, quite frankly.

Size is important for another reason. If you only have 10 people in a cooperative, how do you afford benefits? You don't have that purchasing power to get reasonable rates on health insurance or any other type of insurance. Nor do you have the purchasing power to lower administrative fees for administering a 401(k) plan. And, of course, with 10 people, you have zero chance of having a defined benefit pension plan. So access to benefits has been a real challenge.

"The ones that have been able to survive as employee-owned companies are the ones that started functioning more like a cooperative—that is, **they were companies which had an active union and a company management that listened to its workers**."

SD: *How can these challenges best be addressed?*

RW: Some of the first steps are already being made. A lot of these co-ops are collaborating more and pooling their purchasing power.

We think being affiliated with a union takes it a step further, because a primary function of what we are able to do as a union is to pool the purchasing power of our members. So we have at the Steelworkers a Health & Welfare Fund that can get lower cost insurance in a lot of cases. We have a defined benefit pension plan, the Steelworkers Pension Trust, where the employer puts in a defined contribution and the worker gets a guaranteed defined benefit pension payment on retirement. So that opens the door to having a defined benefit pension for these small co-ops.

SD: *Could you discuss the challenges of financing union-co-ops and how the Steelworkers are seeking to address those challenges?*

RW: In looking at potential projects, there obviously are limited resources for funding worker ownership. For us in manufacturing, one of the reasons why manufacturing jobs pay well is that the labor costs are a small percentage of the overall cost of making the product. On the flip side, that means there are huge capital costs. So, for example, if a small group of workers can afford to buy out a steel mill without financing, they probably wouldn't have needed to work in the steel mill in the first place because it would require a lot of money. That's why we see a lot of service-oriented co-ops—it is the difference of investing, say, $10,000 over time versus $200,000.

I think the other thing that we've learned from our own history is that it's not just about raising money for the buy-out. It is raising money for ongoing investment for liquidity, for withstanding the normal ups and downs of a lot of our sectors. So getting the liquidity to be able to do those things, there is a huge difference between a worker co-op applying for that loan and some venture capital fund manager. They are going to get different rates.

So that's a challenge—accessing that capital.

The other challenge—if we're trying to buy a business out of bankruptcy, how do we do that? You are limited by the amount of money that workers have to invest and, even if you have workers make concessions, the concessions they are able to make aren't likely going to be enough. So in many cases, you are going to need investors. You will need investors who are friendly to the idea of a cooperative model. Even when you can put together the financing for a reasonably sized worker owned business, doing that in bankruptcy and raising the capital quickly enough, it's timing. There is not an existing investing pool out there that is large enough and interested in doing that kind of stuff.

That is why efforts like the Solidarity Fund in Quebec are so intriguing. That was created by the Quebec labor unions in the early 1980s, where individuals put money into it and get some tax credits up to a certain amount on their annual contributions plus they get a return for their investment, which, by the way, has historically gone very well. It has grown to be a $7 billion fund that invests in Quebec businesses that are socially responsible and pass their social audit.

SD: *Could you discuss the state of existing union-co-op business development efforts in Cincinnati, Pittsburgh, Connecticut, and elsewhere?*

RW: In Pittsburgh, there is a growing effort to create a green laundry that would be of pretty significant size. There are definitely people interested in being customers. There are also experienced people that came from a laundry that was closed down a couple of years ago who would very much like to be part of starting this up. Our main challenge right now is the site location, because the likely site itself is on a brownfield. It would be one of the first projects of a larger redevelopment plan for that site. So that has kind of slowed things down at the moment.

In Cincinnati, there is a group that started off as a study group after we announced our collaboration with Mondragón. They decided this union co-op idea sounded interesting. That has since become the Cincinnati Union Co-op Initiative (see http://www.cincinnatiunioncoop.org). They started with three project ideas. I think that they are up to five now. One of those projects they launched last year. It is going to be a food hub—it is called Our Harvest. They started out at the beginning with the farming and developing the farming capacity, but the idea would be that they would locally grow the food, do their own wholesale distribution, maybe some light processing, like canning, and possibly have some food retail outlets, in partnership with the United Food and Commercial Workers (UFCW) union.

In Connecticut, there is a group of people that are working on trying to create jobs for veterans using this model as a way to deconstruct buildings and create modular buildings, including housing, out of the materials that are saved.

And then there are a whole lot of other projects. There is stuff going on all over the country. One of the nice problems that we have is trying to keep track of it all. There are projects in Seattle, Denver, and New York, to name a few.

SD: *What more can the cooperative and community wealth building communities do to support union co-op development?*

RW: What Gar Alperovitz and The Democracy Collaborative have been talking about and working on is part of a growing body of interesting ideas and work that is starting to emerge—namely, how do cities deal with the problems that they have? Not only with keeping jobs in the city, but remaining financially stable as an entity, dealing with development and redevelopment in a responsible way. This emerging idea of keeping money in the community seems to be gaining a lot of steam, especially with groups like Business Alliance for a Local Living Economy (BALLE). Worker ownership can be a key part of that.

Where I think existing co-ops could use help is in the ability to grow. We need to increase the ability for other people who have an idea or are facing some difficult situation to think of worker ownership as a viable option. It is still, for a lot of people, just not on their radar.

So spreading the idea of worker ownership is itself important. In fact, this is one of the interesting things that unions can bring to the table. Unions have an enormous network of people all over the

"It makes sense for us to also think about how can we create our own jobs and **how we create jobs that are sustainable**."

country, working with all sorts of different employers, who can raise the idea. What if we all did this?

Then we need to grow and strengthen the support network that can help turn that idea into reality.

SD: *You've written about the challenges of the labor movement. Could you highlight what some of the key challenges are and how union-co-ops fit into a broader strategy for addressing those challenges?*

RW: This week at the AFL-CIO executive board meeting, they were very public about needing to think about how to be more effective, how to make the labor movement matter to more people. [AFL-CIO President Richard] Trumka was very clear about wanting suggestions and ideas about things that unions could do differently. Because we engage daily in these struggles to maintain benefits, maintain pensions, for job security, for nondiscrimination. And our ability to do that has been diminished some over time, as our density has gotten smaller. They are forming committees to examine these issues and will report back to the AFL-CIO's national convention, which will occur this coming September.

As is well known, we've had these very public battles in Wisconsin, Michigan, Indiana, and Ohio. Some have gone our way, but most have not. There is a pretty well-organized and well-funded opposition to what it is that we do.

And if we go back to that primary concept of what it is that we should be doing—workers helping each other to improve our standard of living—that opens the doors to trying this stuff. And opens the doors to thinking about it—in addition to trying to convince workers of an existing employer that they would be better off joining the union, it probably makes sense for us to also think about how can we create our own jobs and how we create jobs that are sustainable; where the rug does not get pulled out from under us because the company can make something five cents cheaper in China.

SD: *If you had to highlight a few key accomplishments of the union-co-op effort to date, what would they be?*

RW: We announced our collaboration in 2009 without a specific plan or specific pilot project as a demonstration. We announced it because we thought that we had a pretty good idea. And for us to not talk about that idea and just try to work to create a pilot project behind closed doors didn't make a lot of us sense to us. That idea has really caught on.

The initial interest was pretty overwhelming. And as we have stuck with it and thought more carefully about all of the details, I think we're creating more validity to the idea. And so we've gone from, "Hey that sounds really strange. How does that work?" to "I think that might work. How do I apply that idea?" That's a pretty big step.

I think about it in similar terms as our work with the Blue-Green Alliance. When the USW co-founded it with the Sierra Club in 2006, people had a hard time thinking about what it was that people in the labor movement and the environmental movement might have in common. And now we take it for granted that we do have a lot in common and should be working together and doing this kind of work. I think that is where we are getting to on worker ownership and labor unions—because we are natural allies.

And the projects—as I said earlier—we get asked to help on projects that pop up every day. People are out there doing stuff that we don't know about. We are running across new people all the time. Can you give us some help or some ideas?

We have tried not to overemphasize any particular pilot project, because we want this to be something that is replicated. We want it to be tried over and over. Sometimes it will be successful and sometimes not. Launching the idea as a real alternative is the goal. Now we have lots and lots of people working to put those ideas into practice.

SD: *Has there been any interest in co-ops that you are seeing in other unions?*

RW: The United Farm and Commercial Workers (UFCW) union has been very active. They just did a big employee-ownership buyout with Homeland Grocery. They have also been active in supporting the Cincinnati project. They have other projects around the country—more consumer food co-ops than worker co-ops, but they do seem to be pretty active in that general area.

The SEIU [Service Employees International Union] has had some interest. They represent workers at the largest union worker co-op that currently exists in the United States, with Cooperative Home Care Associates (CHCA). I believe the Machinists (IAM) may be working on a project as well.

Another interesting development is a newly formed purchasing co-op. It just launched in December. The Machinists (IAM) and Painters (IAPAT) have launched a purchasing co-op. It's called the Cooperative for Union Services and Products.

Molly Hemstreet

Molly Hemstreet is the organizer, developer, and now worker-owner who got the ball rolling on Opportunity Threads, a worker cooperative cut-and-sew factory in Morganton, North Carolina. Started in late 2008, Molly's leadership story is an inspiring example of how democratic ownership in manufacturing can create jobs, empower workers, and even rebuild the value chains that sustain a community economically.

Interviewed in 2014 by John Duda

John Duda: Can you tell me a little bit about the backstory, first—where did Opportunity Threads come from?

Molly Hemstreet: Opportunity Threads is based in Burke County in western North Carolina. This is the county I grew up in—I've lived most of my life here. We're kind of on the edge of the Appalachian mountain range, and really, in many of our communities, we've been makers. We can produce just about anything, especially textiles and furniture.

Those industries are the lifeblood around which our economy has developed. I see them as sister industries—they've supported the growth of each other because for so much of furniture making, there's a lot of sewing involved. The heart of furniture making in the United States has always been here in the Carolinas for various reasons.

So coming out of school—I went to Duke—I came back home and I became really interested in alternative labor models, because at the point when I was coming back (I had gone into teaching), this was when a lot of the offshoring started happening and a lot of NAFTA (North American Free Trade Agreement) was hitting the fan, so to speak.

And we were feeling the effects of it. In our county, it seemed like almost every day there would be a plant that would close. But not just a plant of 25 or 50 people—it'd be a plant of 1,200 people or 500 people. People were leaving work on Friday and then not going into work on Monday. All these workers—the people who had built these entities for years after years after years—they weren't told that this work was leaving. They didn't have another plan. When something is sold or offshored, those people who have worked those machines for years have no access to the wealth that's been built up—there's no capital left for them.

I was seeing that happening again and again and again. Because of this kind of ownership structure, even in a bad economy where these companies are offshoring, the owners are potentially becoming wealthy. But still it's that workforce that's always left behind. And it's the workforce that has the skills, the workforce that has the vision, and it's the workforce that's often left with nothing even though they've built multi-million, billion dollar companies for people.

We just saw that happen over and over again, and it became a question for me, coming back into my community, what does something different look like? And how do you scale something that's different? How does it not just remain a cottage industry? It's the same question that I think a lot of people are asking, and I think those are healthy questions.

So that was the question I asked. I came back to my community, I taught school for a while, then I started doing community organizing in rural Appalachia, thinking about these questions of how you can build economic power, particularly in marginalized communities. We tried a lot of different things. But it all came back to the question: how do you build, not just secondary incomes like you might in a farmer's market, but how do you build primary income? How do you build structures around primary income? And how do you do it in entities like manufacturing, in a plant? Because you know, manufacturing is very scalable—it's where there's more access to capital on a lot of different levels.

JD: **And how did this all lead you to start a worker cooperative?**

MH: When I came back to North Carolina, I became interested in this model of worker ownership. We worked a lot with the Highlander Center out of east Tennessee, who helped us start to think about these questions: what does worker ownership look like, and can it be scaled in something like manufacturing?

At the time, Frank Adams, who wrote *Putting Democracy to Work*, and who is very well-known in the worker-owner movement, was living up in Asheville, so I sat down with him. And what he said was, "You know, the best way to try to understand this model is just to try it." He had been working with Maggie's Organics, who had started a cooperative in Nicaragua, and he told me that they were looking to do some domestic work. So I reached out to them, and they said that they would like to try something domestically.

My husband had been doing labor organizing—he had been working a lot in the poultry industry and the meatpacking industry—so I was looking at this from a labor perspective. I knew how hard it was to do organizing in a place like North Carolina, where you're not going to necessarily unionize because we're a right-to-work state. We just started putting the pieces of the project together. We knew workers that had some consciousness about labor, and some workers that had stood up in the workplace, and so we pooled together an initial group of people. We had this market with Maggie's, and this leadership with Frank, and so we were able to put these conversations together, and start in on the idea of building a cooperative.

We looked at our assets, our communities' history—what is it that our communities can do? The answer was sewing and textiles—that's what we can do. Even though that industry had taken a real hit, it was still what people had the skills to do, and it was still the infrastructure we had. The building we're in now was a textile factory when I was growing up, and then it sat here empty for many years. And the workers that we had, whether they were immigrant or non-immigrant workers, a lot of them had that textile skill.

There's a significant Guatemalan community that has come into Morganton—there's actually a pretty cool book called *The Maya of Morganton* about what drew the Mayan community here. A lot of them in their home countries had worked in textiles, sewing or weaving. Many had come through Los Angeles, and had a background in the textile industry. And their parents and relatives back home had even been part of artisan cooperatives, so they understood this idea of collective ownership. This immigrant history merged with our own history of textiles in North Carolina—it's a neat story, and it was the base for building Opportunity Threads.

We launched the project in 2009. We incubated in a Workers' Center, and we had one sewing machine, and we were all volunteers. But since then, we've been able to gain a lot of traction. I stopped doing other organizing work and came on as a worker and an owner: I'm one worker-owner, one vote as well. We have 20 full-time people now, and we're in about 6,000 square feet. We need about 10,000 square feet and we're actually looking right now to potentially build some of our own facilities.

JD: *Can you talk a little bit about the kind of work the business takes on?*

MH: We work with people from all over, sewing mainly sustainable products and lot of "upcycled" products, but crucially we help people with scaling that kind of thing. We've found really good ways to work with entrepreneurs and have been able to help them scale: we've had a lot of learning about that. Someone might have a great idea, might even have some capital, but they have no clue on how you scale. We've made a lot of mistakes and I think we've figured out a lot of things as well.

JD: *Who are the 20 folks working in the project? How do they become worker-owners?*

MH: Right now we have 20 people. Eight of those people are part of the ownership—there are six that are full owners and then we have three people who are what we call pre-members. And then we have everyone else, who are kind of en-route—we have a long vetting period. It's up to about two years, and people also have to buy in at $5,000, so it's a pretty significant commitment—and that's what we want it to be.

Again, everyone comes on as an employee. They're usually employees between nine or ten months, and then they're voted in by their peers as pre-members. And then after pre-membership, they're voted in as full members of the cooperative. That's also when they pay in, they put down their payment. That part is pretty standard in the cooperative movement.

JD: *It's a really great model. Are you able to pay at or above the industry average?*

MH: Yes, but it depends on where people are in the process. When they've made it to cooperative level, their pay is above industry average, and includes benefits that they've been able to elect themselves. When they come in as employees, they're more at industry average. We want to have that carrot for people to become part of the cooperative: we don't want to just have people, we want people to be part of the cooperative. We don't want to create some people that are cooperative members and then some that are not cooperative members. We want everyone to be part of the cooperative.

We're also working with Self Help, which is our cooperative credit union. They're coming in two weeks to help us set all of this up—cooperative members are going to have 529 plans for their kids, which is a college savings account, as well as a retirement fund. And we're trying to figure out a health benefits plan as well. These are the three types of benefits that the current workers elected that they wanted and that's where we are right now.

JD: *How about the business end of things? What does the future look like for the business?*

MH: We are in a place of profitability, so hopefully at the end of the year we will either turn that back into dividends to people, or we're also in this growth phase, so we might really take that next leap and purchase more machinery and grow the business. We are basically out of debt, so that's a good thing. In two months, we'll be completely out of debt. So we don't have any debt that we're servicing—we've been able to really be a strong business at the end of the day.

And that's what we want to do. It's great that we're a cooperative, but that alone isn't going to change this industry. First and foremost, we have to be good at what we're doing, particularly because this industry is so cut-throat. It's so hard, particularly with so much that's offshore. We have to really find those pieces that we can onshore or that we can be competitive on—a lot of it is about customization, a lot of it is about quick turn-around work. A lot of it is about how you take something that's very handcrafted, and then make it at scale, but produce it so that it's still very unique and still one of a kind.

That's something that we've really gotten good at—the mass production of customization. A great example of this is a t-shirt blanket project that we have with Project Repeat, where each t-shirt blanket that comes out at the end of the day is different and unique, but at the end of the week we can make up to 300 of them. We're scaling, but still doing customizations.

JD: *To what extent are you able to tell this story about your mission—revitalizing an industry and building cooperative wealth—to the consumers who eventually buy the things you manufacture?*

MH: That's an interesting question. Sometimes it's tricky and we have to walk an interesting line with that. We have a Highlander fellow here with us this year, and part of her job is to tell our story—she actually used to work at Appalshop, a documentary filmmaking project that's told a lot of the story of Appalachia. So she's helping us tell our story.

But quite honestly, what we're trying to do, day in and day out, is get our product out the door. We can't just be a cooperative and think people will be drawn to us. What we have to do is be good at what we do. We have to be on time. We have to have high quality. We have to meet deadlines—if we say we're going to ship something today, it has to be shipped out.

"We have to re-infuse this idea of valuing labor, you know? **That's why I got into this—it was about valuing labor**. There's a lot of education that needs to happen in the entrepreneurial community about interfacing with manufacturing."

So first and foremost, we have to be just a good sew shop if we're going to be competitive. Our hope is that then being a cooperative and really having the authenticity that comes with our model is the icing on the cake. A lot of the entrepreneurs that we're drawing in are coming to us because of our story, and we have to be very careful about how we market that—we've gotten burned quite a few times. The movement now is that you should tell the story of your makers and your relationship with them, but it also has to be deeply authentic. We've gotten burned a lot of times when people will make something and they'll say they're working with us, but they're really not. Or they market us and they market our pictures—but this can be just another form of extraction—our product is also our story. We've worked hard to build a model that's very unique within this industry and in this region. It's working well; it's not just a cottage industry. So we think that our commodity right now is our story, and we're just trying to be very careful about it—we don't want it just to be anybody's story to tell. The only people that should be able to tell it are people that really earn our respect and build an authentic relationship with us.

So we have to just be careful about how our story is sold, because it's selling other people's products. We want to be sure that if we're benefitting somebody else, we're sure that there's reciprocity included in that. Reciprocity looks like people honoring payments due to us, for one thing. If we're building volume for you and you're getting more traction because of our story, we want to be sure that volume is coming back to us. So we just have to be sure that someone else using our story doesn't become another form of extraction—contract work in and of itself has somewhat of an extractive quality to it already. We've just got to be sure that if somebody's telling our story, it's on our terms.

JD: *It's exciting that you are thinking not just about your business, but about transforming and rebuilding a whole industry, on different terms. Can you tell me a little about your involvement in the Carolina Textile District?*

MH: We helped start the Carolina Textile District. What we did is realize that so many people that were coming in were just not organized. They have a great idea, they've gotten some traction, but often their supply chain is not 100 percent together. What was happening to us was that we would get into production, and then there would be problems because they hadn't used a good pattern maker and they hadn't figured out the right amount of fabric, so we'd have 500 t-shirts cut and no fabric for the sleeves because they didn't estimate right.

So I helped start the Carolina Textile District as a way to get entrepreneurs ready and really hoping that it would benefit us in production. And that's what we've seen. In the past, we might have gotten 20 samples and five of them would have actually made it to production. Now, we have five or six samples and all of them will make it to production—because we're sending these entrepreneurs through the District, and the District is helping to organize them. When they get to us, they're more successful in production and they're having a lot more success in the marketplace.

The District now has its own staff, and I'm trying to kind of spin it off more and more. To some extent, it kind of lives in Opportunity Threads often because we're willing to take on those entrepreneurs. We'll just have them come in for several days and spend time with us, so they get to really see the process—the benefit is that the entrepreneur understands that leap from them sewing this in their house to putting this into a production facility. We're small enough where they can experience that, but we're sophisticated enough where it really is true production.

Because of this pipeline, right now our capacity is basically full—we're taking on clients for January, February, March because we've fast-tracked a lot of these clients that came through the Carolina Textile District. And instead of coming back to us for 200 or 300 units, they're coming back for 1,500 and 1,800 units, or they're coming back with new orders very quickly. The nice thing about that is just the consistent flow of opportunity all the time. But the problem is that we'll get five or six calls a day from people wanting to work with us, and we don't have the capacity to do it. We've ended up actually passing work to other mills because in the past, they've passed us work. And so we're trying to build more connections with those other mills, so at least if somebody comes in, we can try to not just say, "No, we can't help you," but, "Hey, this other mill has capacity. They could take you on." It's trying to build a collaborative industry versus one where everybody is just in it for themselves.

JD: *What are the big challenges? What do you need to keep doing the work that you're doing? What other things do you wish you had had when you were getting this off the ground? Building these value chains across the whole sector, regionally, what are the needs there?*

MH: A big problem for us is the way our industry is framed. What we're always up against is "textiles is dead, textiles is dead, textiles is dead." Well, if it's dead, why did all these people call us this week? Why are we booked six months out?

The other thing is we've learned, more by trial and error and really just by complete chance, is who the good clients are. The bottom line is that our workers are the best that there possibly are. They're good at what they do, they're exceptional sewers, they can sew anything, and they also understand the versatility of what they need to do. Nobody ever just handed us a giant contract. We had to scrap for it, and we had to learn how to work with entrepreneurs—the demand is coming from entrepreneurs, but that's not necessarily where volume is. So we had to learn to cash in on entrepreneurial demand. There's a lot of education that needs to happen for entrepreneurs, especially around costs. They need to know that they're going to have to pay, because we're taking a great risk that they might not be able to scale. Even though they've sold 200 cute little things, that's just two days' work for us—so we're taking on risk bringing them into our shop.

But if they understand the value that we bring, particularly if they come and spend time with us, see what we do, get outside their heads and understand that they're passing their product onto us and that we need to know how to make it—when they develop this kind of relationship with us and see the quality of work that we do—then there's a lot more value. They understand that they're going to pay us at an hourly rate. They understand that there's a value to the hourly rate.

We're up against an old school industry that we're trying to infuse with new ways of working. In the past you would never, ever charge anybody for a sample. But we always charge people for the sample. We have to re-infuse this idea of valuing labor, you know? That's why I got into this—it was about valuing labor. There's a lot of education that needs to happen in the entrepreneurial community about interfacing with manufacturing. There needs to be a reciprocal conversation about exchange of labor and exchange of capital. It could be said in different language—but basically you've got to value the people that are going to be the muscles that are going to drive your business's bottom line.

On our end, I think people have to see that we need more storytelling about what we're doing in this industry—it's not just a resurgence of a trend, it's really a kind of reclaiming of our ability to make things. There's a new generation of makers, but it's not just the people that design and maybe make something. The real makers in my heart and my book are the people behind the machines all day. They're like the kingmakers and the queen-makers, and they make beautiful products for other people to sell. I think those people need to be included in the conversation because, at the end of the day, they're driving a lot of the worth. We need to infuse this whole maker conversation with the context of labor—that's really, really important.

JD: *How did you raise the capital to start Opportunity Threads? Especially when you said, "Hey, we know textiles are dead, but we're going to start a worker co-op to do manufacturing"? Did you have problems raising money to get this off the ground?*

MH: We originally started working with Maggie's Organics, who we still sew for. I'm sitting here right now looking at their skirts that are about to go out to Whole Foods. They gave us $5,000 to get started. At the time, I was working with a community organization, the Center for Participatory Change out of Asheville and western North Carolina, and so my time was covered as I did a lot of the initial organizing. But then people just donated time—a lot of it was donations of time. We incubated in a donated space, and then we had a $30,000 startup loan that got us into the building where we are now.

From the beginning we were just very cost-effective at what we did. We didn't try to elevate salaries too high; people worked minimum wage just to get it off the ground so that we could not go into a lot of debt. We're not debt averse, but we want to be sure we could keep our debt in check. I was able to get a few strategic grants, which is difficult because a lot of people won't grant to cooperatives because they are businesses—we are an LLC, not a 501(c)(3). But one of our biggest supporters has been the Catholic Campaign for Human Development—they will fund cooperatives. We got three years of funding from them, and now in our third year we can completely stand on our own. We're profitable and they really drove us to have that kind of cushion of funds to be able to do things like pay higher wages and buy machines and so on. Now we're running on our own, and we've built good relationships with funders, both community development funds and more commercial lenders. Which is good, because we're looking right now at potentially building our own space because the space we have just isn't adequate for the type of volume we're starting to draw. If we needed to draw down and pay higher loan amounts, we now have the relationships. We've been building those relationships.

And actually, through the Carolina Textile District we were able to build a loan fund from that same startup loan that we got initially—we used ourselves as a model and a pilot. That loan was Golden Leaf money—North Carolina tobacco buyout money—provided through a local loan pool called VEDIC. We had this $30,000 loan, which we were about to pay off about eighteen months early. And I went back to them, and I said, "You know, what we need is a line of credit. It's great to have a loan, but I'd rather have a line of credit. If we needed to buy a machine or we need to bring on an influx of workers before we know that we're going to have the payment on the back end, we'll need a line of credit." So we actually worked with them and the USDA to build a more flexible loan pool, and we have now about $1.2 million that can be loaned out just to people in the District or people that are in textile-related companies. That's a great success, too, because at some point you just have to

"How do you build cultures of cooperatives? That to me is more important than reading a financial statement."

build your own system of funding, because you're not going to be able to go to a bank for all of this. So we just built our own lending system. That's just happened in the last few weeks, but it's good. We already have people signed up that are getting into it.

JD: *A lot of the questions around scale really resonate with what we've learned in Cleveland with the Evergreen Cooperatives, especially about having to be good at what you do as the first and foremost concern—you don't get a magic pass on being a successful business just because you're a cooperative. Do you have any thoughts on worker cooperatives and manufacturing in general?*

MH: I think there's this interesting question of scale. One the one hand, you can scale by getting bigger and bigger as an entity: Opportunity Threads can get bigger, and it's important that it does. But beyond that, you can scale by transforming an industry: you can create change, deep change, throughout an entire industry. I think we've seen that with the cleaning cooperatives like Prospera in the Bay Area: they started changing their industry because they begin to assert the control of labor within an industry.

The textile industry has such deep roots here. This is where the National Guard was called in to quell labor unrest. If we can look back thirty years from now, and see that most of the companies—whether they're making fabric or they're dye houses or whatever they are—are owned by the workers themselves, I think that would be an incredible shift of just consciousness in an industry. We're starting to see this transformation. We've been a really good pilot as a startup, and now we're starting to work with producers that are also transitioning to worker ownership, as are a lot of the clients that we're bringing in.

If you can interface with somebody that's really educating you, then you can start to adopt these more democratic models—even if it's two or three workers that own the company or they're an

LLC with a cooperative operating agreement or something like that. This kind of dialogue needs to be happening. What we see is the people that are really successful are those entrepreneurs that we work with that know us really well and know their supply chains really well. There's less friction—it's like the lines between client and producer start to merge a little bit, and I think when there's more transparency there everybody has more success. There's got to be more people that are inventing and dreaming and designing, getting their hands a little dirtier.

And that's why on our social media, we're trying to tell the story of what it is to live in a manufacturing facility—that it can be fun, and it can be creative, and it can be energetic. It can have a lot of the same dynamics that somebody in design sees themselves wanting. We're trying to say that this is the kind of life that someone inside a factory all day can have, too. How do we start to see those stories, and have more transparency and more dialogue between designers and producers? It would be great for you all to come and start to interview the workers here—come at a time when they can participate. Hearing them articulate their own stories is very powerful.

JD: *One of the things that we're working on right now is a report on folks who have managed to take different kinds of cooperatives and other community wealth building projects to scale, and looking specifically at the role that education has played. It'd be great to hear what your strategies have been for how to take people who have been hired and bring them up to the point where they're able to take a full ownership stake in such an exciting, transformative, worker-owned business.*

MH: I think that's a really good question. I think that's probably where we could still use a lot of help—it's really like you never get there. Learning is just something you're always, always, always doing. A combination of just some luck and some real searching too has given us the benefit of having really good mentors. Hilary Abell has been a really good mentor for me—if we have questions, we can look to her; she's been really awesome. We also have one of the best cooperative development lawyers in the United States, Thomas Beckett. He's been with us since the very, very beginning. We have great people that understand the accounting, not just the consensus model, but really the nuts and bolts of cooperatives, and they know our folks, and they'll come and sit down with us.

I also think, however, that a lot of folks that we work with have a real innate ability to understand kind of this idea of consensus and working together. I don't know if it's because a lot of people we work with are Mayan—they're indigenous Guatemalan. And I think sometimes we bump up against the tendency that in the southern, traditionally white community—you're kind of in it for yourself, you're in it for your production numbers. There's this whole culture that has to be developed around what it means to really be collaborative at something, and that's a skill you work at, and it's a skill you monitor, and it's a skill you learn.

What you have to do is kind of build a core group of people that can provide something like positive peer pressure. That's a lot of the training we have—it's just you have your leaders and they're all on the same page. You see this group of people that want to start to emulate them and you give them the tools to do that. We have a lot of folks who don't read and write very well, but they have incredible decision-making powers and abilities to sit in a conversation and weigh positives and negatives. How do you build cultures of cooperatives? That to me is more important than reading a financial statement. Now we do all that too, and we've found people within the cooperative that really want to take on that skill. But you know—I'd rather have our folks here than most people that have been through cooperative development boot camps because our folks live it day in and day out, day in and day out. We've found the best training is just the longevity of somebody being in our permeated culture. If you have a good group of people at the top—well, not at the top!—but if you have a good group of people leading this process, a very self-sacrificial kind of leadership that says, "We're in this and even though maybe we've been here the longest, we've got to push from the bottom and work the hardest"—that's the kind of culture you want. And if you can set that culture up, I think then that's the best training ground.

Then what we do is strategically bring these experts in that can teach us how to do awesome operating agreements that are understandable to somebody that has a fifth-grade education. We bring those people in that just are awesome allies. So you build this culture, you create these leaders, they permeate the next group of people coming in, and then strategically you bring in these awesome allies—the best of the best. That's what we've tried to do.

JD: *I especially like the part about people who have been there the longest needing to recognize that they have to work the hardest.*

MH: Yeah, it's funny because we're training this new woman. She said, "You know, I thought the workday ended at 3:30 P.M., but then I noticed that nobody stopped working. Why is that?" And we explained, "Okay, they're going to work until they're done. And that's not to say you have to do that, but they understand that they're the owners of this business. It has to get out the door. They're going to put in an extra fifteen minutes."

We have this little bell that rings and nobody stops working—and it's not exploitation. It's different than when you work and you're looking over your shoulder, because we have no supervisors. This is something we do in orientations—I don't do the orientations, the workers do the orientations themselves, and I'm just at the table with everybody. We explain how you've got to inculcate yourself with this idea of being your own supervisor—you have to understand your quality measures and you have to understand your productivity measures.

The workers have some really interesting tools that they've developed to help here. They go around on an hourly basis and check everybody's productivity. Everyone is paid by the hour, but everyone also gets an hourly check-in on their productivity, and they get a daily score, and this goes on this big whiteboard: are you making your productivity or are you not? This isn't just telling people you have to be productive and you have to watch quality, but actually helping them do that by giving them the tools they need. Really, it's just simple feedback on a regular basis—and it's all imperfect. We're learning, you know? We make mistakes all the time, but we sit down every week for an hour-and-a-half, and we hash through it all. We're just making it up as we go, honestly.

Emily Kawano

Emily Kawano is Co-Director of the Wellspring Cooperative Corporation, which is seeking to create an engine for new, community-based job creation in Springfield, Massachusetts. Wellspring's goal is to use anchor institution purchases to create a network of worker-owned businesses located in the inner city that will provide job training and entry-level jobs to unemployed and underemployed residents through worker-owned cooperatives. Kawano also serves as Coordinator of the United States Solidarity Economy Network. An economist by training, Kawano served as the Director of the Center for Popular Economics from 2004 to 2013. Prior to that, Kawano taught economics at Smith College, worked as the National Economic Justice Representative for the American Friends Service Committee and, in Northern Ireland, founded a popular economics program with the Irish Congress of Trade Unions.

Interviewed in 2015

Steve Dubb: Could you talk about your background and how it led to a career advocating for economic justice?

Emily Kawano: I have been interested in social justice and economic justice issues from a young age. I decided to go to graduate school in economics because it seemed like something that I couldn't learn on my own. I wanted to get a background in economics in order to be a more effective activist. But while I did some teaching, I found that there was a continual pull back to activism and being involved in a social justice organization.

While I was in graduate school at University of Massachusetts, Amherst, I joined the Center for Popular Economics, which is a collective of economists. Our target audience is grassroots organizations and activists who can be more effective by understanding the economy. I have been a member for about 25 years. When I finished graduate school, I worked at the American Friends Service Committee, doing economic justice work. Then I did popular economics education work in Northern Ireland for five or six years.

When I came back to the United States, I became the director for the Center for Popular Economics. At that time, we went through a strategic planning process and we decided to focus on the need for examining economic alternatives. We realized that the Center does a great job critiquing the capitalist economic system, but at the end of the day, often people felt discouraged in the face of this seemingly monolithic system and seeing no viable way out. If you don't help people see and explore the practical economic alternatives, then there is a danger that people feel hopeless. So we started looking much more seriously at what we first called economic alternatives, and we ended up embracing the framework of solidarity economics. It is grounded in the democracy, sustainability, solidarity and equity (in all dimensions)—it is not a one-size-fits-all strategy. It can accommodate many views. We worked on developing an analysis and relationship with solidarity economics. The Center for Popular Economics was at the center of founding the U.S. Solidarity Economics Network at the 2007 U.S. Social Forum in Atlanta. It has been an important part of my work—going from education that was primarily focused on critique to a much more balanced approach that provides both the critique and the solutions.

SD: *What led you to work in Northern Ireland?*

EK: It involved personal reasons. My partner was covering Irish events for a Boston newspaper. We moved to Belfast in 1998. We had a three-month-old baby, and I was taking maternity leave. So it was a good time to transition. While I was in Northern Ireland, I developed a relationship with the Northern Ireland Committee of the Irish Congress of Trade Unions, which is their equivalent of the AFL-CIO. I began working with their education director, which was a great relationship. We did a lot of work with the unions and local community economic development organizations. I also worked in the south of Ireland as well women's economic development groups in Europe.

I was part of the Northern Ireland Social Economy Network, which was my first exposure to the social economy, which is a sector of the economy that includes enterprises that are collectively owned and managed. The common definition of the social economy includes cooperatives, mutuals, associations and foundations, which is sometimes referred to by the acronym CMAF. There are different definitions, but this is pretty common.

People sometimes think social economy and the solidarity economy are the same, but they are different. Social economy is a sector and is not necessarily about system change. It can be promoted as one of the pillars of capitalism. It can be seen as ameliorating some of the problems of capitalism such as delivering social services, or employing people with disabilities, or away to create jobs for hard to employ people so they can transition to capitalist businesses. At the other end of the spectrum of social economy practitioners it is seen as a step toward transitioning the political and economic system.

The solidarity economy is about transformation of the system, based on principles of democratic ownership, equity in all dimensions (race, class, etc.), sustainability, and democratic decision making and control. The focus is on all spheres of the economy including production, distribution and exchange, finance, consumption, and governance. Transforming the entire economy system is what the solidarity economy is about, which requires building practical, on-the-ground alternatives.

SD: *Could you describe the role played in this work by the Center for Popular Economics that you used to direct?*

"We build on the Evergreen model, but **our path has been different**. For example, we've started on a smaller scale and have had to leverage existing opportunities."

EK: We were one of the founders of the U.S. Solidarity Economics Network at the 2007 Social Forum in Atlanta. The Center for Popular Economics agreed to provide some core staffing to help build out that work. At the time, I was wearing the hat of the director of Center for Popular Economics and of coordinator of the Solidarity Economics Network. It was an important role. The network needed some staff to coordinate the network. After a while we did get a bit of funding to help support our work of covering that role.

SD: *What is the current breadth of activities for the U.S. Solidarity Economics Network today?*

EK: What we're focused on now is a North American Social Solidarity Economy Forum in the spring of 2016 in Detroit. The last time we organized a national conference was in 2009 at the University of Massachusetts, Amherst, which brought together 400 people. It was a great event and the energy and enthusiasm was really high. It did generate some spin-off organizing. Solidarity New York City, for instance, drew inspiration from that event and formed their network after the conference. In Worcester, Massachusetts, not far from where I work today, the Solidarity and Green Economy (SAGE) Coalition coalesced out of that meeting. So there were lots of seeds that were planted.

We are excited to now put together a North American Solidarity Economy Forum. This event will include both the United States and Canada and we will make a great effort to make sure the Mexican solidarity economy folks are present. Mexico has opted to work with the Latin America and Caribbean section, for both linguistic and cultural reasons. We want to ensure they are a strong presence nonetheless. That will be a major area of focus. We would like to have a number of gatherings and meetings leading up to the international conference.

For example, I am working on solidarity economy education and anticipate pulling together a number of meetings in the lead up to the Forum to lay the groundwork for concrete outcomes.

I will mention another project that is connected to solidarity economy. We are working on mapping the solidarity economy. There is a team of four academics and myself who are involved. We got a National Science Foundation grant to do the mapping, as well as other kinds of solidarity economy research, such as an estimation of economic impact, GIS (geographic information systems) analysis, and qualitative interviews.

The map of the solidarity economy aims to raise its visibility, promote the growth of solidarity economy supply chains, allow consumers to find solidarity economy providers and generate data for researchers interested in solidarity economy. We are building a website that will link up with a global solidarity economy map and are working closely with people doing mapping in other countries. Italy and Brazil are models for what we are working on.

SD: *I would like to switch gears now and talk with you more about your local work with the Wellspring cooperative network that you are seeking to build. Could you talk about the factors that led to its formation?*

EK: We started four years ago with the idea of creating a collaborative of anchor institutions, labor and community organizations to develop a network of worker-owned cooperatives for underserved communities in Springfield, Massachusetts. We are now incorporated as the Wellspring Cooperative Corporation. We drew a lot of inspiration from Evergreen. We reached out to the major institutions and all of them were pretty receptive. We also connected with Ted Howard [President of The Democracy Collaborative] very early on. And we had him come and make a presentation on the Collaborative's work in Cleveland, which was very important. The Cleveland example made people feel that developing employee-owned cooperatives in Springfield wasn't completely a pipe dream. In the spring of 2012, we brought a delegation of eighteen people from Springfield to Cleveland. That again was very important.

From the get-go, we set a table for anchor institutions, community organizations and labor groups. Given that Springfield is a mid-sized city, we don't have any foundations with the deep pockets of the Cleveland Foundation. We build on the Evergreen model, but our path has been different. For example, we've started on a smaller scale and have had to leverage existing opportunities.

For example, our first business is an upholstery co-op. It comes out of a partnership with the local jail, which has an upholstery shop inside and was looking for someone who could establish an upholstery shop where some ex-prisoners could get employment. It seemed like a good opportunity and at the same time could meet anchor institution needs around upholstery. And it was an industry with relatively low capital intensity. We were lucky to find a skilled upholsterer who was on board with the vision.

SD: *When did the business open and how many people does it employ?*

EK: The upholstery co-op was launched in mid-December 2013, but really 2014 was the year we really got our business under way. We had our first profitable quarter in August. Up until very recently, we have had five workers.

We have had some turnover due to issues around job performance. One of the challenges with upholstery is that it is a very specific skill. Our skilled upholsterer says that people either have "magic in the fingers" or they don't. It involves being able to do very fine work, very precise. It is patient work. It requires attention to detail and just having a feel for it. I would never have imagined that upholstery production takes such very specific skills, but it does. Not everybody is an upholsterer. We have had a number of people who have washed out because they just don't have that magic in the fingers. If all we were doing was the most simple upholstery, say, auditorium seating, we would be fine. But we have a mix. Some of our jobs are hospital recliner chairs, with lots of tricky matching patterns. You need to have a much higher level of skill for that. And not everybody has the potential.

So finding people with the right aptitude and a team that gels, securing enough work, getting productivity up to a good level, these typical start-up issues has been challenging. We are happy that we turned a corner in August from struggling on all fronts to still struggling, but definitely feeling that we are on target with projections. The business started turning a profit in the third quarter of its first year, which is pretty good.

SD: *What is the level of worker-owner participation in business decision making and what do you do delegate to a professional basis?*

EK: People who are hired at Wellspring come on, on a trial basis, for at least a month. If they pass that, they are on the worker-owner track. They are eligible to become a worker-owner after a year. We have one person who has been on staff for over a year and has now become a worker-owner. He is involved in the board meetings and the small huddles on management decisions.

We hired a manager, Evan, who has been in the business for 30 to 40 years. He ran his own upholstery shop. The one person who has become a member-owner is now part of the decision-making process, though because Evan has this depth of experience, clearly he still has the final word on a lot of things. He is formally the manager.

That said, we do meet every week with all of the workers and there are a lot of the things that we try to decide jointly. We talk about policies like talking on the phone, distractions that come from listening to music with your ear buds. We talk about all kinds of things—what if there is a slow down and not enough work, how do we handle that? Even though people are not officially members, we are trying as much as possible to build that experience and give them decision-making power.

SD: *Could you talk about the role of anchor institutions at Wellspring?*

EK: We spent quite a while, maybe six months to three quarters of a year, doing research on anchor institution purchasing and met with purchasers. We looked at a whole array of ideas: the idea of a laundry is still alive, and we're looking at a partnership with folks in Greenfield, Massachusetts. Food is something that from the get-go, the anchor institutions have been interested in. The second business in the pipeline is a hydroponic greenhouse, although on a much smaller scale than Evergreen. Baystate Health is really keen on local, fresh, and hydroponically grown produce. So they have been really supportive.

On a broad level, anchor participation has just been critical for making the whole initiative believable, which was is really important. There are a few key ones: STCC (Springfield Technical Community College, the University of Massachusetts, Amherst (even though they are not in Springfield), Western New England

University, and Baystate Health. Baystate and STCC in particular have been important and strong supporters. They are very well respected and influential members of the Springfield community. It was really critical to have their support.

SD: *How have you financed the upholstery co-op?*

EK: It was a mix of some loans, some grants, some private social investment and patient capital. The private equity investment is treated as non-voting shares, essentially preferred shares. Outside equity investors do not have a vote or decision-making authority.

SD: *How much money did you raise to launch the upholstery business?*

EK: It was a fairly modest amount: about $160,000. For the greenhouse, we are looking at more like $2 million with the same kind of mix of financing sources. We have identified a group of lenders and investors and have talked to all of them. The financing door is open. We have been talking to the same social investment firm that helped out with the Upholstery Co-op. And there are a number of foundations that we have identified and had preliminary conversations with some of them.

We are finding the site question to be challenging. We have finished the business plan, which is very detailed, but we can't raise the capital until we have a site. We are very interested in a six-acre site. It has lots of room, not only for a greenhouse but also a biodigester that might provide energy for the greenhouse and maybe for the grid. It's possible that we would build it with enough capacity for organic waste disposal, which is being phased out of landfills in Massachusetts. We are looking at food processing facility. That kind of thing would be great for a six-acre site. The complication is that it's a brownfield; there used to be auto salvage and metal recycling there. The city owns it and is doing a Phase I environmental assessment. Then there is a Phase II assessment and remediation. This is likely to take at least a year. So we are looking at a smaller site to start with, closer to downtown, to build the initial greenhouse and hopefully by the time we are ready to expand, we will have settled things with the larger site.

SD: *How are using your popular education experience and knowledge to build the cooperatives?*

"Finding people with the right aptitude and a team that gels, securing enough work, getting productivity up to a good level, **these typical start-up issues has been challenging**."

EK: In the weekly trainings at the upholstery shop, we are using a popular education approach to the training as much as possible. Our discussions build from their experience and explore topics that are relevant to developing a cooperative way of working. In terms of popular economics, we certainly want to include some analysis of where this fits into the big picture—worker ownership as an alternative strategy of economic development and promoting a democratic practice that encourages people to become active decision-makers. I would say we have so much practical stuff to deal with, we really haven't spent much time on this front, but we want people to have a sense of the larger cooperative movement, as well as of the cooperative movement as part of a broader social movement to give birth to a more just and sustainable world. But for the time being, we have done more about the basics of what is a worker co-op, its history, breaking down the financials of specific jobs, workplace policies, and conflict resolution.

SD: *Even with the practical work, are there tools from your popular education work that you find applicable?*

EK: Yes, absolutely. We break down the financials in a participatory way. We did an analysis of one job where they were just starting. Rather than the manager just telling them how long each component of the job should take to do, we asked them what they thought. Then they hashed it out with the manager. It was very participatory. And we engage with workers in problem solving, very much in the popular education mode. We supplement that with outside expertise and we have talked about bringing them to visit some of the longstanding worker co-ops in western Massachusetts. We are also planning on bringing folks to the Eastern Conference on Workplace Democracy in Worcester, which is close by, so that will be a great opportunity.

SD: *How have you dealt with workforce development challenges?*

EK: We have been working with the Hampton County Regional Employment Board or REB. They do workforce development. They were very helpful with navigating the process to access OTJ (on-the-job) training funds, which were critical in the early start-up phase. They have also been useful in helping us figure out the ACT WorkKeys system of assessing whether someone is a good candidate or not. The next time we hire a worker, we will apply that. The framework assesses conceptual skills, fine motor coordination, spatial skills: we will give it a try and see how it works. Otherwise, it means trying people out for a while until our manager Evan can make a well-informed decision about their potential.

SD: *Could you talk about some of the partnerships that you have developed?*

EK: We have worked a little bit with Toolbox and Education for Social Action (TESA) and have had conversation with Cooperative Development Institute (CDI). The Industrial Corporation Association (ICA) group has provided a lot of assistance with business plans and financial assessments. They have been great, working as a mentor more than a consultant. They have helped us build our capacity, so that has been an important relationship. We have also had a close relationship with Cooperative Fund of New England and they represented on our Board. We got a loan from them for the upholstery co-op. They have been helpful connecting to the cooperative world in general. There have been many really useful relationships with organizations that have been supportive.

SD: *Have you enlisted local government support for your cooperative development work?*

EK: We got some funding from the city for the Upholstery Co-op, a small business grant. Springfield's Economic Development Department has been supportive of the greenhouse. They actually agreed to take on the cost of Phase I environmental assessment for the six-acre parcel, which is very helpful. We have also been working pretty closely with Patrick Sullivan, the City's Director of Recreation and Facilities (parks and school facilities). He has been helping us to find a site. We may do at least some of the greenhouse development on park land. Part of the plan, for example, is to develop a community and educational greenhouse. We have been exploring doing that with the parks. We've also been talking about getting the possibility of working with a big tree company that is looking at the adjacent parcels to the six-acre site that we are interested in. This tree company is thinking about putting in a facility that would process the City's tree waste. Patrick Sullivan is putting together a meeting with them, which might possibly lead to a biochar facility.

SD: *What is biochar?*

EK: It is almost like making charcoal. At the very least, it is a strategy for sequestering carbon. When you bury it, it is incredibly good for the soil and at the same time removes carbon from the atmosphere. There is cutting-edge technology that is being used to not only produce biochar but also generate energy. This is very new technology, but this is a possibility. We were interested to see if organic waste can be used for biochar, but we learned that it isn't suitable so we had shelved that idea. With the possibility of a woody source of fuel, we are re-visiting the idea. It is just an example of the enthusiastic response we have gotten from different quarters of the city.

SD: *How else has government supported your work?*

EK: There is a nonprofit, almost semi-public organization called "Develop Springfield"—they are very closely tied into the city. They also have been working with us to identify and tour sites for the greenhouse. The Mayor has been supportive and come to our events, and the Springfield Department of Economic Development has been supportive in helping us look at sites. We received quite a positive response to our letter of inquiry regarding the six-acre site. It's been sitting vacant for quite a few years.

On a regional level, we have worked with the Pioneer Valley Planning Commission on site issues as well as on the issue of food and building a sustainable regional food system. On a state level, we have connected mostly around food. Sustainable food system work is being supported by a state initiative, and we work with the western

"It certainly would be powerful if in the United States we could start pulling together sectoral policies and **knit them together into a more comprehensive platform that supports whole system change**, rather than sector by sector."

Massachusetts local initiatives. In the beginning, we had a lot of contact with the Boston Federal Reserve. They were interested in Wellspring, as they have a focus on some special projects in Springfield. They were coming to meetings, and we went out and met with them. Certainly they have been supportive in whatever ways they can, and included Wellspring in their research and publications.

SD: *What do you see as the potential of Wellspring and the U.S. Solidarity Economy Network going forward?*

EK: For Wellspring, the hope is to create a lot of businesses—dozens of businesses and hundreds of jobs. The upholstery cooperative is exploring producing meditation cushions and animal pet beds that could also use up leftover fabric. Inevitably, the sales go up and down and there are going to be slow periods. If we had a product that workers could continue to make during the slow periods, we could keep them busy all the time. One of the workers has been developing a prototype, which is almost ready to shop around. Alongside the greenhouse, we are also projecting developing alternative energy production, food processing and a food service. Other spin-off ideas include transportation for the businesses, back end business support like bookkeeping, database management and the like.

Some of the businesses that we are developing have been spawned more spontaneously. My co-director, Fred Rose, has a relationship with a group that does landscaping at a big company. They are interested in starting their own cooperative business. We have had discussions about whether it would make sense to be part of Well-spring and how we can assist in that business development. In cases like this, we are not taking all of the initiative of building the businesses but rather aim to provide support to new startups businesses and bring some of them into the Wellspring network.

It is really exciting how receptive everyone has been—from the institutions to the city level to the community and labor organization level. The biggest challenge is people finding the time to engage. We have pretty much encountered nothing but positive reception and openness to an extent that was surprising, but pleasantly surprising.

In terms of the U.S. Solidarity Economy Network, I see my work with Wellspring as part of building the solidarity economy. And, for me, it is nice to be grounded in the actual practice of at least a piece of the solidarity economy. It is about marrying the theory with the practice and continually learning from both aspects. This has been really important. I think there has been a lot of upsurge in activity around solidarity economy. Some people are using that terminology and some are not. Some might not be using the framework, but they are working in a specific sector. There has been growth in worker co-ops and food co-ops, and credit unions have been getting stronger. Community land trusts, the sharing economy, and local currencies are flourishing.

Participatory budgeting and the commons framework are spreading. Those are all practices that solidarity economy embraces: democratic and collective, hopefully pursuing aims of equity and sustainability as well. In some areas, there are local movements that are using solidarity economy as their framework. This is true in Worcester, New York City and Boston. And in Jackson, Mississippi, Cooperation Jackson and that whole movement uses the framework of a solidarity economy. It is one of their pillars. Connected to that is the Southern Economic Grassroots Project. Elandria Williams of Highlander is one of the founders. She has been on the Solidarity Economics Network board for many years. The Southern Economic Grassroots Project has a focus on cooperatives, but they bring in the solidarity economy perspective as well.

In California, there are groups that use the solidarity economy, such as Community to Community in the Seattle area and a San Francisco Bay Area group called People Organizing to Defend Environmental and Economic Rights (PODER). They sent somebody to an international gathering in the Philippines last year. Compared to 2009, I think there has been a significant increase in grassroots engagement in the solidarity economy. I'm very excited about the 2016 North American Solidarity Economy Forum and having the continental Canadian and Quebec participation will be important.

SD: *Could you talk about the role of public policy in providing a supportive environment?*

EK: A lot of the public policy work related to the solidarity economy is sectoral—cooperatives, credit unions, sustainable food systems, for example. What we haven't really yet engaged in, is following the lead of other countries to develop framework legislation—comprehensive legislation—to create a supportive environment for the social solidarity economy. Countries that either have or are in the process of developing framework social and solidarity economy legislation include France, Luxembourg, Portugal, Spain, Greece, Mali, Cameroon, Quebec, Brazil, Mexico, Colombia, Ecuador, Argentina, and Honduras. Some of these countries, such as France and Brazil, have government ministries for the solidarity economy and others, such as Ecuador and Bolivia, have included solidarity economy in their constitutions. It certainly would be powerful if, in the United States, we could start pulling together sectoral policies and knit them together into a more comprehensive platform that supports whole system change, rather than sector by sector.

SD: *If you were to highlight the key accomplishments of your work to date that you are most proud of, what would they be?*

EK: Well, I'm very proud of being one of the founders of the U.S. Solidarity Economy Network and being one of the initiators of Wellspring. The Solidarity Economy Network is very broad—trying to pull together various sectors of the solidarity economy together—to encourage the various practices to recognize each other as being part of a common project to build a just and sustainable world. That work is very broad and somewhat more abstract. And Wellspring is very concrete, very practical, and seeks to primarily benefit under-served, low-income communities of color. I love that combination of broad and concrete. It can be exhausting, but it's great.

SD: *Anything else you would like to add?*

EK: The U.S. Solidarity Economy Network is very deliberate about thinking about race and class. Right now, a lot of alternatives are relatively ghettoized in relatively privileged, well educated, white communities. If we do not deliberately make sure that these models are relevant and workable in poor communities and communities of color, we are not really creating the systems change that we seek to achieve. That is really, really important. We recently organized a webinar entitled "Decolonizing Our Solidarity Economy" that addressed exactly these kinds of issues. I believe that we had around 150 people participate in that webinar. So it goes to show that there is tremendous interest, and it's important to continue to discuss and strategize on these issues.

About the Author

Steve Dubb *is a Senior Fellow at The Democracy Collaborative. Steve has been with the Collaborative since 2004, where he has written a wide body of work, and served as Director of Special Projects and Senior Advisor to the President. In 2005, Steve was the lead author of* Building Wealth: The New Asset-Based Approach to Solving Social and Economic Problems, *published by The Aspen Institute. This book served as the basis for the original Community-Wealth.org website, which has expanded greatly since in its initial launch in May 2005, whose development Steve oversaw for many years after its launch.*

*Since 2005, Steve has written on many themes, including the role of public policy in supporting community wealth building (*Rebuilding America's Communities*), the importance of community wealth building in meeting sustainability goals (*Growing a Green Economy for All*) and has written extensively on how universities and hospitals can adopt an "anchor mission" that aligns economic and human resources to be more effective community partners. Steve's work in this area includes being a co-author (with Rita Axelroth Hodges) of* The Road Half Traveled: University Engagement at a Crossroads *(published by MSU Press in 2012) and, in 2013, leading the research team that produced* The Anchor Dashboard, *which aims to provide a framework for hospitals and universities to assess and improve their impact in low and moderate-income communities. Steve has also facilitated the Anchor Dashboard Learning Cohort, in which seven universities are working to adapt andimplement the Dashboard framework on their campuses.*

Steve has also been engaged in a wide range of community wealth building projects, which brought him into contact with many of the people interviewed in this book. This includes working with Democracy Collaborative President Ted Howard in 2007 on the initial strategic planning that help lead to the development of the Evergreen Cooperatives initiative in Cleveland, Ohio, as well as subsequent work on community wealth building strategy in more than a dozen cities. In addition, Steve has worked as a part of the Collaborative's Learning/ Action Lab team that is partnering with the Northwest Area Foundation and Native American organizations to develop employee-owned businesses and social enterprises in Indian Country.

About the Democracy Collaborative

The Democracy Collaborative, a nonprofit founded in 2000, is a national leader in equitable, inclusive, and sustainable development that works to build community wealth and create a next system anchored in democratic ownership. Our work as community wealth builders encompasses a range of advisory, research, policy development, and field-building activities aiding on-the-ground practitioners. Our mission is to help shift the prevailing paradigm of economic development, and of the economy as a whole, toward a new system that is place-based, inclusive, collaborative, and ecologically sustainable. A particular focus of our program is assisting universities, hospitals, and other community-rooted institutions to design and implement an anchor mission in which all of the institution's diverse assets are harmonized and leveraged for community impact.

Learn more:
http://democracycollaborative.org
http://community-wealth.org

CPSIA information can be obtained
at www.ICGtesting.com
Printed in the USA
LVOW03s0402071017
551452LV00001B/5/P